THE
LEWIS
MUMFORD
READER

BOOKS BY LEWIS MUMFORD

THE
LEWIS
MUMFORD
READER

Edited by

Donald L. Miller

PANTHEON BOOKS
New York

Library of Congress Cataloging-in-Publication Data

Mumford, Lewis, 1895–
The Lewis Mumford reader.

1. Civilization. 2. Cities and towns—History.
3. Architecture. 4. United States—Civilization.
5. Technology and civilization. I. Miller, Donald L.,
1944–. II. Title.
CB151.M83   1986   901   86-42617
ISBN 0-394-55526-0
ISBN 0-394-74630-9 (pbk.)

Since this copyright page cannot legibly accommodate all permissions
acknowledgments, they appear on pages 375–76.

Manufactured in the United States of America

Text design by Marsha Cohen/Parallelogram

Contents

Acknowledgments

Besides Lewis Mumford, who asked me to undertake this project, two people, above all others, made this book possible. Sophia Mumford helped me at every stage of my work. She is the most perceptive living student of her husband's life and work, and one of the most remarkable women I have ever met. This book was born in the mind of Sara Bershtel, my editor at Pantheon Books, and she helped me pilot it to print. I would also like to thank the superbly competent Helena Franklin, of Pantheon Books, for helping me to put the manuscript into final form, and Martin Filler, Alan Trachtenberg, Sam Bass Warner, Wolf von Ekhardt, and Gina Maccoby, my agent, for their valuable advice and suggestions.

THE
LEWIS
MUMFORD
READER

INTRODUCTION

Great havoc makes he among our originalities.
—Ralph Waldo Emerson

This book brings together a representative selection of the major writings of Lewis Mumford, one of the most influential thinkers of our time. Mumford is a writer of audacious reach. His contributions to history, philosophy, literature, art and architecture criticism, urban planning, and the study of cities and technology have opened for fresh consideration large areas of the human achievement. Over a lifetime of steady effort, he has produced a body of cultural criticism and commentary that for its range and richness is unmatched in modern American letters. "It may be," Malcolm Cowley has suggested, "that Lewis Mumford is the last of the great humanists."[1]

Mumford's literary output has been prodigious. In the course of his sixty-year career as a writer, he has produced some thirty books and over a thousand essays and reviews: twenty-three of these books are still in print, a remarkable testimony to his continuing influence. He has received almost every major literary award this country can bestow on a writer of nonfiction, including the National Medal for Literature, the National Book Award, and the Smithsonian Institution's rarely awarded Hodgkins Gold Medal for his pioneering work in bringing together the sciences and the humanities. He has also played a major role in some of the most important public policy debates of our time, including those on urban development, transportation policy, land planning and the environment, nuclear disarmament, and the problems and promise of technology. Lewis Mumford has had "a deeper and more lasting impact on the thinking of his generation," Henry Steele Commager, Jr., commented recently, "than almost any other figure in public life."[2]

Mumford was born in Flushing, Queens, on October 19, 1895, and his career has spanned the century, from the opening decades of soaring social confidence to our own age of diminished expectations. His work has in large part been an exploration of the question of how the world of his youth became the world we now live in. Whatever his other claims, Lewis Mumford is preeminently the interpreter of the century of science, war, and the machine.

Mumford's aim, however, has been to change history, not simply to record it. The renewal of life—the creation of a new kind of personality and a new pattern of community living—is the challenge he has set for our age. But the very possibility of renewal, he has cautioned, hinges on an informed understanding of the sources of our problems. Our future is thus inextricably bound up with our past, and it is to a deeper understanding of the past that Mumford has turned his energies as a writer and a public philosopher.

In all of Mumford's work there is an Emersonian emphasis on moral reform. He has argued consistently that the good life will involve more than a redistribution of the fruits of affluence, more than a humane reshaping of public policy. By urging an almost religious refashioning of values, Mumford has isolated himself from most of the organized liberal and radical groups of his time. He has stood alone, on the solid foundation of his own ideas and principles, which have remained firm and steady over the years.

"Balance" and "wholeness": these two words sum up Mumford's approach to life. He is this century's leading proponent of what he calls synoptic or ecological thinking, which is a way of seeing life whole, in all its variety and interconnectedness. Like a biologist at work in nature, he ceaselessly searches for links and interrelationships, and he always places the subject he is writing about, whether it is a book or a building or an entire city, within its wider cultural context. Art, in his view, cannot be properly understood in isolation from society; cities and architecture must be perceived in relation to the civilizations that produced them. Mumford urges us, as well, to view reality with "a double vision which sees with both eyes—the scientific eye of actuality and the illuminated eye of imagination and dream."[3] He calls for the development of the total person, of all our capacities for reason and calculation, passion and poetry, mental work and full-bodied living.

In his own life, Mumford has tried to hew closely to this ancient Athenian ideal of balance. He brings to his writing the imaginative daring of the artist, the close-focused exactitude of the scholar, and the scientist's reliance upon direct observation and field research, particularly in his architectural and urban writings, which are based on his firsthand surveys of cities and buildings. His ideal community is one that combines the dynamism and diversity of the city with the enduring values of the village—order, neighborhood stability, and community closeness. While he is an urban man to the core, a product of Walt Whitman's "mettlesome, mad, extravagant"[4] New York, he has lived half of his life in a reconverted farmhouse in the quiet village of Amenia, in Dutchess County, New York, a hundred miles and a world away from the city in which he grew up and made his career. He moved to Amenia with his family in 1936 not to escape the city but because, like Whitman, he found ever-active New York a "good place for the harvest" but "a bad place for literary farming."[5] Here in the country he has lived the life of "handsome bareness and simplicity" he calls for in his books, writing in the mornings, and walking, gardening, and sketching in the afternoons.[6] Out of this deep-layered understanding of the best features of these two opposite worlds—the village and the city—Mumford wove his vision of the good life.

Mumford's commitment to the balanced life is evident in yet another way. Few writers have enjoyed the solitude of the study more than he, but he has not been merely a sitting sage, calling for reform and pronouncing judgment from a distance. He helped to organize this country's first nuclear disarmament movement immediately after the Hiroshima holocaust; he spoke out fearlessly against Senator Joseph McCarthy at the height of his influence; he took part in several organized efforts in New York City to stop Robert Moses' neighborhood-destroying highway projects; and he was one of the first Americans in public life to denounce the government's involvement in Vietnam, taking his credo from Shakespeare's *King Lear*:

> The weight of this sad time we must obey:
> Speak what we feel, not what we ought to say.

A strong-willed, impassioned man, Mumford has lived his ideas as few outstanding thinkers do.

Mumford never received a college degree, nor has he ever held a long-term academic appointment. Rather, like Carlyle's central character in *Sartor Resartus,* he has been professor of things-in-general; his "duty," he once said, "is to tear down the fences and the 'no trespassing' signs that keep people from taking advantage of wider views and more significant prospects."[7] He has helped to keep alive in our age of specialization the spirit of the complete man, for whom the whole is more important than the sum of the parts.

But Mumford, of course, has been much more than a generalist, bringing "the scattered specialisms together to form an integrated pattern."[8] He has made his mark as a specialist, too, in at least half a dozen firmly established fields.

He is best known as a writer on cities and architecture—as the author of two landmark works on urban civilization, *The Culture of Cities* (1938) and *The City in History* (1961), and as this century's greatest architecture critic. His pioneering work on the origins and evolution of urban culture helped to establish the city as a subject of scholarly concern, and drew attention to the formative role of the city in the development of Western culture. The noted American sociologist William F. Whyte has called *The City in History* "the greatest book ever written on the city."[9]

Better than any other writer in our time, Mumford has taught us how to understand cities by observing their architecture and design, not solely through the study of books and photographs, but by walking through the city's streets and neighborhoods with our senses alert, just as he himself gained an architectural and urban education. The book on the city that does not take the reader out into the city itself, Mumford has often said, is not worth consulting. In a succession of books and essays on architecture and the city, beginning with his sharply observant classic, *Sticks and Stones* (1924), the first general history of American architecture, he pointed out a new way of looking at the built environment, brilliantly establishing the connection between architecture and civilization. In these writings, and in his "Sky Line" column for *The New Yorker*, which he wrote, with occasional interruptions, from 1931 to 1963, he consistently urged architects to shape their work to the social, psychological, and physical needs of human beings. For Mumford, the chief mission of architecture, the art of good building, is the making of "a new home for man."[10]

Mumford's close attention to human needs and to human scale, his preference for small plans and projects over monumental ones, led him in the 1940s and 1950s to denounce the massive urban renewal, highway, and high-rise building projects that have disfigured and damaged the downtowns of our major cities. The cities that Mumford has always favored are lively, neighborhood-centered cities where people can go on their feet and meet face-to-face in a sidewalk café or a shaded park. "The first lesson we have to learn," he observed in an early indictment of the federal government's program to bring highways into the heart of the city, "is that the city exists, not for the facile passage of motorcars, but for the care and culture of men."[11]

Aside from his architectural and urban work, Mumford has made his most important contributions in the fields of American cultural criticism and the history of Western technology. The four books he wrote in the 1920s on American culture—*Sticks and Stones, The Golden Day, Herman Melville,* and *The Brown Decades*—led to the rediscovery or reappraisal of Melville, Emerson, Thoreau, Whitman, and Hawthorne. Mumford also revived the reputations of a number of American architects, engineers, and environmentalists, among them Henry Hobson Richardson, Louis Sullivan, Frederick Law Olmsted, George Perkins Marsh, and John A. and Washington Roebling, builders of the Brooklyn Bridge—"a poem," Mumford called it, "in granite and steel."[12] Mumford never completed the one-volume study of American culture he started to write on a number of occasions, but, considered together, these four books present a unified, interwoven interpretation of the entire course of American civilization. They are independent ventures over largely unsurveyed terrain, works that established Mumford as one of the founders of what is currently called American studies.

In the 1930s, Mumford widened his field of vision to take in all of Western civilization, beginning a project it would take him two decades to complete, his four-volume Renewal of Life series. In this world-encompassing work, and in the follow-up two-volume study he wrote during the 1960s, *The Myth of the Machine,* he set out to reinterpret the entire history of human development and to reappraise the role of technology and science in Western civilization. These works challenged many of our most fundamental assumptions about Western progress and, for the first time, placed the history of science and technology in a broader cultural frame.[13]

Mumford has never been interested in writing so-called objective history, and what he gives us here is "usable history," history as a guide to present and future conduct. His purpose is to lay bare the sources of what he considers the major problem of twentieth-century Western culture: our life-denying commitment to unlimited power and economic growth—to the goods life, as he put it, rather than the good life. While these books of his later years can be excessively preachy, with analysis often giving way to moral assertion, few writers in our time have recorded with greater sensitivity and suggestive force the rise and triumph of machine civilization in the West, and its often debasing impact on imagination, free choice, and creative living.

Mumford's work of the 1950s and 1960s, his most productive years as a writer, is united by one insistent claim: that the development of the mind and its greatest creations, language and ritual, were more important to human development than the introduction and utilization of the first primitive tools.[14] Man fashioned himself, Mumford suggested, before he fashioned his first sophisticated tools. In this daringly speculative rereading of human origins, Mumford shifted the emphasis from physical survival to cultural and mental development. He had a strong personal reason for doing this. If his theory is correct, he wrote to a friend when he first began to seek supporting evidence for it (he had his conclusions before he had his proof), then man still has sufficient resources to alter the direction of modern technology, and is not, as Jacques Ellul argues, a passive victim of technological society.[15]

Mumford maintains, then, that the promise of man resides within himself. It is up to him to regain and reassert the freedom and the creative capacities he has too readily surrendered to his machines. Man as interpreter and symbol-maker, as maker of meanings and values, is the image on which Mumford erected his philosophy of history—a theory of human development, not coincidentally, in perfect accord with his own chosen role as writer and vision-maker. In Mumford's highly personalized reading of history, the word and the symbol, the writer and the artist, truly matter, and the arts take a central place in life.

This unshakable faith in the possibility of renewal is evident even in Mumford's apocalyptic writings of his later years, with their premonitions of technological regimentation and nuclear disaster. "It seems to me," Mumford wrote in 1975, "that . . . *if the forces that now dominate us continue on their present path* they must lead to collapse of the whole historical fabric, not just this or that great nation or empire."[16] Yet Mumford refused to accept this fate as inevitable. Trend, he continued to insist, is not destiny. This is a man who into his tenth decade, too enfeebled to go on with his writing, continued to quote his favorite line in poetry, from Tennyson's *Ulysses*: "Come my friends, / 'Tis not too late to seek a newer world."

Lewis Mumford has put together several anthologies of his writings on various themes. This is the first book, however, to give representative selections from his writings on all the central concerns of his life—cities, architecture, technology, and American culture. Although I have organized the book thematically, I have tried to present Mumford's ideas developmentally so as to give a sense of a man and a mind in the making. My aim has been to produce a book that has the continuity of an original and interconnected piece of work. Mumford had a genuis for bringing together long-neglected, widely scattered materials into new, imaginative configurations. In making my selections for this reader, I have tried to follow his lead, drawing together into a harmonious whole the best of his wide-reaching works.

Lewis Mumford gave me, as his literary executor, complete editorial freedom in the preparation of this volume. I have made cuts in almost all of the selections, and severely pruned some of them, in order to eliminate repetition and overlap with other essays and to achieve concision and thematic unity. Wherever I have made a cut, I have indicated it by ellipsis points. As a rule, I have used the original title for the texts. Where I have made a change or combined two or more essays or chapters as one selection, I have indicated the change in a bottom note on the first page of the selection, as well as in the information given in the List of Sources on pages 371–74.

The year before Lewis Mumford married Sophia Wittenberg he wrote to her on her twenty-first birthday: "When [people] talk about happiness, they think it is pleasure or comfort, or 'having all you want in the world.' . . . [But] when I say that I wish you happiness, I mean that I hope as you grow older you will become more intensely alive."[17] That intensity of life is what I have tried to capture in this book.

Notes

1. Malcolm Cowley to Julian Muller, October 19, 1978, Lewis Mumford Collection, Van Pelt Library, University of Pennsylvania (hereafter cited as LM MSS).

2. Henry Steele Commager, Jr., in *A Tribute to Lewis Mumford* (Cambridge, Mass.: Lincoln Institute of Land Policy, 1982), 10.

3. Mumford, *Herman Melville* (New York: Harcourt, Brace, 1929), 194.

4. Harold W. Blodgett and Sculley Bradley, eds., *Leaves of Grass,* Comprehensive Reader's Edition (New York: New York University Press, 1965), 294.

5. Whitman quoted in Van Wyck Brooks, *The Times of Melville and Whitman* (New York: E. P. Dutton, 1947), 324.

6. Mumford, Radcliffe Commencement Address, June 13, 1956, LM MSS.

7. Mumford, "From Revolt to Renewal," in Lewis Mumford et al., *The Arts in Renewal,* introd. Sculley Bradley (Philadelphia: University of Pennsylvania Press, 1951), 1.

8. Interview with Lewis Mumford, December 13, 1979, Amenia, New York.

9. William F. Whyte, in *A Tribute to Lewis Mumford,* 31.

10. Mumford, "Architecture as a Home for Man," *Architectural Record,* 143, no. 2 (February 1968): 113–16.

11. Mumford, "The Highway and the City," *Architectural Record* 123, no. 4 (April 1958): 186.

12. Mumford, *The Brown Decades: A Study of the Arts in America, 1865–1895* (New York: Harcourt, Brace, 1931), 43–48.

13. Mumford, *The Myth of the Machine,* vol. 1, *Technics and Human Development* (New York: Harcourt, Brace and World, 1967); *The Myth of the Machine,* vol. 2, *The Pentagon of Power* (New York: Harcourt Brace Jovanovich, 1970).

14. Mumford to Benton MacKaye, May 31, 1934, Benton MacKaye Collection, Dartmouth College Library. Interview with Lewis Mumford, November 15, 1985, Leedsville, New York.

15. Mumford to MacKaye, May 31, 1964, MacKaye MSS.

16. Mumford, "Reflections: Prologue to Our Time," *The New Yorker,* March 10, 1975, 51.

17. Lewis Mumford to Sophia Wittenberg, October 8, 1920, LM MSS.

I

A CHILD OF THE CITY

This is the city and I am one of
the citizens. Whatever interests
the rest interests me, politics,
wars, markets, newspapers, schools,
The mayor and councils, banks,
tariffs, steamships, factories,
stocks, stores, real estate and
personal estate.
—Walt Whitman

Introduction

New York City was a decisive influence on Lewis Mumford's early life and thought. The port of New York became his "Walden Pond," he writes in his autobiography, and as a young boy, on leisurely weekend walks with his German grandfather, he explored New York's streets and buildings and neighborhoods with the same keen-eyed curiosity that Thoreau brought to his explorations of the rural scene. The multitudinous urban world that his grandfather introduced him to "exerted a greater and more constant influence on me," he recalls, "than did my family."[1]

The New York that Mumford knew best as a young man was a small corner of the city, the predominantly German-Irish district of the Upper West Side that stretched its monotonous brownstone corridors up the cross streets from Riverside Drive to Central Park West. The illegitimate, and only, child of Elvina Baron Mumford, a native New Yorker of German Protestant ancestry who ran a series of modest boardinghouses, Mumford was a withdrawn, bookish boy, slight of build and never robustly healthy. As a mature man he would possess steel-firm self-confidence, but it took many years and much effort to acquire it. Even in late adolescence he could not raise the courage to press his mother about the facts of his birth. Not until he was forty-seven years old, in fact, did she finally reveal to him her long-held secret—that he was the son of a Jewish businessman she had had a brief affair with while she was a housekeeper in the home of this young man's uncle, the man she really loved, and who Mumford, as a child, secretly suspected was his father.

As a boy of nine or ten Mumford experimented with wireless radio sets and dreamed of becoming an electrical engineer. This drew him to New York's Stuyvesant High School, which had a reputation for preparing students for careers in the sciences and engineering. At Stuyvesant he published his first professional articles in electrical magazines and acquired his lifelong interest in technology. But for young Mumford, Stuyvesant offered more than an absorbing technical education; it opened to him a different side of city life.

15

The school was located on the Lower East Side, the heart of New York's immigrant quarter and the home of Tammany Hall, Tom Starkey's saloon, and the painted prostitutes of Forsyth Street. Here he made new friends, the sons of Jewish immigrants, and through them was exposed to the vibrant street life and village-like sociability he would always consider the blood and soul of urban living. This was also one of his earliest encounters with poverty, with foul-smelling, clotted tenement quarters he would later compare to those of Juvenal's Rome. "The absence of space, order, intelligent design, even sunlight and fresh air—the sense of all the human qualities that were missing— taught me, by contrast," he observed in retrospect, "what to demand in every work of humane architecture."[2]

At Stuyvesant, in his English classes, Mumford encountered the work of George Bernard Shaw, who became the inspiration of his adolescence. After reading almost all of Shaw, and writing and acting in the school's dramatic society, he abandoned plans to enter engineering school and decided to be a writer, preferably a playwright or a novelist. While he worked on his writing with monkish dedication, unable for a number of years to get any of his offerings published or produced, he attended classes at the City College of New York. There, one afternoon in the biology library, he came upon the work of Patrick Geddes, the Scottish botanist, sociologist, and town planner. This was an encounter that changed Mumford's entire life. From this point on Geddes became the single most important personal influence on Mumford's development, "a Jovian father," as Mumford once described him, "stern and practically omniscient."[3]

A biologist who turned later in his life to city planning, Geddes had begun a series of civic surveys and town revitalization projects in Edinburgh in the 1890s, publishing his results in a succession of books and reports that fired young Mumford's interest in the city. Mumford did not set out to be a city planner or an architect, however. His task, he decided after reading Geddes's *Cities in Evolution,* would be "to enlarge the vision" of those who did the actual planning and building.[4]

Patrick Geddes taught Mumford a new way of looking at the cities, an approach based upon direct observation and a biologist's sensitivity to organic relationships. Geddes never began a planning project without first spending at least a week wandering on foot through a city, letting it "speak" to him, absorbing as much as he could of its history and habits from its buildings, terrain, and people. To Geddes, education —real education—was not something one got from a book or in a lecture hall. *Vivendo discimus* (By living we learn) was his motto.

Geddes was also sensitive to the connection between city and country, insisting that the problems of the city could be successfully attacked only on a regional basis. He saw the entire city-region as a complex, interconnected ecosystem that one had to understand before suggesting alterations that might upset its delicate natural balance.[5] Mumford's classic works on the urban condition, *The Culture of Cities* and *The City in History*, are among the finest examples we have of this holistic, ecological approach to the study of human communities.

Mumford could not have found Geddes at a more propitious moment in his emotional development. An erratic heart and what his doctors diagnosed as the first stages of tuberculosis forced him, in 1915, to suspend his education at City College. This temporary release from formal education, along with the influence of Geddes, led him to re-examine his entire approach to life and learning. Whereas in the past he had led a sheltered, bookish existence, living, as he wrote at the time, "at second hand,"[6] he was now determined "to be fully alive, alive in every pore, at every moment, in every dimension."[7]

Almost from the moment he encountered Geddes's writings, Mumford began to use the city itself as his university. Every afternoon he set out alone to explore New York on foot. On these walks he would stop here and there to do a pencil sketch of a tenement or a water tower or one of New York's arching bridges. All of his later architectural and urban writing is grounded in these early firsthand surveys of his native city and region. The city, he would write years later, "is the point of maximum concentration for the power and culture of a community. . . . Here is where the issues of civilization are focused."[8] Here is where this wide-eyed son of Manhattan went for his first real education.

Notes

1. Lewis Mumford, *Sketches from Life: The Autobiography of Lewis Mumford* (New York: Dial Press, 1982), 25, 1–12.

2. Mumford, "Architecture as a Home for Man," *Architectural Record*, 143, no. 2 (February 1968): 113; Mumford, "A New York Adolescence: Tennis, Quadratic Equations, and Love," *New Yorker*, December 4, 1937, 86–94.

3. Mumford, in Georges Schreiber, *Portraits and Self-Portraits* (Boston: Houghton Mifflin, 1931), 119; Mumford, *Sketches*, 144.

4. Mumford, autobiographical essay, no date, LM MSS, 11–22.

5. Patrick Geddes, *Cities in Evolution* (London: Williams & Norgate, 1914); Geddes, *City Development: A Study of Parks, Gardens, and Culture-Institutes* (Edinburgh: Geddes, 1904).

6. Mumford, "The Invalids," an unpublished play, LM MSS.

7. Mumford, "A Disciple's Rebellion: A Memoir of Patrick Geddes," *Encounter*, September 1966, 11–21.

8. Mumford, *The Culture of Cities* (New York: Harcourt, Brace, 1938), 3.

EAST SIDE, WEST SIDE

I was a child of the city, and for the first thirty years of my life I knew the country only as a visitor, though the occasional summers I spent on a Vermont farm before 1910 had first and last an influence on me that offset my long incarceration in what Melville called "the Babylonish brick-kiln" of New York. Not merely was I a city boy but a New Yorker, indeed a son of Manhattan, who looked upon specimens from all other cities as provincial—especially Brooklynites. Deep down, I suppose, some of that original sense of metropolitan superiority, which has nothing to do with me personally, still lurks.

My first dream-swift memory brings forth a sunlit room, with the neighbors' children gaping at goldfish swimming about in a bowl. This dates back, my mother once told me, to our fleeting refuge in a flat on Amsterdam Avenue at the corner of Ninety-seventh Street when I was two. But my earliest clear picture is at three—that of the backyard behind a four-story brownstone front on West Sixty-fifth Street, where my mother, in spring, would thrust a few pansy plants into the ground, not because she wanted a garden, but because she loved pansies. That was before the High School of Commerce was built across the way and long before the Lincoln Arcade—which still later became a refuge for penurious artists—was razed to make way for Lincoln Center. Until the new subway tore up Boss Tweed's tree-lined Boulevard ("Bullavard" is what my young ears heard), as Broadway above Fifty-ninth Street was called, this was a quite respectable street and gave no hint of becoming the sordid red-light area it later turned into.

It was in this typical New York brownstone that my conscious life begins. I clearly recall our front parlor, dominated by a fashionable rubber plant, as well as the back parlor, with its heavy walnut furniture, where my grandmother, Anna Maria Graessel, and her husband were lodged. Even better, I can still feel myself lying in bed alongside my mother in what was originally the "music room," between back and front parlors. I would wake regularly at six-thirty or so—I've always been an early riser—chanting in monotonous singsong: "I want my toast and coffee." The last two syllables were drawn out in proportion to my impatience, and the coffee was, of course, slightly tanned milk.

At this point my grandmother steps momentarily into the picture: I see her adjusting her bonnet, with a grimace, in front of the pier mirror of the great walnut wardrobe. A few months later she died of Bright's disease.

The backyard, where I played, was safe from all intruders but cats, by reason of one of the high wooden fences with which New Yorkers always enclosed those dreary areas, though its paved path was too uneven to encourage even tricycle riding. From Sixty-fifth Street up, Broadway was still full of vacant lots, with visible chickens and market gardens, genuine beer gardens like Unter den Linden, and even more rural areas. Since for the first quarter of a century of my life I lived between Central Park and Riverside Drive, wide lawns and tree-lined promenades are inseparable in my mind from the design of every great city; for what London, Paris, and Rome boasted, New York then possessed . . .

Since I have spent no small part of my life wandering about cities, studying cities, working in cities, stirred by all their activities, this original envelopment by the city constitutes an important clue to my life. Certainly Manhattan provided a far from ideal environment during the years I was growing up in it; but it still had many rewarding features, natural and man-made, that have since dropped away or been wiped out. This has come about partly through the profitable congestion of tenements and skyscrapers, partly through the more ominous spread of violence and lawlessness, which, in the city of my youth, used to be confined, like a carbuncle, to certain self-enclosed areas, like the Bowery and Hell's Kitchen. Such quarters had not yet poured their infection into the whole bloodstream of the city.

For one thing, it was possible then for men, women, or children, even when alone, to walk over a great part of the city, and certainly to walk through Central Park or along Riverside Drive at any time of the day or evening without fear of being molested or assaulted. This is no longer true, even though the poverty and misery that festered in large areas of New York at the beginning of this century have now been mitigated by social legislation, labor union organization, and indeed by the general rise in the material standard of life even in the lowest income groups.

There was a kind of moral stability and security in the city of my youth that has now vanished even in such urban models of law and order as London, where for long the police performed their duties without even the threat of a nightstick. So deep was this sense of security in a period that had not yet multiplied all the current forms of insurance against the mischances of life that the word "security" did not have a place in our vocabulary. More than once lately in New York I have felt as Petrarch reports himself feeling in the fourteenth century, when he compared the desolate, wolfish, robber-infested Provence of his maturity, in the wake of the Black Plague, with the safe, prosperous region of his youth.

That breakdown of law and order at the very peak of metropolitan power and prosperity is, as Barbara Tuchman has discovered, one of the chronic puzzles of history. . . .

This discovery has nonetheless not robbed me of my love of cities or made me forget my quiver of anticipation when I stepped off the train in a strange city and, while waiting perhaps for a taxi, caught my first glimpse of its skyline or my first jumbled earful of sounds from its characteristic activities—the high-pitched whistle of the Chicago traffic policemen, at least of old, or the frantic toots of the taxis in Paris, before those sounds were officially suppressed. The overhead whoosh or sonic boom of a plane today unfortunately wakens no such happy expectations.

I was an Upper West Side boy. The area where I grew up then stretched roughly from 59th Street to 110th Street: beyond that, though overeager speculators or homemakers had here and there set down scattered rows of defiantly urban houses, was a sort of no-man's-land, already spoiled for agriculture, neither country or city, still less suburbia. Even in built-up areas there were still many vacant lots, sometimes vacant blocks, until well past 1900. On some of these there were not merely squatters' shacks but thrifty market gardens; indeed, I remember that there was still such a leftover in the lower Nineties as late as 1912, on the Astor estate. And above 125th Street there lingered many tracts that could still be called farms, interspersed as they were with roadhouses and beer gardens where the thirsty cyclists who then filled the highways on Sundays could rest in the shade and down a schooner of beer for five cents.

The two main outdoor excursions of my elders—going to the racetrack and going to the cemetery—were always welcome diversions in my youth, on account of the journey itself if not its somber destination. As to the latter, for long this was at least a monthly visitation, often made in the company of uncles and aunts, for my maternal grandmother had died when I was there, and the regular visit to her grave combined piety with pleasure—and was also favored as good for the health. Above MacComb's Dam Bridge, along Jerome Avenue, was then almost open country, but the monument makers' yards thickened as one got closer to Woodlawn Cemetery. My elders would comment on how well or ill the hired florist was keeping the grave bed in order, on what sort of inscription was to be put on the tombstone when my grandfather died, or on how—dear me!—the cemetery was filling up so fast. After that there would be beer and sandwiches, with glasses of sarsaparilla for the children, before starting home.

But the trip to the horse races at Belmont Park or Sheepshead Bay or Brighton was, of course, far more exciting. East of Prospect Park the houses gave way to wide meadows and farms, and the open Brooklyn trolley cars, with their formidably high steps, used to whizz through this placid countryside, with the south wind bringing the delectable odors of new-mown grass and far-off salt spray.

My area of the city was relatively compact. The rows of brownstone fronts that had been so popular in the third quarter of the nineteenth century—an ugly chocolate-colored sandstone from the quarries around Hartford had displaced the warm reddish-brown sandstone from Belleville, New Jersey, which one may still find on Brooklyn Heights—were giving way to a more variegated type of domestic architecture, first influenced by Richardson, then by McKim, Mead, and White, with fine ocher Roman bricks and classic details; and then, on West End Avenue, this was followed by gabled houses in the Dutch style, as a new shelf of civic-history books brought back into the consciousness of New Yorkers their own Dutch heritage.

On Riverside Drive itself the houses, often spreading mansions, were done in rustic stone and had enough shrubbery around them to give them a suburban air, though in the early part of the present century Bishop Potter's new residence, near the Soldiers' and Sailors' Monument, and a few other palatial houses introduced a more urbane Italian note. Never have rich people in New York had more garden space than they did for a decade or so at this time: the steel magnate Schwab—familiar to my grandfather as Charlie Schwab—even built a Renaissance "castle" set in the middle of a whole block. But these early settlers had not reckoned with the fact that their handsome Riverside Drive quarters were not sealed against atmospheric pollution. They were soon to find that the fresh west winds that blew across the Hudson also blew the fumes and smoke from noisome factories on the Jersey shore, to say nothing of the odors from the long trains of cattle cars that used to pass down to the slaughterhouses in the West Thirties, along the open tracks between Riverside Park and the Hudson.

Those trains, and those cattle cars particularly, were my delight as a child, and not least because, despite their ugly smell, the plaintive lowing of the cattle, and the grunting of the pigs, they brought a touch of wildness into the tame city. But I can understand the dejection that grew to desperation when a prosperous family, after investing heavily on Riverside Drive, belatedly discovered that the grand sweep of the river did not offset the putrid odors and harsh west winds.

Within twenty years this domestic loss was written off by the building of a great palisade of apartment houses for a less choosy economic group; and within another thirty years scarcely a vestige of these suburban palaces remained on Riverside Drive: one of a hundred examples that bear witness to the swift tempo of construction and destruction that has characterized my native city. If someone were to ask me now for directions in the neighborhoods where I lived the first twenty-five years of my life, I could only say, with a helpless smile: "I'm a stranger here myself." New Yorkers over fifty are all Rip van Winkles.

My memories embrace a series of neighborhoods, from 65th Street to 105th Street; but unlike Greenwich Village, Yorkville, or Manhattanville, none of them had ever been a village, and so they were only faintly identifiable in either their physical or social structure. My part of the West Side had taken shape in the late eighties and nineties; and its class structure had a diagrammatic neatness. The poorer classes lived on Amsterdam and Columbus Avenues, in the "old law" tenement houses —crowded structures with the majority of their rooms on airless airshafts and lightless light wells. Here lived the cabmen and clerks, the mechanics and the minor city employees, the widows who rented their extra rooms and went out sewing or washing or cleaning by the day. Only the rich lived off Central Park or on Riverside Drive; while between them on the cross streets, in their row houses, sometimes uniform for a whole block, sometimes with playful architectural variations —inset balconies, oriels, bay windows—lived the well-to-do and the more ambitious middle classes.

Like most New Yorkers in those days, we seemed to be always moving; and it was not till I was twelve years old that we finally settled down in the apartment house on Ninety-fourth Street at the southwest corner of Columbus Avenue, where I was to live for the next dozen or so years. This shifting of residences was typical of the old city, at least among those who did not own their houses; it was due to the fact that, far from there being a housing shortage in middle-class quarters, there was actually a constant vacancy of around 4 percent—if I remember correctly the figure I once stumbled on.

People were tempted to move not merely for the sake of "modern conveniences," like electricity and "open plumbing," or to lower their expenses by getting the standard concession of a free month's rent;

sometimes they even moved, it would seem, as the simplest way of getting through a spring cleaning. At all events, they moved; and Moving Day, the first of May or the first of October, saw vans loading and unloading on every block. This whole scheme of moving, this game of musical chairs in domestic real estate, was based on the scandalously low wages that everyone who assisted in the game received: plasterers, painters, wallpaper hangers, moving men.

As a result of our many moves, I came to know from within the quality of the space in an old brownstone, and in a smaller, shallower kind of brown brick house we lived in for a few years on West Ninety-third Street, between Columbus Avenue and Central Park West; I have lived in an old "railroad flat," and in a better kind of flat with a central passage, bedrooms on one side, living rooms on the other; I have lived on the top floor of a walk-up and on the second floor of an elevator apartment, to say nothing of a more ancient and dingy flat house on West Fourth Street, where my wife and I started our married life.

In only one of my childhood homes did we have a view over any kind of open space other than the backyards: we were lucky if an ailanthus tree or two raised its head in the distance. Visually my domestic memories are mostly bleak and stuffy; and I hate to think how depressing the total effect would have been had not Central Park and Riverside Park always been there to gladden my eyes and to beckon my legs to a ramble. . . .

ALL AROUND
THE TOWN

My grandfather, Charles Graessel, introduced me to the city. He was really my mother's stepfather, but our relations were as solid as blood could have made them; and . . . I had no other visible grandfather. The fact that this genial soul had leisure time to be my daily companion for almost half a dozen years, from 1899 on, tells something about the social background of that period. At sixty he became a "gentleman of leisure," for he voluntarily retired from the post he had held for, I suppose, some dozen or more years, as head waiter at Delmonico's, a restaurant that then boasted perhaps the finest cuisine in the city. (The great Delmonico cookbook that its onetime chef and epicure Ranhofer produced in the nineties is still in my possession. It is a book full of fabulously rich and time-consuming recipes that pampered the appetites and taxed the stomachs and livers of the restaurant's patrons.) By that time my grandfather had saved what seemed to him then a sufficient sum of money to ensure a decent old age. In all, I don't think that this amounted to as much as twenty thousand dollars; but in purchasing power, of course, it was the equivalent of many times that sum today—and that is more than I could show in savings at the same age. . . .

My grandfather was a man of middle height, portly but solid, with a big head, a high forehead, and sideburns which he kept darkened by daily dabs of a vile-smelling liquid: but no mustache covered his broad upper lip. His heavy eyebrows, brushed upward, gave him a roguish look even in old age, though it is more evident in an earlier photograph. For me he was the dear *Doppelgänger* of my favorite childhood comic-strip character, Foxy Grandpa, who was always up to counter-mischief against his own mischievous imps.

Despite his obvious dignity in the Prince Albert coat he regularly

24

wore on our afternoon sorties, he was always up to sly jokes and teases, like suddenly vanishing behind a tree when one's back was turned, or at home, planting a huge sprig of parsley the day after I had planted parsley seed in the backyard garden and pretending that the plant had shot up while I was at school. When I was little, some of his tricks used to frighten me. The false faces and masks he brought home from Delmonico's—those were still the days of masked balls—always filled me with unmitigated terror at the sudden disappearance of the person I loved; even the Santa Claus mask upset me, though I delighted to make my own face disappear in the same terrifying way. But I still remember the taste of boned turkey with truffles or lobster à la Newburg which he sometimes brought home in generous samples.

My grandfather was undeviatingly kind and good-humored; and his willingness, on our afternoon walks, to look at his watch repeatedly, so that I might guess the time—he usually rewarded me with a penny or a candy when I guessed right—is probably responsible for what might otherwise seem my uncanny sense of time, which still operates. . . .

Until I was eight or nine I spent almost every afternoon in the company of my grandfather, in saunters around Central Park or along Riverside Drive. These walks furnished the aesthetic background of my childhood. Along Fifth Avenue or Riverside Drive my grandfather could tell me who lived in nearly every great mansion. Often we would sit down on a bench before the west carriage drive in Central Park to watch the regular afternoon procession of broughams, victorias, and hansom cabs in a sort of parkwide carrousel, which mingled self-display with "taking the air." . . . My grandfather could identify by name, sometimes with a little personal history, almost everyone of consequence who passed by: the Astors, the Vanderbilts, the Goelets, and the rest of the Four Hundred, as well as rich outsiders, like Russell Sage, who usually drove in an unfashionable surrey with a fringed top. ("A miser," my grandfather once said of Sage. "He watches every penny; but the Old Lady is very nice.")

Oddly enough I still recall the getup of an Astor—or was it a Vanderbilt?—who often drove through the park in a four-in-hand tallyho, with a coachman on the box behind, blowing a horn: a fresh-looking man, with red cheeks and a black, pointed beard above a white stock. Chauncey Depew remains in memory, too: he whose white sideburns contrasted with my grandfather's gray. Depew was so feeble, back in 1904, that he had to be accompanied by an attendant; and my grandfather, looking down at him from the parapet on Riverside Drive, said: "Poor devil, he hasn't long to live." Two years later my grandfather was dead, while Depew continued to fence with death for not a few more years.

On Saturdays or Sundays my grandfather would take me on much farther excursions to visit friends or old cronies like the Bastians. Old Bastian, a kindly white-bearded bookbinder, with a head a little like General Grant's, was one of those gentle, idealistic Germans who came to the New World lured less by the promise of a better income than by the desire for freedom, a desire nourished mainly by Cooper's *Leatherstocking Tales*; and it was Bastian indeed who, when I was only eight, urged me to read James Fenimore Cooper. I have him to thank for my early initiation into *The Spy*, *The Pilot*, and my favorite Leatherstocking novel, *The Pioneers*. . . .

Such visits took us to every part of the city; for we might go down to Canal Street, where my grandfather's boots were made, or over to the East Fifties to pick up the box of moderately expensive handmade cigars he always bought direct from the manufacturer, Keyser and Klug. Sometimes we would go to Brooklyn, on a Saturday afternoon, to listen to a band concert in Prospect Park with my granduncle Louis Siebrecht and his orphaned grandchild, Hewel, a somewhat sissy lad almost my own age. Sometimes my grandfather would encounter one or another of his old Delmonico cronies strolling in Central Park; and they would be as rigorously dressed and as finely polished in manner as he: particularly the debonair Phillipini, then chef at Delmonico's, in a gray Prince Albert and a gray high-crowned hat to match (a perfect Ascot costume!), setting off his gray Napoleonic imperial. I remember the torrential flow of his French! . . .

These excursions gave me my first impression of the city that lay beyond my neighborhood. . . . When, from 1915 on, I began to walk systematically over every neighborhood of my city and its surrounding regions, beholding its life with my own eyes, reading the buildings as if they were so many pages of a book, I was but continuing in solitude these early rambles.

All in all there was a reassuring solidity and poise about my grandfather, the poise of a "man of the world"; and the saddest thing about his long final illness was the shriveling up of his body as he lost the use of his legs and wasted away into a gray shadow. But a flickering sense of humor remained to the end. When I said good-bye to him one morning in late July 1906—he died in September—he knew it was our final parting, and he said: "Remember, Lewlie, all the things your mother used to blame me for, she'll blame on you when I am gone. . . . Be good to her and take care of her."

Much as I loved my grandfather, I had a child's self-protective callousness about his death. When the telegram announcing it came to Mrs. Josephine French's farm in Vermont, where I was again spending the summer, I took it coolly and talked matter-of-factly about what would happen to my mother and our household. Never a tear. He had been out of my active life for well over a year, and it was only in maturity that I at last, contemplating my childhood, realized all he had meant to it, and not least to my studies of the city.

Though my grandfather's presence is central to these youthful memories, other parts of the city revealed themselves to me under other auspices, and these more fragmentary impressions long sustained me, too. My Irish nurse, Nellie Ahearn—for a decade she was our cook and maid of all work—introduced me to the Middle West Side, the grimy tenements in the Forties, and those along nearer Amsterdam and Columbus Avenues, where her relatives and friends lived. My nose still wrinkles in disgust at the unsavory smell in the hallways of those tenements, compounded of overcooked cabbage and furniture polish, mingled with the most ugly smells of all, those of the bedbug poisons and the disinfectants that were supposed, in proportion to the offensiveness of the odor, to fortify the sanitary work of soap in cleaning. . . .

In time I was to know even poorer quarters from the inside, for, as a lad of nineteen, I would visit my friend Irwin Granich, later Michael Gold, the author of *Jews without Money,* who lived far down on the East Side on Chrystie Street. There only one room received outside light and, the tenement being older, whole colonies of cockroaches and bedbugs had had time to entrench themselves in the woodwork. But even in the most elegant parts of the West Side, I must add, just as in Carlyle's Chelsea, these insect companions of man were then far from scarce. The difference between the better apartments and the inferior kind was due partly to the fact that the former were regularly visited by exterminators. (In those halcyon days no one thought of exterminating anything but rodents and insects: human beings were still supposed to be immune.)

Thanks to these contacts, I grew up in the real world, aware of its many social stratifications and faults; not least aware of its poverty, its sordor, and the unflinching efforts of so many of the poor to maintain their respectability and decency in the face of odds one might have thought overwhelming. Later, in the mid-thirties, this underlying experience of the human diversity of New Yorkers made it easy for me, once the ice was broken, to get closer to my Tammany colleagues on the Board of Higher Education. They might call me Professor at first, but they would soon recognize that I was one of them in my understanding and boyhood love of the city. Like them I had gone through the public schools and was at home everywhere.

. . .

Looking back now, I can see how deeply my walks with my grandfather influenced my later life; not least, how important they were in counteracting the narrow, secondhand learning and the bureaucratic routines of the elementary schools I attended. Being a passive, timid child, weakened before seven by a prolonged case of measles followed by mastoiditis and a long, violent bout of whooping cough, I might have found my life completely desiccated by the current academic drilling, but for the peephole glimpses into other lives and other ways that these walks under the tutelage of my grandfather had given me.

During the period when I was growing up, a series of gigantic shifts and upheavals took place in the urban scene around me; and many of these were, astonishingly, changes for the better. It was then that the first new patch of open play space was carved out of one of the worst slum areas on the East Side, to become Jacob Riis Park; it was then that the first freestanding skyscraper, the Flatiron Building, was built by Daniel H. Burnham, the successor of Burnham and Root, the Root who had built that other freestanding office building, the Monadnock Block, in Chicago. It was then that the series of bridges north of the Brooklyn Bridge was built, culminating in the most handsome one after the Brooklyn Bridge, the Hellgate Railroad Bridge. In the first decades of the twentieth century, Park Avenue likewise achieved a moment of exemplary urbanity and good form, with a broad green strip down the middle that made a pleasant pedestrian walk; and it was then that a great tidal movement of population took place, into the Bronx for the lower-income groups and out into the suburbs for the well-to-do. . . .

The city I once knew so intimately has been wrecked; most of what remains will soon vanish; and therewith scattered fragments of my own life will disappear in the rubble that is carted away. I have not Frank Lloyd Wright's consolation, when he designed that overmassive pillbox, the Guggenheim Museum, that the building made in his image would survive a nuclear bombing, so that even though the rest of the city was destroyed, his spirit would still be present to survey the ruins. In that sense I share the fate of my generation. Whether hilarious or sad, we are all displaced persons. . . .

[When I was a boy in New York,] even the intimate daily events of the city had a special domestic color: this somehow was most in evidence on a late spring or summer evening, along the streets where private, middle-class row houses prevailed. Each family, or the occupants of each boarding house, would swarm on the high stoops, usually sitting on straw mats, often on hot nights burning incense or acrid Chinese punk to keep off the mosquitoes, waving palm-leaf fans, chatting among themselves, occasionally exchanging greetings with neighbors, whilst keeping an eye on the children having a last game of tag or running a buckboard wagon lighted by a candle in a cigar box, with a little boy as human motor to push it from the rear, up and down the block.

That picture, as I bring it back, has a kind of bucolic innocence and neighborliness which recalls that vanished age. Through fluttering lace curtains a lonely piano might be pleading the cause of love, but except for that and the rumble of the elevated or the clop-clop of a cab horse on the cobblestones, the human voice struck the dominant note: chuckling, laughing, just idly talking, sometimes whistling and even singing. But if some dire event or some criminal outrage had occurred later in the evening, the raucous shout of a newsboy crying "Uxtry! Uxtry! All about the great explosion!" might chill the spine for a moment.

This life, without motion pictures, without telephones, without radios, without television sets, without motorcars, without the vast volumes of standardized goods that must nowadays be bought promptly and consumed rapidly, was not destitute of amusement and color: but it found its variety in little changes, little differences. The neighborhood grocery store may fittingly symbolize this. Every grocer's boasted a row of black lacquered bins holding tea and coffee in bulk, which were identified by their place of origin. One bought coffees—Santos, Rio, Maracaibo, Java, Mocha—knowing their special flavors and gauging the quality against a wide range of prices.

That colorful, still selective middle-class world began to disappear in New York after the First World War; and since the fifties has been disappearing in Europe, where it clung tenaciously until after the Second World War. (The Monoprix chain in Paris—and Le Drug Store—sounded the new ominous note.) Nothing so well indicates to me the difference between my own generation and the present one as the fact that I do not, without a certain inner resistance and resentment, accept a system of marketing in which all the decisions have been taken out of the hands of both the shopkeeper and the customer and put under the remote control of the market researcher and the packaging expert, the advertising agency and the wholesale distributor. Those who have grown up in this packaged world accept such external controls and compulsions as normal: their loss of choice, their loss of taste, they do not even notice, for they have never known anything different. We have now exchanged autonomy for automation.

· · ·

But one thing is missing from this nostalgic picture. What I cannot quite recapture is the little boy who first took this in: or rather, I cannot get inside him, for he, too, flits across my "finder" as merely part of the scene: much more scenery than person. For the rest, I behold that child as an outsider might, now squatting on the floor, making drawings of battleships or horses, now calling out "Good night! What time is it?" repeatedly, after going to bed, to make sure of the presence of his mother or grandfather in the next room. Often enough the whole family is playing pinochle, and his wakeful inquiries are trying their patience. Or again, he is playing red rover or buttons with the little gang on the block, like any other West Side boy.

Oh! but where is that bright lad himself, growing year by year in his own consciousness of himself? Somehow he eludes me, and I now begin to guess the reason: he is indissolubly part of the self I have become and therefore cannot be viewed from a vantage point outside. When I look too intently at him, I have the horrifying sense one sometimes has if one looks too long at one's image in the mirror. If one keeps on staring, nothing will remain except a mocking mask, detached from any living reality.

OUR
METROPOLITAN
PAGEANTS

. . .Two . . . aspects of the city captivated my early adolescence: the theater and the tennis courts. Between them they lifted the gray blight that would, without them, have crept over my youth.

Well before my college days I tapped a source of delight that penetrated even deeper than had tennis: the theater in all its forms, from the circus and the Wild West Show to vaudeville, from the parades on Fifth Avenue to the great naval pageants on the Hudson and, later, the masques and musical festivals that became popular in the years before the First World War. . . .

Central to all these special experiences was the vaudeville show; for, like so many West Side boys of my age and background, I used even before adolescence to go occasionally, on Saturday afternoons, to Proctor's or Keith's, particularly to the old Colonial Theater on Broadway and Sixty-second Street.

Like the circus, the vaudeville show was then an international performance: a single program might offer, besides our American clog dancers and monologists, an Italian acrobatic team; a London music-hall performer, like Little Tich; a Scots comedian, like Harry Lauder; a French chanteuse, like Yvette Guilbert; a troupe of Japanese jugglers; and by turns one identified oneself with each of them and conceived a new role and a new life. How colorful, how suggestive of the world's own variety—and of its oneness, too—were these variety acts!

My youth coincided with the last great days of vaudeville. I saw Vesta Victoria and the swagger Vesta Tilley, and Anna Lloyd, who sang "There Was I, Waiting at the Church," and some of the best of the old-time monologists and magicians. But it was all magic. One walked home under the sparkle of Broadway lights, with a lift of the heart and

31

a gleam in the eye, imitating in fantasy the juggling and dancing, the pattering and drawling in a style that daily life had never presented. . . .

In the autobiographic chapters of the final volume of Arnold Toynbee's *A Study of History,* he reveals the part that the great museums of London played in his own intellectual development, not least those in South Kensington, which adjoined his neighborhood to the north. My own youth was spent in precisely the equivalent area of New York, and to the extent that I was later cut off from formal academic studies, I made even fuller use of the two great museums of art and natural history that stand almost opposite each other, with Central Park coming between them.

These museums were old haunts of mine from childhood on, but now I went to them for solid food, not merely to get occasional refreshment. The American Museum of Natural History was, back in 1915, just on the point of turning from a showcase museum, full of detached specimens, into an ecologically ordered museum, dramatically presenting organisms functioning in their natural environments, in visible association with other species in a symbiotic, if necessarily static, relationship. All this was being done with the aid of artists like Charles Robert Knight, as well as naturalistic taxidermists, in a way that had never been attempted in the past. In the Hall of Evolution the curators had made the beginnings of a connected presentation of the whole course of evolution; they were not yet embarrassed by the confused wealth and muddled proliferation of the later decades, from which a semblance of order is only now beginning to emerge.

The Metropolitan Museum of Art had a more personal effect upon my life, in ways that those who are interested in art only as detached aesthetic experience would not suspect: above all, by putting before me a personal ideal of bodily beauty. There was one particular figure that had, unaccountably, a special influence on me: a handsome Roman copy of, I think, a Greek athlete, a rather mature man with a beard, using a strigil to wipe the cleansing oil off his body. I wanted to look like him, though I stopped short of the beard! That statue used to stand near the old south entrance, and the museum never seemed quite the same to me when they removed it sometime in the twenties, probably to the cellar. But it played a part in my general physical rehabilitation during this period. Perhaps such noble nude statues produced a similar response in the ancient world: did not their gods serve as models?

. . .

I began to use the great central library on Fifth Avenue in 1912, shortly after it was opened, and I have memories of its original space and amplitude, its bright marbled freshness, the soul-filling silence that once pervaded its halls, the sense of a building lifted above the rush, the congestion, the pressures of the teeming city outside. If I may paraphrase the poet, the museums were but my visits: this was my home. With a lordly gesture of hospitality that great library invited me to use what was then and perhaps still is—despite the staggering difficulties of keeping it so—the best organized catalog in the world, and what was for long the quickest service of books. . . .

The new building itself, designed by Thomas Hastings (Carrère and Hastings), was conceived primarily as a great classic monument, in the same fashion as the Pennsylvania Station, done about the same time. But no sufficient allowance was made in that design for the continued expansion or alteration of the facilities of the library, for the need for internal flexibility, for the requirements of stack space and readers' space in the future years. So within a decade the special rooms of the library began to overflow into the corridors, and this process has kept on, through sheer inner pressure, until one of the greatest qualities of the building, its repose, its inviting emptiness, has disappeared, even in the two rooms that held out the longest: the Catalog Hall and the great Main Reading Room, where now a second stack of books prevents one from reaching, without the help of an attendant, the volumes along the walls that used to be accessible at will. Here as elsewhere in our culture excessive quantity has eroded quality.

The spaciousness of this monumental building was not in itself an error on Hastings's part; quite the contrary, it had an immediate effect on the mind which favored all the proper offices of the library. If the decoration was a too sedulous mixture of classic motifs, with such atavistic features as lions' heads spouting water for a drinking fountain—a sanitary aberration soon to be absurdly corrected by triggered taps issuing from the same mouths—my reproaches even on this score would not be too heavy; for I can remember what a blessed relief it was, after an hour of close reading, to lean back in my chair and pick out some intricate figure on the ceiling, so much better than a blank space or a spot on the plaster, on which to rest my eyes: indeed, there was a nude girl, whose beautiful trunk tapered into a leafy scroll design, who became a sort of platonic mistress and sometimes served as the center of my still youthful erotic dreams. I even once wrote a sticky poem to her. But it was while waiting for the indicator to call me to the delivery desk that I first read Emerson's *Journals* and James Legge's edition of the Chinese classics.

· · ·

During this early period of manhood (1914–19) I began to experience the waterfront of New York, by repeated rides on ferryboats, in a fashion that has now become impossible. Everywhere the wholesale commitment to bridges and tunnels across and under the rivers and bays, for the sake of speed alone, is depriving us of this primal source of recreation, causing us to go farther in search of enlivening change —and often to fare worse.

But surely the ferryboat was one of the great inventions of the nineteenth century: that great turtlelike creature—plodding through waters often iridescent with scum near the ferry slips, doggedly meeting the hazards of time and weather, sometimes serving as a summer excursion boat to Staten Island, sometimes bumping and cracking through the ice floes in the surly black water, so that the salt spray would tingle in one's nostrils.

What endless variations on the simple theme of "passage" by water! Even the short trips to Jersey City from downtown New York provided a touch of uncertainty and adventure, allowing for the tide, dodging other boats and ships, all with a closeness to the sea and sky and the wide sweep of the city itself that no other form of locomotion could boast.

Ferryboats would have been worthwhile for their value as a source of recreation alone: no, I would go further, they were worth running if only to give sustenance to poets and lovers and lonely young people, from Walt Whitman to Edna St. Vincent Millay, from Alfred Stieglitz and John Sloan to myself. Ferries had uses beyond the ordinary needs for transportation, and their relative slowness was not the least part of their merit—though as to speed, it has often taken far more time to cross by motorcar from Manhattan to Brooklyn or from San Francisco to Oakland during the rush hour, amid poisonous fumes and irritating tensions, than it once did by ferry. Those who put speed above all other values are often cheated even of speed by their dedication to a single mode of mass locomotion.

No poet, hurtling by plane even as far as Cathay, has yet written a poem comparable to "Crossing Brooklyn Ferry"; no painter has come back with a picture comparable to John Sloan's *Ferryboat Ride*, which, for me, in its dun colors, recalls one of the moments I liked best on the North River: a lowery sky, a smoke-hung skyline, and the turbid waters of the river. When I read Whitman's poem now, I realize the special historical advantage of belonging to a generation that is "ebbing with the ebb-tide," for I am old enough to have felt every sensation he described, to have seen every sight—except the then-bowered heights of Hoboken—with a sense of identification that even the most active imagination could hardly evoke now.

Those wonderful long ferry rides! Alas for a later generation that cannot guess how they opened the city up, or how the change of pace and place, from swift to slow, from land to water, had a specially stimulating effect upon the mind. But if I loved the ferries, I loved the bridges, too; and one after another I walked over all the bridges that linked Manhattan to Long Island, even that least rewarding one, the Queensboro. But it was the Brooklyn Bridge that I loved best, partly because of its own somber perfection of form, with its spidery lacing of cables contrasting with the great stone piers through which they were suspended: stone masonry that seemed in its harmony of granite pier, classic coping, and ogive arch to crystallize the essence of Roman, Romanesque, and Gothic architecture; while its cables stretched like a bowstring to shoot a steel arrow into our own age.

Since we lived on Brooklyn Heights between 1922 and 1925, I took every possible occasion to walk back and forth across the Brooklyn Bridge; and I knew it in all weathers and at all times of the day and night: so it is no wonder that when I came to write *Sticks and Stones* in 1924, I gave perhaps the first critical appreciation of that achievement since Montgomery Schuyler's contemporary essay, published in his *American Architecture* in 1893.

At that period, as it happened, Hart Crane and I—then personally unknown to each other—were living on Brooklyn Heights, and he, in his poet's way, was engaged in a similar enterprise: indeed, some time later, after I had moved away, he consulted me about biographic materials on the Roeblings, the builders of the Bridge. Thousands of people must have felt the same as we in our different ways had felt, ever since the Bridge was opened; but no one had freshly expressed it until the twenties. . . .

So deeply did the Bridge itself capture my imagination that before I had abandoned my aim of becoming a playwright (as late as 1927), I wrote the first draft of a long play on the theme of the Bridge: a play that I recognized, even while writing it, could be produced only when done over into a motion picture. Fragments of that play still haunt me: not least a love scene, at night, high up on one of the piers of the half-finished structure, with a sense of giddy isolation heightening the passion of the lovers—and the muted whistles and hoots from the river below, in the spreading fog, underscoring with the note of the city itself their private encounter. . . .

There was a slightly older contemporary who, as it seemed in 1915, had caught the very beat of the city, a beat that had begun to pulsate with quickening consciousness in all of us. This was Ernest Poole, who in *The Harbor,* through his choice of scenes, characters, social issues, said something for my generation that no one else had yet said, though he was never—that was perhaps his tragedy!—to say it so well again.

Brooklyn Heights and *The Harbor* took shape almost entirely in Poole's imagination. But he captured the contrast between the depths of Furman Street, on the level of the waterfront, rimmed by a jumble of warehouses and docks, and the top of the stone-walled escarpment, with its seemly rows of brick or serpentine houses which commanded the whole harbor. There on Furman Street in the middle of the afternoon I had already seen an aged, drunken slattern, foul with whiskey and fouler with words—exhibiting the destitution and squalor that the gardens and mansions above both actually and figuratively overlooked.

I hardly dare to look at *The Harbor* to find out how the printed pages would compare now with the sensations I had in 1915, when I first read the book. Somehow that novel seethed with my own hopeful excitement over the contemporary world of factories and steamships, of employers and labor unions, of political strife and private ambition, giving me much the same reaction I had felt earlier when reading H. G. Wells's *The New Machiavelli* or his *Tono-Bungay*—both books that influenced my youth. *The Harbor* satisfied my appetite for the concrete and the contemporary, which was a very real appetite in those quickening days. The fact that Poole saw the city in much the same way I was beginning to see it gave moral backing and political support to my own efforts.

Not that I needed much backing! We all had a sense that we were on the verge of translation into a new world, a quite magical translation, in which the best hopes of the American Revolution, the French Revolution, and the Industrial Revolution would all be simultaneously fulfilled. The First World War battered and shattered those hopes, but it took years before the messages received through our eyes or felt at our fingers' ends were effectively conveyed to our brains and could be decoded: for long those ominous messages simply did not make sense. Until well into the 1930s we could always see the bright side of the darkest cloud. We did not, while the spirit of our confident years worked in us, guess that the sun upon which we counted might soon be in eclipse.

Yes: I loved the great bridges and walked back and forth over them, year after year. But as often happens with repeated experiences, one memory stands out above all others: a twilight hour in early spring— it was March, I think—when, starting from the Brooklyn end, I faced into the west wind sweeping over the rivers from New Jersey. The ragged, slate-blue cumulus clouds that gathered over the horizon left open patches for the light of the waning sun to shine through, and finally, as I reached the middle of the Brooklyn Bridge, the sunlight spread across the sky, forming a halo around the jagged mountain of skyscrapers, with the darkened loft buildings and warehouses huddling below in the foreground. The towers, topped by the golden pinnacles of the new Woolworth Building, still caught the light even as it began to ebb away. Three-quarters of the way across the Bridge I saw the skyscrapers in the deepening darkness become slowly honeycombed with lights until, before I reached the Manhattan end, these buildings piled up in a dazzling mass against the indigo sky.

Here was my city, immense, overpowering, flooded with energy and light; there below lay the river and the harbor, catching the last flakes of gold on their waters, with the black tugs, free from their barges, plodding dockward, the ferryboats lumbering from pier to pier, the tramp steamers slowly crawling toward the sea, the Statue of Liberty erectly standing, little curls of steam coming out of boat whistles or towered chimneys, while the rumbling elevated trains and trolley cars just below me on the Bridge moved in a relentless tide to carry tens of thousands homeward. And there was I, breasting the March wind, drinking in the city and the sky, both vast, yet both contained in me, transmitting through me the great mysterious will that had made them and the promise of the new day that was still to come.

The world, at that moment, opened before me, challenging me, beckoning me, demanding something of me that it would take more than a lifetime to give, but raising all my energies by its own vivid promise to a higher pitch. In that sudden revelation of power and beauty all the confusions of adolescence dropped from me, and I trod the narrow, resilient boards of the footway with a new confidence that came, not from my isolated self alone, but from the collective energies I had confronted and risen to.

I cannot hope to bring back the exaltation of that moment: the wonder of it was like the wonder of an orgasm in the body of one's beloved, as if one's whole life had led up to that moment and had swiftly culminated there. And yet I have carried the sense of that occasion, along with two or three other similar moments, equally enveloping and pregnant, through my life: they remain, not as a constant presence, but as a momentary flash reminding me of heights approached and scaled, as a mountain climber might carry with him the memory of some daring ascent, never to be achieved again. Since then I have courted that moment more than once on the Brooklyn Bridge; but the exact conjunction of weather and light and mood and inner readiness has never come back. That experience remains alone: a fleeting glimpse of the utmost possibilities life may hold for man.

II

ARCHITECTURE AS A HOME FOR MAN

If man is created, as the legends
say, in the image of the gods, his
buildings are done in the image of
his own mind and institutions.
—Lewis Mumford

Introduction

Mumford first made his reputation as a writer in the field of architecture criticism, and although he never devoted himself exclusively to this subject, he has produced a body of architecture criticism of unrivaled quality and prescience. He has probably done more than any other writer in our time to heighten the American public's awareness of architecture, teaching us how to approach buildings, what to expect from them, and what to demand from those who design them.

Mumford has used architecture, moreover, to illuminate the history of the human achievement as a whole. *Sticks and Stones,* his first book on American architecture, is a study not just of architecture but also of architecture and civilization; it has been Mumford's consistent claim that the two are inseparable. From John Ruskin he learned that every stone has a tongue and every tongue tells a story, that buildings are so many records of a community's life and spirit. "Each generation," as Mumford once remarked, "writes its biography in the buildings it creates." But whereas Ruskin confined himself to the great landmarks and masterpieces of architecture, Mumford reached out to consider, as well, simple, commonplace structures—houses, barns, factories, bridges, post offices, even street corner luncheonettes—as reflections of a people's purposes and aspirations.[1]

Mumford had no formal architectural education, and this perhaps explains his refreshingly human approach to buildings. He learned about architecture by studying it firsthand, on his early walking surveys of New York, excursions that eventually took him beyond his native Manhattan to cities, towns, and hamlets up and down the northeastern seaboard. To those seeking a sound architectural education his advice has always been the same—experience the building itself.[2]

Mumford brought to the appreciation of architecture the visual sensitivity of the artist; and it was not unusual for him to make a quick pencil sketch of a building or a city scene before he began to take down notes for one of his early essays on architecture for magazines like the *Freeman* and *The American Mercury* (a practice he continued intermittently throughout his life). Yet Mumford never considered architecture as solely, or even primarily, an art form. Unlike painting or poetry, architecture must be shaped to useful human purposes. Its first responsibility is a social one—to serve the people who use it, to elevate the quality of everyday living.

It was his undeviating attention to basic human needs that led Mumford to criticize the skyscraper, as early as the 1920s, as a promoter of urban congestion and inflated land values, and as a building form more expressive of technical virtuosity than of social function. Mumford did not, however, oppose the skyscraper in all its forms. He accepted it as an unavoidable fact of modern urban life, and as a critic he assessed its strengths and weaknesses as a building style. In the 1920s, for example, he was sharply critical of the showy historicism of such skyscrapers as New York's Woolworth Building, Gothic and classic imitations that were, he once said, "born old." Yet in the more straightforward, deliberately modern tall buildings of Chicago architects like John Wellborn Root and Louis Sullivan, buildings that he first encountered in 1927, he found the beginnings of a distinguished American architecture.[3]

In *The Brown Decades: A Study of the Arts in America, 1865–1895*, from which the second essay of this section is taken, Mumford gave his fullest appraisal of the great Chicago builders, re-introducing his countrymen to a powerful and handsome building style. The concluding section of this essay, on Frank Lloyd Wright, is probably Mumford's most concise statement of his views on what modern architecture should be. In Wright's ground-hugging prairie houses, open to sunlight and the environment and built to conform to the characteristics of the terrain, Mumford found the promise of a new organic architecture combining function and feeling.

In his earliest writing Mumford campaigned for a distinctly modern style in architecture and the arts. The machine had produced new physical materials and techniques, and he urged architects and artists to use these in their work—to follow in the tradition of those great nineteenth-century master builders John A. and Washington Roebling, whose Brooklyn Bridge he hailed as the supreme engineering achievement of the age, a Chartres Cathedral of the epoch of steam and steel. Mumford, accordingly, was one of the first champions of the new International Style of Walter Gropius, Ludwig Mies van der Rohe, Adolf Loos, and Le Corbusier, seeing in the early work of these avant-garde architects and designers a healthy concern for functional clarity and social need.

Yet Mumford was one of the first critics on either side of the Atlantic to detect in modernism what would become all too apparent in its more mature manifestations: an almost fanatical fascination with purity of form. In one of his first essays on the new minimalist style, he argued that while the absence of ornament and the clear expression of form-in-function "is what constitutes the modern feeling . . . there must be something more." That "something more" included "feeling," decoration, and, most crucial of all, a more complex appreciation of human needs—of people's occasional desire, for example, for the lyrical and the unexpected.[4]

Le Corbusier proclaimed that we live in a machine age, so our buildings must be machines to live in. Mumford pointed out, in his famous essay "The Case against Modern Architecture," that it was only a short step from buildings as *machines à habiter* to buildings as characterless air-conditioned boxes. Mumford saw his fears realized when sterile imitations of Mies van der Rohe's elegantly proportioned glass towers began to appear in midtown Manhattan in the 1950s. "Architecture," he had written in his notes in the early 1930s, "is either the prophecy of an unformed society or the tomb of a finished one."[5] We do not have to guess where he placed the new skyscraper architecture.

Mumford's great fear was that this recent surge of high-rise development would destroy the city itself. He has argued consistently that to function well, a city must encourage social intimacy, face-to-face meetings in parks, shops, cafés, and other public areas. "You might say . . . that the city is a place for multiplying happy chances and making the most of unplannable opportunities," he remarked in a speech before a group of architects in 1961. But when you put people in enormous glass boxes with narrow windy spaces between them "you lose the possibility of this kind of interchange." A livable city, in other words, requires an appropriate architectural form. In redesigning our cities, architects and planners should build "on the human scale for lovers and for friends."[6]

Notes

1. Mumford, *Architecture*, Reading with a Purpose, no. 23 (Chicago: American Library Association, 1926), 9, 25; Mumford, "The Modern City," in Talbot Hamlin, ed., *Forms and Functions of Twentieth-Century Architecture*, vol. 4, *Building Types* (New York: Columbia University Press, 1952), 802.

2. Mumford, *Architecture*, 34.

3. Mumford, "American Architecture To-day," *Architecture* (New York), 57 (April 1928): 181.

4. Ibid., 181–88.

5. Mumford, Random Notes, 1934, LM MSS.

6. Mumford, "Culture of the City," *American Institute of Architects Journal*, n.s., 35, no. 6 (June 1961): 54–60.

THE BROOKLYN
BRIDGE

From the standpoint of art and nature, the gross inefficiencies of industrialism in its earliest stages were recorded in the general loss of form in the landscape and in the various works of man that appeared on it. Was industrialism synonymous with ugliness? Could steel be used as effectively as stone? Up to the middle of the nineteenth century there was no sure answer to these questions. Cast iron had been used in bridge construction in London with a little practical success, but with no decisive aesthetic results. The great glass and iron conservatory that [Joseph] Paxton built for the London Exposition of 1851 seemed to promise something; but a similar building, done a little later in New York, made the issue seem dubious.

A stunning act was necessary to demonstrate the aesthetic possibilities of the new materials, and to give people confidence in that side of engineering which the engineer had least concerned himself with: its human and aesthetic effect. That act was the building of the Brooklyn Bridge—not merely one of the best pieces of engineering the nineteenth century can show anywhere, but perhaps the most completely satisfactory structure of any kind that had appeared in America. Coming into existence in an "era of deformation," it proved that the loss of form was an accident, not an inescapable result of the industrial processes.

The Brooklyn Bridge was the conception and achievement of two men: John A. Roebling and his son Washington, loyally supported by a corps of workers whose dangers and difficulties they intimately shared.

This selection was originally part of "The Renewal of the Landscape," a chapter in *The Brown Decades*. (Editor's note)

In order to understand the monument itself, one must know a little of the characters and personalities that stood behind it.

John A. Roebling was born in Mühlhausen, in Thuringia, in 1806. He received his degree as an engineer at the Royal Polytechnic Institute in Berlin in 1826, after having studied architecture, bridge construction, and hydraulics: according to [a] biographical memoir, he studied philosophy with Hegel, "who avowed that John Roebling was his favourite pupil." After spending three years in obligatory service with the state, as superintendent of public works in Westphalia, John Roebling emigrated to the United States in 1831. He had $3,000 in capital, and with a few fellow immigrants he founded the village of Saxonburg, about twenty-five miles from Pittsburgh. Here Washington Roebling was born in 1837.

Those were the days when the canal boats made their way through the Alleghenies by means of long overhill portages, the whole boat being pulled up the steep incline: the ordinary ropes used in such hauls frayed too quickly, and Roebling, whose first job was that of assistant engineer on the slack-water navigation of Beaver River, invented the steel cable to take the place of the weak hemp, and set up a cable manufacturing plant. Roebling had first seen a chain suspension bridge on a student tramp at Bamberg, and suspension bridges formed the subject of his graduation thesis. He presently invented a suspension aqueduct to make the portage of a canal over a river, using cable instead of chains; and he built it in record time. Another step brought him to the first cable suspension bridge at Pittsburgh in 1846. In 1849, he removed his wire-rope factory to Trenton, New Jersey. Without these wire-ropes vertical transportation would have come tardily and been more dangerous.

Roebling was the architect of his own plant; he designed every piece of machinery in it. Like many other early industrialists—people like Robert Gair, the paper-box manufacturer, for example—Roebling was a man of iron regularity and inflexible will: he would call off a conference with a man who was five minutes late. He disciplined his family, apparently, with equal rigor. Indeed, he anticipated the customs of Erewhon by regarding illness as a moral offense and penalizing it severely. But he was also an eager student of the new scene: in the midst of his inventions, he read Emerson and wrote a long manuscript volume entitled "Roebling's Theory of the Universe." His son, after being graduated from the Rensselaer Polytechnic in 1857, assisted his father on the Allegheny suspension bridge. During the Civil War, Washington built suspension bridges for the Union Army and did balloon observation.

Manhattan Island needed a bridge connection with Long Island to supplement the ferries. The bitter winter of 1866–67, which froze over the East River entirely and blocked ferryboat traffic, brought to a head the plan for a bridge, which John Roebling had broached in 1857. Nothing but Roebling's experience, his personal power, and his immense authority could have made this plan go through: a suspension bridge with towers 276 feet high and almost 1,600 feet in the central span had not been built anywhere in the world: Stephenson, one of the great English engineers, had declared against this form. By 1869 the design had come into existence. Unfortunately, as a result of an accident on a ferry, John Roebling acquired lockjaw and died, leaving behind little more than the outline that Washington was to work up into their masterpiece, provided he had the power to grapple with the many unsolved problems of tactics and construction.

Washington Roebling's heavy bullet head reminds one a little of Grant's: what it lacked of his father's granite intellectuality was made up for by an equally massive will. Washington threw himself into the work. In 1871 the foundations for the Brooklyn tower were sunk. The building of the New York tower involved a drastic decision: should he waste a year and possibly many lives in digging to bedrock, or should he let the sand distribute the weight of the caisson on the uneven rock, a few feet away? He risked his reputation and his fortune on the decision; but he boldly faced the possibility of seeing his tower slip into the river. That possibility cannot have been absent from his mind until the cable and span were set.

The whole work of building the bridge was full of martial decisions, heroic sacrifices: the Civil War itself had been easier on Colonel Roebling. A fire broke out in the caisson in 1871; and Roebling, who had spent more time than any other workman under pressure, and who directed the fighting of the fire, acquired the bends, or caisson disease. He retired to a house on Columbia Heights; his wife sat at the window with a telescope and reported on the progress of the work; and from his bed Washington Roebling directed every detail through letters. In 1872, fearing that he might not live to finish the bridge, and knowing how incomplete all the plans and instructions were, he spent the winter writing and drawing in all the details; and a year later, after a cure in Wiesbaden, he was still too weak to talk for more than a few minutes. Such heroism was not lost: the work went with a will: the little man on a white horse who commanded at Austerlitz never had a more devoted army. When the carriage for winding the cable was ready for trial, the first man to test it out was not a common workman, but Frank Farrington, the master mechanic. As many as six hundred men were employed at one time. More than twenty were fatally hurt. Several succumbed to caisson disease. But the granite towers rose: the nineteen strands of cable were spun and anchored: the girders were riveted: the bridge stood. Cars and processions passed over it. It still stood.

In 1883 the battle was over. The bridge was opened, and the Brooklyn Bridge took its place with the Eads Bridge at St. Louis and the Pont Garabit in France as one of the victories of modern engineering. But it was more than that. If anyone doubts that a bridge is an aesthetic object, if anyone doubts that it reveals personality, let him compare the Brooklyn Bridge with the other suspension bridges on the same river. The first bridge is in every sense classic. Like every positive creative work, the Brooklyn Bridge eludes analysis, in that its effect is disproportionate to the visible means, and it triumphs over one's objections even when it falls short of its highest possibilities.

I know no better appreciation of the bridge than Montgomery Schuyler's contemporary estimate. His whole appraisal, in *American Architecture*, is worth examination; but here is the nub of it. "It is an organism of nature. There was no question in the mind of the designer of 'good taste' or of appearance. He learned the law that struck its curves, the law that fixed the strength of the relation of its parts, and he applied the law. His work is beautiful, as the work of a ship-builder is unfailingly beautiful in the forms and outlines in which he is only studying 'what the water likes,' without a thought of beauty. . . . Where a more massive material forbade him to skeletonize the structure, and the lines of effort and resistance needed to be brought out by modelling, he has failed to bring them out, and his structure is only as impressive as it needs must be."

Still, to say that the masonry might have been better is a different thing from being able to point out a single architect who might have done it better: the [Henry Hobson] Richardson of 1885 might have qualified, but the young romantic architect of 1870 would, I fear, have made a horrible botch of it. Schuyler objected to the towers on the ground that the stone does not reflect the passage of the cables over the cushions on which they rest: but perhaps the greatest weakness is in the heavy rustication of the granite and the character of the stone cornice. But, particularly from the waterfront below, the piers are simple and convincing: at all events, they are the highwater mark of American architecture in the period between the design of the Washington Monument and the last phase of Richardson. The stone plays against the steel: the granite mass in compression, the spidery steel in tension. In this structure, the architecture of the past, massive and protective, meets the architecture of the future, light, aerial, open to sunlight, an architecture of voids rather than solids.

The Brooklyn Bridge was both a fulfillment and a prophecy. In the use of steel in tension it disclosed a great range of new possibilities: for the great mission of steel as a building material is essentially to span and enclose space, and to remove the inconvenient bulkiness of bearing walls and stone columns. In its absence of ornament, its refusal to permit the steel to be other than its own unadorned reality, the Brooklyn Bridge pointed to the logic and aesthetics of the machine; and it did this far more rigorously than its later rival, the Eiffel Tower in Paris, with its early Art Nouveau treatment of the base. Finally, the bridge existed in its own right, independent of its influences and potentialities, as a work of art, a delight to the artist and the poet, but equally well appreciated by the man in the street.

This was not the first work of engineering to be a work of art; but it was the first product of the age of coal and iron to achieve this completeness of expression. It needed a man of John Roebling's intellectual and philosophic capacities to conceive such a clean, untrammeled work; it needed Washington's courage to make it an actuality. Washington Roebling lingered on, once his great life-work was fulfilled, a soldier who had not the good fortune to die on the battlefield: he collected minerals, and found life a little bitter and sardonic, according to reports, in the final years before his death in 1926. The firm that these men founded remains, too; but the heroism and the exploit of an untried problem has been diminished a little by routine: the new Hudson River bridge is doubtless a mighty work, but in comparison with the knowledge, experience, and mechanical powers available in 1869, the first is still the grander accomplishment.

If the lesson of the Brooklyn Bridge has been less potent in our engineering and architecture than it should have been, it is perhaps because our engineering schools have had a narrower conception of the engineer's vocation and culture than John Roebling had. Their simple factual statements, their respect for materials, their willing anonymity, are all fine qualities: in them is the making of a modern architectural vernacular. What is needed is an application of the method and attitude to something more than the bare mechanical problem. But the lesson of the Brooklyn Bridge has not altogether been lost: far from it. Dams, waterworks, locks, bridges, power plants, factories—we begin to recognize these as important parts of the human environment. They are good or bad, efficient or inefficient, by something more than quantitative criteria. The Roeblings perhaps never used the word "aesthetics" in this relation; but it was their distinction to have made it visible.

TOWARDS
MODERN
ARCHITECTURE

When the Civil War broke, architecture in America had been sinking steadily for a generation. "Order," "fitness," "comeliness," "proportion," were words that could no longer be applied to it: construction was submerged in that morass of jerry-building, tedious archaicism, and spurious romanticism that made up the architectural achievement of the nineteenth century.

In the American farmhouses, the open fireplaces were already being boxed up to permit the more efficient operation of the iron stove, with its bulgy firebox and its ornamented legs; the simple Windsor chairs were retreating to the attic; the newly added porches were presently embellished with scroll-saw caprice; the fine proportions of wall and window were lost; and in the seventies, the mansard roof came, a crowning indignity. In the eastern parts of the country a chocolate-colored sandstone replaced brick for dwellings, while cast-iron façade became the synonym for modernity in office buildings and department stores.

Partly under the pressure of higher land values, the rooms in city houses became narrower, as the house crawled over the remaining backyard space; and the interiors became dark and airless: instead of being two rooms deep, as was the practice in the provincial city, they were now three and sometimes four deep on the lower floors: in New York the very rich even achieved back-to-back houses. If the upper classes did not fully realize the dreadful housing problem that existed in the slums of every large city, to say nothing of many small ones, where a multitude of poverty-stricken people lived in damp, sunless, airless rooms, it was partly because they were gaily and rapidly building slums of their own, with almost as little concern for their own hygiene as they showed in their tenement properties.

Beauty was defined in terms of visible possessions: no house was thought fit to live in that did not contain truckloads of ornament and bric-a-brac. With the steady growth of European travel among the richer classes, the acquisitive spirit throve; and presently the most fashionable architect of the Gilded Age, R. M. Hunt, was building French châteaux on Fifth Avenue, while less eminent rivals were designing Rhine castles for brewers, or weird combinations of architectural souvenirs—an eclecticism that reached its climax in a brilliant design, unfortunately not executed, for a building exhibiting a different historical style on every story.

Before the Civil War no one had emerged who was capable of facing the problems of building in the spirit that Walt Whitman had sought to face those of poetic expression. There was a great deal of loose talk about an architecture appropriate to industrial society; many people thought that iron and glass were the coming materials; but it was almost useless to look to the architects of the day for leadership in such experiments: they had forgotten even to use stone or brick with any confidence and adroitness. . . .

. . . Architecture, on the downgrade since the twenties, had by 1860 touched bottom. Before every new manifestation of industrial society in cities and buildings, the word "ugly" became inescapable.

Within thirty years the situation had changed: the foundations of a new architecture had been laid. Architecture was reunited to city development in the boulevards and parks designed in New York, Baltimore, Boston, Chicago, Kansas City, and many other communities; and in the eighties, for the first time if one excludes such happy accidents as the mills at Manchester, New Hampshire, the problem of architectural comeliness was considered in relation to workers' housing in the well-intentioned but misdirected plans for Pullman, Illinois. Sculptors, painters, and workers in glass and iron appeared as accessory to the architect in a country where only sixty years before a poor wretch was released from jail since he was the only person in New York competent to cut the marble for City Hall.

More than this: between 1880 and 1895 the task and method of modern architecture were clarified through the example of a group of American architects whose consistent and united efforts in this line antedated, by at least a decade, the earliest similar innovations in Europe. Modern architecture had its beginning in this period; and though no one has taken the trouble to investigate the totality of work done during these years, one needs only to walk about the central business portion of Boston, or, a few years ago, the Loop of Chicago, or to keep one's eyes open here and there in almost every center, to see beneath years of grime, many alterations, and the disfigurement of competitive advertisements, the first experimental efforts to work out the form of an office building, an urban factory, a hotel, in terms of their inherent needs and their new possibilities.

How did this change come about? In back of it stands a colossal man, Henry Hobson Richardson, an architect who almost single-handed created out of a confusion which was actually worse than a mere void the beginnings of a new architecture. No single mind since Wren's has perhaps left such a large impress of his own personality, not alone through his work, but through that of his disciples and successors; and no one has demonstrated better in practice the qualities that are necessary for a complete orchestration of all the personalities and forces concerned in building. His life merits a brief recapitulation.

Richardson was born in Louisiana in 1838. His mother was a daughter of Joseph Priestley, the famous eighteenth-century radical; and Richardson would have entered West Point had he not had, like his grandfather, an impediment in speech. He was graduated from Harvard in 1858, and in 1859 he went over to France to prepare himself for the Ecole des Beaux-Arts, to which he was admitted in 1860. Being out of funds during the war, he never left Paris; but he had the good fortune to gain a living working under [the architect] Labrouste while he pursued his studies. When Richardson came back to America in 1865 he brought with him, unlike R. M. Hunt, no obvious French tags or labels: what he had absorbed was a method of analysis and a capacity for intense work.

Richardson was an architect in his bones: a solid worker with a respect for all his fellow workers, making his presence felt in every department of building. In stature, ideas, and habits of mind he was a curiously close counterpart of William Morris: he had the same bulky figure and large head and bluff, full beard—the build and driving force of a bison. All his appetites were as positive and gargantuan as the great stones he first played with. His love of good food, his capacity to drink champagne, his yellow waistcoat, his tireless energy, became bywords in the Brown Decades. Unlike Morris, however, Richardson did not write; and such ideas as he had about his art were articulated chiefly in the act of building. But though the makings of a great architect were in young Richardson, he had much to learn; and during his first ten years of practice, he went through the usual Victorian experience of working in Gothic, from which he felt his way back to the more elemen-

tary masonry forms of the Southern French Romanesque. Trinity
Church in Boston, his most important achievement before 1880, still
belongs to the period of preparation.

Richardson had escaped from the dominant styles of his period,
those which a later critic facetiously referred to as the Victorian Cathar-
tic, the Tubercular or Queen Anne Style, and the Cataleptic Style, with
its complete suppression of all that would indicate life; but he had still
to find a modern idiom, and meanwhile his own efforts with the heavy
Romanesque earned, not altogether unjustly, the epithet "dropsical."
The most obvious features of his design were the heavy courses of
rough-finished stone, often in contrasting colors; the rounded arches for
entrances and the romantic towers. . . . He was, without doubt, for the
greater part of his life purely a Romantic architect, seeking to create
by traditional devices an effect comparable to that produced by other
cultures and remoter ways of life: the effect of age, antique strength,
endurance, religious energy.

So far Richardson was on the wrong track. Had he died before
1880, he would have to be classed with Pugin, Scott, Viollet-le-Duc, and
Cuypers, men who respected sound building, who adored the early
Middle Ages, and who wished to renew other than classic harmonies
and proportions—an honest but wholly derivative architect, the precursor of that vast tribe of eclectics who now beg and borrow from the
ragbags of the past the details and feelings which will cover up their
own inability to conceive strictly or carry out competently any genuine
aesthetic problem. His influence would still have been respectable: his
design for the Albany Cathedral curiously anticipates the Kaiser Wil-
helm Gedächtniskirche in Berlin; but it would not have been capable
of development.

But Richardson grew steadily both in architecture and in his comprehension of the needs and opportunities of modern life: he was still
growing when his career was cut short by his death in 1886. His latent
powers are even more important for us than his achievements.

Richardson was the first architect of distinction in America who was
ready to face the totality of modern life. As soon as he began to design
railroad stations for the Boston & Albany line in 1881, he was already
on the road toward a new conception of architecture, since, search
where he would, he could find nothing in the nature of a suburban
railroad station even dimly to remind him of other architectural solutions. In designing such a structure, one was forced either to face the
elements and work with them, or become stultified.

It was part of the "Victorian compromise" to evade this problem
by confining Gothic architecture to churches and schools, to use classic
or Renaissance motifs on public buildings, and to turn over structures

like factories, offices, and railroad stations to engineers and contractors who had no particular concern with beauty. Richardson rejected that compromise. In a series of designs, he showed that such a rejection was not merely inevitable, but that it afforded the starting point for a new architecture which, like all the valuable examples of the past, would belong to its own day and grow out of current needs.

Richardson was already at the beginning of this conception in his interior plans for public libraries; he went farther in his railroad stations, with their emphasis upon the covered platform and their bold effort to achieve a maximum of daylight in the waiting rooms. In a similar spirit, he turned in 1880 to the simple cottage of wood and created one that, for the first time, blended with the reds, greens, and browns of the Northern landscape. Domesticity and industry, culture and work, were in Richardson's mind on a common platform: the utilitarian and the romantic emerged from their futile and crippling opposition.

The criticism of Richardson's architecture as purely Romantic is not correct even when it is applied to his earlier and, from the standpoint of his later achievements, weaker buildings. It comes, indeed, from critics who are themselves more romantic than the architect, for they are put off by literary allusion and symbolism, and neglect to examine the evolution of Richardson's plans, the bold functional disposition of the parts, and above all his highly inventive use of the window. Richardson, more perhaps than any other architect, was responsible for abandoning the window as a repetitive unit, as in Renaissance design, and making it an integral part of the interior development—placing it and establishing its dimensions by the needs of the interior, rather than by the purely formal requirements of the façade. In the Glessner House in Chicago, on an L-shaped corner plot, Richardson designed a street façade with a minimum of windows, in order to keep out the dust and noise: in his libraries, the stacks are properly lighted and well disposed: this factualism, this attention to the basic program, characterized even his outwardly Romantic period. In the fenestration of Austin Hall, at Harvard (1881), he established the standards of a functionalist architecture. One can comprehend now what Richardson meant when he said, in his circular to inquiring clients: "In preparing the architectural design I agree, after consultation with the owner, to use my best judgement. I cannot, however, guarantee that the building, when completed, shall conform to his ideas of beauty or taste, or indeed to those of any person or school. I can only agree to examine and consider this matter well and carefully, and to recommend nothing which is inconsistent with my own ideas upon these subjects."

· · ·

When one begins to make a tally of Richardson's qualities, one discovers that he had uniquely all the elements that make up a great architect. What other architect before or since in America has had such a complete equipment? This armory of qualities included a strong sense of color, which perhaps tempted him too far in his use of contrasting stones; it embraced a hitherto unique sense of place, so that he himself said that architecture "cannot be fully judged except in concrete shape and colour, amid actual lights and shadows and its own particular surroundings," a sense which placed him apart from the designers whose work is always best on the drawing board; and it even extended to an appreciation of the ancillary arts, so that he had the taste to recognize and use some of the best artists his time offered: Saint Gaudens, La Farge, W. M. Hunt. More than this: Richardson worked equally well with his clients, the municipal officials and industrialists and businessmen, as difficult a collection of patrons as ever an artist was blessed with. If one looks for the secret of Richardson's success here, one will not be too easily satisfied with the explanation that his love of good food and good wine brought them swiftly on a common footing, although one cannot doubt that it helped. The main point was that Richardson had an authentic intuition of his society and his age. Mr. Charles Moore in his biography of Richardson's pupil Charles McKim says curiously that Richardson's style was not adapted to American conditions: but what is the mark of adaptation? Contemporary jobs? Richardson had them. Durability? His works have lasted better than his successors'. Power to serve as a foundation for later work? That is Richardson's eminent claim to our attention. Richardson did not grovel before practical conditions: he did not think of himself as a mere handyman of business interests, enclosing rentable space: nor did he view the practical needs of his day with contempt. . . . The wind is rising again in Richardson's point of the compass; for what he brought to architecture, finally, was an interest, not in an exotic past, not in dead forms, not in the external flourish, but in the inherent nature of the building itself and its relation to society.

Richardson died just as the transition from masonry to steel frame construction was being made: he died too early to carry this transition beyond its first stages, and to apply to it his own powerful masculine imagination. But there is little doubt that the man who welcomed the problem of the railroad station, whose pencil was busy with sketches for ice plants and similar industrial establishments, who wished to design the interior of a river steamboat, who had already, on the Marshall Field Building . . . , reduced the cornice and subordinated ornament to the expression of the whole—there is little doubt that this man would have made the transition from one system to another with even more decisiveness than his successors. The gap between stone and steel-and-glass was as great as that in the evolutionary order between the crustaceans and the vertebrates. . . .

Unfortunately, Richardson's architectural contemporaries largely muffed their opportunity. They had not yet caught up with his latest work, and while they acknowledged that he had solved the problem of masonry expression for them, they mistakenly thought that steel construction nullified his achievements—and they hastily abandoned their dead master at the moment when he could have taught them most. The fact was, we can now see, just the opposite of their impression: in his final years Richardson was already seeking in masonry qualities that could be triumphantly incorporated only with the aid of steel.

Richardson beheld the promised land, and as the most influential architect of his time, he tasted the grapes of success; but he did not enter it. That realization was granted to a group of architects in Chicago, through three of whom the tradition for which Richardson laid the foundation was widened and modified until it became, in effect, the basis of modern architecture throughout the world. . . .

Richardson's influence in Chicago was a happy one. There were, in particular, two architects who had felt it when it was for them chiefly a tendency towards Romantic expression, and who, in the eighties, encountering Richardson's mind in its most mature phase, drew from it the inevitable lesson.

One of these architects was John Wellborn Root. Root was, like Richardson, a Southerner. His father, a New Englander, had wished to study architecture, but had instead opened a dry-goods shop in Lumpkin, Georgia. Born in 1850, Root was trained in the office of one of the leading exponents of Gothic architecture, that of Renwick, the designer of St. Patrick's Cathedral in New York, and like Daniel Burnham he was drawn to Chicago in response to the vast opportunity created by the Chicago fire. In 1873, Root and Burnham, who had been working in the same office, formed a partnership on the prospect of doing a large suburban development for a realty company; and the firm of Burnham and Root, combining the adroit business imagination and practical enthusiasm of one with the sound aesthetic ideals of the other, rapidly rose to eminence.

John Root's life as an independent architect was even shorter than Richardson's; and his original training and culture were not nearly so broad, although he had studied for a while at New York University and had a deep love for music. His many city mansions and office buildings do not show the steady logical progression of Richardson's enlarging imagination. But Root was intellectually more articulate than Richardson, and he took part in that general ferment of ideas which made the better architects of Chicago conscious of their civil mission and willing to impose upon themselves the discipline necessary to its fulfillment. The Cataleptic Style, the trance of dead forms, had never taken root in that city; if the architecture was often crude and barbarous, it was nevertheless alive.

"In America," Root said once in a lecture, "we are free of artistic traditions. Our freedom begets license, it is true. We do shocking things; we produce works of architecture irremediably bad; we try crude experiments that result in disaster. Yet somewhere in this mass of ungoverned energies lies the principle of life. A new spirit of beauty is being developed and perfected, and even now its first achievements are beginning to delight us. This is not the old thing made over; it is new. It springs out of the past, but it is not tied to it; it studies the traditions, but is not enslaved by them. Compare the best of our recent architecture—some of Richardson's designs, for example—with the most pretentious buildings recently erected in Europe. In the American works we find strength and fitness and a certain spontaneity and freshness, as of stately music, or a song in the green woods."

Root's observation was not farfetched or inaccurate; it was echoed, too, by the one real critic of architecture that America had produced, Montgomery Schuyler, whose *American Architecture* is a neglected landmark in architectural criticism. In the Monadnock Building, still working in a masonry tradition, Root took Richardson's example one step farther, and carried the design of the tall building—it was fifteen stories—as far as it was possible to go without reconstructing the terms of the problem. Its actual design shows the important part that was played in establishing a sound foundation by the businessmen who corrected the architect's whimsies and vagaries by a strong sense of practical needs. I quote from Miss Harriet Monroe's biography of Root:

> For this building [the Monadnock] Mr. Aldis, who controlled the investment, kept urging upon his architects extreme simplicity, rejecting one or two of Root's sketches as too ornate. During Root's absence of a fortnight, Mr. Burnham ordered from one of the draftsmen a design of a straight up-and-down, uncompromising, unornamented façade. When Root returned, he was indignant at first over this project of a brick box. Gradually, however, he threw himself into the spirit of the thing, and one day told Mr. Aldis that the heavy sloping lines of an Egyptian pylon had gotten into his mind as the basis of this design, and that he thought he would throw the whole thing up without a single ornament.

It was a wise decision; even the gradation of the bricks from a deep brown at the bottom to a yellow at the top, which Root was prevented from doing only by a lack of time, might have marred the fine severity of the design, whose sole interest, apart from the strong silhouette, was derived from the projecting bays of windows that increased the sunlit space in rooms that would have been lost in darkness behind piers fifteen feet thick at the bottom. At the time, Montgomery Schuyler pronounced the Monadnock Building the best of all tall office buildings. He was right. It was by far the best thing done in masonry; and its windows were more inventively planned than those of the Auditorium Building, which followed close on its heels. . . .

While Root had finally stripped the face of the office building, making it as austere as a steamship, as nicely adapted to its purpose as the elevators that had begun to glide up and down in the eighties, after many experimental makeshifts and failures in the seventies, a final clarification of the structure was going on from within. The heavy masonry walls necessary for a fifteen-story building took away both light and valuable space. Meanwhile, the cheapness of cast iron and later rolled steel had suggested the use of steel beams for floors and steel columns to assist the masonry piers. Two Chicago architects, Messrs. Drake and Wight, contributed the invention of steel columns with air chambers and fire-clay around them; finally, the complete steel skeleton was articulated in William Le Baron Jenney's Home Insurance Building (1885), and the outside walls, instead of being supporting members, became only a fireproof curtain, each segment supported at each floor.

The priority for the invention of steel frame or skeleton construction has been disputed; it was claimed by, among others, L. H. Buffington, Minnesota architect, who applied for a patent; but the whole question becomes a little absurd when one remembers that the traditional American frame house is based on an exactly comparable method of construction. The new elements were the fireproofing of the component materials, and the more exact calculations made possible through the use of steel, along with the opportunity of increasing the height of the structure, which was limited only by the strength of the foundations and the expense of vertical transportation. Socially, the skyscraper gave encouragement to all our characteristic American weaknesses: our love of abstract magnitude, our interest in land gambling, our desire for conspicuous waste: it did this to such an extent that it is almost heresy to call attention to the defects of the tall building: the dubious economy of vertical transportation at the magnificent maximum rate of nine miles per hour: the waste of cubage in the unused sections of express elevator shafts—to say nothing of the shutting out of sunlight and air, and the intensification of congestion on the streets and in the subways.

But the skyscraper is one thing, and steel-framed construction, though it was first developed for use in this type of building, is quite another. To admit the manifold deficiencies of the skyscraper under our present system of credit, land increment, and unregulated city growth is not to lessen the boldness and inventiveness which characterized the Chicago architects and the steelmasters and engineers who aided them. It was one with the spirit that created the grain elevators, the continental railroad systems, the great bridges, the steelworks themselves. Root formulated the aesthetic of these new structures. "In them," he said, "should be carried out the ideals of modern business life—simplicity, stability, breadth, dignity. To lavish upon them profusion of delicate ornament is worse than useless, for this would better be preserved for the place and hour of contemplation and repose. Rather should they by their mass and proportion convey in some large elemental sense an idea of the great, stable, conserving forces of modern civilization."

From the point of clarified expression that Root formulated, and that he and Richardson and Wells had demonstrated, there has been little real advance. Every later effort to evade the logic of modern civilization by insincere gestures of respect to the culture, the feelings, the ornamental systems of previous ages, or to simulate their effect by "modern" systems of ornament merely reduces the dignity and sincerity that these older structures achieved. Attempts to make a business building a cathedral or a temple deny the order that belongs to the essential function: the Chicago Tribune Tower is miles below the best office buildings of the eighties in all that constitutes aesthetic rightness and good form. Business, and not the fake religion of business, was what the earlier skyscrapers expressed. Their conception can be summed up in a word: the builders *meant business.* Could one give either the architects or their clients higher praise?

The fact is that the architects of the Brown Decades reached an appropriate solution for the office building more quickly than they knew, or anyone could anticipate. This solution had no equivalent in the aesthetic vocabulary of the age; and instead of clinging to it, developing it, bringing out to the last degree the virtues of simplicity and directness, and playing only with the fundamental units of construction, the architects of America, having scaled the heights too quickly, poised for a dizzy moment and then fell—fell into the easy mechanical duplication of other modes of architecture, frigidly predicted by the Chicago Exposition of 1893 . . . turning out a rapid succession of Roman temples and baths, Florentine villas and French palaces and Gothic churches and universities, to say nothing of office buildings which retained ill-chosen souvenirs from all these crumbled civilizations.

So low had American taste sunk in the generation after the [Chicago] World's Fair that people habitually characterized as an advance what was actually a serious retrogression. Had Richardson lived, had Root lived another fifteen years, the results might have been different: one original man can lead, two men of the same mind are an army, and three men directed toward a single objective might possibly have conquered the dull and inert forces that stood in their way: at all events, they would have made a glorious fight. But in 1891, only one of this early trio was left. His name was Louis Sullivan.

Louis Sullivan. The name has become a symbol, and the symbol has been one to conjure with. I approach this man with reverence; for even his enemies have respected the fierce sincerity of his mind and his passionate affirmations of life and art: they have called him the father of the modern skyscraper and they have paid tribute to the originality of his ornament, even when they had no desire to emulate it.

As an architect and a man, Louis Sullivan is a figure for whom one must make allowances, and correct for both enmities and partialities, before coming to a just estimate; but he remains an important personality, even when full justice has been done. The influence of his example was almost as wide as Richardson's; that of his writings was far more important than Root's. His *Kindergarten Chats* and his *Autobiography of an Idea*, for all their turgidities, will long remain a witness to his spirit. He was willful, capricious, sometimes grandiloquently mystical; even before poverty and defeat created compensatory needs, his belief in his own unique illuminations kept him from having the most fruitful contact with other men; and his weaknesses were accentuated in the solitude of his last years, spent miserably in a third-rate Chicago hotel, with only a few unimportant jobs coming his way, sometimes through the kindness of despairing friends. But Mr. Frank Lloyd Wright still habitually refers to him as *der Meister*—and he was all of that.

Sullivan's was perhaps the first mind in American architecture that had come to know itself with any fullness in relation to its soil, its period, its civilization, and had been able to absorb fully all the many lessons of the century. One might call him the Whitman of American architecture. If his vision outstripped his own accomplishment, it was large enough to outstrip any immediate program; for it had the force and drive of a whole civilization.

Louis Sullivan was of French-Irish ancestry. He was born in Boston in 1856. After studying at the English High School under a redoubtable master, Moses Woolson, in 1870 he took examinations for the Massachusetts Institute of Technology and passed them: he showed precocity.

Very early in life he decided upon architecture as a career, and he went from the Institute to the Ecole des Beaux-Arts in Paris, by way of the office of Furness and Hewitt in Philadelphia. Frank Furness was the designer of a bold, unabashed, ugly, and yet somehow healthily pregnant architecture. It was of work such as his that Montgomery Schuyler remarked: "It is more feasible to tame exuberances than to create a soul under the ribs of death. The emancipation of American architecture is thus ultimately more hopeful than if it were put under academic bonds to keep the peace. It may be freely admitted that many of its manifestations are not for the present joyous but grievous."

The panic of 1873 robbed Sullivan of his job and sent him to Chicago; in 1874 he sailed for France, and stayed there almost four years. It was a heady experience for this sensitive young man; and in his autobiography he has given only one aspect of it, the effect of French logic and discipline upon an eager self-confident American. Sullivan's mathematics was at first inadequate, and he studied it under a French master. This man, M. Clopet, scanned the mathematical textbook that Sullivan had purchased in advance and said: "Now observe: here is a problem with five exceptions or special cases; here a theorem, three special cases; another nine, and so on and on, a procession of exceptions and special cases. I suggest you place the book in the wastebasket; we shall not need it here; for our demonstrations shall be so broad as to admit of no exceptions!"

These words, however they were uttered or repeated, made a deep impression on the young man. Here was the voice of a real teacher, and he had crystallized for Sullivan, in a sentence, the aim of a genuine system of architecture—to arrive at a method so broad as to admit of no exceptions. "If this can be done in mathematics," said Sullivan to himself, "why not in architecture? The instant answer: it can and it shall be!"

Louis Sullivan returned to Chicago, a thriving city, busy, hospitable, building itself out of the wreck of the fire, a brutal network of industrial necessities, railroads, grain elevators, bridges, stockyards, business offices, brutal and chaotic, but full of an electric vitality which, if it made the errors grosser, made its triumphs even more colossal. The pressure of financial interests in the Loop was already creating the gratuitous congestion of the skyscraper; vast railroad yards swung across the lakefront in blithe contempt for any other uses than the convenience of iron and wheels; but grappling with this brawling ugliness were men equally huge, and the architects of the day were not dwarfed by the businessmen, but stood shoulder to shoulder with them, supplementing their deficiences and sharing their strength. In this environment, an idea might be an act.

There were other men, like John Edelman, to share Sullivan's interest in the historians of art like Taine, in such poets as Whitman, the Whitman who had said: There is no more need of romances; let facts and history be properly told. These sentiments took hold of Sullivan. In 1879 he went into the office of an able architect and organizer, Dankmar Adler, and in 1881, at twenty-five, he became Adler's partner. A rapid rise, in all probability too rapid: Sullivan was not toughened like Richardson by a long period of probation, but suffered from an elation of ego that made him perhaps too easily satisfied with his own philosophy and his own achievements—the psychology of the spoiled child. The world was at his feet. At the age of thirty he began to work on the enormous Auditorium Building and Theatre, a work so huge and difficult that it took almost four years to finish. That building, like the Monadnock, stands at the parting of the ways between the older forms of Richardson's masonry and the lighter, more supple forms of steel construction. It is a great pile. Following Richardson's precedent in the Marshall Field Building, the face is notably devoid of ornament, although the auditorium itself and other parts of the interior exhibited the delicate lacy stuff that Sullivan's hand turned out so quickly. It was Adler and Sullivan's strongest and best-integrated building—though, unlike some of Sullivan's later buildings, it opened no new paths.

In the World's Fair that followed, this healthy native growth was cut down: the joe-pye weed and the swamp maple and the locust tree were extirpated in favor of a few elegant, sickly shrubs which could not flourish in the common soil of our life. It is conceivable that had Root been the master designer, as was at first projected—he was partly responsible for the choice of a park site with watercourses and he contemplated the use of color more lavishly than had hitherto been attempted—it is conceivable that Louis Sullivan would with Root have dominated the situation. The Chicago architects were, however, largely crowded out by the suave classic and Renaissance practitioners whom Burnham brought in, and Sullivan was notable in the fair only for the Transportation Building, the one structure that departed from precedent in its golden portal, its obviously plaster façade. Incidentally, his work resulted in the award of a gold medal, on the recommendation of the French government commission, by the Société Centrale des Arts Décoratifs.

Up to this time, Sullivan and Root had ridden on the crest of the wave. The minor arts themselves began to reflect their efforts: the Yale and Towne Lock Company employed them to make designs for hardware; and as late as 1897 these designs were still popular. In 1891 Root died, and in 1895 Sullivan and Adler parted company. This was to prove a great misfortune; for, unlike Richardson, Sullivan alone lacked some of the necessary ingredients for architectural mastery: he was at his best with the tactful, practical, painstaking Adler at his side, to serve as buffer between the imperious artist and his clients. Sullivan's buildings, though often original in conception, began in a subtle way to disintegrate: the masculine and the feminine elements, form and feeling, drew apart; and finally, in the work of his declining years, Sullivan's ornament often ruined the logic of his design. Social changes accented these individual deficiencies. Building revived slowly after the panic of 1893. Two large skyscrapers, designed by Sullivan at the end of the decade and approved by his clients, were abandoned for lack of financial resources. The breaks were against him. Some of his closest clients and old friends lost their faith in him when their own taste deteriorated. The tide set against sound design. Styles took the place of style, as the builders of industry gave way to the salesmen and financial manipulators. Thorstein Veblen's *Theory of Business Enterprise* reflects a conflict that was written with particular clearness on the stones of Chicago. Buildings and furnishings did not call for creative effort: they demanded vulgar waste, costly antiques, historic loot. Sullivan refused to deal in these cheap-jack wares. So his detractors damned him as an "expensive" architect.

Like Root, Sullivan formulated a theory of the tall office building, and tested it out on the Wainwright Building in St. Louis (1891), the Prudential Building in Buffalo (1895), and the Schiller Building (1892) and the Gage Building (1898) in Chicago. Let us examine his analysis. "The practical considerations," said Sullivan, in an article in *Lippincott's Magazine* in 1896, "are, broadly speaking, these, Wanted—First, a storey below ground, containing boilers, engines of various sorts, etc. —in short, the plant for power, heating, lighting, etc. Second, a ground floor, so-called, devoted to stores, banks, or other establishments requiring large area, ample spacing, ample light, and great freedom of access. Third, a second story readily accessible by stairways—the space usually in large subdivisions, with corresponding liberality in structural spacing and in expanse of glass and breadth of material openings. Fourth, above these an indefinite number of stories of offices piled tier upon tier, one tier just like another—an office being similar to a cell in a honey-comb, merely a compartment, nothing more. Fifth and last, at the top of this pile is placed a space or a story that, as related to the life and usefulness of the structure, is purely physiological in its nature—namely, the attic. . . . Finally, or at the beginning, rather, there must be on the ground floor a main aperture or entrance common to all the occupants or patrons of the building. . . . What is the chief character of the tall office building? And at once we answer, it is lofty. This loftiness is to the artist-nature its thrilling aspect. It is the very open organ-tone in its appeal. . . . It must be every inch a proud and soaring thing, rising in sheer exultation that from bottom to top it is a unit without a single dissenting line—that is the new, the unexpected, the eloquent peroration of most bald, most sinister, most forbidding conditions."

Between Sullivan's fine factual analysis and his desire for a romantic thrill there was a conflict, and this division is written upon his office buildings. Sullivan was one of the first architects to emphasize the vertical lines of the skyscraper: in the Wainwright Building he did this by inserting a pier between the main columns of each bay, even though there was nothing in the actual function of the building to dictate this arrangement. This accentuation of the vertical was in both its immediate and its ultimate effects an unfortunate solution: I say this with due deference to such excellent critics as Mr. Claude Bragdon, who have hailed Sullivan as the first adequate designer of the skyscraper. The objections are manifold.

For one thing, the steel cage is not in itself a vertical system of construction: it is rather a system of articulated cubes. A brick wall will stand after a fire though the connecting beams have been gutted away: without its horizontal ties a steel wall must come down. The temptation to accentuate the vertical leads to the use of piers or mullions, which indicate masonry construction; whereas the curtain wall, with shallow reveals, . . . expresses the system of construction. Again: the vertical lines conflict with the need for unbroken window space on the lower two floors; hence on Sullivan's skyscrapers the horizontal accent at the base contradicts the vertical system above; and the result, taken with the overhang that caps the Wainwright Building, or the outward curving at the top as in the Prudential Building, is curiously like the classic conception of base, column, and capital—which has precious little to do with the logic of the tall building, and is full of dissenting lines.

More than anything, the mischief lay in the notion that on the foundation of practical needs the skyscraper could or should be translated into a "proud and soaring thing." This was giving the skyscraper a spiritual function to perform: whereas, in actuality, height in skyscrapers meant either a desire for centralized administration, a desire to increase ground rents, a desire for advertisement, or all three of these together—and none of these functions determines a "proud and soaring thing." It was but a step from Sullivan's conception to the grandiose and inefficient tower buildings that mark the last two decades of American skyscraper development. These towers accentuate the vertical lines well enough: but they cannot be compared, as practical economic plans and elevations, with the Monadnock Building.

Just as the idea of accentuating the vertical lines spoiled the logic of the tall business building, so the desire to embellish the façade was a step backward from the solution indicated at such an early date by the Monadnock Building, to say nothing of Sullivan's own Auditorium Building. Ornament, however, was Sullivan's claim to originality as distinguished from great technical competence: he represented that surviving tradition in architecture which differentiated buildings as much through their symbolic effects in ornament as through their structural means of expression. Sullivan's ornament was frequently not related to the forms and materials of the building: it was as arbitrarily applied as acanthus leaves. It was, moreover, a drafting-room ornament. Although not derived from books and pictures, it represented the architect's originality, not that of the painter, the modeler, the sculptor; and it was restless and assertive, without being in a sculptural sense entertaining. Sullivan found a justification for these lacy forms of his in nature: if one objects to their use it is only because nature, at first hand, in trees and bushes and flowers, is so much more delightful than stone or iron—and where there is no place for nature, the pressed or carved designs are less exhilarating than an unbroken surface. Ornament was for Sullivan the great realm of individuality. If his ornament means less to the present generation than any other part of his work, it is only because we have begun to see that the nineteenth-century quest of "individuality" and "personality" in architecture was a last step in disintegration, since architecture is a social art, and must stand or fall by its collective achievement. "Individuality" cannot be the foundation of a common rule: it is only the irreducible residue that remains after the common rule has been established.

But one cannot call the roll of Sullivan's works without paying a tribute to the one outstanding building of his later years: the Schlesinger and Mayer Building, now that of Carson, Pirie and Scott. This is a department store, and the date of its first unit on Madison Street is 1899; that of the second unit, on the corner of State and Madison Streets, is 1903. Here Sullivan used a bold system of horizontal windows and gained a legitimate accent at the corner by a rounded glass bay: a clean, logical solution for the problem, more decisive in every way, it seems to me, than his skyscrapers. In departing from this logic on the lower two stories, to the extent of using a lacy snowflake grille, he destroyed the unity of expression and distracted attention, by his own exhibition, from the exhibitions behind the windows. Despite this weakness, the design was an expressive and salutary one: nothing comparable to this appeared in department stores in Europe until after 1920. The final section of the building, it is true, was taken from Sullivan by D. H. Burnham, when the store changed hands; but that architect recognized, apparently, the work of a superior hand, and he kept in the main close to Sullivan's design.

The neglect of this precedent, like the neglect of Richardson's last office building twenty years before, pointed to the essential shallowness of architectural practice in America, to say nothing of the life it enthroned. It was not for lack of adequate appreciation that this work went so long for nothing: Montgomery Schuyler, although a little tamed by the overwhelming omnipresence of the eclectic school, and far too kind to such manifestations of it as the Woolworth Building, was still as alert in 1912 as he had been in Root's day: "It is hard," he said then, "to see how an unprejudiced inquirer can deny that such designers as Mr. Sullivan and Mr. Wright have the root of the matter, and their works are of good hope, in contrast with the rehandling and rehashing of admired historical forms in which there is no future nor any possibility of progress."

I have granted a little more freely than most of Sullivan's critics or admirers his own personal weaknesses: I have not attempted to conceal the fact that they accounted in part for the mean and bedraggled ending of what had set out as a great career. But there is a continuity between the individual and society which will not let any honest analysis stay at this point: one must point out that the Brown Decades, for all their sordidness, had certain healthy characteristics which were lacking in the more refined but no less rapacious society that followed. What Sullivan said as a critic of social architecture was correct: "What the people are within, the buildings express without; and inversely, what the buildings are objectively is a sure index of what the people are subjectively. In the light of this dictum, the unhappy, irrational, heedless, pessimistic, unlovely, distracted, and decadent structures which make up the great bulk of our contemporaneous architecture point with infallible accuracy to qualities in the heart and mind and soul of the American people that are unhappy, irrational," and so forth.

Sullivan's original observation in the *Kindergarten Chats* is true for the longer span that we have been examining: it is true for the two generations that have followed the Civil War: "We are at that dramatic moment in our national life wherein we tremble evenly between decay and evolution, and our architecture, with strange fidelity, reflects this equipoise. That the forces of decadence predominate in quantity there can be no doubt; that the re-creative forces balance them by virtue of quality and may eventually overpower them is a matter of conjecture. That the bulk of our architecture is rotten to the core, is a statement that does not admit of one solitary doubt. That there is in our national life, in the genius of our people, a fruitful germ, and that there are a handful who perceive this, is likewise beyond question."

One sees these forces, balancing, thrusting, fighting, sometimes clear and sometimes confused, in Sullivan's own work: no one can lift himself up by his bootstraps, and the best architect survives or stifles in the same milieu that surrounds his lesser contemporaries. Even when he stands out against these forces, as Sullivan sought to do and as Wright in a measure did by turning to the design of country houses when more critical and important works of architecture were denied to him, he pays almost as great a price for his recalcitrance as he would for his submission. For architecture is, through and through, a social art, and all its interesting and valid answers must be couched in response to the demands of society. The only kind of tower that the architect must deny himself the privilege of building is a Tower of Ivory. . . .

What, then, was Louis Sullivan's contribution? Sullivan was the first American architect to think consciously of his relations with civilization. Richardson and Root both had good intuitions, and they had made effective demonstrations; but Sullivan knew what he was about, and what is more important, he knew what he ought to be about. "Once you learn," he said, "to look upon architecture not merely as an art more or less well or more or less badly done, but as a *social manifestation*, the critical eye becomes clairvoyant, and obscure, unnoted phenomena become illumined." Sullivan had this sense of the forces at work in society, in industry, in the human personality. He "found himself drifting into the engineering point of view, or state of mind, as he began to discern that the engineers were the only men who could face a problem squarely; who knew a problem when they saw it. Their minds were trained to deal with real things, as far as they knew them, as far as they could ascertain them, while the architectural mind lacked this directness, this simplicity, this singleness of purpose—it had no standard of reference, no bench-mark one might say."

Sullivan saw that the business of the architect was to organize the forces of modern society, discipline them for humane ends, express them in the plastic-utilitarian form of building. To achieve this purpose, the architect must abandon the tedious and unmeaning symbolism of older cultural forms: a modern building could no more wear the dress of the classic than the architect could wear a peruke and sword. The whole problem of building, Sullivan saw, must be thought out afresh, and the solution must be of such a nature that it would apply to every manner of structure, from the home to the factory, from the office to the tomb: no activity was too mean to escape the ministrations of the architect. While Sullivan manfully faced the problem of the tall building, he saw that the spirit that produced such congestion was "pro-

TOWARDS MODERN ARCHITECTURE · 67

foundly antisocial . . . these buildings are not architecture but outlawry, and their authors criminals in the true sense of the word." So, though Sullivan respected the positive forces of his age, democracy, science, industry, he was not a go-getter, and he refused to accept an architecture which showed a "cynical contempt for all those qualities that real humans value."

Sullivan's own relative failure in carrying through his conceptions does not vitiate them. In his final years, his thought sometimes became misty and vague; there are passages in *The Autobiography of an Idea* in which an eloquent and obsessive rhetoric conceals a certain emptiness, in which a platitude is put forward as with a fanfare of trumpets announcing a puppet king. But Sullivan was not simply a creature of his environment. He had absorbed the classic discipline of French thought, he had lived with Michelet, Whitman, Taine, Darwin, and this fusion of the Romantic, scientific, and classical impulses in the man gave him a special power to react upon his environment. Breaking loose from the Romantic phase of Richardson, Sullivan made a real beginning. On Richardson's solid foundations, he laid the cornerstone of the new organic architecture. Sullivan was the link between two greater masters, Richardson and Frank Lloyd Wright; and with the development of Wright's architecture the last stage in the transition was made: modern architecture in America was born. From that point on the Chicago school entered into the general stream of a world movement. In Wright, Sullivan's best ideas found actual expression more completely and convincingly than in his own work.

To understand better the immense accomplishment of the Brown Decades in architecture, one must be aware of the two continuous lines of movement which were started then, but which have become more visible and better defined in our own day. One involved the application of the machine to architecture—the introduction of new utilities for heating, ventilating, cooling, bathing, cooking, communicating, and the creation of new materials and methods of construction. This has changed both the problem and the outlook of architecture. The other movement, typified by the work of Richardson, Sullivan, and Wright, has been a conscious orientation of architecture toward new forms of expression, forms which comprehended, not merely the automatic developments of the mechanical age, but the role of the land itself, human habits, human desires, human institutions. Imagination disciplined by necessity, new necessities carried through to a final clarification in the mind: these are the poles of the modern spirit in architecture.

While Sullivan was finishing the Auditorium Building, he took on a young draftsman, Frank Lloyd Wright, who had just been a student in the engineering school at the University of Wisconsin. Wright was born in 1868, and he worked in the office of Adler and Sullivan from 1889 to 1895. Like his master, Wright was one of the few American artists who, in the face of the snobbishness and timid taste of the well-to-do in America, refused to participate in the revivalism and eclecticism that followed the World's Fair: he continued to seek an organic architecture.

Wright took the fashionable American house of the early nineties, with its high-pitched roof and spindly chimneys, its numerous dormer windows, and its crazy turrets and towers, and brought this wild, shambling, pseudo-Romantic creation, half Pegasus and half spavined selling plater, down to earth. On his very first house, he widened the windows and introduced more light: after that, pursuing more zealously Richardson's lead in treating the window as the original component of sound design, he fashioned the window in horizontal banks, doing away with the guillotine sash window. Wright called the houses he built during the next twenty years in Oak Park and the various tributaries of Chicago "prairie houses": with their low-pitched roofs, their rambling plans, their marked horizontality, they were deliberate adaptations to the landscape. At the very time when the archaic note of colonialism was being emphasized by the fashionable architect, Wright was showing his respect for the actual landscape and the actual problems of his day and locality.

Out of the ground, into the sun, has been the emblem of his work: no one, up to this time, had torn down the wall as a dividing unit and had dared to introduce so much glass and sunlight. His façades, instead of consisting of masonry walls punched with windows, were rather windows backed or connected by concrete, steel, or brick. Wright carried this essential principle to its logical conclusion in his design for the apartment house for St. Mark's-in-the-Bouwerie, where the supporting steel serves as a spinal column and the glass walls are the skin of the building; but the principle was implicit in the work he did in the nineties, and in the Steffens House and the Roberts Cottage it became manifest.

Wright has embodied in his work two qualities which can never permanently leave architecture—a sense of place, and a rich feeling for materials. This sense and this feeling have been momentarily lost in architecture, under the stress of clarifying form; but, boldly or surreptitiously, they are bound, I think, to make their way back into building; and Wright has left the way open for them. His architecture, though he has pioneered with modern methods of construction and delighted in mechanical techniques, is not merely a passive adaptation to the machine age: it is a reaching toward a more biotechnic economy, better grounded in the permanent realities of birth, growth, reproduction, and the natural environment than is the dominant order of paper values and merely mechanical efficiencies.

A hygienist has pointed out that our boasted mechanical age, with its knowledge of physical science and its control of delicate industrial processes, has not in the course of a hundred years yet learned the proper height for a toilet seat—with the result that sanitation and constipation are almost synonymous terms. One could criticize the latest achievement in mattresses in the machine age on similar grounds: the manufacturers seem unaware that the soft resilience of their product, if possibly conducive to sleep, is an obstacle to satisfactory sexual intercourse, and, paying attention to the physical processes of manufacture, they have not reckoned with the complete set of biological conditions their product must meet. No architecture can be efficient in the total situation which forgets the essential character of our humanity: human impulses cannot be flouted without their taking revenge in unexpected places. Frank Lloyd Wright's strong sense of human needs is a necessary complement to technical innovations.

One can sum up the effect of Wright's many innovations in design by saying that he altered the inner rhythm of the modern building: effecting these alterations on the most traditional form of building, with the most stable and traditional requirements, he opened the way for a fresh attack on all the problems of modern architecture. His own opportunity to work upon the school, the office building, the factory, the hotel, has been limited: his most powerful influence has therefore been effected in the domain of the country or suburban house, and with respect to the mass of building this represents only a minor problem— in some respects one that is tangential to our civilization. Those who think of Wright, however, solely in terms of the country house forget that as early as 1915 he had made a series of designs for type houses, whose parts were to be factory-made: here, as elsewhere, he was in advance of European precedent, and his failure to exert more influence has come from the inability of his fellow countrymen to make sufficient demands upon him. For this reason, it is all the more important to keep in mind Wright's fundamental contribution, which has nothing to do with the specific forms in which he worked.

Wright kept alive the tradition of experiment. He introduced sunlight and the glass opening, to take the place of the opaque and light-belittling wall: he widened the gamut of materials with which the architect worked; and at a time when all the successful practitioners were doing their best to revive handicraft, or to find some way of imitating by machinery and standardized methods the texture or finish of handicraft, Wright deliberately embraced the machine and the new products which were being added to the architect's store by the manufacturer. His speech on behalf of the machine, delivered at Hull House in 1903, was the first wholehearted word that was said in its favor, the first hint that the results which Morris hoped to achieve by going back to the Middle Ages might be attained by going forward to a new destination.

No American architect, not even Richardson, has had the command over materials that Wright has exercised, or the understanding of the specific use and beauty of each material, steel, copper, glass, concrete, brick, stone, wood. It may well be that the way toward a coherent form in the work that lies ahead will be through the deliberate restriction of materials and the methods of building: but before we establish narrower limits, it is important that someone should have ranged over the whole field and explored the whole range of possibilities in structure, function, and ornament: and more than with anyone else, this has been Mr. Wright's function.

Wright was ahead of his time. He lacked, therefore, the support of an underlying convention, and the actualization of each building required not merely an individual conversion of his clients to his particular method and point of view: it required equal adaptations on the part of the building trades and the manufacturers: resistance in this department is almost as fatal as lack of understanding or courage on the part of the patron. Wright's very originality and fertility of imagination were something of a handicap, and possibly, in reaction against the resistance he met, he accentuated the element of idiosyncrasy in his work. As the vigorous impulses of the Brown Decades slackened, Wright found himself more and more alone. Though he had disciples and imitators, his buildings were individual solutions. From these solutions, a hundred important lessons can be learned: the beauty of earth colors and natural finishes: the manifold possibilities of glass: the importance of living plants as a final element in decoration: the principles of horizontal composition—lessons from which Wright's foreign admirers derived invaluable suggestions.

There is, however, one great weakness in Mr. Wright's architecture, a weakness inherent in the transitional state of his society: far too great a burden rested on the architect. It was not merely necessary that he should design the building: he had to invent the methods of construction, alter established rules of procedure, create new types of furniture, rugs, chinaware; everything, from the foundation table to the roof, must bear the imprint of his personality. A man of genius delights in such a load: but architecture as a social art cannot depend upon the existence of men of genius: when it is in a healthy state, it relies upon the commonplace efforts of the carpenter, the builder, the engineer, the manufacturer, and the task of the architect is not to usurp the work that is done in these departments but to organize it intelligently and to create out of it an orderly composition. Mr. Frank Lloyd Wright's genius carried architecture as far as any single man could carry it. He was the seedbed of the new architecture in America. Some of his young shoots would live; others would die; others would undergo unexpected mutations and start a new species; but living or dying, stabilizing or changing, efflorescing or seeding, no work in modern architecture has been more necessary and significant. . . .

While the path towards an appropriate modern architecture was kept open by the excellent individual work of Frank Lloyd Wright, a corresponding communal advance was being made by the engineers who standardized building processes, invented new units of heating and plumbing, and occasionally, almost without knowing it, threw up fine engineering structures of their own, such as the Ford Plant at Baton Rouge or the ventilator units of the Holland Tunnel in New York. Conscious of quantitative relations alone, impervious to the human effects of their processes, innocent of the aesthetic result, the engineer nevertheless had a real contribution to make. It was through his inventions and processes that architecture ceased to be the concern solely of the carpenter and the stonemason: a new battalion of trades and techniques entered it.

It was the engineer who hastened the use of the steel skeleton building; it was he who made possible the building with open walls. Despite Richardson's precedent and Wright's efforts, the architect had battled against the engineer and belittled his achievements: when he could not do without his iron and glass structure, as in the railroad station, he hid it behind an imposing masonry front. Fortunately, there were other exceptions besides Wright and Sullivan during this period; some of Ernest Wilby's designs for Albert Kahn showed a happy recognition of the inherent possibilities of the new materials. But it is only in our own day that the integration has begun to go farther and to touch the problem of the dwelling house itself. Since every new mechanical utility, however indispensable, has increased the cost of the modern dwelling, by diverting to machinery energy and money that used to go into the bare shell, the critical problem of modern architecture has become:

How to restore by good design in the community the spaciousness, the color, the interest that is lacking in the environment of the individual house? Once we face the problem of housing decently the great mass of the population—a problem which Western civilization has flinched from during the entire industrial period—we must recognize that the means are strictly limited. Sunlight, air, gardens, play space, outlook: these are the main requirements of the modern house; and in providing these elements on a communal scale, the architect can no longer work for the single individual: his individual house will be a type-unit, adapted to the special whole in which it functions. Plainly, then, the integrated modern house cannot be created by a single hand; above all, it cannot be integrated merely from within. It requires an adequate type of community plan, properly oriented to sunlight, with publicly maintained open spaces and gardens and insulation from unnecessary traffic and movement: its bare severe interior—so necessary for simplified housekeeping—requires the presence of sunlight and living plants, pictures, and people to be fully humanized. The way to the new architecture requires the weaving together of the several lines of initiative which were first started during the Brown Decades: the attempt at community planning which marked the building of Pullman, Illinois, the experimental effort towards new forms which was exhibited in Richardson, Sullivan, and above all Wright, the effort to integrate the playground and the park with the city as a whole which characterized the work of [Frederick Law] Olmsted . . . and the effort to raise standardized industrial production to a higher aesthetic level which marked the work of the last generation of plumbing and kitchen utility manufacturers. No one of these elements by itself is sufficient to create a fine architecture; but once they are comprehensively united and directed, once the new architecture becomes the medium, not of some one individual's tastes and desires, but the informed, positive consensus of the community, form will cease to be a sporadic possibility and become instead the mark of our whole civilization. Such a change implies a real revolution in our economic and social ideas; and no revolution would be worth working for if it did not imply, among other things, such concrete and comprehensive changes.

THE CASE AGAINST "MODERN ARCHITECTURE"

Three-quarters of a century ago, the tides of modern architecture were rising, as the great technical resources that engineers like Telford, Paxton, and Brunel had introduced were applied, at last, to other forms of building. This was the period when Jenney, Sullivan, and their colleagues developed steel frame construction and found a form for the skyscraper, when Eiffel produced his tower and Freyssinet his Hall of Machines, and when the new spirit that Richardson had brought to the design of traditional domestic buildings in stone and wood was spreading everywhere, from the houses of Ashbee, Voysey, and Parker in England to the far shores of California, where at the turn of the century Maybeck had begun work.

For reasons that no one has successfully uncovered, this wave spent itself during the decade before the First World War: except in the design of purely utilitarian structures, there was a return to the pseudo-historic and outwardly traditional, at least in the decorative facing of buildings: skyscrapers with Gothic pinnacles vied with those that were crowned with Greek temples of love; and the splendid train hall of Grand Central Station, now effaced by a loud smear of advertisement, was betrayed earlier by its imitative Renaissance façade. When modern architecture came back in the twenties, first in France with Le Corbusier and Lurçat, and in Germany with Mendelsohn and Gropius, it was forced to refight the battle that had already seemed won in 1890.

Within the last thirty years, modern architecture has swept around the world. The victory of the modern movement over its traditional enemies has been so complete that special courses must now be offered, outside the usual architectural school curriculum, to provide architects with sufficient historical knowledge to maintain and restore ancient monuments preserved for their historical value. Yet many ominous signs have appeared, during the last fifteen years, that indicate that the victorious forces do not know how to make full use of the victory. . . .

The order and the consensus that modern architecture seemed ready to establish in the thirties is still far to seek: indeed, some of the most brilliant exponents, like the late Eero Saarinen, boasted a theory of form that denied the need for continuity and made of each separate project an essay in abstract design, without any affiliation to the work of other architects in our period or to the architect's own designs, before or after. As in the advertising copy of our period, the successful modern architects have been saying, in effect: "And now! a new taste sensation." Or, "You, too, can be *years ahead* with the latest model."

This situation has given hope and comfort to minds that are so radically committed to past forms that they would solve the problems that modern architecture faces by merely erasing the history of the last century and going back to the classic shells of antiquity, particularly Roman antiquity. This is the last hope of Henry Reed; too empty and vulnerable to merit more than a passing smile. But though Mr. Reed's remedies are absurd, the situation in modern architecture is in fact profoundly unsatisfactory: almost as chaotic and irrational as the political situation of the modern world, in which the heads of state solemnly threaten each other to solve their problems, if the other side does not yield, by mutilating the human race and wiping out civilization.

The very fact that one can make such a comparison points to certain underlying errors about the nature of technical and social progress that crept into modern architecture almost from the moment that the conception of new forms, which reflected the needs and ideals of our period, became articulate in the writings of a few architectural critics and thinkers, like Adolf Loos and, much later, Le Corbusier. The moment has come to examine these conceptions and to reformulate the ideas and ideals that have, up to this moment, governed the development of the whole movement. We shall perhaps find, when we do so, a need for restoring some of the values that were too ruthlessly discarded in the development of modern form.

THE BASIS OF MODERN FORM

Beneath the belief in modern architecture lay certain preconceptions about the nature of modern civilization; and these preconceptions have proved so inadequate that it is time to give them a thorough overhauling.

Perhaps the most central of these beliefs was the belief in mechanical progress. Concealed within this notion was the assumption that human improvement would come about more rapidly, indeed almost automatically, through devoting all our energies to the expansion of scientific knowledge and to technological inventions; that traditional knowledge and experience, traditional forms and values, acted as a brake upon such expansion and invention, and that since the order embodied by the machine was the highest type of order, no brakes of any kind were desirable. Whereas all organic evolution is cumulative and purposeful, in that the past is still present in the future, and the future, as potentiality, is already present in the past, mechanical progress existed in a one-dimensional time, the present. Under the idea of mechanical progress only the present counted, and continual change was needed in order to prevent the present from becoming passé, and thus unfashionable. Progress was accordingly measured by novelty, constant change, and mechanical difference, not by continuity and human improvement.

In every department, the nineteenth century ruthlessly swept away old ideas, old traditions and institutions, and not least old buildings, confident that nothing would be lost that the machine could not replace or improve. Have we forgotten that the central shrine of our independence and our Constitution, Independence Hall, was almost sold off to the highest bidder in the early part of that century? But this anti-traditionalism imposed a penalty upon modern architecture; and that is, it was deprived by its own assumptions of either recognizing its essential continuity with the past or of building upon its own tradition. In wiping out the past, unfortunately, the cult of the machine surreptitiously destroyed its own future—and left only an underdimensioned present, scheduled like any speculative building investment, for quick replacement.

Beneath this belief in mechanical progress as an end in itself was still another conviction: that one of the important functions of architecture was to express its civilization. This conviction was a sound one; and indeed, even without conviction, that condition whether openly recognized or unconsciously fulfilled is unavoidable. But those of us who insisted upon the value of this expression were perhaps unprepared for what it would reveal about "modern times." We used the word "modern" as a "praise-word," in Robert Frost's vocabulary; and we overlooked the possibility that modern technics, which had given us instant communication, would also provide us with instantaneous mass extermination: or the fact that in its hospitals and medical services and sanitary precautions it would reduce diseases and allay pain; but it has also polluted our food, befouled the air with smog, and produced new tensions and new diseases and new anxieties, as crippling as those that have been banished. Modern psychology has introduced man to the depths of his own nature, in all its immense variety and creative potentiality; but it has also produced the bureaucratic personality, sterilized, regimented, overcontrolled, ultimately hostile to every other form of life than its own: cut off from human resources and human roots.

Since modern architecture has begun to express modern civilization, without the hypocrisy and concealment that the eclectic architects used to practice, it is not perhaps surprising that the unpleasant features of our civilization should be as conspicuous as its finest and most admirable achievements. We have been living in a fool's paradise, so far as we took for granted that mechanical progress would solve all the problems of human existence, by introducing man into the brave new, simplified, automatic world of the machine. If we look at our buildings today, with open eyes, we shall find that even in handling the great positive forces of our time, with admirable constructive facility, the greater number of them have neglected even the scientific data they need for a good solution. There is hardly a single great innovation in building this last thirty years—total air conditioning, all-day fluorescent lighting, the all-glass wall—that pays any respect to either the meteorological, the biological, or the psychological knowledge already available, for this knowledge calls for radical alterations in their use. And still less do these innovations heed human activities or personal desires.

In so far as modern architecture has succeeded in expressing modern life, it has done better in calling attention to its lapses, its rigidities, its failures, than in bringing out, with the aid of the architect's creative imagination, its immense latent potentialities. The modern architect has yet to come to grips with the multidimensional realities of the actual world. He has made himself at home with mechanical processes, which favor rapid commercial exploitation, and with anonymous repetitive bureaucratic forms, like the high-rise apartment or office building, which lend themselves with mathematical simplicity to financial manipulation. But he has no philosophy that does justice to organic functions or human purposes, and that attempts to build a more comprehensive order in which the machine, instead of dominating our life and demanding ever heavier sacrifices in the present fashion, will become a supple instrument for humane design, to be used, modified, or on occasion rejected at will.

FROM THE MACHINE TO THE PACKAGE

Despite the shallowness of the theory of mechanical progress, the first erections of modern architecture, beginning with the Crystal Palace in 1851, rested on a firm foundation: the perception that the technology of the nineteenth century had immensely enriched the vocabulary of modern form and facilitated modes of construction that could hardly have been dreamed of in more ponderous materials, while it made possible plans of a far more organic nature than the heavy shells that constituted buildings in the past.

In their pride over these new possibilities, the engineers who turned these processes over to the architect naturally overemphasized this contribution; and when Louis Sullivan proclaimed that form followed function, his successors falsely put the emphasis on mechanical form and mechanical function. Both are in fact essential to the constitution of modern architecture; but neither by itself—nor both together— is sufficient. Frank Lloyd Wright understood this from the beginning, and insisted, quite properly, that he was something more than a "functionalist," though in the last phase of his great career, as in the Johnson laboratory and the Guggenheim Museum, he succumbed to the fascination of an elegant mechanical solution, treated as an end in itself.

In the new beginning that dates from Le Corbusier's *Vers une Architecture*, the machine occupied a central place: its austerity, its economy, its geometric cleanness were proclaimed almost the sole virtues of the new architecture. Thus the kitchen became a laboratory, and the bathroom took on the qualities of a surgical operating room; while the other parts of the house, for a decade or so, achieved excellence almost to the degree that they, too, were white, cleanable, empty of human content. This was in fact a useful period of cleansing and clarification. A few critics, notably Henry-Russell Hitchcock, recognized that this was the primitive state in the evolution of a historic style; and that, at a later date, certain elements, like ornament, that had been discarded in this new effort at integrity might return again—though in fact they had never been abandoned by Wright.

Unfortunately, this interpretation of the new mechanical possibilities was in itself dominated by a superficial aesthetic, which sought to make the new buildings *look* as if they respected the machine, no matter what the materials or methods of construction; and it was this superficial aesthetic, openly proclaiming its indifference to actual mechanical and biological functions or human purposes that was formally put forward, by Philip Johnson and his associate Hitchcock, as the International Style, though it was Alfred Barr who coined the dubious name. From this, only a short step took the architect, with Mies van der Rohe to guide him, from the Machine to the Package. Mies van der Rohe used the facilities offered by steel and glass to create elegant monuments of nothingness. They had the dry style of machine forms without the contents. His own chaste taste gave these hollow glass shells a crystalline purity of form: but they existed alone in the Platonic world of his imagination and had no relation to site, climate, insulation, function, or internal activity; indeed, they completely turned their backs upon these realities just as the rigidly arranged chairs of his living rooms openly disregarded the necessary intimacies and informalities of conversation. This was the apotheosis of the compulsive, bureaucratic spirit. Its emptiness and hollowness were more expressive than van der Rohe's admirers realized.

Here perhaps was the turning point in the development of modern architecture. The principle of functionalism, stated even in its crudest terms, was sound as far as it went; and if modern architecture was to develop further, that principle needed to be applied to every aspect of architecture. It was necessary to develop functional analysis to its limits, not merely embracing the physical elements of building, but the internal services; not merely the external structure, but the plan, and the relation of the building to its site; and the site itself to the rest of the urban or rural environment. And even this is only a beginning, because human purposes modify all these functional characteristics; so that the so-called open plan for the dwelling house turns out to be far from acceptable as a universal solution, once one takes account of the need for privacy, solitude, withdrawal, or of the differences between the extroverted, the introverted, and the integrated personality. As one adds biological and social functions, and personal desires and needs, to those of the purely physical requirements of structure, one must get, as a resultant design, a much more complex and subtle result than if one centered attention upon only one set of conditions.

How far modern architecture has withdrawn from the effort to achieve such organic richness one learns from recent architectural exhibitions, which have shown modern buildings as spatialized abstractions, in utter isolation. Some of the most famous architects of our time defiantly throw away their best opportunities: thus more than one new business building has been placed in the middle of a large country estate, with all the advantages of a lovely landscape, only to turn its back completely to its surroundings, defiling the approach with an acre of parking lot, whilst the building itself, air-conditioned and curtained in venetian blinds, mocks its open site, its possible exposure to sunlight and fresh air, by turning inward upon a closed court. The result is the characterless package, which has become the main hallmark of fashionable architecture for the last decade.

Is Le Corbusier's Unity House at Marseille an exception to this rule? Far from it. Its powerful concrete façade, with variations produced by the ill-conceived and almost abandoned market area, aesthetically distinguishes it from the less expensive and less sculptural façades of similar buildings; but for all that, it is a mere package, because the plan of the individual apartments is cramped and tortured to fit the arbitrary allotment of space, in a fashion that is as archaic as that of a New York brownstone front that has been built over the backyard and is full of narrow, dark rooms, without exposure. The genius of Le Corbusier here consisted in making a mere package look like a real building; and the feebleness of current architectural criticism is recorded in the chorus of praise that this extravagant piece of stage decoration still calls forth.

THE PACKAGE AND THE FASHION PLATE

Meanwhile, the advance of technology has presented the architect with a vast array of new metallic alloys and new plastics, with new structural materials like prestressed concrete, with new large-scale elements useful for modular designs, and with new mechanical devices that add to the total cost of the structure, as well as the upkeep. On the assumption that mechanical progress is itself more important than human purposes, the architect has felt, it would seem, almost a moral obligation to use all these materials and methods, if only to maintain his status as a creative designer. In this respect, the architect finds himself in almost the same unfortunate position as the physician, overwhelmed by the enormous number of new antibiotics and other drugs that are thrust on the market by the great pharmaceutical organizations, and often unable to follow through one remedy before a new one is thrust on him.

But the advances of technology, which have opened those possibilities for the new forms that Eric Mendelsohn so brilliantly anticipated in his imaginative sketches back in the twenties, have also revealed the possibility of two new architectural perversions. One of them is the utilization of sensational methods of construction merely to produce equally sensational forms, which have no purpose other than that of demonstrating the aesthetic audacity of the designer. The external shell of the new opera house at Sydney reveals this order of design; so, for that matter, does the too-often quoted Guggenheim Museum in New York, and even more Wright's new municipal building in Marin County; and all over the country today, one finds new churches whose very form of construction reveals nothing except a desire to compete on equal aesthetic terms with the supermarket and the hot-dog emporium. This is not functional and purposeful creativity: it is the creativity of the kaleidoscope, so far the most successful of all inventions for imitating creativity by juggling mechanical forms.

When a child is bored or an adult is ill, the aesthetics of the kaleidoscope is enchanting; and I do not underestimate its fascination. Nor would I deny that, related to our emergent needs, many new forms

must and will appear in modern architecture, which will reveal meanings and values, intuitions about the nature of the cosmos or the condition of man, that are not present in any earlier architectural system. But
creativity, in order to be assimilated, requires an underlying basis of
order; and what is more, the most original form needs to be repeated,
with modifications, if its full value is to be absorbed by the user and the
spectator. The desire for architectural originality through a succession
of kaleidoscopic changes, made possible by modern technological
agents, when the inner purpose and contents are ruled out of the
equation, inevitably degrades the creative process. Such technical facility, such aesthetic audacity, poured forth on a large scale, promises only
to enlarge the domain of chaos. Already the architectural magazines
show projects, and even buildings, that look as if they were ingeniously
cut out of paper and twisted together, shapes full of fantasy and capable
of giving childish pleasure—provided they are not carried out in more
solid constructions.

One may explain this excessive virtuosity, with which modern architecture is now threatened, by two conditions. This is plainly, on one
hand, a revolt against the excessive regimentation that has gone on in
every part of our lives: that regimentation whose symbol is the vast
repetitive inanity of the high-rise slab. And on the other hand, it is due
to the fact that genuine creativity, which takes into account all the
possibilities of structure, the nature of an institution's function and
purposes, the values that the client draws from the community and in
turn must give back to the community, is a slow process. Because such
knowledge and such facility cannot be improvised in a few weeks, the
creative architect must build from structure to structure on his own
experience, and absorb that of other architects, past and present. It is
far easier to create a sensational shell, with the constructive facilities
now available, than to fulfill all the functions of architecture. An engineer of genius, like [Pier Luigi] Nervi, has shown the way toward more
solid achievement; but even he has succeeded best when the inner
content of the building was as simple as tiers of spectators watching
sport, or an exhibition or market hall whose contents could be adequately enclosed by a mere shell.

But there is an alternative to kaleidoscopic creativity that would be
equally disastrous to architecture and to the human spirit, though the
threat comes from the opposite point of our machine economy. Instead
of an endless succession of superficial new forms, dazzling Christmas
packages that have no relation to contents, we are threatened by another form of technological facility, whose present favored form is the
geodesic dome. Under this potential technical triumph, buildings as
such would disappear, except perhaps as improvised rooms within a

mechanically controlled environment, dedicated to producing uniform temperature, lighting, and ultimately, with the aid of drugs, surgery, and genetic intervention, uniform human beings. Whether above ground or below ground, this development would bring to an end, in a world of colorless uniformity, the long history of man's building: he would return to the cave from which he originally emerged, none the richer or wiser for his experience. I will not examine this particular possibility in detail, except to note that many minds are now busily engaged in preparing for this grand act of suicide. So committed indeed are many architects in our day to the automatism of the machine that they fall under a compulsion to follow the process to its limit, even though that final stage is a colorless and dehumanized existence, just one breath more alive than the world that might emerge from a nuclear catastrophe.

POLYTECHNICS AND MULTI-FUNCTIONALISM

If modern architecture is not to continue its disintegration into a multitude of sects and mannerisms—international stylists, empiricists, brutalists, neoromantics, and whatnot—it must rest on some principle of order; and that order must ally architecture to an equally coherent theory of human development. The notion of mechanical progress alone will not do, because it leaves out the one element that would give significance to this progress: man himself; or rather, because it makes the human personality a mere tool of the processes that should in fact serve it.

Man himself is an organism whose existence is dependent upon his maintaining the delicate balance that exists between all the forces of nature, physical and organic, from sunlight and air and the soil, the bacteria, the molds, and growing plants right up to the complex interaction of thousands of species. Despite the great advances in technology, man controls only a small part of these processes: for neither destruction nor mechanical substitution is in fact a mode of control. From this complex biological inheritance man extracts and perfects those portions that serve his own purposes. Organic order is based on variety, complexity, and balance; and this order provides continuity through change, stability through adaptation, harmony through finding a place for conflict, chance, and limited disorder, in ever more complex transformations. This organic interdependence was recognized and expressed in every historic culture, particularly in its cosmic and religious conceptions, with their genuinely sacred buildings, and though these buildings have outlived their technologies they still speak to the human soul.

[Horatio] Greenough's original analysis of form, on a basis of the biological and physiological nature of organisms, did justice to both process and function, but overlooked their transformation through a still higher and more complex category, that of human purpose. Man is not just an actor and a fabricator: he is an interpreter and a transformer. On the higher levels of existence, form determines function, no less than function form. At this point the continued development of the whole man takes precedence over the continued development of his instruments and his machines; and the only kind of order that can ensure this is one that provides a many-sided environment capable of sustaining the greatest variety of human interests and human purposes. An environment or a structure that has been reduced to the level of the machine, correct, undeviating, repetitious, monotonous, is hostile to organic reality and to human purpose: even when it performs, with a certain efficiency, a positive function, such as providing shelter, it remains a negative symbol, or at best a neutral one.

There are three sources for this larger order: nature is one; the cumulative processes of history and historic culture are another; and the human psyche is the third. To turn one's back upon these sources, in the name of mechanical progress, for the sake of purely quantitative production, mechanical efficiency, bureaucratic order, is to sterilize both architecture and the life that it should sustain and elevate. An age that worships the machine and seeks only those goods that the machine provides, in ever larger amounts, at ever rising profits, actually has lost contact with reality; and in the next moment or the next generation may translate its general denial of life into one last savage gesture of nuclear extermination. Within the context of organic order and human purpose, our whole technology has still potentially a large part to play; but much of the riches of modern technics will remain unusable until organic functions and human purposes, rather than the mechanical process, dominate.

An organic approach will handle, with equal dexterity, but with greater freedom of choice, every kind of function: it will not automatically reject daylight in favor of a facile mechanical substitute, or fresh air, renovated by vegetation, for a purely mechanical system of modifying the air. But neither will it turn banks into frivolous glass-enclosed pleasure palaces, office-building entrances into cathedrals, or churches into airport hangars. On the contrary, purpose and function will provide an organic criterion of form at every stage of the design process; and in the end this will produce, not merely an aesthetic variety and exuberance that are now almost unknown, but even mechanical economies that have been flouted by our compulsive overcommitment to the machine.

There are two movements now visible that indicate a beginning in the right direction, which will lead, not away from functionalism, but toward a multi-functional approach to every architectural problem.

One of these movements, visible in the architectural schools today, is the students' demand for architectural and town-planning history. The desire behind this is not for forms to imitate, but for experience and feeling to assimilate, for spiritual nourishment beyond that which is offered by the immediate environment or a brief present moment. This is a healthy reaction against the notion that the experience of a single generation, or a single decade in a generation, is sufficient to provide the knowledge and insight man needs to create a human environment of sufficient richness and depth.

The other movement became visible last summer in the meeting of the younger architects who have broken away from the old masters of the C.I.A.M.* In their attempt to redefine the province of architecture today, they expressed many differences with the generation of Le Corbusier and Gropius, as well as personal and characterological differences within their own ranks; but at the end they were united, in a large degree, on one final conclusion: that architecture was more than the art of building: it was rather the art of transforming man's entire habitat. This concept had already struck root in California, when the school of architecture at Berkeley was reconstituted and renamed as the School of Environmental Design.

If human development does not become sterile and frustrated through an excessive effort to conquer nature without drawing upon all the resources of history and culture to rehumanize man, the architecture of the future will again be a true polytechnics, utilizing all the resources of technics, from the human hand to the latest automatic device. It will be closer in spirit and form to the earlier work of Frank Lloyd Wright . . . than to the masters of the C.I.A.M.; and it will go beyond them, because it will draw upon the richer human resources now worldwide in cultural scope, which are happily available for collective as well as individual expression.

*Congrès International d'Architecture Moderne (International Congress of Modern Architecture). *(Editor's note)*

SYMBOL AND FUNCTION IN ARCHITECTURE

. . . The one great domain where, in the very nature of things, [art and technics] have always been united in the closest sort of domestic union . . . [is] architecture. In that art, beauty and use, symbol and structure, meaning and practical function, can hardly even in a formal analysis be separated; for a building, however artless, however innocent of conscious speech on the part of the builder, by its very presence cannot help saying something. Even in the plainest aesthetic choices of materials, or of proportions, the builder reveals what manner of man he is and what sort of community he is serving. Yet despite this close association in building between technics and art, doing and saying, the separate functions are clearly recognizable in any analysis of an architectural structure: the foundations, the inner drainage system, or in later days the heating and cooling systems, plainly belong exclusively to technics; while the shape and scale of the structure, the elements that accentuate its function or emphasize its purpose in order to give pleasure and sustenance to the human spirit, is art.

On one side there is the engineering side of building: a matter of calculating loads and stresses, of making joints watertight and roofs rainproof, of setting down foundations so solidly that the building that stands on them will not crack or sink. But on the other side there is the whole sphere of expression, the attempt to use the constructional forms in such a way as to convey the meaning of the building to the spectator and user, and enable him, with a fuller response on his own side, to participate in its functions—feeling more courtly when he enters a palace, more pious when he enters a church, more studious when he enters a university, more businesslike and efficient when he enters an office, and more citizenlike, more cooperative and responsible, more proudly conscious of the community he serves, when he goes about his city and participates in its many-sided life. Architecture, in the sense that I here present it to you, is the permanent setting of a culture against which its social drama can be played out with the fullest help to the actors. Confusion and cross-purposes in this domain—such confusion as has existed in the recent past when businessmen thought of their offices as cathedrals, or when pious donors treated university buildings as if they were private mausoleums—all this brings about disruption in our life; so that it is of utmost importance that symbol and function in architecture should be brought into an effective harmony.

Once upon a time a great motion-picture palace was opened; and an array of notable New Yorkers was invited to the first night. For at least ten minutes, but for what seemed the better part of an hour, the audience was treated to a succession of lighting effects, to the raising and lowering of the orchestra platform, and to the manifold ways in which the curtain could be lifted and parted. For a while, the audience was delighted by the technical virtuosity displayed: but when nothing further seemed about to happen, they were bored: they were waiting for the real performance to begin.

Modern architecture is now in a state similar to that of the Radio City Music Hall on the opening night. Our best architects are full of technical facility and calculated competence: but from the standpoint of the audience, they are still only going through the mechanical motions. The great audience is still waiting for the performance to begin. Now, in all systems of architecture, both function and expression have a place. Every building performs work, if it is only to keep off the rain or to remain upright against the wind. At the same time, even the simplest structure produces a visual impression upon those who use it or look at it: unconsciously or by design, it says something to the beholder and modifies, in some slight degree at least, his organic reactions. Functions that are permanently invisible remain outside the architectural picture; hence a building below ground may not be called architecture. But every function that is visible contributes in some degree to expression. In simple monuments like obelisks, or even in more complex structures like temples, the function of the building is subordinate to the human purpose it embodies: if such structures do not delight the eye and inform the mind, no technical audacity can save them from becoming meaningless. Indeed, ideological obsolescence is more fatal than technical obsolescence to a work of architecture. As soon as a building becomes meaningless, it disappears from view, even though it remain standing.

Modern architecture crystallized at the moment that people realized that the older modes of symbolism no longer spoke to modern man;

and that, on the contrary, the new functions brought in by the machine had something special to say to him. Unfortunately, in the act of realizing these new truths, mechanical function has tended to absorb expression, or in more fanatical minds, to do away with the need for it. As a result, the architectural imagination has, within the last twenty years, become impoverished: so much so that the recent prize-winning design for a great memorial, produced by one of the most accomplished and able of the younger architects, was simply a gigantic parabolic arch. If technics could not, by itself, tell the story of the pioneer, moving through the gateway of the continent, the story could not, in the architectural terms of our own day, be told. . . .

By now, many architects have become aware of a self-imposed poverty: in absorbing the lessons of the machine and in learning to master new forms of construction, they have, they begin to see, neglected the valid claims of the human personality. In properly rejecting antiquated symbols, they have also rejected human needs, interests, sentiments, values, that must be given full play in every complete structure. This does not mean, as some critics have hastily asserted, that functionalism is doomed: it means rather that the time has come to integrate objective functions with subjective functions: to balance off mechanical facilities with biological needs, social commitments, and personal values. And to understand the new prospects that open before architecture, we must first do justice to functionalism and see how it came about in our time that the mechanical part was taken for the whole.

As so often happens, functionalism came into the world as a fact long before it was appraised as an idea. The fact was that for three centuries engineering had been making extraordinary advances in every department *except* building; and it was high time that the interest in new materials and technical processes, associated in particular with the fuller use of iron and glass, along with the mass production of standard units, should find its way into building. Functionalism resulted in the creation of machines, apparatus, utensils, structures, completely lacking in any expressive intention, but designed with utmost rigor for effective operation. Even before the machine exerted its special discipline, functionalism tended, in other departments of building, to produce strong geometric or organic forms. A barn or a haystack or a silo, a castle, a bridge, a seaworthy sailing vessel—all these are functional forms, with a certain cleanness of line and rightness of shape that spring, like the shape of a gull or a hawk, from the work to be performed. By and large, people do not stop to contemplate or enjoy such structures until they have ceased to use them, or at least until they pause to take in the meaning of what they have done. But these buildings have at least the quality of all organic creations: they identify themselves and so symbolize the function they serve. When a steam locomotive is fully developed, for example, so that all its excrescences and technological leftovers are absorbed in a slick overall design, "streamlined" as one now hesitates to say, that locomotive not merely *is* more speedy than the primitive form, but it says speed, too. All these developments had a special message for architecture; for the expressive effects of architecture in all its great periods had been due in large part to the absorption and mastery of these engineering elements: pure building.

One of the first people to understand both the symbolic implications and the practical application of functionalism was an American sculptor, Horatio Greenough. He published his thoughts, at the end of his all-too-brief life, on his return to America, in a series of papers that were first unearthed—they had been lying quietly on library shelves—by Mr. Van Wyck Brooks and have lately been republished. But since Greenough's mind powerfully affected contemporaries like Emerson, it is very likely that his contribution worked quietly under the surface of American life, affecting later critics like James Jackson Jarves and Montgomery Schuyler, even when they were unaware of their sources or negligent in acknowledging their debt. It was Greenough who carried further, as a student of anatomy as well as sculpture, the great theorem of Lamarck: form follows function. This principle carries two corollaries: forms change when functions change, and new functions cannot be expressed by old forms. Greenough saw that this applied to all organic forms, even man-created ones. He recognized that the effective works of art in his own day, the primitives of a new era, were not the current specimens of eclectic decoration and eclectic architecture but the strong virile forms, without any other historical attachment than to their own age, of the new tools and machines, forms that met the new needs of modern life. The American ax, the American clock, the clipper ship—in every line of these utilities and machines necessity or function played a determining part. They were without ornament or decorative device of any kind, except perhaps for a surviving ship's figurehead: like the naked body, when harmoniously developed, they needed no further ornament or costume to achieve beauty. For what was beauty? "The promise of function."

As expressed by Greenough, that was a breathtaking, a spine-tingling thought; and in the minds of Greenough's successors, such as the architect Louis Sullivan, who might well have breathed in Greenough's words with his native New England air, this doctrine provided a starting point for the new architecture. Until the twentieth century, however, the movement toward functionalism in architecture went on almost in spite of the architect, rather than through his eager efforts. The great new constructions of the nineteenth century were as often as not the work of engineers: the Crystal Palace of 1851, the Brooklyn Bridge of 1883, and the Paris Hall of Machines of 1889 were all works of engineering, though some vestigial remnants of early expressive elements remained even in structures as pure as Roebling's masterpiece, in his choice of a Gothic arch in the stone piers, capped by the remains of a classic cornice.

But though all these new works tended toward a certain starkness, a certain severity and simplicity, that quality was not altogether the work of the new engineers, nor even the automatic result of the new industrial process. Economy and simplicity have their roots in the human spirit, too. The desire to slough off symbolic excrescences, to avoid ornateness of any sort, to reduce even speech to its simplest forms,and to remain quiet when one has nothing to say—behind all that is something else, a religious sense of life, to which those who have dealt with architecture have hardly yet done justice. But the fact is that the new functionalism in architecture owed something to a fresh religious impulse, that of the Society of Friends, those sincere Christian souls who sought to get back to the unadorned innocence of the primitive Christian Church. They rejected ornament of any kind either in dress or in speech, as offensive to an inner purity of spirit; their directness, their matter-of-factness, their underemphasis, their severity and probity, had an effect upon modern ways out of all proportion to their numbers. Democratic simplicity in dress and in manners passed over into architecture, only to disappear once more in our day as technological overelaboration takes the place of more obvious forms of symbolic superfluity. . . .

But while Greenough's doctrine was a salutary one, it was incomplete; for it partly failed to do justice to those human values that are derived, not from the object and the work, but from the subject and the quality of life the architect seeks to enhance. Even mechanical function itself rests on human values: the desire for order, for security, for power; but to presume that these values are, in every instance, all-prevailing ones, which do away with the need for any other qualities, is to limit the nature of man himself to just those functions that serve the machine.

Perhaps it would be profitable at this point to contrast Greenough's doctrine of functionalism with the conception of architecture that John Ruskin advanced in *The Seven Lamps of Architecture.* Contrary to popular misinterpretation, Ruskin had a very healthy respect for the functional and utilitarian triumphs of the Victorian age, and even his complaint against the barbarous effects of the new railroad trains, though petulant and often childish in tone, was only the voice of a good conservationist who understood that filth and dirtiness and land erosion and stream pollution were not evidences of industrial efficiency. But Ruskin insisted that building was one thing and architecture was another: a building became architecture, in his theory, when the structure was enhanced and embellished with original works of sculpture and painting.

This theory of architecture—which would make architecture dependent upon the symbolic contributions of the nonarchitectural arts —seems to me, in the form Ruskin gave it, a downright false one; and certainly it is impossible to reconcile with Greenough's conception of functionalism. But it has the virtue of pointing to the expressive and symbolic aspects of architecture and underlining their importance. The basic truth in Ruskin's statement comes out just as soon as one replaces the restricted notion of painting and sculpture applied to an otherwise finished building with the larger concept of the building as itself an expressive work of multi-mural painting and architectonic sculpture. By his choice of materials and textures and colors, by the contrasting play of light and shade, by the multiplication of planes, by the accentuation, when necessary, of sculpture or ornament, the architect does in fact turn his building into a special kind of picture: a multidimensional moving picture, whose character changes with the hours and seasons, with the functions and actions of spectators and inhabitants. Similarly, he creates in a building a unique work of sculpture, a form one not merely walks around but walks into, a form in which the very movement of the spectator through space is one of the conditions under which the solids and voids of architecture have a powerful aesthetic effect, not known in any other art. The most daring innovations of the sculptor Henry Moore are in fact the aesthetic commonplaces of architecture. And only when a building can be conceived and modeled so as to achieve a maximum degree of expression by the use of the material elements proper to building, only when the architect has sufficient means to play freely with the structure as a whole, modeling plan and elevation into a plastic unity, emphasizing its special meanings, intensifying its special values, does architecture in fact emerge from building and engineering. At that moment, Ruskin and Greenough, symbolic beauty and functional beauty, are reconciled.

Now, no matter how rapidly our technical processes change, the need for expression remains a constant in every culture; without it the drama of life cannot go on, and the plot itself becomes pointless and empty. Life must have meaning, value, and purpose, or we die: we die standing on our feet, with our eyes open, but blind, our ears open but deaf, our lips moving but speechless. And we cannot, by any mechanical duplication of old symbols, come to a realization of the vital meanings in our own life. Our intercourse with other ages can only be of a spiritual nature. Everything we take over from the past must disappear in the act of digestion and assimilation, to be transformed into our own flesh and bones. Each age then must live its own life. But because of the need for finding meaning and value in our own works and days, our civilization can no more forgo symbolic architecture than could any earlier civilization.

So it came about that symbolic expression, driven out the front door by the doctrine that form follows function, came in by the rear entrance. The conscious theories of functionalists from Greenough to Sullivan, from Adolf Loos to Gropius, have by now succeeded in eliminating almost every historic or archaic mode of symbolism. They established the fact that a modern building cannot be imitation Egyptian, imitation Greek, imitation medieval, imitation Renaissance, or imitation hodgepodge. Their new structures were not refurbished traditional forms, improved with modern plumbing and elevator service; they were naked, clean, properly devoid of extraneous ornament. *But still they said something.* They were not merely products of the machine; they revealed that the machine itself might become an object of veneration; and that an age that despised and debunked symbols might nevertheless, like the hero of a forgotten play by Eugene O'Neill, find itself worshiping a dynamo. Feelings and emotions that hitherto had attached themselves to organisms and persons, to political and religious concepts, were now being channeled into machine forms. These new forms not merely revealed function: they reveled in function, they celebrated it, they dramatized the mathematical and the impersonal aspects of the new environment. And so far forth the new buildings were symbolic structures.

My point here is that much of what was masked as strict functionalism during the last generation was in fact a sort of psychological if not religious fetishism: an attempt, if I may use Henry Adams's well-worn figure, to make the dynamo instead of the Virgin serve as an object of love and devotion. Since both the true functionalist and the fetishist have used the same kind of technical means, it sometimes requires acute insight to distinguish one from the other at first glance; though with a little further acquaintance with the building itself one readily discovers whether it actually stands up well and works well, or whether it only is an aesthetic simulacrum of structures that do such things. In short, those who devaluated the human personality, and in particular subordinated feeling and emotion to pure intellect, compensated for their error by overvaluing the machine. In a meaningless world of sensations and physical forces, the machine alone, for them, represented the purposes of life. Thus the machine became a symbol to contemplate, rather than an instrument to use: it was (mistakenly) identified with the totality of modern life. That error was an easy one to fall into; for a large part of the modern world has been created, with the aid of mathematics and the physical sciences and mechanical invention; and no honest construction in our time can avoid in some measure expressing this discipline and acknowledging this immense debt.

Naturally, a certain unified method of approach, a certain common way of thinking, a certain common technical facility, must underlie the forms of our age. But to assume that the machine alone should dominate the forms of twentieth-century architecture, symbolically as well as functionally, does not show any real insight into either the dangers of mechanization or into the pressing need of bringing other human motives and purposes back into the center of the picture. The machine, treated as a symbol, was used as a substitute for the whole. To assume that seaside houses should look like ocean steamships, as Le Corbusier did in his cruder moments, or to assume that a building should look like a cubist painting or constructivist abstraction, is not a functional assumption at all. As a symbol, the machine might properly have represented the partial, lopsided culture of early nineteenth-century industrialism. But we know in 1951, as men did not know in 1851, that the machine is only a limited expression of the human spirit: that this is not just the age of Faraday and Clerk Maxwell and Einstein; it is also the age of Darwin and Marx and Kropotkin and Freud, of Bergson and Dewey and Schweitzer, of Patrick Geddes and A. J. Toynbee. In short, ours is an age of deep psychological exploration and heightened social responsibility. Thanks to advances in biology, sociology, and psychology, we begin to understand the whole man; and it is high time for the architects to demonstrate that understanding in other terms than economy, efficiency, and abstract mechanical form.

In the multidimensional world of modern man, subjective interests and values, emotions and feelings, play as large a part as the objective environment: the nurture of life becomes more important than the multiplication of power and standardized goods, considered as ends in themselves. The machine can no more adequately symbolize our culture than can a Greek temple or a Renaissance palace. On the contrary, we know that our almost compulsive preoccupation with the rigid order of the machine is itself a symptom of weakness: of emotional insecurity, of repressed feelings, or of a general withdrawal from the demands of life. To persist in the religious cult of the machine, at this late day and date, is to betray an inability to interpret the challenges and dangers of our age. In this sense, Le Corbusier's polemical writings, beginning with his publication of *Towards a New Architecture,* were in no small measure a reactionary influence: retrospective rather than prophetic.

Now all this is not to say that the doctrine that form follows function was a misleading one. What was false and meretricious was the narrow applications that were made of this formula. Actually, functionalism is subject to two main modifications. The first is that we must not take function solely in a mechanical sense, as applying only to the physical functions of the building. Certainly new technical facilities and mechanical functions required new forms: but so, likewise, did new social purposes and new psychological insights. There are many elements in a building, besides its physical elements, that affect the health, comfort, and pleasure of the user. When the whole personality is taken into account, expression or symbolism becomes one of the dominant concerns of architecture; and the more complex the functions to be served, the more varied and subtle will the form be. In other words—and this is the second modification—expression itself is one of the primary functions of architecture.

On hygienic grounds, for example, the architect may calculate the number of cubic feet of space necessary to provide air for a thousand people in a public hall; and with the aid of the exact science of acoustics —plus a little luck—he may design a hall which will enable every person to hear with a maximum of clarity every sound that is made for the benefit of the audience. But after the architect has made all these calculations, he has still to weight them with other considerations that have to do with the effect of space and form on the human soul. In the cathedrals of the Middle Ages economy, comfort, and good acoustic properties were all cheerfully sacrificed to the magnification of glory and mystery, in a fashion designed to overwhelm the worshiper. In terms of medieval culture, that was both effective symbolism and true functionalism. In the strictly graded aristocratic society of the Renaissance, in which music itself was subservient to the ostentatious parade of upper-class families, seeking to impress each other and the populace, the Palladian horseshoe form of opera house, with poor acoustic properties but excellent visibility for the box holders, likewise did justice to the functions of the building in the order of their social importance, within that culture.

In other words, every building is conditioned by cultural and personal aims as well as physical and mechanical needs. An organic functionalism, accordingly, cannot stop short with a mechanical or a physiological solution. So in the rebuilding of the House of Commons, Mr. Winston Churchill wisely insisted that the seating space should be considerably smaller than the actual membership, in order to preserve the closeness and intimacy of debate in the House, under normal conditions of attendance. That decision was as wise as the medieval decoration that went with it was inept and meretricious; though an original modern architect might have found a means of echoing, in works of

original sculpture, the traditional ceremonies and symbols so assidu-
ously preserved in the British Parliament, beginning with that medieval relic the Speaker's mace.

The architecture of Frank Lloyd Wright was subjected to a considerable amount of arbitrary critical disparagement during the 1920s
when mechanization and depersonalization were regarded, with Le
Corbusier, as the all-sufficient ingredients of contemporary form. But
this disparagement was based on the very qualities that made Wright's
architecture superior to the work of Le Corbusier's school. In Wright's
work, the subjective and symbolic elements were as important as the
mechanical requirements. From his earliest prairie houses onward,
both the plan and the elevations of Wright's buildings were informed
by human ideals, and by a sense of what is due to the person whose
varied needs and interests must be reflected in the building. It was the
idea of the organic itself, the desire to embrace nature, that led to the
introduction of the garden into the interior; it was the idea of horizontality as an expression of the prairie that led Wright to emphasize
horizontal lines in his early regional houses. So, too, in Wright's later
work, a geometrical figure, a circle or a hexagon or a spiral, the expression of a subjective human preference, supplies the ground pattern for
the whole building. In such instances, as the late Matthew Nowicki
pointed out, the old formula is reversed—function follows form: man
dictates to nature.

Now, when subjective expression is overplayed the results are not
always happy—any more than was the case in Renaissance buildings,
where the idea of axial balance and symmetry determined both plan
and elevation. But to say this is only to admit that, if mechanical functions, taken alone, do not fulfill all human needs, so subjective expressions, if divorced from practical considerations, may become willful,
capricious, defiant of common sense. Accordingly, the more sensitive
the architect is to expression, the more capable he is of transforming
"building" into "architecture," the greater the need for his own self-
knowledge, self-control, self-discipline: above all, for subordinating his
own inner willfulness to the character and purposes of his client.

On this latter score, Frank Lloyd Wright's work is sometimes not
impeccable; for all too rarely has he been faced with a client sufficiently
strong in his own right to stand up to Wright's overbearing genius, in
a way that will do justice to every dimension of the problem. But one
thing is usually in evidence in Wright's architecture—not the machine
but the human person has taken command. Hence Frank Lloyd
Wright's wealth of designs is marked, not by any mechanical uniformity, but by an endless diversity and variety, held together by the underlying unity of Wright's own very positive personality; and whatever

criticisms one may make of his buildings in detail—and I have made sundry criticisms in my time—one finds that as a whole they stand preeminent among the structures of our time precisely because they unite the mechanical and the personal. Here form follows function and function follows form, in a rhythmic interplay between necessity and freedom, between construction and choice, between the object-determined self and the self-determined object. In Wright's fertile and inventive use of the machine, combined with a refusal to be cowed by it or intimidated by it into a servile disregard of his own purposes, his work has been prophetic of a future in which art and technics will be effectively united.

How hard it is to achieve such structures, at once functional in all their offices and arrangements and duly symbolic of their own human purposes, we can see when we examine a building near at hand: the new Secretariat Building of the United Nations. That great oblong prism of steel and aluminum and glass, less a building than a gigantic mirror in which the urban landscape of Manhattan is reflected, is in one sense one of the most perfect achievements of modern technics: as fragile as a spiderweb, as crystalline as a sheet of ice, as geometrical as a beehive. On this structure almost a score of the best architectural and engineering minds of our day were at one time or another at work. But unfortunately, the genius presiding over this design was an architectural doctrine altogether too narrow and superficial to solve the actual problem itself. The very decision to make the Secretariat Building the dominant structure in this complex of buildings reveals at the start either a complete indifference to symbolism, or a very wry reading of the nature and destiny of the United Nations. With relation to the city itself, a forty-two-story building cannot possibly express dominance: it is just another skyscraper in an urban heap of skyscrapers, actually seeming even lower to the eye than it is in fact, because the river front where it stands drops sharply below the escarpment above it. With relation to the General Assembly Building, the overwhelming dominance of the Secretariat is ridiculous—unless the architects conceived it as a cynical way of expressing the fact that [James] Burnham's managerial revolution had taken place and that the real decisions are made in the Secretariat, by the bureaucracy.

Has this building then been conceived with a strict regard to its functions as an office building? Did the architects seize the opportunity to create, for the example of the rest of the world, an ideal office building, freed as they were from the constraints of realty speculation, constricted building lots, and metropolitan overcrowding? Unfortunately, as a functional unit, the Secretariat Building is even more lacking in merit, if this is possible, than as a symbol. This structure, as the chief architect has explained, is really three separate office buildings, each with its own elevator and ventilating machinery, piled one on top of the other. In other words, there is no functional reason whatever for its present height. For the purely aesthetic purpose of creating an unbroken glass surface for the façade, as much money must be spent on washing the spandrels between the windows as for washing the windows themselves; and that high cost of upkeep, added to the excessive cost of artificial ventilation, takes away income sorely needed for other purposes. But this is not all. In order to create the purely abstract aesthetic effect of an unbroken marble slab on the north and south ends of the building—and in order incidentally to give a large expanse of window space to the women's lavatories, for reasons no one can explain —about a quarter of the perimeter of the building, which might have been used to give natural lighting to the offices, has been sacrificed. And what is the functional result? The result is that a large number of secretaries, instead of working under ideal conditions, as they should in such a building, work in dreary interior cubicles that lack sunlight and air and view: advantages they might have enjoyed if functional considerations had been sufficiently respected. Surely that was a disreputable blunder to make in providing working quarters for an organization that is attempting, on a worldwide scale, to improve the conditions of the worker. In such a building bad working conditions mean bad symbolism.

In short, the sound functional requirements of the Secretariat Building were sacrificed so as to give aesthetic purity to a symbol that is not a symbol, unless we accept this skyscraper as an eloquent but unintentional symbol of the general perversion of life values that takes place in a disintegrating civilization. The Secretariat Building—or, rather, the complex of modest buildings that might have formed the Secretariat—should have been treated neither as a monument nor a symbol, still less as an imitation of a commercial New York skyscraper. The Secretariat should have been planned on the human scale, subordinated in its placement and design to the Assembly Building. The office buildings should have been designed with something more than lip service to economy, to mechanical function, above all, to the actual working needs of their occupants. Instead of having their substance wasted on elaborate mechanical utilities, introduced to counteract the massive errors in general design, the buildings should have been correctly oriented for sun and wind, and surrounded by trees and lawns that would have provided a pleasant microclimate for both winter and summer, with due architectural provision for intervals of recreation and social intercourse that are denied the inmates of the present building. By departing from the meretricious errors of New York speculative building—the pattern and model of the present structure—the architects of the Secretariat might have established a model for all future office buildings, in whose design human considerations would predominate above profit or prestige or mechanical fetishism.

Conceived in this fashion, the very functions of the Secretariat would have produced the correct symbol, one duly subordinated to the main effort to hold the eye and elevate the spirit through the development of the Assembly Building and the design and gardening of the site as a whole. Instead, the designers of the Secretariat Building sacrificed both mechanical efficiency and human values in order to achieve an empty abstract form, a frozen geometrical concept, that reflects the emptiness and purposelessness of modern technics, as now conceived. Certainly it expresses nothing about the purposes and values of a world organization, dedicated to peace and justice and the improvement of human life. In short, the Secretariat Building exhibits both a breakdown of functionalism and a symbolic blackout. Though mechanically new, it is architecturally and humanly obsolete. That is almost a definition of the pseudo-modern.

The architect who perhaps came closest among our contemporaries to resolving function and expression was Matthew Nowicki, he whose early death in an airplane accident in 1950 was a loss comparable to the one architecture sustained when John Wellborn Root died at an equally early age. In the course of some forty intense years of life, Nowicki had passed through the various phases of modern architecture represented by cubism, by mechanical functionalism and *Sachlichkeit*, by Le Corbusier's "International Style." Firmly rooted in our own age, he regarded the standard unit, the module, as an essential discipline for the modern architect: the minimum ingredient for form. In such designs as that for the great amphitheater in the State Fair Grounds at Raleigh, North Carolina . . . he used that typical modern form, the parabolic arch, to enclose the facing ranks of the grandstand: an acrobatic feat of great audacity and beauty, appropriate to the functions it served.

But Nowicki knew that all buildings speak a language, and that this language must be understood by the people who use it. When he worked on the preliminary designs for the library and the museum that were to be erected near the State House in Raleigh, he took into account the love and affection the people of North Carolina feel toward that fine piece of provincial classicism. For the sake of meeting their sentiment halfway, he was ready to utilize artificial lighting throughout the new buildings in order to create a solid masonry structure which, in its own modern way, would carry on the theme of the beloved older building. That tact, that understanding, and that human sympathy stand in full contrast to Le Corbusier's constant demand for people cut to the measure of his own architecture: like old Procrustes, he would amputate the human leg or stretch the human soul to fit the form he has arbitrarily provided for it.

So, again, when Matthew Nowicki went to India to work on the design of a new capital for the East Punjab . . ., he brought with him no ready-made stereotypes from the West, but absorbed, with his marvelous sensitivity and intuitive grasp, the Hindu way of life, sympathetic even to the fathomless richness and complexity that expressed itself traditionally in ornament. In the intimate plans for housing and neighborhood units, above all in one of the sketches for the Capitol itself, Nowicki translated this richness into patterns and plans that were wholly in the vernacular of modern building, yet were native to the scene and in resonance with the Hindu personality and with Hindu family life.

Rigorous in its physical foundations, Nowicki's architecture rose above them to the plane of the social and the personal. Through his humility and human sympathy, through his reverence for all genuine expressions of life, he was equipped as no other architect of his generation perhaps was to effect a fuller reconciliation of the organic and the mechanical, the regional and the universal, the abstract-rational and the personal. Along the path that he began to blaze, modern architecture, if it is to develop and grow, must follow, creating forms that will do justice to every aspect of the human organism, body and spirit in their living unity. . . .

III

THE CITY IN CIVILIZATION

He saw many cities of men, and learnt
their mind.
—Homer

Introduction

The mark and measure of Mumford's architecture criticism is its emphasis upon the whole human complex into which a building is set. A building, for him, is not a free-standing, self-contained structure to be appraised on its aesthetic merits alone. It is but one element in a larger civic or landscape design. Inspired architecture, then, demands inspired city planning.

This conclusion drew Mumford, in 1923, to a group of young architects, planners, and environmentalists who were preparing to build several new towns based on the most advanced thinking on urban design. They called themselves the Regional Planning Association of America (RPAA), and their leaders were three of the outstanding figures in twentieth-century American planning, Clarence Stein, Henry Wright, and Benton MacKaye. Within a year after joining the RPAA, Mumford became its leading spokesman and theoretician.

From Ebenezer Howard, the British urban visionary, Mumford and his RPAA colleagues borrowed the idea of garden-city planning. In *Garden Cities of Tomorrow,* published in 1898, Howard outlined a plan to stop the unbounded growth of the industrial city and restore it to human scale by relocating its excess population in new medium-sized cities situated in the outlying countryside. These regional cities would be ringed by greenbelts of farm- and parkland placed so as to prevent urban sprawl. Land would be communally owned, and the towns and their surrounding region planned as an interlocking whole. Howard built two such "garden cities," just north of London—Letchworth and Welwyn Garden City. Inspired by his ideas and example, the RPAA constructed two planned communities of its own in the New York City area—Sunnyside Gardens, Queens, and Radburn, New Jersey. Although neither of them is a complete garden city, both are harmoniously designed communities that have greatly influenced urban planning in the United States and Europe.

It was this passionate interest in the cities of the future that inspired Mumford's interest in the cities of the past. The creation of new cities requires the creation of a new image of the city, and as Mumford points out in one of the opening essays of this section, "The Disappearing City," this cannot be formed without a clear understanding of the soundest features of historic cities, as well as of the mistakes of past urban planners. In this spirit, and to this end, Mumford wrote his two classic works on the city: *The Culture of Cities,* published in 1938 and the first book to give him an international reputation; and *The City in History,* a more somber book completed over twenty years later, when he had lost some of his faith in the possibilities of worldwide urban revitalization.

It is the younger Mumford we glimpse in the essays of this section,* the more confident Mumford of *The Culture of Cities.* Like his writing on architecture, this book draws extensively on Mumford's firsthand knowledge of cities, on the enormous body of notes he had made in two decades of urban observation in America and Europe. The book, in fact, is like a great city in itself, packed with all the vitality, striking imagery, and pulsating energy of the urban spectacle it describes. Here Mumford brings into play all his visual and architectural skills. His overriding concern, however, is with the city as a human community, as a stage or physical setting for the complex drama of living. He puts social, not aesthetic, questions first, as he does in his architecture criticism. Is this city worthy of man? Is it compatible with basic human needs? Does its design foster pedestrian movement and face-to-face communication? Such are the questions that interest him most.

The Culture of Cities is a work of history, certainly, but it is history with an unmistakable didactic thrust. The entire book is shaped into an intricately woven argument for the kind of city Mumford had been advocating in his work for the RPAA. The book's unifying theme is consistent with everything of importance he had written up to this point: it is a study of the erosion of a balanced, decentralized civilization and its replacement by one with an oppressive metropolitan centralization of power, people, and culture. The story begins in the medieval town, here depicted as an earlier version of the garden city—a compactly designed community, limited in size and surrounded by open countryside—and then proceeds to describe all of subsequent urban history as a fall from grace, a long plunge into chaos and moral confusion.

While Mumford's depiction of the medieval city is wonderfully evocative, if perhaps too idyllic, the most captivating chapters are those

---

*Although the selections for this reader on the medieval city and the baroque city are taken from *The City in History,* these chapters first appeared in almost the same form in *The Culture of Cities.*

describing the baroque or imperial city. Drawing on the work of Oswald Spengler, that hard-souled Prussian meta-historian, Mumford detects between the fifteenth and eighteenth centuries a movement from universality to uniformity, from localism to centralism, from the absolutism of God to that of the temporal sovereign and the new nation-state. Mumford's powerfully suggestive, if somewhat unbalanced, critique of the baroque city deserves close examination, for in the culture that produced it he found the sources of many of the problems afflicting twentieth-century cities and civilization.

In Washington, D.C., a city he often visited in the 1920s, he saw many of the errors of baroque-style planning tediously repeated, with a concern for show and spectacle, and for the convenient movement of wheeled traffic, overriding neighborhood needs and human scale. "The framework [is] excellent," he wrote after one of his first visits to Washington, "if cities [can] live by government alone."[1]

Twentieth-century planners like Le Corbusier, Mumford points out in *The Culture of Cities,* continued to work in the spirit of the baroque builders because such sweeping plans have a "showy decisiveness" that gives them an edge over smaller, less costly projects.[2] Yet Mumford concludes the book on a hopeful note, calling for a new City of Man even more closely tailored to human needs than the great cities of the age of Abelard and Aquinas. Throughout this long, complex argument, we confront again and again that bewildering mix of despairing indignation and tenacious optimism that characterizes Mumford.

Notes

1. Mumford, *Sticks and Stones: A Study of American Architecture and Civilization* (New York: Boni and Liveright, 1924), 67.
2. Mumford, *The City in History: Its Origins, Its Transformations, and Its Prospects* (New York: Harcourt, Brace, 1961), 401, 406.

WHAT IS A CITY?

The city, as one finds it in history, is the point of maximum concentration for the power and culture of a community. It is the place where the diffused rays of many separate beams of life fall into focus, with gains in both social effectiveness and significance. The city is the form and symbol of an integrated social relationship: it is the seat of the temple, the market, the hall of justice, the academy of learning. Here in the city the goods of civilization are multiplied and manifolded; here is where human experience is transformed into viable signs, symbols, patterns of conduct, systems of order. Here is where the issues of civilization are focused: here, too, ritual passes on occasion into the active drama of a fully differentiated and self-conscious society.

Cities are a product of the earth. They reflect the peasant's cunning in dominating the earth; technically they but carry further his skill in turning the soil to productive uses, in enfolding his cattle for safety, in regulating the waters that moisten his fields, in providing storage bins and barns for his crops. Cities are emblems of that settled life which began with permanent agriculture: a life conducted with the aid of permanent shelters, permanent utilities like orchards, vineyards, and irrigation works, and permanent buildings for protection and storage.

Every phase of life in the countryside contributes to the existence of cities. What the shepherd, the woodman, and the miner know becomes transformed and "etherealized" through the city into durable elements in the human heritage: the textiles and butter of one, the moats and dams and wooden pipes and lathes of another, the metals and jewels of the third, are finally converted into instruments of urban

This selection is an excerpt from the Introduction to *The Culture of Cities.* *(Editor's note)*

living: underpinning the city's economic existence, contributing art and wisdom to its daily routine. Within the city the essence of each type of soil and labor and economic goal is concentrated: thus arise greater possibilities for interchange and for new combinations not given in the isolation of their original habitats.

Cities are a product of time. They are the molds in which men's lifetimes have cooled and congealed, giving lasting shape, by way of art, to moments that would otherwise vanish with the living and leave no means of renewal or wider participation behind them. In the city, time becomes visible: buildings and monuments and public ways, more open than the written record, more subject to the gaze of many men than the scattered artifacts of the countryside, leave an imprint upon the minds even of the ignorant or the indifferent. Through the material fact of preservation, time challenges time, time clashes with time: habits and values carry over beyond the living group, streaking with different strata of time the character of any single generation. Layer upon layer, past times preserve themselves in the city until life itself is finally threatened with suffocation: then, in sheer defense, modern man invents the museum.

By the diversity of its time structures, the city in part escapes the tyranny of a single present, and the monotony of a future that consists in repeating only a single beat heard in the past. Through its complex orchestration of time and space, no less than through the social division of labor, life in the city takes on the character of a symphony: specialized human aptitudes, specialized instruments, give rise to sonorous results which, neither in volume nor in quality, could be achieved by any single piece.

Cities arise out of man's social needs and multiply both their modes and their methods of expression. In the city remote forces and influences intermingle with the local: their conflicts are no less significant than their harmonies. And here, through the concentration of the means of intercourse in the market and the meeting place, alternative modes of living present themselves: the deeply rutted ways of the village cease to be coercive and the ancestral goals cease to be all-sufficient: strange men and women, strange interests, and stranger gods loosen the traditional ties of blood and neighborhood. A sailing ship, a caravan, stopping at the city, may bring a new dye for wool, a new glaze for the potter's dish, a new system of signs for long-distance communication, or a new thought about human destiny.

In the urban milieu, mechanical shocks produce social results; and social needs may take shape in contrivances and inventions which will lead industries and governments into new channels of experiment. Now the need for a common fortified spot for shelter against predatory attack draws the inhabitants of the indigenous village into a hillside fortification: through the compulsive mingling for defense, the possibilities for more regular intercourse and wider cooperation arise. That fact helps transform the nest of villages into a unified city, with its higher ceiling of achievement and its wider horizons. Now the collective sharing of experience, and the stimulus of rational criticism, turn the rites of the village festival into the more powerful imaginative forms of the tragic drama: experience is deepened, as well as more widely circulated, through this process. Or again, on another plane, the goldsmith's passive repository for valuables becomes, through the pressure of urban needs and the opportunities of the market, the dynamic agent of capitalism, the bank, lending money as well as keeping it, putting capital into circulation, finally dominating the processes of trade and production.

The city is a fact in nature, like a cave, a run of mackerel, or an ant heap. But it is also a conscious work of art, and it holds within its communal framework many simpler and more personal forms of art. Mind *takes form* in the city; and in turn, urban forms condition mind. For space, no less than time, is artfully reorganized in cities: in boundary lines and silhouettes, in the fixing of horizontal planes and vertical peaks, in utilizing or denying the natural site, the city records the attitude of a culture and an epoch to the fundamental facts of its existence. The dome and the spire, the open avenue and the closed court, tell the story, not merely of different physical accommodations, but of essentially different conceptions of man's destiny. The city is both a physical utility for collective living and a symbol of those collective purposes and unanimities that arise under such favoring circumstance. With language itself, it remains man's greatest work of art.

Through its concrete, visible command over space the city lends itself, not only to the practical offices of production, but to the daily communion of its citizens: this constant effect of the city, as a collective work of art, was expressed in a classic manner by Thomas Mann in his address to his fellow townsmen of Lübeck on the celebration of the anniversary of Lübeck's foundation. When the city ceases to be a symbol of art and order, it acts in a negative fashion: it expresses and helps to make more universal the fact of disintegration. In the close quarters of the city, perversities and evils spread more quickly; and in the stones of the city, these antisocial facts become embedded: it is not the triumphs of urban living that awaken the prophetic wrath of a Jeremiah, a Savonarola, a Rousseau, or a Ruskin.

What transforms the passive agricultural regime of the village into the active institutions of the city? The difference is not merely one of magnitude, density of population, or economic resources. For the active agent is any factor that extends the area of local intercourse, that engenders the need for combination and cooperation, communication and communion; and that so creates a common underlying pattern of conduct, and a common set of physical structures, for the different family and occupational groups that constitute a city. . . .

Historically, the increase of population, through the change from hunting to agriculture, may have abetted this change; the widening of trade routes and the diversification of occupations likewise helped. But the nature of the city is not to be found simply in its economic base: the city is primarily a social emergent. The mark of the city is its purposive social complexity. It represents the maximum possibility of humanizing the natural environment and of naturalizing the human heritage: it gives a cultural shape to the first, and it externalizes, in permanent collective forms, the second.

"The central and significant fact about the city," as [Patrick] Geddes and [Victor] Branford pointed out, "is that the city . . . functions as the specialized organ of social transmission. It accumulates and embodies the heritage of a region, and combines in some measure and kind with the cultural heritage of larger units, national, racial, religious, human. On one side is the individuality of the city—the sign manual of its regional life and record. On the other are the marks of the civilization, in which each particular city is a constituent element.". . .

THE
DISAPPEARING
CITY

Nobody can be satisfied with the form of the city today. Neither as a
working mechanism, as a social medium, nor as a work of art does the
city fulfill the high hopes that modern civilization has called forth—or
even meet our reasonable demands. Yet the mechanical processes of
fabricating urban structures have never before been carried to a higher
point: the energies even a small city now commands would have roused
the envy of an Egyptian Pharaoh in the Pyramid Age. And there are
moments in approaching New York, Philadelphia, or San Francisco by
car when, if the light is right and the distant masses of the buildings are
sufficiently far away, a new form of urban splendor, more dazzling than
that of Venice or Florence, seems to have been achieved.

Too soon one realizes that the city as a whole, when one approaches
it closer, does not have more than a residue of this promised form in an
occasional patch of good building. For the rest, the play of light and
shade, of haze and color, has provided for the mobile eye a pleasure that
will not bear closer architectural investigation. The illusion fades in the
presence of the car-choked streets, the blank glassy buildings, the glare
of competitive architectural advertisements, the studied monotony of
high-rise slabs in urban renewal projects: in short, new buildings and
new quarters that lack any aesthetic identity and any human appeal
except that of superficial sanitary decency and bare mechanical order.

In all the big cities of America, the process of urban rebuilding is
now proceeding at a rapid rate, as a result of putting both the financial
and legal powers of the state at the service of the private investor and
builder. But both architecturally and socially the resulting forms have
been so devoid of character and individuality that the most sordid
quarters, if they have been enriched over the years by human inter-

course and human choice, suddenly seem precious even in their ugliness, even in their disorder.

Whatever people made of their cities in the past, they expressed a visible unity that bound together, in ever more complex form, the cumulative life of the community; the face and form of the city still recorded that which was desirable, memorable, admirable. Today a rigid mechanical order takes the place of social diversity, and endless assembly-line urban units automatically expand the physical structure of the city while destroying the contents and meaning of city life. The paradox of this period of rapid "urbanization" is that the city itself is being effaced. Minds still operating under an obsolete nineteenth-century ideology of unremitting physical expansion oddly hail this outcome as "progress."

The time has come to reconsider the whole process of urban design. We must ask ourselves what changes are necessary if the city is again to become architecturally expressive, and economically workable, without our having to sacrifice its proper life to the mechanical means for keeping that life going. The architect's problem is again to make the city visually "imageable"—to use Kevin Lynch's term. Admittedly, neither the architect nor the planner can produce, solely out of his professional skill, the conditions necessary for building and rebuilding adequate urban communities; but their own conscious reorientation on these matters is a necessary part of a wider transformation in which many other groups, professions, and institutions must in the end participate.

The multiplication and expansion of cities which took place in the nineteenth century in all industrial countries occurred at a moment when the great city builders of the past—the kings and princes, the bishops and the guilds—were all stepping out of the picture; and the traditions that had guided them, instead of being modified and improved, were recklessly discarded by both municipal authorities and business enterprisers.

Genuine improvements took place, indeed, in the internal organization of cities during the nineteenth century: the first substantial improvements since the introduction of drains, piped drinking water, and water closets into the cities and palaces of Sumer, Crete, and Rome. But the new organs of sanitation, hygiene, and communication had little effect on the visible city, while the improvements of transportation by railroad, elevated railroad, and trolley car brought in visual disorder and noise and, in the case of railroad cuts and marshaling yards, disrupted urban space as recklessly as expressways and parking lots do today. In both the underground and the aboveground city, these new gains in mechanical efficiency were mainly formless, apart from occasional by-products like a handsome railroad station or a bridge.

In consequence, the great mass of metropolitan buildings since the nineteenth century has been disorganized and formless, even when it has professed to be mechanically efficient. Almost until today, dreams of improvement were either cast into archaic, medieval, classic, or Renaissance molds, unchanged except in scale, or into purely industrial terms of mechanical innovations, collective "Crystal Palaces," such as H. G. Wells pictured in his scientific romances, and even Ebenezer Howard first proposed for a garden-city shopping mall. In America, despite the City Beautiful movement of the nineties, urban progress is still identified with high buildings, wide avenues, long vistas: the higher, the wider, the longer, the better.

Current suggestions for further urban improvement still tend to fall automatically into a purely mechanical mold: gouging new expressways into the city, multiplying skyscrapers, providing moving sidewalks, building garages and underground shelters, projecting linear Roadtowns, or covering the entire area with a metal and plastic dome to make possible total control of urban weather—on the glib theory that uniform conditions are "ideal" ones. So long as the main human functions and purposes of the city are ignored, these subsidiary processes tend to dominate the architect's imagination. All the more because the resulting fragments of urbanoid tissue can be produced anywhere, at a profit, in limitless quantities. We are now witnessing the climax of this process. . . .

Not the weakest of the destructive forces are those that operate under the guise of "up-to-date planning," in extravagant engineering projects, like the new motorways along both banks of the Seine—a self-negating improvement just as futile as the motorways that have deprived Boston and Cambridge of access to their most convenient and potentially most delightful recreation area along the Charles. This new order of planning makes the city more attractive temporarily to motor-cars, and infinitely less attractive permanently to human beings. On the suburban outskirts of our cities everywhere in both Europe and America, high-rise apartments impudently counterfeit the urbanity they have actually left behind. Present-day building replaces the complex structure of the city with gray masses of gritty "urbanoid" tissue.

This formless urbanization, which is both dynamic and destructive, has become almost universal. Through it utilizes one kind of structure in metropolitan renewal projects and a slightly different kind in suburbia, the two types have basically the same defect. They have been built by people who lack historical or sociological insight into the nature of the city, considered as anything but the largest number of consumers that can be brought together in the most accessible manufacturing and marketing area.

If this theory were an adequate one, it would be hard to account for the general exodus that has been taking place from the center of big cities for the last generation or more; and even harder to account for the fact that suburbs continue to spread relentlessly around every big metropolis, forming ever-widening belts of population at low residential density per acre, ever further removed from the jobs and cultural opportunities that big cities are by their bigness supposed to make more accessible. In both cases, cities, villages, and countryside, once distinct entities with individuality and identity, have become homogenized masses. Therewith one of the main functions of architecture, to symbolize and express the social idea, has disappeared.

During the last generation an immense amount of literature on cities has belatedly appeared, mostly economic and social analysis of a limited kind, dealing with the subsidiary and peripheral aspects of urban life. Most of these studies have been entirely lacking in concrete architectural understanding and historical perspective. Though they emphasize dynamic processes and technological change, they naïvely assume that the very processes of change now under observation are themselves unchanging; that is, that they may be neither retarded, halted, nor redirected nor brought within a more complex pattern that would reflect more central human needs and would alter their seeming importance.

For the exponents of aimless dynamism, the only method of controlling the urban processes now visible is to hasten them and widen their province. Those who favor this automatic dynamism treat the resultant confusions and frustrations as the very essence of city life, and cheerfully write off the accompanying increase in nervous tensions, violence, crime, and health-depleting sedatives, tranquilizers, and atmospheric poisons.

The effect of this literature has been, no doubt, to clarify the economic and technical processes that are actually at work in Western urban society. But that clarification, though it may help the municipal administrator in performing his daily routines and making such plans as can be derived from five-year projections, has so far only served to reinforce and speed up the disruptive processes that are now in operation. From the standpoint of the architect and the city planner, such analysis would be useful only if it were attached to a formative idea of the city; and such an idea of the city is precisely what is lacking.

"Idea" comes from the original Greek term for "image." Current proposals for city improvement are so imageless that city-planning schools in America, for the last half-generation, have been turning out mainly administrators, statisticians, economists, traffic experts. For lack of an image of the modern city, contemporary "experts" covertly fall back on already obsolete clichés, such as Le Corbusier's Voisin plan for Paris. Following the humanly functionless plans and the purposeless processes that are now producing total urban disintegration, they emerge, like the sociologist Jean Gottmann, with the abstract concept of "Megalopolis"—the last word in imageless urban amorphousness. And unfortunately, people who have no insight into the purposes of urban life have already begun to talk of this abstraction as the new "form" of the city.

The emptiness and sterility of so much that now goes under the rubric of modern city design is now being widely felt. Hence the interest that has been awakened by books like Jane Jacobs's *The Death and Life of Great American Cities*, with its keen appreciation of some of the more intimate aspects of urban life, and with its contrasting criticism, largely deserved, of radical human deficiencies in the standardized, high-rise, "urban renewal" projects.

The fact is that twentieth-century planning still lacks a fresh multidimensional image of the city, partly because we have not discussed and sorted out the true values, functions, and purposes of modern culture from many pseudo-values and apparently automatic processes that promise power or profit to those who promote them.

What has passed for a fresh image of the city turns out to be two forms of anti-city. One of these is a multiplication of standard, de-individualized high-rise structures, almost identical in form, whether they enclose offices, factories, administrative headquarters, or family apartments, set in the midst of a spaghetti tangle of traffic arteries, expressways, parking lots, and garages. The other is the complementary but opposite image of urban scatter and romantic seclusion often called suburban, though it has in fact broken away from such order as the nineteenth-century suburb had actually achieved, and even lacks such formal geometric coherence as Frank Lloyd Wright proposed to give it in his plans for Broadacre City. As an agent of human interaction and cooperation, as a stage for the social drama, the city is rapidly sinking out of sight.

If either the architect or the planner is to do better in the future, he must understand the historical forces that produced the original miscarriage of the city. . . .

THE MEDIEVAL
CITY

By the thirteenth century the main forms of the medieval city were fixed: what followed was an elaboration of detail. But the new institutions that began to dominate the town curtailed the older influence of the abbey and the castle, and the theme of the next three centuries was not authority, withdrawal, and security, but freedom, involvement, challenge, adventure. Crusades, missions, explorations opened up a wider world.

New dynamic elements entered the town, creating tensions and pressures that are well symbolized in the structure of the new Gothic cathedrals, which sacrificed the stability of the wall in order to throw open the interior to a flood of light. One would behold this dynamism on the periphery, in the batteries of windmills that surrounded the towns, and again, at the very center, as the new preaching orders and protestant laymen, oriented toward urban life, established their friaries and their *béguinages* in such open spaces as were left. . . .

In general, there were three basic patterns of the medieval town, which corresponded to their historical origin, their geographic peculiarities, and their mode of development. Behind these urban patterns were still older rural ones, such as we find in the "street" village, the crossroads village, the commons village, and the round village, which could be represented graphically by =, +, ×, and 0.

The towns that remained from Roman days usually retained their rectangular system of block platting, in the original center, modified by the building of a citadel or a monastery, which might alter the even

This selection combines several sections of "Medieval Urban Housekeeping," in *The City in History. (Editor's note)*

113

parceling out of the plots. Towns that grew by slow stages out of a village or a group of villages lying under a monastery or a castle would conform more closely to topography, changing slowly generation by generation, often preserving in their plan features that were products of historic accident rather than conscious choice.

This second kind of town is often regarded as the sole truly medieval type: some historians even deny the title of plan to its actual conformation. Those who refer to the winding streets of such a town as mere tracings of the cowpath do not realize that the cow's habit of following contours usually produces a more economical and sensible layout on hilly sites than any inflexible system of straight streets. Finally, many medieval towns were designed in advance for colonization: frequently, though not always, these would be laid out on a strict checkerboard plan, with a central place left open for the market and public assembly. All three modes were medieval. In separation or combination they produced an inexhaustible variety of forms.

At the very beginning of the Middle Ages one discovers, indeed, a certain partiality for the regular, geometric plan, with the rectangle as the basis of subdivision: see the ideal ground plan for the monastery of St. Gall in the ninth century. Kenneth Conant has shown, too, that the original buildings of Cluny were set in rectangular formation, within a three-hundred-foot square. Plainly Oswald Spengler's interpretation of the checkerboard plan as purely the product of the final hardening of a culture into a civilization is an unsupportable generalization. But though a geometric layout was more characteristic of freshly founded towns, it did not always follow that, as in the classic bastide of Montpazier, it would be coupled with a rectangular outline for the city as a whole. Sometimes the rectangles are placed within a circular bounding wall; sometimes, as at Montségur or Cordes in France, a basically rectangular plan was intelligently adapted to the contours and natural boundaries of the site.

I emphasize these points because the checkerboard or gridiron plan has been subject to a constant stream of misleading speculation and interpretation. Sometimes such plans are referred to as peculiarly American or New World types; sometimes, in the face of the brilliant pre-Communist Peiping, as a synonym for dullness. Even town-planning theorists have made such errors, largely because of their failure to grasp the difference, familiar to students of biology, between homologous and analogous forms. A similar form does not necessarily have a similar significance in a different culture; again, similar functions may produce quite different forms. . . . The rectangle meant one thing to an Etruscan priest, another to Hippodamos, a third to the Roman legionary, spading his camp for the night, and a fourth to the city plan commissioners for New York in 1811, seeking to provide in advance the maximum number of building lots. To the first, the rectangle might symbolize cosmic law; to the last, it meant simply the most favorable possibilities for real-estate speculation.

There is indeed a sound reason for thinking of medieval plans as usually more informal than regular. This was because rugged rocky sites were more frequently utilized, for they had decisive advantages for defense until effective cannon fire became possible in the sixteenth century. Since streets were not adapted to wheeled traffic and neither water pipes nor sewage drains needed to be provided for, it was more economical to follow nature's contours than to attempt to grade them down; note the tilt of the broad marketplace in Siena. By building on barren hilly sites, moreover, the thrifty citizens did not encroach on the richer agricultural bottomland.

In organic planning, one thing leads to another, and what began as the seizure of an accidental advantage may prompt a strong element in a design, which an a priori plan could not anticipate, and in all probability would overlook or rule out. Many of the surviving irregularities in medieval towns are due to streams that have been covered over, trees that were later cut down, old balks that once defined rural fields. Custom and property rights, once established in the form of lots, boundaries, permanent rights of way, are hard to efface.

Organic planning does not begin with a preconceived goal: it moves from need to need, from opportunity to opportunity, in a series of adaptations that themselves become increasingly coherent and purposeful, so that they generate a complex, final design, hardly less unified than a preformed geometric pattern. Towns like Siena illustrate this process to perfection. Though the last stage in such a process is not clearly present at the beginning, as it is in a more rational, non-historic order, this does not mean that rational considerations and deliberate forethought have not governed every feature of the plan, or that a deliberately unified and integrated design may not result.

Those who dismiss organic plans as unworthy of the name of plan confuse mere formalism and regularity with purposefulness, and irregularity with intellectual confusion or technical incompetence. The towns of the Middle Ages confute this formalistic illusion. For all their variety, they embody a universal pattern; and their very departures and irregularities are usually not merely sound, but often subtle, in their blending of practical need and aesthetic insight.

Each medieval town grew out of a unique situation, presented a unique constellation of forces, and produced, in its plan, a unique solution. The consensus is so complete as to the purposes of town life that the variations in detail only confirm the pattern. That consensus makes it look, when one views a hundred medieval plans in succession, as if there were in fact a conscious theory that guided this town planning.

The agreement was deeper than that. But toward the close of the Middle Ages, the rationale of this planning was expressed by the highly reflective intelligence of Leone Battista Alberti, in his *De Re Edificatori.*

Alberti was in many ways a typical medieval urbanist. In his concern for functionalism, the localization of business, curved streets, "he did no more," as [Pierre] Lavedan observes, "than register approval of what he saw under his eyes." Even when Alberti justifies the continuously curving street, with its gently blocked yet ever-changing vistas, he was only giving conscious expression to something his predecessors recognized and valued, too. The slow curve is the natural line of a footwalker, as anyone can observe if he looks back at his tracks in the snow across an open field, unless he has consciously tried to overcome this tendency. But the pleasure in that curve, once laid out by the pedestrian, is what gives character to medieval building, on such a consummate piece of late-medieval and renascence building as the High Street in Oxford. There a single tree whose branches jut out beyond the building line enriches the picture more than would a whole arcade of streets.

The other source of the organic curves in the medieval town was the emphasis on its central core. Lavedan goes so far as to say that "the essential fact of medieval urbanism is the constitution of the city in such a fashion that all the lines converge toward a center, and that the contour is usually circular: this is what contemporary theorists call the radio-concentric system." Unfortunately, the term "radio-concentric" calls to mind the spiderweb. What one finds, rather, in most towns, is a central quarter or core, surrounded by a series of irregular rings, which have the effect of enclosing and protecting the core, while, by devious passages, approaching more closely to it. Where there is something that approximates a continuous circular street, it is almost surely the indication of a wall that has been torn down. Even in a little town like Bergues, as seen in Blaeu's great *Atlas,* with its almost geometric precision in its central core, only three streets come together at the center. The resulting plan is generated by the two opposing forces of attraction and protection: the public buildings and open places find security behind a labyrinth of streets, through which the knowing foot nevertheless easily penetrates. It is only with the baroque planners who worked to overcome the medieval pattern that the street drives headlong into the town center, as in the asterisk plan—though Alberti himself, as it happens, anticipated this new scheme, which symbolized the collection of public power in a centralized institution or a despotic prince.

The determining elements in the medieval plan hold both for an old town on a Roman foundation, like Cologne, and for a new town like Salisbury. The wall, the gates, and the civic nucleus determine the main lines of circulation. As for the wall, with its outside moat, canal, or river, it made the town an island. The wall was valued as a symbol as much as the spires of the churches: not a mere military utility. The medieval mind took comfort in a universe of sharp definitions, solid walls, and limited views: even heaven and hell had their circular boundaries. Walls of custom bounded the economic classes and kept them in their place. Definition and classification were the very essence of medieval thinking: so that philosophic nominalism, which challenged the objective reality of classes, and presented a world of unrelated atoms and disconnected events, was as destructive to the medieval style of life as cannonballs proved to be to the walls of the town.

The psychological importance of the wall must not be forgotten. When the portcullis was drawn and the town gates were locked at sundown, the city was sealed off from the outside world. Such enclosure helps create a feeling of unity as well as security. It is significant—and a little disturbing—that in one of the rare modern communities where people have lived under analogous conditions, namely in the atomic-research community at Oak Ridge, the protected inhabitants of the new town grew to value the "secure" life within, free from any sort of foreign invasion or even unauthorized approach—though it meant that their own comings and goings were under constant military surveillance and control.

But once again, in the medieval community, the wall built up a fatal sense of insularity: all the more because the poor state of road transport increased the difficulties of communication between towns. As had so often happened in urban history before, defensive unity and security reversed their polarity and passed over into anxiety, fear, hostility, and aggression, especially when it seemed that a neighboring city might prosper at its rival's expense. Recall Florence's shameless assaults on Pisa and Siena! This isolationism was in fact so self-defeating that it gave sanction to forces of exploitation and aggression, both in Church and in State, that sought at least to bring about some more inclusive unity, by turning the all-too-solid wall into a more etherialized frontier boundary, outlining a far wider province.

One may not leave the wall without noting the special function of the town gate: far more than a mere opening, it was a "meeting place of two worlds," the urban and the rural, the insider and the outsider. The main gate offered the first greeting to the trader, the pilgrim, or the common wayfarer; it was at once a customs house, a passport office and immigration control point, and a triumphal arch, its turrets and towers often vying, as in Lübeck, with those of the cathedral or town hall. Wherever the river of traffic slows down, it tends to deposit its load: so it would be usually near the gates that the storehouses would be built, and the inns and taverns congregate, and in the adjoining streets the craftsmen and merchants would set up their shops.

Thus the gate produced, without special zoning regulations, the economic quarters of the city; and since there was more than one gate, the very nature of traffic from different regions would tend to decentralize and differentiate the business areas. As a result of this organic disposition of functions, the inner area of the city was not burdened by any traffic except that which its own needs generated. The original meaning of "port" derives from this portal; and the merchants who settled in this port were once called porters, till they passed the name on to their menial helpers.

Finally, one must not forget an ancient function of the wall, which came back in the Middle Ages: it served as an open promenade for recreation, particularly in the summer. Even when the walls were no more than twenty feet high, they gave a point of vantage over the surrounding countryside, and permitted one to enjoy summer breezes that might not penetrate the city.

CIVIC NUCLEUS AND NEIGHBORHOOD

No town plan can be adequately described in terms of its two-dimensional pattern; for it is only in the third dimension, through movement in space, and in the fourth dimension, through transformation in time, that the functional and aesthetic relationships come to life. This holds particularly for the medieval city; for the movement it generated led not merely through horizontal space, but upwards; and to understand the plan one must take in the mass and profile of its dominant structures: especially the disposition of the nuclear components, the castle, the abbey or friary, the cathedral, the town hall, the guildhall. But if one building may be taken as the key structure in the medieval town plan, it is the cathedral; so much so that [Wolfgang] Braunfels even suggests that the master builders in charge of the cathedral also, in fact, exercised a pervasive influence over other public buildings.

With certain notable exceptions, the dominant medieval buildings did not exist in empty spaces; still less did one approach them along a formal axis. That type of space came in with the sixteenth century, as in the approach to Santa Croce in Florence; and it was only with the nineteenth century that urban "improvers" who were incapable of appreciating the medieval system of town planning removed the smaller structures that crowded around the great cathedrals, to create a wide parklike area, like that in front of Notre Dame in Paris: bleak staring emptiness. This undermines the very essence of the medieval approach: the secrecy and the surprise, the sudden opening and the lift upwards, the richness of carved detail, meant to be viewed near at hand.

Aesthetically, a medieval town is like a medieval tapestry: the eye, challenged by the rich intricacy of the design, roams back and forth over the entire fabric, captivated by a flower, an animal, a head, lingering where it pleases, retracing its path, taking in the whole only by assimilating the parts, not commanding the design at a single glance. For the baroque eye, that medieval form is tortuous and the effort to encompass it is tedious; for the medieval eye, on the other hand, the baroque form would be brutally direct and overunified. There is no one "right" way to approach a medieval building: the finest face of the Chartres cathedral is the southern one; and though perhaps the best view of Notre Dame is from across the Seine, in the rear, that view, with its engirdling green, was not opened up till the nineteenth century.

Yet there are exceptions. There is a handful of minsters—to say nothing of countless village churches—that are free-standing buildings, set in the midst of an open green, quite detached from the busy life of the town: Salisbury and Canterbury are almost suburban in their free use of space and greenery, while Pisa's Campo Santo is equally detached and open. Often an original graveyard accounts for such openness.

In the main, the great church is central to the town, in every sense but a geometric one; and since it drew to itself the largest crowds, it needed a forecourt to provide for the entrance and exit of the worshippers. With the theological orientation of the church, its altar pointing toward the east, the church would often be set at a nonconforming angle to a more regular pattern of streets. When one finds the marketplace either spreading in front of the cathedral or opening a wedge or a square for itself nearby, one must not assign to these institutions the same values they have today: it was the market that was occasional, while it was the church whose services were constant and regular. As with the original growth of the city, the market settles close to the church because it is there that the inhabitants most frequently come together.

One must think of the church, indeed, as one would now think of a "community center": not too holy to serve as a dining hall for a great festival, as a theater for a religious play, as a forum where the scholars in church schools might stage oratorical contests and learned disputes on a holiday, or even, in the early days, as a safe-deposit vault, behind whose high altar deeds or treasures might be deposited, safe from all but the incorrigibly wicked.

In one manner or another, a constant procession of people, alone, or by twenties or by thousands, wound through the streets to the portals of the church. Here is where one set out on one's journey; here is where one returned. If it were otherwise, how could one account for the riches lavished on the building of a Bamberg, a Durham, an Amiens, a Beauvais, an Assisi, in communities of ten thousand inhabitants or less. Such communities today, with all our mechanized facilities and capital accumulation, would find it hard to raise funds for a prefabricated parish house, bought at a discount.

As for the open places of the medieval city, even the big market-places and cathedral places were anything but formal squares. More often than not, in towns of organic growth, the marketplace would be an irregular figure, sometimes triangular, sometimes many-sided or oval, now saw-toothed, now curved, seemingly arbitrary in shape because the needs of the surrounding buildings came first and determined the disposition of the open space. Though sometimes the market may be but a widened street, there are other examples, in Brussels or Bremen, in Perugia or Siena, where the proportions of the place are ample: big enough not merely for many stalls, but for public gatherings and ceremonies. The marketplace recaptured, in fact, the function of the earliest forum or agora.

In the marketplace the guilds set up their stages for the performance of the mystery plays; here the savage punishment of criminals or heretics would take place, on the gallows or at the stake; it was here that at the end of the Middle Ages, when the serious occupations of feudalism were transformed into urban sports, great tourneys would be held. Often one marketplace will open into another subordinate place, connected by a narrow passage: Parma is but one of many examples. The dry-goods and hardware market was usually separated for very natural reasons from the provisions market. Many a square we now admire purely for its noble architectural frame, like the Piazzetta San Marco in Venice, originally was carved out for a utilitarian purpose—in this case a meat market.

Apart from the cathedral and, sometimes, the town hall, where mass and height were important symbolic attributes, the medieval builder tended to keep to modest human dimensions. Almshouses would be founded for seven or ten men; convents might begin with the apostolic dozen; and instead of building a single hospital for the entire town, it was commoner to provide a small one for every two or three thousand people. So, too, the parish churches multiplied throughout the growing town, instead of letting a few big edifices wax at the center. In London in the twelfth century, according to Fitz Stephen, there were 13 conventual and 126 smaller churches, for a population of possibly twenty-five thousand people; and [John] Stow notes some three centuries later from two to seven churches in each of the twenty-six wards.

This decentralization of the essential social functions of the city not merely prevented institutional overcrowding and needless circulation: it kept the whole town in scale. The loss of this sense of scale, in the oversized burgher houses of the north, or in the crazily competitive fortress towers of Bologna or San Gimignano was a symptom of social pathology. Small structures, small numbers, intimate relations—these medieval attributes gave the town special qualitative attributes, as against large numbers and mass organizations, that may help account for its creativity.

The street occupied in the medieval town a quite different place than in an age of wheeled transportation. We usually think of urban houses as being ranged along a line of predetermined streets. But on less regular medieval sites, it would be the other way about: groups of trades or institutional buildings would form self-contained quarters or "islands," with the building disposed without relation to the public ways outside. Within these islands, and often outside, the footways marked the daily goings and comings of the inhabitants. The notion of a "traffic network" was as absent as constant wheeled traffic itself. "Islands" formed by the castle, the monasteries or colleges, the specialized industrial section of the more advanced towns, like the Arsenal at Venice, interrupted the closer pattern of small-scale residential blocks.

In medieval new towns, the charters often distinguished between traffic streets—traffic being mainly carts—and lesser streets; and in uniform Montpazier, as centuries later in Philadelphia, the houses had a two-street frontage, one on a broad street twenty-four feet wide and one on an alley seven feet wide. But in general, the street was a line of communication for pedestrians, and its utility for wheeled transport was secondary. Not merely were the streets narrow and often irregular, but sharp turns and closures were frequent. When the street was narrow and twisting, or when it came to a dead end, the plan broke the force of the wind and reduced the area of mud.

Not by accident did the medieval townsman, seeking protection against winter wind, avoid creating such cruel wind tunnels as the broad, straight street. The very narrowness of medieval streets made their outdoor activities more comfortable in winter. But likewise, in the south, the narrow street with broad overhangs protected the pedestrian against both rain and the sun's direct glare. Small variations in height and building material and rooftop profile, and variations in window openings and doorways, gave each street its own physiognomy.

Though Alberti favored straight and broad streets for noble and powerful cities, to increase their air of greatness and majesty, he wrote a most perceptive apology for the older medieval type of winding street. "Within the heart of the town," he observed, "it will be handsomer not to have them strait, but winding about several ways, backwards and forwards, like the course of a river. For thus, besides by appearing so much longer, they will add to the idea of the greatness of the town, they will likewise be a great security against all accidents and emergencies. Moreover, this winding of the streets will make the passenger at every step discover a new structure, and the front door of every house will directly face the middle of the street; and where as in larger towns even too much breadth is unhandsome and unhealthy, in a smaller town it will be both healthy and pleasant to have such an open view from every house by means of the turn of the street." No one, not even Camillo Sitte, has done better justice to the aesthetics of medieval town planning.

The medieval town thus had a character in its residential quarters that the blank walls of a classic Greek city, for example, certainly lacked. But the town enjoyed still another happy feature, perhaps carried over from the ancient city: for frequently the street would be edged on each side with an arcade, which formed the open end of a shop. This gave better shelter than even a narrow open street, and one finds it not merely in France and Italy, where it might in fact be a conscious continuation or resumption of the classic portico, but in towns like Innsbruck in Austria, in the street leading up to Das Goldene Dachl. One must not forget how important physical protection against the weather was, for the stalls and booths of handicraftsmen and merchants were not generally put behind glass till the seventeenth century; in fact, the greater part of the business of life, even cooking, was conducted more or less outdoors. The closed narrow street, the arcaded front, and the exposed shop were in fact complementary. Not till cheap glass enclosed the second could new conceptions of town planning open up the first. . . .

Note one more feature: the neighborhood unit and the functional precinct. In a sense, the medieval city was a congeries of little cities, each with a certain degree of autonomy and self-sufficiency, each formed so naturally out of common needs and purposes that it only enriched and supplemented the whole. The division of the town into quarters, each with its church or churches, often with a local provision market, always with its own local water supply, a well or a fountain, was a characteristic feature; but as the town grew, the quarters might become sixths, or even smaller fractions of the whole, without dissolving into the mass. Often, as in Venice, the neighborhood unit would be identified with the parish and get its name from the parish church: a division that remains to this day.

This integration into primary residential units, composed of families and neighbors, was complemented by another kind of division, into precincts, based on vocation and interest: thus both primary and secondary groups, both *Gemeinschaft* and *Gesellschaft,* took on the same urban pattern. In Regensburg, as early as the eleventh century, the town was divided into a clerical precinct, a royal precinct, and a merchant's precinct, corresponding thus to the chief vocations, while craftsmen and peasants must have occupied the rest of the town. To this constellation, university towns, like Toulouse or Oxford, would also add their college precincts, each relatively self-contained; while as convents and nunneries were drawn into the city, a movement that went on steadily from the thirteenth to the eighteenth century, a scattering of conventual precincts, different from the cathedral precinct, would likewise follow, adding their gardens and open spaces, however private, to the sum total of open spaces in the city. In London, the Inns of Court, like the Temple, formed still another kind of enclosed precinct.

The significance of the functional precinct has been too tardily recognized, even by planning theorists: in fact, perhaps the first modern planners to have done justice either to the historic form or its modern variations were Henry Wright and Clarence Stein. But these precincts were the first translation of the spatial qualities of the sacred precinct of the original city into the vernacular of everyday life. At the present moment, when the very existence of the city today is threatened by the overexpansion of wheeled traffic, the tradition of the medieval precinct, released from the street and the major traffic artery, comes back as a new form at a higher point in the spiral of development.

One cannot leave the medieval city, in its unity and diversity, without asking a final question about its planning: how far was it pursued as a conscious effort to achieve order and beauty? In formulating an answer, it is easy to overestimate both spontaneity and accidential good looks, and to forget the rigor and system that were fundamental qualities in the education of both scholar and craftsman. The aesthetic unity of the medieval town was not achieved any more than its other institutions without effort, struggle, supervision, and control.

No doubt most of the supervision was personal; most of the agreements probably came from face-to-face discussions of interested parties, which left no record behind. But we know that when the Town Hall of Siena was built in the fourteenth century, the municipal government ordered that the new buildings put up on the Piazza del Campo should have windows of the same type. And though much work remains to be done in medieval archives to bring out all the functions of the town architect, we know, too, that in Italy the office was an old one. We need not doubt Descartes in his *Discourse on Method* when he observes that "there have been at all times certain officers whose duty it is to see that private buildings contributed to public ornament."

What the nineteenth-century admirer of medieval art regarded as the result of effortless spontaneity and artless unconsciousness was done in fact with method and conscious intention in urban planning, precisely as any other art is carried through. Lavedan, it is true, in his admirable appreciation of the medieval town, is inclined to regard its beauty as a mere by-product of its practical and symbolic concerns. But the city was no more innocent of intentional aesthetic order than it was of geometric order, though its discipline was pliant enough to allow for the new, the spontaneous, the different.

As a result, the same "medieval" town plan could, by the eighteenth century, hold together Romanesque, High Gothic, Florid, Renascence, and Baroque structures, often jostling together on the same street, without any dulling of the aesthetic moment: indeed, with just the contrary effect. The aesthetic mixture corresponded with the historic social complex. This was a mode of planning that met the requirements of life, and yielded to change and innovation without being shattered by it. In the deepest sense of the words it was both functional and purposeful, for the functions that mattered most were those of significance to man's higher life.

Under such a canon of planning, no one was tempted to deny either the old form that still served well or the new form that represented a new purpose; and instead of wiping out buildings of different styles in order to make them over wholesale in the fashionable stereotype of the passing moment, the medieval builder worked the old and the new into an ever richer pattern. The bastard aestheticism of a single uniform style, set within a rigid town plan, arbitrarily freezing the historic process at a given moment, was left for a later period, which valued uniformity more than universality, and visible power more than the invisible processes of life.

CONTROL OF GROWTH AND EXPANSION

Many people think of medieval life as sluggish and the medieval town as static. But though the tempo was different from that of the twentieth century, whose dynamism is often disruptive and self-defeating, the Middle Ages was a period of constant, sometimes violent, change. Towns multiplied and grew, from the tenth century to the fifteenth. So we must ask: How did the medieval town accommodate its increasing population? And what if any were the limits of its growth?

The limit that originally defined the physical town was the wall. But as long as a simple wooden palisade or a masonry wall sufficed for military defense, the wall was no real obstacle to town extension. Technically, it was a simple matter to tear down the wall and extend the city's boundaries, to provide inner space; and the circular streets of many medieval towns testify, like the annual rings of trees, to the successive periods of growth, marked by extensions of the wall. Florence, for example, enlarged its wall circuit for the second time, in 1172, and not more than a century later built a third circuit that enclosed a still greater area. When the pressure of the overfilled belly became uncomfortable, the Florentine municipality, so to say, loosened its belt.

As the suburbs spread, the wall would engirdle them. This was common practice in growing towns up to the sixteenth century, when the new system of fortification made necessary by accurate artillery fire made such simple forms of town extension impossible. But even at its widest, no medieval town usually extended more than half a mile from the center; that is, every necessary institution, every friend, relative, associate, was in effect a close neighbor, within easy walking distance. So one was bound every day to encounter many people by coincidence whom one could not meet except by pre-arrangement and effort in a bigger city. The Historic Mile of Edinburgh stretched between the extreme limits of the castle top and the Holyrood Abbey at the outskirts. When these limits were overpassed, the medieval town, as a functioning organism, ceased almost by definition to exist; for the whole community structure was a system of limitations and boundaries; and their breakdown in the city revealed an even wider dismantling through the whole culture.

The restrictions on the medieval town's growth were due partly, of course, to natural and social conditions, rather than to the cincture of the wall: limitations of water supply and local food production; limitations by municipal ordinances and guild regulations, which prevented the uncontrolled settlement of outsiders; limitations of transport and communication, which were overcome only in advanced cities, such as those of the Low Countries, which had waterways instead of roadways for heavy traffic. For practical reasons alone, the limits of horizontal expansion were speedily reached. As a result, in the early centuries of medieval city development, the surplus population was cared for by building new communities, sometimes close by, but nevertheless independent and self-sufficient units. This practice was followed as late as the seventeenth century in New England. So Charleston threw off Woburn, Dedham Medfield, and Cambridge Belmont, each no mere scattering of houses, but a civil and religious community, with a central meeting house for religion and a local system of government. As late as the nineteenth century, Ipswich founded Marietta, Ohio.

In short, the limitation on area and population did not make the medieval town static: that is an illusion. Not merely were thousands of new urban foundations made during the early Middle Ages, but settled towns that found themselves physically hampered or inconveniently located moved boldly to better sites. Thus Lübeck changed its original site, in order to better its means of trade and defense, and Old Sarum left its wind-beaten, inconvenient hill-site, to settle at Salisbury, by the river. Town building was prosecuted, in general, with a ready expenditure of energy and constructive zeal for which there are few modern parallels outside devastated areas. But this vast urban movement was not governed by the covetousness of the modern real-estate speculator, seeking quick and inordinate gains. Even for urban investments, long-term security was of more concern than short-term profits; and the feudal conception of land, as a stewardship and trust, in a different category from more mobile forms of property, was so deeply rooted that in Europe it has never altogether disappeared.

The general pattern of medieval town growth, then, was radically different from the period of concentration and consolidation around great political capitals, which immediately followed it. The medieval pattern was that of many small cities and subordinate villages in active association with their neighboring towns, distributed widely over the landscape. Elisée Reclus discovered, indeed, that the villages and towns of France could be plotted with amazing regularity, forming the pattern of a day's walk from the most distant point to and from the market. In other words, the pedestrian's needs dominated: he who could use his legs had access to a city. The urban pattern conformed to the economic one; and both favored the small unit and direct face-to-face communication.

As to population distribution, the facts are plain. The medieval town ranged in size from a few thousand to forty thousand, which was the size of London in the fifteenth century. Populations above a hundred thousand, achieved earlier by Paris, Venice, Milan, Florence, were highly exceptional until the seventeenth century. Toward the close of the period, Nürnberg, a thriving place, had about twenty thousand inhabitants, while Basel, no mean town, had around eight thousand. Even on the productive soils of the Lowlands, supported by the highly organized textile industries, under a rigorous system of capitalist exploitation, the same limitation holds: in 1412 Ypres had only 10,376 inhabitants, and Louvain and Brussels, in the middle of the same century, had between 25,000 and 40,000. Bruges, the biggest, may have held 70,000. As for Germany, town life there was concentrated in some 150 "large" cities, of which the largest did not have more than 35,000 inhabitants.

All these statistics, it is true, dated from the century after the Black Death, which in some provinces carried off half the population. But even if one doubled the figures for the towns themselves, they would still remain, in terms of modern population massings, small and scattered. In Italy alone, partly because of the old Roman foundations and because capitalism there had an earlier start, these figures have to be enlarged. Overcrowding and overbuilding, with increasingly extortionate rents and increasingly constricted dwelling space—as well as suburban expansion and scatterment—did not become common until the capacity for building new cities had greatly diminished. . . .

THE BAROQUE
CITY

Between the fifteenth and the eighteenth century, a new complex of cultural traits took shape in Europe. Both the form and the contents of urban life were, in consequence, radically altered. The new pattern of existence sprang out of a new economy, that of mercantilist capitalism; a new political framework, mainly that of a centralized despotism or oligarchy, usually embodied in a national state; and a new ideological form, that derived from mechanistic physics, whose underlying postulates had been laid down, long before, in the army and the monastery.

Until the seventeenth century all these changes were confused and tentative, restricted to a minority, effective only in patches. In the seventeenth century the focus suddenly sharpened. At this point, the medieval order began to break up through sheer inner corruption; and thenceforth religion, trade, and politics went their separate ways.

In order to understand the post-medieval town, one must be on guard against the still-fashionable interpretation of the renascence as a movement toward freedom and the re-establishment of the dignity of man. For the real renascence of European culture, the great age of city building and intellectual triumph, was that which began in the twelfth century and had achieved a symbolic apotheosis in the work of an Aquinas, an Albertus Magnus, a Dante, a Giotto. Between that revival and the classical revival of the fifteenth century a great natural disaster had taken place: the Black Death of the fourteenth century, which wiped out between a third and a half of the population, according to the most conservative estimates. By the sixteenth century, these losses

This selection is composed of excerpts from "The Structure of Baroque Power" and "Court, Parade, and Capital," in *The City in History. (Editor's note)*

had been repaired; but the breach in continuity that resulted from the plague was accentuated by a lowering of communal vitality, like that which comes after an exhausting war.

In the social disorganization that followed, power came into the hands of those who controlled armies, trade routes, and great accumulations of capital. With the rise of military despotisms came the suppression of academic freedom in the universities, and the studious suppression of the independence of the spiritual powers, in the interests of the temporal rulers. All this has a familiar ring today: it parallels what went on in Russia, Germany, Italy, and various other parts of Europe after the First World War, and what went on, even in the physically remote United States, after the Second World War. The transformation of the medieval universities from international associations of scholars to nationalistic organizations, servile to the new despots, impervious to "dangerous thoughts," bound by loyalty oaths, went on steadily; and it had its parallels in the Church and the city.

Within a few centuries, all the older medieval institutions gave evidence of their profound demoralization. Huizinga, in *The Waning of the Middle Ages,* has documented this change with a wealth of examples. In the fifteenth century, according to [George Anton Hugo] von Below, there was the beginning of organized gambling in Germany in houses provided by the municipality. And the same tendencies appeared in the Church: not merely the buying of offices and the sale of blessings, but the general recrudescence of superstition. Belief in witchcraft, rejected by Saint Boniface in the eighth century, was given final sanction of the Church in 1484: perhaps because there had been in fact a recrudescence of earlier pagan earth cults that inverted Christian morality. And it was in the seventeenth century, marked by the appearance of the exact methods of the physical sciences, that the persecution of witches became popular. Some of the most vicious offenders in this respect were the new scientists and philosophers themselves: people like Joseph Glanvill who almost in the same breath were predicting the complete transformation of the physical world by science and technics.

But the very shock of the Black Death also produced a quite different reaction: a tremendous concentration of energies, not on death, eternity, security, stability, but on all that human audacity might seize and master within the limits of a single lifetime. Overnight, six of the seven deadly sins turned into cardinal virtues; and the worst sin of all, the sin of pride, became the mark of the new leaders and society, alike in the counting house and on the battlefield. To produce and display wealth, to seize and extend power, became the universal imperatives: they had long been practiced, but they were now openly avowed, as guiding principles for a whole society.

From medieval universality to baroque uniformity: from medieval localism to baroque centralism: from the absolutism of God and the Holy Catholic Church to the absolutism of the temporal sovereign and the national state, as both a source of authority and an objective of collective worship—there was a passage of four or five centuries between the old and the new constellations. Let us not obscure the essential nature of this change by referring only to its aesthetic accompaniments. The unearthing and the measurement of classical monuments, the discovery of Plato and Vitruvius, the reverence for the Five Orders in Architecture, the sensuous delight in antique ornaments and in newly unburied statues—all this threw a garment of aesthetic decency over the tyrannies and debaucheries of the ruling powers. Connoisseurs like Hippolito Vitellesco might embrace and talk to his classic statues—John Evelyn reported—as if they were alive: but living men were being turned into automatons, obedient only to external command: a recrudescence of the earliest practices of king-centered cities.

The underlying tendency of this new order did not become fully visible until the seventeenth century: then every aspect of life departed from the medieval pole and re-united under a new sign, the sign of the prince. Machiavelli's work *The Prince* provides more than one clue to both the politics and the plan of the new city, and Descartes, coming later, will re-interpret the world of science in terms of the unified order of the baroque city. In the seventeenth century the intuitions of precursors like Alberti were finally realized in the baroque style of life, the baroque plan, the baroque garden, and the baroque city. . . .

OPENNESS AND CLARIFICATION

Before baroque organization had gained control of almost every aspect of the scene, there was an intermediate stage in which the new and the old mingled and reciprocally gained by their very contrast and opposition. This phase still unfortunately is called "the" renascence: a term too solidly established to be discarded easily, yet almost as misleading in its connotations as "the" Industrial Revolution. At this point in urban building, the now-meaningless enclosure, and the disorder and clutter that often characterized the late medieval city, had become intolerable. Even on practical grounds, crooked streets and dark alleyways had become suspect as abettors of crime: King Ferrante of Naples in 1475 characterized narrow streets as a danger to the State.

In order to breathe once more, the new planners and builders pushed aside the crowded walls, tearing down sheds, booths, old houses, piercing through the crooked alleys to build a straight street or an open rectangular square. In many cities, people must have had the sense of the shutters being suddenly opened in a musty room hung with cobwebs.

But to call these fifteenth- and sixteenth-century changes a "rebirth" is to misunderstand both the impulse and the result. We are dealing rather with a kind of geometric clarification of the spirit that had been going on for many generations, and that sought, not a wholesale change, but a piecemeal modification of the historic city. In cities like Florence and Turin, whose original Roman outlines were still visible, the new style was so deeply organic that it seems a continuation of its own past, rather than a renunciation of it. The Loggia dei Lanzi in Florence, for example, was completed in 1387. Though by the calendar it belonged to the Middle Ages, in form it is definitely "renascence"— open, serene, with its three round arches and its classic columns. A rebirth? No: a purification, an attempt to get back to the starting point, as a painter might paint over the smudged colors and confused forms of his canvas to recover the lines of his original sketch.

If one uses the term precisely, there is no renascence city. But there are patches of renascence order, openings and clarifications, that beautifully modify the structure of the medieval city. If the new buildings, with their impersonal gravity and decorous regularity break up the harmony of the medieval pattern, they established a contrapuntal relationship which brings out, by contrast, otherwise unregarded, often invisible, aesthetic qualities in the older streets and buildings. The theme itself remained medieval; but new instruments were added to the orchestra and both the tempo and the tonal color of the city were changed.

The symbols of this new movement are the straight street, the unbroken horizontal roof line, the round arch, and the repetition of uniform elements, cornice, lintel, window, and column, on the façade. Alberti suggested that streets "will be rendered much more noble if the doors are built all after the same model, and the houses on each side stand on even line, and none higher than the other." The clarity and simplicity was enhanced by the two-dimensional façade and the frontal approach; but the new order, while it was still alive, never was carried through with any overriding consistence, such as the seventeenth century introduced, with its strict rules of composition, its endless avenues, and its uniform legal regulations. It is, indeed, just in this pliancy, in this avoidance of regimentation, that the new renascence builders prove their debt to the medieval order. The height of Sansovino's new library in the Piazza San Marco is not exactly that of the Ducal Palace; so, too, the height of the buildings around the Piazza Santissima Annunziata in Florence is only roughly the same. However strict the order of the renascence street, it does not go far enough to be rigid or oppressive.

One of the first of these new streets, that built by the Big Four in Genoa, was actually called the Strada Nuova: it was designed, Vasari tells us, by Galeazzo Alessi of Perugia, for the purpose of being the most magnificent street in Italy; and it was lined with enormous palaces, free-standing, also designed by him, with hillside gardens behind them, big enough to house a private army—and with correspondingly high rooms. But this bold new street, if wider than the old lanes and alleys, is still only twenty feet across; and it is less than seven hundred feet in length. Thus in the beginning the pattern of the old city was not substantially altered, even at the command of ruthless and powerful magnates. Most of the renascence palaces in Florence were erected on narrow Roman and medieval streets: one of the great exceptions is the Pitti Palace across the river—a suburban site, yet still close to the old Via Romana.

Not merely were the ambitions of the new urban planners of the sixteenth century still limited and modest: it was this very modesty that brought out what was best in the old order as well as the new. There was no attempt by the new planners to harmonize their design with old medieval patterns: that would have been self-defeating. But because so much of the old was still standing, the new buildings created a rich, complex order, often more satisfying aesthetically than the uniform, single-minded compositions of a later period. The classic example of this visual achievement is the straight, narrow street formed by the two sides of the Uffizi in renascence Florence. They are a sort of diagrammatic illustration of the new order. The classic composition of these buildings, with their repeating motifs and their converging horizontal lines, would soon become dull, if they did not promptly reveal a different kind of building: the tower of the old Palace of the Signory in the piazza beyond.

Once the planner was free to design an entire city on the same principles as the Strada Nuova or the Uffizi, the aesthetic limitations of this wholesale regimentation of space, and this equally wholesale disregard for the variety of human functions, became manifest. In the first case, order was still an instrument of life; in the second, life had become an instrument of order. But in small measures the new order of the renascence design often added to the beauty of the medieval city, giving it, as in the Piazza Santissima Annunziata, some of the inner spatial repose of the monastic cloister. . . .

Up to the seventeenth century the new tradition in building, using old classic forms again to express new intuitions and feelings, produced a fresh sense of openness, clarity, and formal order. Visual disarray that had been tolerated in the ancient city gave way to a formal costume. Raw, eroded sites like the Capitoline Hill in Rome were plated with stone, and the steep goat path turned into a grand flight of stairs. Not the least contribution of the renascence tradition, indeed, was its street furniture: stone and brick paving, stone stairs, sculptured fountains, memorial statues. In its sense of vertical movement, the upward play of the fountain and the ascent of the steps, these innovations added a spatial liveliness to the functions they served. The Spanish Steps in Rome, at once a flower market, an arena, and a penitential approach to the Trinitá above, perform a service of liberation that must be measured not by the area occupied but by intensity of use.

Some of this spirit lingered in the best work of the baroque period: particularly in the sculptured fountains and squares by Bernini in Rome. But these patches of beauty and order gain not a little by the contrasting clutter around them. As soon as baroque order became widespread, uniform, and absolute, when neither contrast nor evasion was possible, its weaknesses lay revealed. Clarification gave place to regimentation, openness to emptiness, greatness to grandiosity. The solo voice of the planner might be amplified many volumes; but it could never take the place of all the singers in a civic chorus, each holding his own part, while following the contrapuntal score.

Within the shuttered world of specialist art criticism, and even of city design, these changes from renascence to baroque are often interpreted as changes in taste or aesthetic insight alone: but what gave them the influence they have actually exerted on the planning of cities is the fact that they were supported at every point by profound political and economic transformations. The forces that had originally brought the royal cities of the ancient world into existence reappeared once more, with scarcely a change, except perhaps that the new engines of power were even more effective, and the resultant city plans even more ruthless, one-sided, non-cooperative; even more indifferent to the slow, complex interactions, the patient adjustments and modifications, through trial and selection, which mark more organic methods of city development. To understand the baroque plan that took shape finally toward the end of the seventeenth century, creating new urban quarters and even new residential cities for royalty, one must follow the shifts in authority and power that took place at the end of the Middle Ages.

Because all these tendencies finally came to a head in the baroque city, I long ago chose to use this term—originally contemptuous—as one of social description, not of limited architectural reference. The concept of the baroque, as it shaped itself in the seventeenth century, is particularly useful because it holds in itself the two contradictory elements of the age. First, the abstract mathematical and methodical side, expressed to perfection in its rigorous street plans, its formal city layouts, and in its geometrically ordered gardens and landscape designs. And at the same time, in the painting and sculpture of the period, it embraces the sensuous, rebellious, extravagant, anti-classical, anti-mechanical side, expressed in its clothes and its sexual life and its religious fanaticism and its crazy statecraft. Between the sixteenth and nineteenth century, these two elements existed together: sometimes acting separately, sometimes held in tension within a larger whole.

In this respect, one might regard the early renascence forms, in their purity, as proto-baroque, and the neoclassic forms, from Versailles to St. Petersburg, as "late" baroque: while even the careless uncontrolled romanticism of the eighteenth-century gothic revivalists might be considered, paradoxically, as a phase of baroque caprice. None of this makes sense if one thinks of the baroque as a single moment in the development of architectural style. But the widening of the term has gone on steadily during the last generation; and a certain original vagueness and contradictoriness in the epithet adds sanction to this more generalized use. . . .

THE IDEOLOGY OF POWER

The two arms of this new system are the army and the bureaucracy: they are the temporal and spiritual support of a centralized despotism. Both agents owed no small part of their influence to a larger and more pervasive power, that of capitalist industry and finance. One must remember, with Max Weber, that the rational administration of taxation was an accomplishment of the Italian cities in the period *after* the loss of their freedom. The new Italian oligarchy was the first political power to order its finances in accordance with the principles of mercantile bookkeeping—and presently the fine Italian hand of the tax expert and financial administrator could be observed in every European capital.

The change from a goods economy to a money economy greatly widened the resources of the state. The monopoly of rent, the booty from piracy and brigandage, the loot of conquest, the monopoly of special privileges in production and sale through patents granted by the state, the application of this last system to technical inventions—all these resources swelled the coffers of the sovereign. To increase the boundaries of the state was to increase the taxable population: to increase the population of the capital city was to increase the rent of land. Both forms of increase could be translated ultimately into terms of money pouring into the central exchequer. Not merely did the royal governments become capitalistic in their workings, founding industries of their own, in arms, porcelain, tapestry: but they sought, under the notion of a "favorable balance of trade," to create a system of exploitation in which every sovereign state would receive more in exchange, in measure of gold, than what it had given: classic colonial economics.

Capitalism in its turn became militaristic: it relied on the arms of the state when it could no longer bargain to advantage without them: the foundations of colonial exploitation and imperialism. Above all, the development of capitalism brought into every department secular habits of thought and matter-of-fact methods of appraisal: this was the warp, exact, orderly, superficially efficient, upon which the complicated and effulgent patterns of baroque life were worked out. The new merchant and banking classes emphasized method, order, routine, power, mobility, all habits that tended to increase effective practical command. Jacob Fugger the Elder even had a specially designed traveling set made for himself, containing a compact, efficiently organized dining service: nothing was left to chance.

The uniformity of the die that stamped the coin at the national mint became a symbol of these emergent qualities in the new order. Florence gained international fame and special commercial status by coining its gold florin in honest uniform weight. Interests that were later sublimated and widened in physical science first disclosed themselves in the counting house: the merchant's emphasis upon mathematics and literacy—both so necessary to long-distance trade through paid agents acting on written instructions—became the fundamental ingredient in the new education of the grammar schools. It was not by accident that Newton, the physicist, became master of the mint, or that the merchants of London helped found the Royal Society and conducted experiments in physics. These mechanical disciplines were in effect interchangeable.

Behind the immediate interests of the new capitalism, with its abstract love of money and power, a change in the entire conceptual framework took place. And first: a new conception of space. It was one of the great triumphs of the baroque mind to organize space, make it continuous, reduce it to measure and order, and to extend the limits of magnitude, embracing the extremely distant and the extremely minute; finally, to associate space with motion and time.

These changes were first formulated by the painters and architects and scene painters, beginning with Alberti, Brunelleschi, Uccello, and Serlio. While the Flemish realists, working in the medium of the advanced spinning industries, had accurate perceptions of space, it remained for the Italians of the fifteenth century to organize space on mathematical lines, within two planes, the foreground-frame and that of the horizon line. They correlated distance not merely with intensity of color and quality of light but with the movement of bodies through the projected third dimension. This putting together of hitherto unrelated lines and solids within the rectangular baroque frame—as distinguished from the often irregular boundaries of a medieval painting—was contemporary with the political consolidation of territory into the coherent frame of the state. But the development of the straight line and the uniform building line, as a means of expressing uniform motion, took place at least a century before the building of actual façades on visually limitless avenues.

Similarly, the study of perspective demolished the closed vista, lengthened the distance toward the horizon, and centered attention on the receding planes, long before the wall was abolished as a feature of town planning. This was an aesthetic preface to the grand avenues of baroque design, which at most have an obelisk, an arch, or a single building to terminate the converging rays of the cornice lines and the pavement edges. The long approach and the vista into seemingly unbounded space—those typical marks of the baroque plan—were first discovered by the painter. The act of passage is more important than the object reached: there is keener interest in the foreground of the Farnese Palace than in the gawky façade that caps the hill. The new renascence window is definitely a picture frame, and the renascence painting is an imaginary window which, in the city, makes one forget the dull courtyard that an actual opening would reveal.

If the earlier painters demonstrated Cartesian mathematics before Descartes, on their system of coordinates, the general sense of time likewise became more mathematical. From the sixteenth century on, the domestic clock was widespread in upper-class households. But whereas baroque space invited movement, travel, conquest by speed—witness the early sail-wagons and velocipedes and the later *promenades aériennes* or chute-the-chutes—baroque time lacked dimensions: it was a moment-to-moment continuum. Time no longer expressed itself as cumulative and continuous *(durée)*, but as quanta of seconds and minutes: it ceased to be a life time. The social mode of baroque time is fashion, which changes every year; and in the world of fashion a new sin was invented—that of being out of date. Its practical instrument was the newspaper, which deals with scattered, logically incoherent "events" from day to day: no underlying connection except contemporaneity. If in spatial order repeating patterns take on a new meaning—columns on the façades of buildings, ranks of men on parade—in time the emphasis rests on the novel and nonrepetitive. As for the archaeological cult of the past, it was plainly not a recovery of history but a denial of history. Real history cannot be recovered except by its entering into a fresh life in a new form.

The abstractions of money, spatial perspective, and mechanical time provided the enclosing frame of the new life. Experience was progressively reduced to just those elements that were capable of being split off from the whole and measured separately: conventional counters took the place of organisms. What was real was that part of experience which left no murky residues; and anything that could not be expressed in terms of visual sensations and mechanical order was not worth expressing. In art, perspective and anatomy; in morals, the systematic casuistry of the Jesuits; in architecture, axial symmetry, formalistic repetition, the fixed proportions of the Five Orders; and in city building, the elaborate, geometrical plan. These are the new forms.

Do not misunderstand me. The age of abstract analysis was an age of brilliant intellectual clarification. The new system of dealing with mathematically analyzable fragments instead of with wholes gave the first intelligible collective means of approaching such wholes: as useful an instrument of order as double-entry bookkeeping in commerce. In the natural sciences, the method of analytic abstraction led to the discovery of units that could be investigated swiftly and accurately *just because* they were dismembered, fragmentary, incomplete. The gain in the power of systematic thought and in the accurate prediction of physical events was to justify itself in the nineteenth century in a series of mighty advances in technics.

But in society the habit of thinking in terms of abstractions worked out disastrously. The new order established in the physical sciences was far too limited to describe or interpret social facts, and until the nineteenth century even the legitimate development of statistical analysis played little part in sociological thought. Real men and women, real corporations and cities, were treated in law and government as if they were imaginary bodies; whilst artful pragmatic fictions, like Divine Right, Absolute Rule, the State, Sovereignty, were treated as if they were realities. Freed from his sense of dependence upon corporation and neighborhood, the "emancipated individual" was dissociated and delocalized: an atom of power, ruthlessly seeking whatever power can command. With the quest for financial and political power, the notion of limits disappeared—limits on numbers, limits on wealth, limits on population growth, limits on urban expansion: on the contrary, quantitative expansion became predominant. The merchant cannot be too rich; the state cannot possess too much territory; the city cannot become too big. Success in life was identified with expansion. This superstition still retains its hold in the notion of an indefinitely expanding economy. . . .

In the desire for more subjects—that is, for more cannon fodder, more milch cows for taxation and rent—the desires of the prince coincided with those of the capitalists who were looking for larger and more concentrated markets filled with insatiable customers. Power politics and power economics reinforced each other. Cities grew; consumers multiplied; rents rose; taxes increased. None of these results was accidental.

Law, order, uniformity—all these then are special products of the baroque capital: but the law exists to confirm the status and secure the position of the privileged classes; the order is a mechanical order, based not upon blood or neighborhood or kindred purposes and affections but upon subjection to the ruling prince; and as for the uniformity—it is the uniformity of the bureaucrat, with his pigeonholes, his dossiers, his red tape, his numerous devices for regulating and systematizing the collection of taxes. The external means of enforcing this pattern of life lies in the army; its economic arm is mercantile capitalist policy; and its most typical institutions are the standing army, the bourse, the bureaucracy, and the court. . . .

MOVEMENT AND THE AVENUE

Since I am dealing with an age of abstractions, I purpose to follow its style. I shall treat of the part before I discuss the whole. First the avenue: . . . only after that the city, as an aesthetic if not a complete social unit.

The avenue is the most important symbol and the main fact about the baroque city. Not always was it possible to design a whole new city in the baroque mode; but in the layout of half a dozen new avenues, or in a new quarter, its character could be redefined. In the linear evolution of the city plan, the movement of wheeled vehicles played a critical part; and the general geometrizing of space, so characteristic of the period, would have been altogether functionless had it not facilitated the movement of traffic and transport, at the same time that it served as an expression of the dominant sense of life. It was during the sixteenth century that carts and wagons came into more general use within cities. This was partly the result of technical improvements that replaced the old-fashioned solid wheel with one built of separate parts —hub, rim, spoke—and added a fifth wheel, to facilitate turning.

The introduction of wheeled vehicles was resisted, precisely as that of the railroad was resisted three centuries later. Plainly the streets of the medieval city were not adapted either in size or in articulation to such traffic. In England, [James Henry] Thomas tells us, vigorous protests were made, and it was asserted that if brewers' carts were permitted in the streets the pavement could not be maintained; while in France, parliament begged the king in 1563 to prohibit vehicles from the streets of Paris—and the same impulse even showed itself once more in the eighteenth century. Nevertheless, the new spirit in society was on the side of rapid transportation. The hastening of movement and the conquest of space, the feverish desire to "get somewhere," were manifestations of the pervasive will-to-power. "The world," as [John] Stow remarked when the fashion was taking hold in London, "runs on wheels." Mass, velocity, and time were categories of social effort before Newton's law was formulated.

Movement in a straight line along an avenue was not merely an economy but a special pleasure: it brought into the city the stimulus and exhilaration of swift motion, which hitherto only the horseman had known galloping over the fields or through the hunting forest. It was possible to increase this pleasure aesthetically by the regular setting of buildings, with regular façades and even cornices, whose horizontal lines tended toward the same vanishing point as that toward which the carriage itself was rolling. In walking, the eye courts variety, but above this gait, movement demands repetition of the units that are to be seen: it is only so that the individual part, as it flashes by, can be recovered and pieced together. What would be monotony for a fixed position, or even in a procession, becomes a necessary counterpoise to the pace of fast-moving horses.

In emphasizing the demands of wheeled traffic, which became urgent in the seventeenth century, I do not wish to neglect a characteristic need that disclosed itself at an even earlier period: the need of avenues for military movement. To cite Alberti again, he distinguished between main and subordinate streets. The first he called—and the name is important— *viae militares,* or military streets: he required that these should be straight. Anyone who has ever led a company of men through an irregularly planned city knows the difficulty of conducting them in martial order through its windings and twistings, particularly when the streets themselves are upgraded: inevitably, the individual falls out of alignment and the ranks present a disorderly appearance. To achieve the maximum appearance of order and power on parade, it is necessary to provide a body of soldiers either with an open square or a long unbroken avenue.

The new town planners had the needs of the army constantly in mind: Palladio seconded Alberti. In addition to observing that the ways will be short and convenient if planned in a straight line, and so large that horses and coaches be no hindrance to each other when they meet, Palladio says that "the ways will be more convenient if they are made everywhere equal; that is to say, that there be no place in them where armies may not easily march." This uniform oversized street, which was to become such a blight in the development of neighborhoods in new cities, and which was to add so greatly to the expenses, had purely a military basis.

Palladio's further definition of the new military avenue is equally significant: he distinguished it from the nonmilitary kind by pointing out that they pass through the midst of the city and lead from one city to another, and that they "serve for the common use of all passengers for carriages to drive or armies to march." Accordingly Palladio dealt with the military streets alone because nonmilitary streets ought to be regulated according to the same principle as military ways, and the more alike they are the *"more commendable they will be."* In view of the importance of the army to the ruling classes, it is no wonder that military traffic was the determining factor in the new city plan, from the first mutation in Alberti to the final survival in the laying down of Haussmann's boulevards in Paris.

The aesthetic effect of the regular ranks and the straight line of soldiers is increased by the regularity of the avenue: the unswerving line of march greatly contributes to the display of power, and a regiment moving thus gives the impression that it would break through a solid wall without losing a beat. That, of course, is exactly the belief that the soldier and the prince desire to inculcate in the populace; it helps keep them in order without coming to an actual trial of strength, which always carries the bare possibility that the army might be worsted. Moreover, on irregular streets, poorly paved, with plenty of loose cobblestones and places of concealment, the spontaneous formations of untrained people have an advantage over a drilled soldiery: soldiers cannot fire around corners, nor can they protect themselves from bricks heaved from chimney tops immediately overhead: they need space to maneuver in. Were not the ancient medieval streets of Paris one of the last refuges of urban liberties? No wonder that Napoleon III sanctioned the breaking through of narrow streets and cul-de-sacs and the razing of whole quarters to provide wide boulevards: this was the best possible protection against assault from within. To rule merely by coercion, without affectionate consent, one must have the appropriate urban background.

In the new city, or in the formal additions made to old centers, the building forms a setting for the avenue, and the avenue is essentially a parade ground: a place where spectators may gather, on the sidewalks or in the windows, to review the evolutions and exercises and triumphal marches of the army—and be duly awed and intimidated. The buildings stand on each side, stiff and uniform, like soldiers at attention: the uniformed soldiers march down the avenue, erect, formalized, repetitive: a classic building in motion. The spectator remains fixed. Life marches before him, without his leave, without his assistance: he may use his eyes, but if he wishes to open his mouth or leave his place, he had better ask for permission first.

In the medieval town the upper classes and the lower classes had jostled together on the street, in the marketplace, as they did in the cathedral: the rich might ride on horseback, but they must wait for the poor man with his bundle or the blind beggar groping with his stick to get out of the way. Now, with the development of the wide avenue, the dissociation of the upper and the lower classes achieves form in the city itself. The rich drive; the poor walk. The rich roll along the axis of the grand avenue; the poor are off-center, in the gutter; and eventually a special strip is provided for the ordinary pedestrian, the sidewalk. The rich stare; the poor gape: insolence battens on servility.

The daily parade of the powerful becomes one of the principal dramas of the baroque city: a vicarious life of dash and glitter and expense is thus offered to the butcher's boy with a basket on his head, to the retired merchant out for a stroll, to the fashionable housewife, shopping for bargains and novelties, to the idle mob of hangers-on in all degrees of shabby gentility and downright misery—corresponding to the clients of imperial Rome.

"Mind the carriages!" cried Mercier in his eighteenth-century *Tableau de Paris.* "Here comes the black-coated physician in his chariot, the dancing master in his *cabriolet,* the fencing master in his *diable*— and the Prince behind six horses at the gallop as if he were in the open country. . . . The threatening wheels of the overbearing rich drive as rapidly as ever over stones stained with the blood of their unhappy victims." Do not fancy the danger was exaggerated: in France the stagecoach, introduced in the seventeenth century, killed more people annually than the railroad that followed it. This increase in the tempo of life, this rapid motion, these superficial excitements and dangers, were the psychological sweetening of the bitter pill of autocratic political discipline. In the baroque city one might say "The carriages move swiftly," just as people once said, to justify fascism in Italy, "The trains run on time."

There was only one desirable station in this despotism; it was that of the rich. It was for them that the avenue was made and the pavement smoothed out and springs and cushions added to the wheeled vehicle: it was to protect them that the soldiers marched. To keep a horse and carriage was an indispensable mark of commercial and social success; to keep a whole stable was a sign of affluence. In the eighteenth century the stables and mews crept into the less savory quarters of the capitals, behind the wide avenues and the sumptuous squares, carrying there the faint healthy smell of straw and manure. If the fowls no longer crackled at dawn, the restless stomp of a high-bred horse might be heard at night from rear windows: the man on horseback had taken possession of the city. . . .

URBAN FUNCTIONS AS LEFTOVERS

As I have indicated, the city was sacrificed to the traffic in the new plan: the street, not the neighborhood or quarter, became the unit of planning. The uniform avenue brought movement and confusion into parts of the town that had been quiet and self-contained; and it tended to stretch out the market along the lines of traffic, instead of providing local points of neighborly concentration where people could congregate and meet—though in cities like London, less under the sway of baroque ideas than most big capitals, neighborly concentration in a few short market streets would still prevail. Living space, in the baroque plan, was treated as a leftover, after the avenue itself determined the shape of the houseplot and the depth of the block.

With this neglect of urban functions other than traffic went an overvaluation of the geometric figure: a square like the new Freudenstadt, a nine-sided figure with radio-concentric streets, like Palma Nuova, a partial star like Karlsruhe. What does this mean? The abstract figure delimits the social contents, instead of being derived from them and in some degree conforming to them. The institutions of the city no longer generate the plan: the function of the plan is rather to bring about conformity to the prince's will in the institutions. There are, it is true, a few exceptions: but alas! they remained on paper. Filarète's ideal star plan was one exception: its central place was rectangular, with the cathedral and the palace on the short sides and the merchants' quarters and the food markets on the long sides. Likewise medieval in its respect for function is the fact that each of the sixteen radial streets is broken by secondary places, eight of these for parish churches, the other eight reserved for special markets, such as those for wood, straw, grain, wine. Such a plan, with its concern for the everyday life of the parish, was still medieval in spirit, if baroque in outline. One need hardly add that Filarète's ideal city was never built: this type of thinking now lacked authority and influence. The prince and his aides had other considerations in mind.

The subordination of the contents of urban life to the outward form was typical of the baroque mind; but its economic costs were almost as extravagant as its social losses. If the topography was irregular, the terrain must be evened out, at whatever cost in materials and manpower, merely in order to make the plan work: the avenue will not swerve in its course or alter its width by a few feet in order to save a fine tree or keep intact a precious building. In event of a conflict with human interests, traffic and geometry take precedence. So difficult is it to execute a baroque plan on irregular contours that most new city building took place on level sites. Sometimes, indeed, the projector retreated from his original plans when, as in the case of the avenues radiating from the Piazza del Popolo in Rome, one hillside proved to be too rugged to be penetrated by the proposed avenue. (It seems doubtful, in fact, if the planner could have condescended to look at the site when he so projected it: a not uncommon negligence in this type of planning.)

Francesco Martini, it is true, varied his ideal plans by an ingenious application of spherical geometry to fit curved hillsides, with tolerable grades for streets, but even that essay in three-dimensional thinking required that the curve of the solid whose contours he conformed to should be actually more regular than it usually is in nature. Not alone, then, did baroque indifference to topography add greatly to the expense of city development: in addition, the increase of wheeled vehicles added to the cost by entailing a heavier type of paving and more of it. The widening and lengthening of avenues added a further burden; and Pope Sixtus IV in 1480 wisely met this by imposing an extra charge on property owners who profited by improvements made in their neighborhood. Unfortunately, this sound procedure, like his other remarkable innovation—the condemning of private land for such public purposes as street widening—was not taken up seriously by other municipalities till the end of the nineteenth century.

This is not to say that geometric order cannot play a useful part in planning: quite the contrary. An age like ours, which has succumbed to purely capricious and aimless "free forms," may soon have to recover an appreciation of a more rigorous discipline, with its intelligible simplification and order, and its reasonable constraints. The function of geometry in planning is to clarify and guide. Like every other type of useful abstraction, it must be conditioned by the concrete situation in its wholeness and its variety, and give way to specific needs when the latter point to some aspect of life that has escaped the formula. In a period when changes were rapid and when custom could no longer serve as sufficient guide, geometry might well serve as a temporary expedient to produce at least an outward conformity. Unfortunately, baroque planners tacitly assumed that their order was eternal. They not merely regimented space but they sought to congeal time. Their ruthlessness in clearing out the old was equaled only by their stubbornness in opposing the new: for only one order could harmonize with their kind of plan—namely, more of their own.

In short, a baroque plan was a block achievement. It must be laid out at a stroke, fixed and frozen forever, as if done overnight by Arabian Nights genii. Such a plan demands an architectural despot, working for an absolute ruler, who will live long enough to complete their own conceptions. To alter this type of plan, to introduce fresh elements of another style, is to break its aesthetic backbone. Even the superficial contents of a baroque plan can be preserved only by severe administrative regulations. Where these were maintained, as in Paris, order might be preserved on the surface for many generations, even for centuries.

The seventeenth-century feeling for outward unity was perhaps best summed up by Descartes, who is one of the most representative thinkers of the period, not least because he was a soldier as well as a mathematical philosopher. "It is observable," said Descartes, "that the buildings which a single architect has planned and executed are generally more elegant and commodious than those which several have attempted to improve. . . . Thus, also, those ancient cities which from being at first only villages have become, in the course of time, large towns, are usually but ill laid out compared with the regularly constructed towns which a professional architect has freely planned on an open plain; so that although the several buildings of the former may often equal or surpass in beauty those of the latter, yet when one observes their indiscriminate juxtaposition, there a large and here a small, and the consequent crookedness and irregularity of the streets, one is disposed to allege that chance, rather than any human will guided by reason, must have led to such an arrangement. And if we consider that nevertheless there have been at all times certain officers whose duty was to see that private buildings contributed to public ornament, the difficulty of reaching high perfection with but the materials of others to operate on will be readily acknowledged."

There could be no sharper contrast between the two orders of thinking, the organic and the mechanical, than here: the first springs out of the total situation; the other simplifies the facts of life for the sake of an artful system of concepts, more dear to the mind than life itself. One works cooperatively with "the materials of others," perhaps guiding them, but first acknowledging their existence and understanding their purpose; the other, that of the baroque despot, insisting upon *his* law, *his* order, *his* society, is imposed by a single professional authority, working under his command. For those on the inside of baroque life, the courtier and the financier, this formal order was in effect organic: it represented the values they had created for themselves as a class. For those outside, it was a denial of reality.

The essence of this mode of thinking, the most representative symbol of baroque design in both its weakest and its most creative moments, is the seventeenth-century formal garden or park. This is a formal composition in space, in which the natural growths and efflorescences become merely subordinate patterns in a geometrical design: so much carpet and wallpaper and ceiling decoration, artfully put together out of nature's foreign materials. The clipped alley in which the trees are turned into a smooth green wall: the clipped hedge: the deformation of life in the interests of an external pattern of order—here was something at once magnificent and preposterous, as if Procrustes had been given the imagination of a Poussin.

To understand the final limitations of the baroque plan, its failure to deal with any mode of existence except that derived from the court, one must ask: What provisions were made for the civic nucleus? In the neighborhood, none. The local market and the school were not given special sites on the plan; nor does the local park within the big square serve even as a minor playground for neighborhood children, save those who have legal access, by right of ownership, to the square. As for the civic institutions of the municipality, they were subordinate to the prince's palace; and the theory of this civic nucleus was admirably set forth by Palladio.

"To return to the principal squares, to those that ought to be joined to the Prince's palace, or that for the meeting of the states, as the country is either a monarchy or a republic. The exchequer or the public treasury, where the money and treasure of the public is lodged, ought to join them likewise, as well as prisons. These latter were anciently of three sorts; one for such as were debauched or immodest . . . and which we now assign to fools or mad-folks; another was for Debtors . . . and the third was for traitors or wicked persons."

The palace: the exchequer: the prison: the madhouse—what four buildings could more completely sum up the new order or better symbolize the main features of its political life. These were the dominants. Between them stretched the blankly repetitive façades; and behind those façades the forgotten and denied parts of life somehow went on. . . .

REMNANTS OF BAROQUE ORDER

The baroque cult of power has been even more tenacious than the medieval ideology: it remained in being and extended its hold on other departments of life, creating Napoleons not merely in statecraft but in business and finance, though its regimentation progressively lost the lively feeling for aesthetic expression that the great practitioners of its earlier phases actually had. Through the very workings of democracy, baroque absolutism tightened its hold upon society: we must not forget that military service for the entire male population, not for a few months every year, as under feudalism, but for years at a time, dates only from the French Revolution. In modern times, no absolute prince dared impose such universal compulsion: it had hardly been possible, indeed, after the time of the pyramid builders.

Armies, governments, capitalistic enterprises, took the characteristic animus and form of this order, in all its inflated dimensions. Particularly in governmental planning, the baroque image remained dominant: though the "new town" halls of nineteenth-century Europe might often be cast in the mode of the Middle Ages, from Vienna to Manchester, the houses of parliament (with the exception of that at Westminster) and the government offices would be in some dull and pompous version of the baroque, sometimes desiccated into the correctness of the neoclassical. Even the demented exponent of Nazism, with his deliberate regression to the savage gods of Germanism, cast his fantasies of dehumanized power into an appropriately classic extravagance of emptiness.

In Paris, Madrid, St. Petersburg, Vienna, and Berlin, the baroque style in both architecture and planning not merely lingered on but found its greatest opportunities for large-scale application. While royal residence cities ceased to be built after the eighteenth century, the great capitals in their growth and extension followed the same general lines, often with a ruthless disregard of the historic values one might expect to find preserved and piously furthered in national monuments and shrines. Some of the greatest successes in baroque planning were reserved, indeed, for nineteenth-century Paris: proof, incidentally, that an historic phase of urban culture creates a durable archetype that cannot be put neatly within the time boundaries of any single period, for reasons we have already explored.

In Paris the baroque approach served two imperial leaders, Napoleon I and Napoleon III. Each of these leaders carried out and enlarged plans for the improvement of Paris that their less adventurous predecessors had only toyed with. To the degree that these rulers exercised real power, the style itself retained more than a little of its old vitality. Whereas Colbert's plan for Paris in 1665 had stressed the *control* of building and expansion, these new rulers, more royalist than the old kings, were on the side of growth and expansion. Their animus served well the bankers and speculators who profited by the subsequent increase of ground rents and building gains.

Right on into the twentieth century urban planning itself, at least in the great metropolises, meant chiefly baroque planning: from Tokyo and New Delhi to San Francisco. The most grandiose of these projects was Burnham's and Bennett's plan for Chicago, with its parks and its parkways, its diagonal avenues, its elimination of industry and railroads from the riverfront. But here as elsewhere one must note the typically baroque failing: no concern for the neighborhod as an integral unit, no regard for family housing, no sufficient conception of the ordering of business and industry themselves as a necessary part of any larger achievement of urban order. In the same fashion, the San Francisco civic center was conceived, like those at Cleveland and Springfield, without any further control over the townscape that enveloped it—and that openly denied its aesthetic pretensions.

Some of the best and some of the worst examples of baroque planning did not come forth until they had ceased, flagrantly, to be either symbolically or practically appropriate to the age that had constructed them. Without princely powers, stringent control of the surrounding area, heavy capital investments, baroque plans could not cope with the disorderly competitive enterprises of the expanding and towering city. For in baroque schemes half a loaf is actually worse than none: what remains undone or unaffected by the plan is itself a confession of its weakness.

Apart from the incongruity of baroque forms with the purposes and functions of a modern city, there was a further weakness that its later advocates never realized. Its very grandeur was based upon an innocence of, if not a contempt for, practical needs: even the needs of traffic. Thus its most imposing contribution, the long, straight, wide avenue, served indeed to connect distant points quickly; but the very width of the avenue created a barrier between its opposite sides; and until a late date, when traffic lights were introduced, the crossing of such an avenue, even with the aid of pedestrian islands, was a hazard.

For the purpose of shopping, that great post-seventeenth-century pastime, it is the narrow streets, unreceptive to traffic, like Old and New Bond Street in London, the Kalverstraat in Amsterdam, the Calle Florida in Buenos Aires, that flourish best. And if the avenue is a barrier, what shall we say to such wide, windy places as the Place de l'Etoile, whose circumnavigation on foot is nothing less than a pilgrimage? Such extravagances demand a heavy daily sacrifice, disproportionate to the benefits achieved.

What, then, is responsible for the active hold that the baroque plan has so long kept on the planner's mind? Why is so much superficially modern planning still carried out in the baroque spirit, with the same imperious extravagance and the same imperious contempt for human needs—though the grand avenue has turned into an "expressway" and the great roundpoint has become a cloverleaf? Behind all these modes are the assumptions—and superstitions—of unqualified power. The baroque prescription carries with it the same kind of authority that the old-fashioned physician exercised when he automatically prescribed a drastic purgative for his patient, no matter what the symptoms or the nature of the disease: it promised definite results, swift, visible, even striking.

If one compares the handsome geometry of a baroque plan with the kind of patient, piecemeal replacement and modification suggested in Rowland Nicholas's plans for the rebuilding of Manchester, one discovers the specious advantages of this administrative superficiality. It takes both knowledge and imagination to realize that the process the Manchester planner would set in motion would produce a far sounder city than a single impatient razing of a whole quarter, followed by a wholesale cutting through of new avenues and large-scale building projects, with a peremptory diversion of money and effort from other parts of the town equally in need of patient treatment, step by step. The showy decisiveness of the baroque style gives it an edge, in the beginning, over projects that take fuller account of the biological, social, and economic realities.

And yet, there was a measure of deep human insight in Daniel Burnham's famous observation: "Make no little plans, for they have no power to stir men's minds." And there are moments when the audacity of the baroque aesthetics, with its ruthless overriding of historic realities, provides an answer to what would be insuperable difficulties, if one sought a piecemeal solution. No one could accuse W. R. Lethaby, a medievalist by profession, an advocate for a functional modern vernacular, free from style-posturing, as being one who had an a priori fondness for baroque design: just the contrary. Yet, face to face with the indecisive sprawl of Central London, with its incurable tangle of mean streets, its lack of any intelligible order or visible purpose, as formless (he noted) as a London fog, he suggested the plan of the Golden Bow. The curve of the Thames gave the bend of the Bow, with St. Paul's at one end and Westminster Abbey at the other: the arrow was a new avenue, winging over Waterloo Bridge straight into the heart of London, pointing at the British Museum.

Here was a bold solution, as happy as the Regent Street conceived and built by [John] Nash to cut through a similar urban undergrowth. The Golden Bow did not suggest the creation of a wide-flung network of symmetrical streets and diagonal traffic avenues after the Parisian fashion of Haussmann: indeed Lethaby specified that the "arrow," which would open up the view of the river, should be a pedestrian mall, free from vehicles. But he applied this method to make a fresh cut through the urban debris, almost as a surgeon would cut out dead tissue in a festering wound. This was not, of course, the typically baroque approach: it was rather that of the renascence planner, applied with greater force, over greater distances, on the large scale to which the sventeenth-century designers had long acclimated the mind. But what happened to the baroque plan when applied as a whole to a modern city one may find by considering one of the greatest single examples of the method and the style: the plan of Washington [D.C.].

THE LESSONS OF
WASHINGTON, D.C.

Only a century or so separates the design of Versailles, the greatest if not the biggest of the palatial "new towns," from Major Pierre Charles L'Enfant's plans for the building of Washington, submitted in 1791. In the meanwhile, the political order of Western society had been shaken to its foundations. Three revolutions, the English, the American, and the French, had disposed of the whole scheme of irrevocable, centralized power, incarnated in an absolute monarch, whose airs and pretensions had begun to rival his earliest Egyptian prototype. With the downfall of absolutism had gone the overthrow of the feudal estates, the secularization of the state, the removal of the restrictive regulations imposed by the guilds and municipalities; and along with that, the abolition of the guilds themselves, and the transformation of the city into a dependency whose powers had been granted by the state and might be taken away again.

If anything should have modified the baroque pattern, one might think that this wholesale reconstitution of political society would have accomplished that result. Particularly in the early days of the American republic, when the powers of the state were still nebulous and undetermined, limited by the prerogatives of provincial systems of government. But what do we find?

When the new capital was to be designed, as the seat of the federal government, it was a French engineer who was called in to do the job. He was a remarkably competent man, far abler and more foresighted than his patrons and colleagues ever realized: indeed, considering his youth and limited experience, almost a genius. L'Enfant believed, in his

This essay is a section (originally titled "The Lessons of Washington") of "Court, Parade, and Capital," in *The City in History*. (*Editor's note*)

148

own words, that the "mode of taking possession of, and improving, the whole district at first must leave to posterity a grand idea of the patriotic interest which promoted it": so even its squares were to be enshrined with sculptured figures "to invite the Youth of succeeding generations to tread in the paths of those sages or heroes whom their country thought proper to celebrate."

Despite L'Enfant's firm republican convictions, the design he brought forth for the new capital was in every respect what the architects and servants of despotism had originally conceived. He could only carry over into the new age the static image that had been dictated by centralized coercion and control. The sole feature that was lacking was the original sixteenth-century fortifications, since there was no apparent need for military defense. As it happened, this was an embarrassing oversight, for such works alone might have saved the new public buildings in Washington from their destruction by British raiders in the War of 1812. Apart from that, the plan was an exemplary adaptation of the standard baroque principles to a new situation.

Now L'Enfant, with the true planner's insight, began, not with the street system, but with the principal buildings and squares. Between these cardinal points he devised "Lines or Avenues of direct communication," aimed not merely to promote traffic but to "preserve through the whole a reciprocity of sight at the same time," with special attention to convenience and pleasant prospects en route. Washington was thus planned as a series of interwoven traffic spiderwebs, with its main avenues as generous in their dimensions as the Champs Elysées. The principal avenues were 160 feet wide, with 10 feet of pavement on each side, 30 feet of gravel walk "planted with trees on each side," and 80 feet in the middle of the carriage way. Even the lesser avenues, like those leading to public buildings or markets, were 130 feet wide, while the remaining streets, 110 to 90 feet, vie with the largest crosstown streets provided in the 1811 plan for Manhattan, and surpass in generosity anything considered elsewhere in historic cities.

Doubtless it was the very absence of buildings that made L'Enfant's homage to the avenue so profound. But his gridiron pattern of streets was varied in size, not uniform in dimensions like those of Penn's plan for Philadelphia. Apart from the irregularity of the blocks formed by converging diagonals, the difference in their size corresponds to some need not fully explained by L'Enfant. The variations in both block and street dimensions shows that this was no simple drawing-board plan: in conceiving it L'Enfant was able to relate the elements of the plan to the daily functions they served.

While one pays due tribute to the quality of L'Enfant's imagination, one must observe that he was not able to escape the usual baroque sacrifice of all the other functions of the city to space, positional magnificence, and movement. Of the 60,000-odd acres included in his plan, 3,606 were required for highways, while the land required for public buildings, for grounds or reservations, was only 541 acres. By any criterion that apportionment between dynamic and static space, between vehicles and buildings, was absurd. Only a modern highway engineer, with his extravagant intersections, could compete with L'Enfant in this reckless wastage of precious urban land.

As a result, only 1,964 acres, less than two-thirds of the amount required for streets and avenues, were left to be divided into building lots, creating a total of 20,272 building lots. At the generous allowance of six persons per dwelling house, this would not give accommodation to more than a hundred and twenty thousand people, if every lot could in fact have been used solely for residential purposes. The street system demanded a city of at least half a million people to justify it: the plan permitted, on its *own original terms*, something on the order of a hundred thousand.

This, too, shows the limitations, not so much of L'Enfant's imagination, as of the ideology he took for granted. And it is no justification of the original allotment to note that both traffic and density of occupation eventually caught up with L'Enfant and more than excused his extravagance. By the time that happened it had become plain that once wheeled traffic is treated as the chief concern of planning, there will never be enough space to keep it from becoming congested, or a high enough residential density to provide taxes sufficient to cover its exorbitant demands.

On the surface, Washington had all the aspects of a superb baroque plan: the siting of the public buildings, grand avenues, the axial approaches, the monumental scale, the enveloping greenery. With no single big city, not even St. Petersburg, available to serve him as model, L'Enfant had nevertheless succeeded in envisaging what a great capital, conceived in baroque terms, might be. He had heeded Alberti's dictum that "the city, or rather the region of the city, is the greatest and most important among public buildings." And he had even made the most of what was, before the hand of man touched it, a discouraging site: bottomland, bordered by a swamp on the Potomac side, and dissected by a small river, ironically called the Tiber, which soon became a sewer. The framework was there, but the contents were absent. For one thing was lacking: the power to execute the plan by building. The order existed on paper, but not in fact.

The failure was all the more lamentable because no one since the Woods in Bath had accepted more eagerly the challenge of a difficult site. Instead of trying to remove these difficulties, L'Enfant sought to take advantage of them. Thus his plan for a cascade flowing down Capitol Hill, utilizing water from the Tiber, was worthy of Bernini himself. L'Enfant began, adroitly, by siting the essential public buildings, in order to establish the civic cores, the points of attraction, in the most commanding situations. Even his conception of the spinal relation of the Mall and Pennsylvania Avenue, though sadly overblown, was of the same order of thinking as Lethaby's Golden Bow. Only after he made the major dispositions of the buildings, did he proceed to fill up the interstices with streets and blocks. Federal buildings, including a nonsectarian national church for public ceremonies, local building sites for schools and colleges—all were duly established by L'Enfant as determining elements in the plan.

Surely, a wise, foresighted government would not have overlooked these admirable suggestions or forfeited these sites: rather, it would have acquired the whole District of Columbia by purchase, and would have rented, not sold, the land essential to its development as a national capital. Without public control of the land itself, Major L'Enfant's plan was defeated before he had even come within sight of the opposing army.

Even today, after the partial recapture of L'Enfant's conception through the appreciative McMillan Commission of 1901, the reality of some of L'Enfant's grandest proposals has only been partly realized, while others, like the Mall, reveal the sterility of a purely visual approach to planning, when it has no foundations in the functions that it serves: the Mall is actually a greenbelt, at best a fire barrier, which keeps segregated and apart areas that should in fact be more closely joined. In the beginning, the infant city could not fill these adult breeches; and by the time it was ready to, the style of the age had irretrievably changed.

Even the government buildings themselves, with the executive and legislative branches at opposite ends of the grand axis, were too far apart to be effectively related by the eye. The domed Capitol alone, alike by its form, its bulk, and its position, escapes annihilation by L'Enfant's all-too-magnificent distances. In piously emulating the constitutional separation of powers, L'Enfant had gone too far; and even if from the beginning Pennsylvania Avenue in its entire length had been lined with uniform office buildings, like those belatedly introduced into the "Triangle," the result would have been deadly.

As for the Mall, which L'Enfant thought of as a proper place for ambassadorial residences—he reduced the proposed buildings to invisibility by the very breadth of the long green. Unfortunately, so strong is the image of baroque order even today that no one dares suggest that this is perhaps the only part of Washington that might be appropriately lined with ten- or fifteen-story buildings as the only way of redeeming this spatial desolation and saving the rest of Washington for a more human scale.

In its heyday, the strength of baroque planning lay in the fact that the surface plan and the three-dimensional structure of the city, or at least the façades of that structure, proceeded together. Planning and building, in Karlsruhe, Versailles, St. Petersburg, went hand in hand. Under the conditions that governed L'Enfant's work, the paper plan had no influence whatever over the contents: the forces that could make the plan come to life or kill it were not in the hands of either the planner or his client, the new United States government, impecunious, hesitant, committed to a laissez-faire philosophy that nullified the political assumptions that underlay the plan.

There is no question as to what happened in Washington. L'Enfant's bold conception was brutally massacred; and as if that were not sufficient, it was, in time, visually disrupted and defiled by a wide scattering of unkempt and irrelevant buildings. Even to this day, the area immediately around the Capitol is spotted by an outbreak of urban eczema that a baroque architect would at least have been able to hide behind a wall, if his patron lacked sufficient authority to demolish the buildings themselves. Plainly, the plan by itself could not generate the city of gleaming white limestone fronts and uniform roof lines that L'Enfant must have dreamed of. When Dickens visited Washington in 1842, he found it a city of "spacious avenues that begin in nothing and lead nowhere; streets a mile long that only want houses, roads, and inhabitants; public buildings that need only a public to be complete, and ornaments of great thoroughfares that need only great thoroughfares to ornament."

In conceiving the city as a whole, as it would be in its finished form, L'Enfant had dared greatly; and in terms of baroque assumptions and baroque purposes—done over, as in a painting by David, with classic republican symbols—he had planned superbly. But he forgot the strict limits of his assignment. He overlooked the fact that he himself could not build the city he had planned, nor had the political leaders of his generation that power, much though they might recall the classic figures in Plutarch. The country itself would need at least half a century of growth, prosperity, and unification, before it could even begin to fill out such a comprehensive outline; and in the meanwhile, the more modest beginnings which might have been made within a more appropriate frame would be obstructed rather than hindered by the very grandeur of the full-blown scheme.

L'Enfant forgot, in fact, that time is a fatal handicap to the baroque conception of the world: its mechanical order makes no allowances for growth, change, adaptation, and creative renewal. Such a command performance must be executed, once and for all, in its own day. Had L'Enfant respected these narrow limits, he might have achieved as much success in the siting of the main government buildings as Jefferson was to achieve in his University of Virginia campus; but by providing for everything, he lost even the little he might have achieved.

L'Enfant's plan was saved from total obliteration by two things alone. One was the work of Alexander Robey Shepherd, who carried out a series of major public improvements after the Civil War. This commissioner was known as Boss Shepherd: like his near contemporary Haussmann, he had the proper dictatorial qualifications for carrying out a baroque plan. Fortunately, Shepherd also had enough imagination to undertake, at last, the planting of the wide streets and avenues with trees, as L'Enfant had specified. These trees gave the surface plan a stabilizing third dimension. That natural arcade, green for a large part of the year, mercifully hides some of Washington's worst architectural misdemeanors, without seriously obscuring the more comely buildings. But in the case of avenues that lack such embellishment, the sordor is often unrelieved.

The other fact that redeemed L'Enfant's original plan, though it did not add to its beauty, was the filling up of the overload of wide streets with sufficient wheeled traffic to justify their existence: this came in only with the motorcar. Though motor traffic has now caught up with the plan, clogging the most extravagant arteries, and hiding the verdure behind a metallic wall of parked cars, Washington has proved a classic testing station for the question of whether a city dedicated wholeheartedly to traffic could sufficiently survive for any other purposes.

Already it is plain in Washington—and will become plainer as the city receives the inundation of new expressways, which recklessly spoil every view and defile every approach to its finest urban prospects—that when traffic takes precedence over all other urban functions, it can no longer perform its own role, that of facilitating meeting and intercourse. The assumed right of the private motorcar to go to any place in the city and park anywhere is nothing less than a license to destroy the city. L'Enfant's plan, by its very invitation to traffic, has now proved its own worst enemy.

But note: the part of Washington that has become the favored area for residence is not the area that fronts on the grand traffic avenues, with their noise and their poisonous gases. Just the contrary; it is Georgetown, with its narrow streets and its more compact layout, modest enough to serve in the nineteenth century for the little dwellings of mechanics and tradesmen. This area has been converted, during the last generation, into an upper-class residential neighborhood. There one gratefully finds, not the monumental, but the domestic scale.

Yet when all is said, Washington must count as a classic example of baroque planning. If Washington could have been built in twenty years, parading suitable uniform structures, all occupied, it might have been a miracle of the solo town planner's art: a final period piece to close the epoch. Failing this, its very sweep and grandeur invited disorder. Absolute power, republican discipline, and public spirit alike were absent. The fault lay not merely with L'Enfant but with those who had charge of the execution of L'Enfant's plan: beginning with President Washington, who had more respect for his fellow landowner Daniel Carroll, the greatest landlord in the district, than he had for the integrity of L'Enfant's plan.

The dismissal of L'Enfant was a sign that the landowners and commercial speculators, not the government, were to exercise the major control over the development of the capital. Though L'Enfant realized, in his own words, that the "capital city's nourishment, unlike that of other cities, would come out of its public buildings rather than out of its trade centers," it was the traders and speculators whose heedless feet trampled out the best features of L'Enfant's plan, leaving only the bleached outline. But except for his failure to hold at bay the actual forces that would overwhelm his plan, I know no other baroque town planners, not even those in Haussmann's *équipe*, who showed a better grasp of the interrelation of topography, traffic, monuments, and public buildings than L'Enfant did. What was lacking was a responsible form of political control, to replace the often extravagant and irresponsible commands of despotism. But that would in turn have altered the very character of the plan.

In this respect, the smudging of the great Washington plan symbolizes the fate of the whole baroque scheme, as it affected the life of men in cities. In a period of flux and change, the baroque insistence upon outward order and uniformity had at least imposed a common standard, and reminded the upper-class city dweller of the interdependences of the common life. In Europe, a series of building acts established standards of construction, limited heights, and imposed a measure of decency, which limited competition at lower levels. In England, and even more in the United States, these standards seemed irksome to the leaders of the nineteenth century. Thus the sensible English Building Act of 1774 became known as the "Black Act," a synonym for bureaucratic repression and drab monotony. In the name of freedom, the new leaders of commerce and industry, once they were freed from the restraints of baroque taste, invited speculative uncertainty and planless competition. As a result, the great tide of urbanization in the nineteenth century resulted in a strange phenomenon: the progressive submergence of the city. The landscape was filled, instead, with a spreading mass of urban flotsam and jetsam, cast overboard in the storm of capitalist enterprise.

IV

THE URBAN PROSPECT

Civics as an art has to
do, not with imaging an
impossible [utopia] where all
is well, but with making the most
and best of each and every place,
and especially of the city in which
we live.
—Patrick Geddes

Introduction

In all of Lewis Mumford's work there is an active interplay of the past, the present, and the future. We see this most vividly in his culminating survey of urban civilization, *The City in History.* This is history as a form of social prophecy; virtually every page contains lessons and portents and suggestions for renewal. Nowhere, however, does Mumford give a fully formed image of the perfect city. No such city exists, he insists; nor can it exist. And, in any event, "life," as he was fond of saying, "is better than utopia."[1] The architect Harry M. Weese has perhaps shown the most sensitive understanding of Mumford's way of influencing the future of the city. "[Mumford] speaks of values and of living with nature in a reasonable habitat, of family life, and of self-discipline," Weese remarked recently. "Unlike the planners of utopias he does this without offering solutions but by illuminating the virtues of the good life in humane cities."[2]

Mumford calls the type of planning he favors "organic planning." The term, admittedly, is a slippery one, but it is as precise as he can make it: what he has in mind is almost undefinable, since organic planning leaves so much to the future.

The city, in Mumford's view, is a cumulative product, the creation of many lifetimes of creative effort. A lovely historic city like Siena is a collective work of art, made richer and more life-enhancing by a centuries-long succession of small changes. No truly stimulating city, architecturally expressive and culturally varied, can be brought into being in a single generation or by a single architect or architectural conception. In a city, beauty and diversity are introduced, as often as not, by time and not by the planner.

Still, Mumford argues that city planning must be guided by carefully thought-out social, biological, and aesthetic principles. In the opening essay of this section, "The Ideal Form of the Modern City," he gives what is perhaps his most concise summation of what those aims and principles should be.

Here he makes a strong argument for the garden city. Yet it is not

157

Ebenezer Howard's garden city (see above, p. 101) he is describing; it is his own, the garden city of his dreams. Before World War II, Mumford briefly visited Howard's two experimental New Towns, Letchworth and Welwyn Garden City, but not until the 1950s did he have a chance to closely examine Howard's idea in practice, when he visited the New Towns the British government was constructing on the outskirts of London. What he saw profoundly disappointed him. The British New Towns lacked, in his estimation, the cultural variety, liveliness, and handsome architectural form of older historic cities; worse still, they did not even look like real cities. In their understandable reaction against the overcrowded British industrial centers, the planners—many of them, ironically, disciples of Mumford—had sacrificed the urban virtues of sociability and community closeness for privacy and open space. In the garden city the garden had replaced the city.[3]

Considered by many an uncritical apologist of the garden city, Mumford was one of the first and most perceptive critics of the British New Towns. Nonetheless, he never lost faith in the garden-city ideal itself. Into the 1960s he continued to urge the federal government to begin a massive new-towns program in America, and simultaneously to begin rebuilding older cities in a manner suggested by the Regional Planning Association of America at Radburn. He suggested that whenever possible, urban neighborhoods should be reorganized into campus-like "superblocks," sealed off from motor traffic, with many of the houses and other buildings facing inward, away from the street, toward a small park or garden.

Mumford's advocacy of the regional city put him into direct conflict with two of the outstanding minds in twentieth-century planning, Le Corbusier and Jane Jacobs. It was Le Corbusier who drew his heaviest fire, for he and those who worked in his wake, like New York's czar of public works, Robert Moses, had a direct and insidiously damaging influence on modern city building. Although Le Corbusier discarded some of his more procrustean notions about city design later in his career, Mumford's mind remained fixed on the earlier Le Corbusier. In his widely influential "Voisin" plan (1922–25) Le Corbusier proposed to tear down the crowded, run-down historic core of Paris, preserving only the central monuments. In its place he wanted to build a gleaming city of tall office buildings and apartments, spaced far apart so that each glass-enshrouded tower would be surrounded by green space and have a wide and fine view. A city of tall towers, spacious parks, and high-speed motorways: this was Le Corbusier's Radiant City, but it seemed to Mumford to be Robert Moses' grand vision of New York as well. When, in 1962, Mumford wrote that Le Corbusier's "imagination worked like a bulldozer on an urban renewal project" in its eagerness to tear down well-rooted neighborhoods to build his city of tomorrow, he was surely thinking of Robert Moses as well.[4]

By bringing his multitiered expressways directly into the heart of New York City, and rehousing the poor in humanly dispiriting concrete towers, Robert Moses, Mumford charged, inflicted more damage on New York—and, by his far-spreading example, on other cities—than anyone else in our time. For nearly two decades, beginning in the 1940s, Mumford fought almost every one of Moses' major highway and urban renewal projects. He lost nearly all of these battles, but in the process he helped to bring about a slow change in our thinking about highways, mass transportation, and urban renewal. This led eventually to important policy revisions, although not nearly to the kind of comprehensive reforms he repeatedly called for in hard-hitting articles in *The New Yorker* and elsewhere. In these years, when we did so much to destroy our cities, Lewis Mumford was America's urban conscience.

In several of these campaigns against Robert Moses, Mumford's strongest ally was Jane Jacobs, author of one of the most influential books on the modern city, *The Death and Life of Great American Cities*.[5] Her book, however, represents an important reaction against Mumford's ideas on the city—a reaction that began to build up, ironically, in the early 1960s, when he was at the peak of his influence as an urban critic. Jacobs prefers the standard grid-style street design to the enclosed superblock, arguing that a city needs streets, lots of streets teeming with people and activity, if it is to be a safe and lively place. Crowded streets tend to be safer, she argues, because so many eyes are watching, whereas the secluded cul-de-sacs and superblocks are open invitations to the criminal. Jacobs also supports higher urban densities than Mumford is willing to tolerate, claiming that the most dangerous areas of a city are those neighborhoods with the lowest densities. But, as Mumford makes clear in his slashing attack on her book, condescendingly entitled "Home Remedies for Urban Cancer," their differences go well beyond their disagreements on matters of density and neighborhood design. It is a question of order versus disorder, of disciplined, or well-planned urban development versus a more haphazard, hit-or-miss approach. These themes of order and discipline are at the heart of Mumford's mature analysis of the city.

Mumford offers his ideas for a more orderly, decentralized New York in his essay "Restored Circulation, Renewed Life." This essay is his answer to both Robert Moses and Jane Jacobs. He points out here, however, that truly successful city planning must be regional planning; and in the essay that follows he makes it clear that the kind of regionalism he favors aims at a change in living habits, not just a change in living places. It will entail, he says, a movement toward a more settled, cooperative way of life and toward an enhanced concern for the natural environment.

This is the theme he sounded in his very first book, *The Story of Utopias,* which called for a new social philosophy dedicated to measure, balance, and economic sufficiency, not to the achievement of unlimited economic abundance. Inner or value change has always come first for Mumford. Good planning and architecture are important, but any real improvement in the frame of civilization hinges on a transformation that is essentially valuative and psychological.[6] In *The Story of Utopias* Mumford argued for a new humanism, an organic mode of thinking and acting that recognizes the "inner and the outer, the subjective and the objective, the world known to personal intuition and that described by science [as] a single experience."[7] While some radicals expected such a value change to occur after the revolution, for Mumford this value change *was* the revolution.

Mumford's plea for a new humanist synthesis led him straight to an argument for "the regional survey" as the foundation of any urban reconstruction effort. This is an idea he borrowed from Patrick Geddes, who recommended that urban planning be preceded by a comprehensive survey of the city and its surrounding region, examining the region's environmental characteristics as well as its history and cultural heritage. The survey is not just an indispensable tool of the planner; in itself, it is a form of synoptic thinking, Mumford argued, an example of the new humanism in practice. It brings together scientists, social scientists, and creative artists and directs their efforts to the service of community life.

More than Geddes, however, Mumford emphasized the role of the creative artist in the process of social transformation. Attracted as a young man to both sociology and literature, he described a role for the insurgent intellectual that perfectly embodied his twin interests. A systematic sociology, Geddes had taught him, must be linked to a vision of the good life; and in *The Story of Utopias,* Mumford declared it the responsibility of the artists to suggest this. They would be responsible for the first, the most important, step in any general reform—the reconstruction of our inner world—by suggesting images of a more balanced, spiritually satisfying life. These could then be woven into the plans of the regional surveyors, whose job it would be to recommend flexible civic programs for each of the various regions of the country. In this way we could begin to build not Utopia, the perfect world, but Eutopia, the best place possible.

It is a far less sanguine Mumford we confront in the final essay of this section, "The Choices Ahead"—a man who, for reasons he explains here, has lost some of his confidence in social planning as an instrument of reform. By the 1960s Mumford had become convinced that our most pressing urban problems were traceable to a massive breakdown in civilized behavior, a breakdown in communal discipline, family closeness, and neighborhood solidarity. The disintegration of our cities, he warns in his most somber Old Testament tones, is a sign of a disintegrating society.[8] Yet, while there is unquestionably a shift in mood and emphasis here, this is still the Lewis Mumford who argued in Emersonian fashion in his first book that a change in social direction hinged on a prior change in morals and values. Relying on planning or architecture or even money as antidotes to our urban problems, as he observes in his essay on Jane Jacobs, is like "applying a homemade poultice for the cure of a cancer."[9]

Notes

1. Lewis Mumford to Catherine Bauer, July 1930, LM MSS.

2. Harry M. Weese, in *A Tribute to Lewis Mumford* (Cambridge, Mass.: Lincoln Institute of Land Policy, 1982), 31.

3. Mumford to Frederic J. Osborn, August 25, 1957, *The Letters of Lewis Mumford and Frederic J. Osborn: A Transatlantic Dialogue,*, ed. Michael Hughes (New York: Praeger, 1971), 277–78.

4. Mumford, "The Future of the City—Part II: Yesterday's City of Tomorrow," *Architectural Record* 132, no. 5 (November 1962): 139–44.

5. Jane Jacobs, *The Death and Life of Great American Cities* (New York: Random House, 1961).

6. Mumford, *Sticks and Stones: A Study of American Architecture and Civilization* (New York: Boni and Liveright, 1924), 121.

7. Mumford, "Toward a Humanist Synthesis," *The Freeman* 11 (March 2, 1921): 582–85; Mumford, "A Modern Synthesis," *Saturday Review of Literature* 6 (April 12, 1930): 920–21; (May 10, 1930): 1028–29.

8. "A Brief History of Urban Frustration," in Mumford, *The Urban Prospect* (New York: Harcourt, Brace and World, 1968).

9. Ibid., 207.

THE IDEAL FORM
OF THE
MODERN CITY

... The "modern city" cannot be created by mechanical improvements
—a possibility that seemed so promising to utopian writers like [Ed-
ward] Bellamy and [H.G.] Wells when toward the end of the nineteenth
century they envisioned the "city of the future"—and especially if it is
conceived in the childish terms used in the 1920s by various American
skyscraper architects in portraying super-skyscraper cities lived in
largely under artificial light, zoned in horizontal layers according to
incomes, and utilizing every mechanical device that would further
congestion, increase land values, or speed movement. . . .

The architectural embodiment of the modern city is in fact impossible until biological, social, and personal needs have been canvassed,
until the cultural and educational purposes of the city have been outlined, and until all of man's activities have been integrated into a balanced whole. One cannot base an adequate architectural conception on
such a crude sociology as that which led a group of modern architects
and planners to examine the modern city with reference to only four
functions: work, transportation, dwelling, and recreation. The city, if it
is anything, is an expression and symbolization of man's wholeness—a
representation in buildings of his nature and purposes. This wholeness
is not elementary; it emerges from the diversity of man's interests,
activities, and purposes, from the division of labor and the differentiation of associations and institutions, and from all those infinitely varied
human capacities which were perhaps latent but undeveloped in the
primitive village.

What, then, are man's permanent needs, and what are the collec-

This essay was originally titled "The Modern City." *(Editor's note)*

tive urban means for satisfying them? Before we can survey a site or lay a stone, we must achieve a provisional agreement so as to the nature of man and as to the values and potentialities of his present culture.

Historically the city begins in the village—a group of households attached to the soil. Here nurture and neighborly cooperation are the two basic elements; the limited horizon and a repetitive routine give to the growing child security and to the adult the basis of social solidarity, like-mindedness. The "primary group" of families and neighbors, as [Charles Horton] Cooley called such a unit, forms the basis of all other associations; the common locality that is shared and the common biological tasks of nutrition and reproduction create a common general purpose. This community of interest demands face-to-face intercourse, for most of the social values are here transmitted not through intermediate symbols but from person to person by word, gesture, and daily example. Hence the elemental neighborhood unit should cover an area not greater than the normal radius of action of a small child nor greater than the distance—to speak in modern terms—that a mother can conveniently push a baby carriage. From 250 to 1,000 people make up such a natural unit. Such economic functions as are performed here should be those that pertain directly to the home.

The central figures in the neighborhood group are the mother and the child, and the first differentiation of social life beyond the household is in the play group and nursery-school group. All the spatial relationships of such a community must be based on walking distances, almost on crawling distances. Security, quiet, freedom from danger, intimacy of relationship, and opportunities for spontaneous meetings without special effort or the intervention of mechanical agents should give the clue to the architectural treatment. Frank Lloyd Wright's scheme for Broadacre City, in which each family would have a minimum of one acre of land, limits social intercourse on the primary level to a mere handful of neighbors and above that level demands motor transportation for even the most casual or ephemeral meetings. . . .

Architecturally the primary neighborhood unit calls for enclosed private gardens and a few nodal points—a group of trees, a fountain, a pergola—where mothers may refresh their senses, chat and sew, or watch over their offspring without being confined to their isolated domestic cells. When buildings are oriented for sunlight in open rows, then parapets and trellises and foliage should limit the long vistas, contain the movements of the toddler, and add to the visual sense of intimacy by richness of detail in the foreground. At this point in the plan the architect still can learn something from the "innerness" of the medieval city, for it symbolized to the point of exaggeration the fundamental needs of the primary group. Nowhere, perhaps, has this sense of intimacy been better embodied than in Matthew Nowicki's studies ... for the neighborhood units in the proposed capital of the East Punjab in India.

The opposite of the feeling of identification which arises instinctually in the village and more rationally in the modern neighborhood unit —the sense of being disinherited, anonymous, lonely, "not belonging" —is the typical malady in the modern metropolis, and it is accentuated by all the devices that produce mechanically regulated days and by unidentifiable living quarters in neighborhoods that have neither boundaries nor architectural definition. In such cities spontaneous reactions are fostered only by mass activities, which make people temporarily neighbors at football games and motor races and parades. Part of the strength of fascism, in both its open and its disguised forms, consists of playing on the need for solidarity and sympathy and of canalizing it into commercially or politically profitable forms. Proposals now fashionable —and strenuously advocated by Le Corbusier—for putting families and households into tall apartment houses, as in Marseille and Rotterdam and New York, ignore the nature and needs of primary groups and forget human scale in shaping their environment. In big units children must be regimented or kept under the watchful eye of an adult, whereas the essence of good neighborhood planning is to give them the maximum amount of freedom of movement compatible with physical safety.

The visible house and the usable garden are important means of gaining security and stability for the growing child, and good neighborhood planning is an attempt to give a wider range to these qualities. The widespread recognition of this fact has doubtless prompted the movement into suburban areas; unfortunately, however, for those below the highest income levels, the architectural solution of this problem in suburbia usually only caricatures the hope that prompted it.

But a city is more than a collection of primary groups and neighborhoods; a hundred thousand families might be so collected together without forming a city. For, in contrast to the village, the city is a combination of primary *and* secondary groups, of instinctual communities *and* purposeful associations. Whereas one belongs to a village by birth or residence, historically one becomes a member of a city by choice and participates in its life by engaging in an occupation or a profession, by joining a church or a fraternity or a trade union, by enrolling as a student in a school, or by organizing an office or a factory —in short, by banding with people of similar interests to pursue some specialized purpose. Thus the simple melody of village life becomes the complex, four-part, contrapuntal score of the city: the biological, economic, political, and educational themes weave in and out to form a higher but less stable unity. Diversity, conflict, differentiation, deliberate organization, and cooperation characterize city life. Here differentiation might be fatal to social life did not the city itself, as a shell and a symbol, help to restore unity.

Conceivably a city could be built underground, or it might be enclosed within the undifferentiated envelope of a single massive, air-conditioned skyscraper with no window opening to the outer world. Proposals are current for both types. But one important element in social development would be lacking in such a city—the aesthetic symbolization of its contents, its activity, its meaning. For the city, conceived as an architectural entity, is an attempt to make visible the facts of group life, to give them a form suited to their practical needs, and to underline their significance by means of architectural devices. Above all, the city is a symbol of enduring social relationships. The planning of the individual structures of the city is an important contribution to the functions they serve, and the interrelation of these structures in the city plan becomes a means of effecting a further unification—first in the daily imprint made on the mind and second in their actual functioning together. The city is the outward embodiment of a social order which does not itself reach the stage of self-consciousness until the city itself is built.

In cities not only do the social functions exist; they signify. Architecture and city planning are the visible translations of the total meaning of a culture. Each generation writes its biography in the buildings it creates; each culture characterizes, in the city, the unifying idea that runs through its activities. The complexity of even a small city would be baffling were it not for the unifying effect of the whole, which one reads almost at a glance just as one reads in the face of a person his health, his status, his background, his attainments. The medieval city says PROTECTION under the eye of God; the baroque city says POWER under the favor of the prince; the industrial city says PRODUCTION no matter what the human cost; the American metropolis says FINANCE must dominate. Silhouette and street plan, elevation and detail—these all express such elemental but comprehensive terms. In the ideal form of the modern city one must look for a fuller embodiment of human needs than any recent culture has produced.

ACHIEVEMENT OF URBAN BALANCE

Since the middle of the nineteenth century the greater part of urban planning has been a thing of shreds and patches. The first modern attempt to formulate the needs of a city as an integrated whole was the work of a man who was neither an architect nor a city planner—Sir

Ebenezer Howard, the author of *Garden Cities of Tomorrow.* * Howard was both a mechanical and a social inventor, and he applied to the building of cities the same imaginative capacity that has led to the improvement of machines.

Originally Howard's conceptions did not touch directly on the physical problems of planning or on the question of architectural form. With great insight he applied himself first to the more fundamental concerns of the relation of population to industry and to the land, the possibilities of creating a new rural-urban pattern, and a reinterpretation of human needs in terms of twentieth-century political and technical possibilities. By reason of his fundamental approach, Howard provided a principle of order on which architectural conceptions could flourish. The first architect to give these conceptions architectural form was Tony Garnier, whose *Une Cité industrielle* . . .† because of its aesthetic freshness and clarity was closer to the spirit of Howard's proposal than the first actual "garden city," Letchworth, founded five years after the first edition of Howard's book was published.

The first contribution made by Howard was to establish the necessity for limiting the area and the population of a city. He recognized that the indefinite and unlimited growth of cities led not merely to internal decay but to a permanent misuse of valuable agricultural land and a steady depletion of rural life itself. Howard recognized in the city the same limitations on biological growth that is seen in the cell, though he did not use this biological metaphor. Every cell has a norm of development, and when it passes beyond that norm the wall of the cytoplasm will break down, unless growth leads to the reproductive process. When a cell has reached its optimum of growth, its nucleus divides in two, and two new cells are formed. Cities are not biological organisms; hence, except for a primitive dependence on a limited water and food supply, there is no natural limit to their growth—but there is a social limit, marked by lapse of function and disorganization and descent to more primitive social levels, and that limit has been constantly exceeded in the expansion of modern cities.

Howard pointed out that a city should be large enough to sustain a varied industrial, commercial, and social life. It should not be solely an industrial hive, solely an overgrown market, or solely a dormitory; instead, all these and many other functions, including rural ones, should be contained in a new kind of urban organization to which he applied the slightly misleading name of garden city. Howard had no thought of

*(London: Faber & Faber, 1946); first issued as *Tomorrow: A Peaceful Path to Real Reform* (London: S. Sonnenschein, 1902).
†(Paris: Vincent, 1918).

a return to the "simple life" or to a more primitive economy; on the contrary, he was seeking higher levels of both production and living. He believed that a city should be big enough to achieve social cooperation of a complex kind based on the necessary division of labor, but not so big as to handicap or frustrate these functions—as the big city tended to do even when viewed solely as an economic unit. In his ideal scheme the garden city was to have a population of 32,000 persons, 2,000 of whom were to be absorbed by the agriculture of the surrounding green-belt. The entire estate was to consist of 6,000 acres, 1,000 of which were to be dedicated to the city itself; the overall density was 30 persons to the gross acre, or some 90 to 95 persons per residential acre.

Neither Letchworth (1904) nor Welwyn Garden City (1919), the first two towns that were built in accordance with Howard's general formula, grew fast enough to contain 32,000 people by 1947. Mean-while, in the working out of the New Towns policy in Britain, that original number, based on a reasonable guess rather than a statistical analysis, has been revised upward to 60,000. American experience sug-gests that there is a rough correlation between size and certain other characteristics and that cities of over 25,000 do not fully reproduce their population, though the net reproductive ratio of cities of 50,000 is still close enough to 1.0 to make them adequate biological environ-ments. The correct population for a balanced urban community must be worked out experimentally, and it is probable that there are regional and cultural factors which will produce a considerable variation.

Howard's important contribution was the suggestion that the set-ting of limits of population, area, and density of use is the first step in the art of building cities. It is interesting to note that Leonardo da Vinci recognized the evils of congestion and blight that resulted from the overcrowding of Milan at the beginning of the sixteenth century. He proposed to put its 300,000 people into ten cities of 30,000 each—an idea that not only anticipated Howard's but even arrived at approxi-mately the same population figure. Once the optimum size of the city has been reached, further growth must take place not by extension but by reproduction—the planning of another balanced community. This method overcomes one of the gravest effects of indefinite expansion—much faster growth at the periphery than within the nucleus, so that in the course of time unlimited expansion produces characteristic evi-dence of cultural and social impoverishment: the areas beyond the central city, from the standpoint of many essential social needs, are "do without" areas.

The modern way of fixing the city's organic limits was also con-ceived by Howard. A generation earlier John Ruskin had suggested that the boundaries of a city should be clearly defined, as in medieval times, by a wall; but, although the wall had once served in a secondary fashion as an open promenade, he did not suggest any further reason for building such a costly utility. Howard gave the archaic conception of the wall its functional modern horizontal equivalent: he conceived it as a permanent belt of green land dedicated to market gardens, agricultural schools, and other rural pursuits. To make secure both the internal development of the garden city and the external maintenance of the green wall, he proposed to vest the land in perpetuity in the original development company or the municipal corporation that sprang out of it. The common ownership of the land was the key to the plan as a whole—a provision which ensured that such prosperity as the community achieved would return in the form of increased land values not to individual landlords but to the community as a whole.

For Howard, the social control of land was of primary importance. Though he relied on individual enterprise to build the garden city and actually exhibited daring initiative in helping to launch two garden cities, he realized that land is in a category basically different from any other kind of property; also, since one who controls a city's land controls its destiny, Howard held that such control should be vested in a public body responsible for the good of the whole. To expect order, coherence, social foresight, and social responsibility through the "free action" of individual speculators was as self-defeating as to suppose that the mere random throwing of stones would result eventually in the building of a house.

In short, Howard wisely saw that urban design is fundamentally an economic and a political problem. Where control is unified, order is possible. The choice is not between control and no control but between an arbitrary, one-sided control and control exercised by a responsible authority acting in behalf of the entire community. The princes and ground landlords who produced the civilized town planning of the eighteenth century were self-appointed officers, but their plans served something more than a short-sighted private interest, whereas the individual owners of property in the nineteenth century not only had split up power into a thousand parcels but also had renounced any higher consideration than the possibility of achieving private gain. This system, though called free, was actually a despotic and one-sided control, often openly in opposition to the public interest but more unchallengeable than the despot's because it was more diffused. Effective urban order in urban design awaited the unification of economic power and democratic political responsibility, and this is what Howard's program provided. Once this was established, design in the aesthetic and architectural sense was possible.

His third contribution—the most important of all—was his conception of the *balanced community*, relatively self-contained and big enough to provide out of its own resources and activities all that might be needed for the citizen's daily life. The garden city was no "housing project," no dormitory suburb, no trading estate, no industrial satellite; all these separate functions, along with those of recreation, education, and government, were integrated, and balance and integration were the marrow of the organism.

Howard's successors, in stressing the self-contained nature of the garden city, tended to overlook two other masterly contributions of his which round out that conception. The first was his division of the city into six wards or neighborhood units, for within the city he recognized the need for an even simpler pattern of organization. With that proposal Howard anticipated both the sociological and the planning discoveries of a later generation; in the United States, in time, the community-center movement and the social-unit plan—both arising out of the original initiatives that created the settlement house—would call attention to the need for "self-contained" planning on the neighborhood and family level. The second, and even more masterly perhaps, was Howard's perception that a city, no matter how well balanced, can never be completely self-contained. He pointed out that in a group of garden cities united by rapid transportation each would have facilities and resources that would supplement those of the others; so grouped, these "social cities" would in fact be the functional equivalent of the congested metropolis.

His insight here must be emphasized. Balance is a necessary attribute of all organic life, but in the nature of things it is incomplete. An individual's personal balance is forever unstable; it needs family, friends, comrades, and colleagues to maintain even its internal harmony—hence the horror and demoralization of solitary confinement or prolonged isolation. So, too, the domestic community, though it may be complete from the standpoint of the child, is incomplete for the adult; even the adolescent must leave his immediate neighborhood to become a member of a secondary school. The balanced community of from thirty to sixty thousand citizens may take care of the larger number of daily activities, but there remains a whole range of activities of a more occasional or specialized nature which require a wider population base; higher education, certain types of recreation (like opera), specialized surgical or medical services, and comprehensively stocked department stores, for example, call for wider forms of cooperation. Even that balance is not final: certain activities will draw on a whole regional area for support, and these in turn, though still more intermittently or selectively, will call for international collaboration.

For a community, no matter how large, cannot be completely

self-sufficient. The essential problem of modern urban planning is to conceive a series of relatively self-contained units, each of which has an open passage to the next larger and more complex community, so that eventually it will achieve an articulate order leading from the life of the child to the life of the mature man, from the immediate day-to-day activities, involving neighbors, friends, family, and fellow workers, to occasional activities that will enlist the support of men and women in every part of the world or specialized activities that will call for the constant intercourse of special people or groups everywhere. Now, each of these communities should be balanced, each should be mainly self-contained; each should symbolize architecturally its own wholeness. Yet their very functioning and their growth will depend on drawing together special resources and facilities, and above all special people, from other communities; and these wider unifications, this more complex balance, must also be symbolized. That which the overgrown metropolis achieved by mere vastness and juxtaposition of elements within a limited space, at the price of disorganization, must now be achieved by orderly design. The domestic group, the neighborhood unit, the garden city, the "town cluster," the regional city—all these relatively self-contained units are involved in the conception of the modern city; their visible and invisible interrelation is the task of architects, community planners, engineers, and regional planners.

But the chief contribution that modern sociology and technics have made to the concept of the city itself is the possibility of a fuller integration—as first conceived by Sir Thomas More—between town and country as such and between those parts of the social heritage which town and country maintain. No ideal plan can do justice to the potential nature of modern man if it does not further the rhythmic interaction of the urban and the rural patterns of life, bringing gardens, parks, and recreation spaces into the heart of the city and making available for the most isolated country dweller the fullest resources of culture, education, and collective intelligence. Among modern countries, the town-planning tradition of the Netherlands has perhaps gone farthest in creating this urban and regional balance.

IDEAL FORM AND OUTLINE OF THE MODERN CITY

It now becomes possible to define in more concrete terms some of the functions and attributes of the modern city.

Cellular Character.   The modern city is a group of interrelated cells, each cell balanced and partly self-contained but also part of a wider social whole. It is not conceivable as a pattern of highways, streets, and public places, capable of indefinite extension; nor is it a close massing of buildings with an occasional public green punctuating the stony waste. From the air the ground pattern of the modern city is not formed by highways, avenues, and buildings but by parked and gardened open spaces into which the architecture partly dissolves.

The principle of limiting urban growth to an optimum size, related to economic and social functions, governs the entire plan and likewise every choice between high and low buildings. The basic cell of the city is the domestic and neighborhood unit; the city itself must be planned as a related cluster of such units, wards, or quarters, differentiated according to function and defined further by appropriate architectural treatment. Though such a city will have business, industrial, residential, and civic zones, modern planning must not be confused with zoning. Zoning, as practiced in the United States, is an attempt to achieve by law a result that cannot be achieved without planning; by turns it is too loose or too flexible, too indiscriminate or too selective.

Perhaps the worst sin of zoning is that it violates an essential social characteristic of neighborhood planning, namely, that each unit must be balanced—it is the city writ small. Each unit, accordingly, must have a place for the industrial, political, educational, and domestic facilities which pertain to its special purposes. Thus the residential neighborhood must contain more than a collection of houses, in the fashion of a segregated residential zone; it should also have, *as an integral part of the plan,* a place for retail stores, for garages, for small workshops serving the immediate needs of the inhabitants; in short, it should be a representative human community, expressing the variety and cooperation of the larger whole of which it is a part. This principle also holds true for the factory quarter. If that quarter is properly planned, it will provide not merely transportation facilities and storage but also recreational facilities for the lunch hour or for after-work sports, and it will also subserve the political life of the community by providing suitable meeting places and auditoriums for public discussion and conference. In a city designed to encompass the full nature of man the isolation and segregation of his functions, as worked out in the militarist-industrialist pattern of the last three centuries, must be replaced by structures designed for the whole man at every phase of his life.

Social Structures.   The social nucleus, with its institutions serving politics, education, and religion, is essential to the definition of the neighborhood unit or precinct, and no quarter can be called well designed unless those functions have a central place in the plan. These institutions are the chromosomes which transmit the social heritage, and in providing a place for them both their practical office and their symbolic function must be respected. What Sigfried Giedion has termed monu-mentality . . . rests partly on a sufficient dedication of thought, money, and love to the creation of such buildings. . . .

This does not mean that all the higher social functions of the community need be centralized in a single plaza or civic center: certain ecological associations are as marked in the grouping of human institutions as in the grouping of plant species. The school and the library, for example, belong together; but there is no such kinship between the school and the motion-picture theater, which is more effectively associated—as in the Waikiki development at Honolulu—with a group of shops, and these in turn with tearooms, bars, and restaurants. In creating such nuclei, the architect must avoid "locked-in" plans which do not permit an economic expansion or contraction of functions. Even when a norm of growth is established for the community, no amount of calculation can fix absolute limits for the growth or shriveling of a particular function; hence space and open planning must provide the needed factor of safety, particularly when the installation itself is a costly one.

Cell Boundaries. The boundaries of the urban cell must be as clearly defined as those of the city itself. There are two modern methods for establishing such limits, both functional and visual. One is by means of the through-traffic avenue, planned to unite a series of neighborhood units. Instead of serving, as of old, as a river whose banks are lined with houses, such traffic arteries should be enjoined from every other use; the divorce of major highways and buildings must be complete in order to secure speed and safety for the first and freedom from congestion, danger, and noise for the second. Access roads and lanes, which filter out the traffic and finally bring it to a standstill in the heart of the residential district, will further lessen the economic waste that went with the undifferentiated streets of the obsolete standard plan.

The other method of establishing the neighborhood boundary is by means of the park strip—a local greenbelt serving as interstitial tissue within the larger urban greenbelt. Ideally it should be possible to proceed on foot from one part of the city to another by means of such a continuous belt without having to cross, at level, a single major artery. Such belts may be independent of the major roads or may parallel them; in either case they ensure not only a foreground of verdure in the approach to important groups of buildings but also the possibility of a terminal point of green in every open vista. Even when the architecture is as mediocre as that of Radburn, New Jersey, the aesthetic effect of the continuous inner park that binds the superblocks together is extraordinarily charming.

Where the greenbelt is used within the city and where by municipal ownership or by zoning a permanent greenbelt is established around a city in a fashion that puts the whole countryside within ready walking or cycling distance, the need for a central park disappears. Gardens, playgrounds, and recreation fields on a small scale will be allotted to the neighborhood unit; but for the other purposes of the park the greenbelt and the open country suffice. In a city conceived as a group of neighborhood units and functional zones there is no single center and therefore no reason to establish a single point of dominance as the terminus of a major axis. Each part of the city may in turn become the center when it serves as a focus for some particular activity serving the city as a whole, and that functional shifting of the social axis—in deep accord with the principle of relativity—could only be falsified by a centralized and hierarchical scheme.

SCALE IN URBAN DESIGN

This new kind of planning, with its full-fledged differentiation of the city's traffic and residential functions, produces differences in tempo which in turn have an architectural result. The change of speed from the through-traffic highway (safe average speed 45 mph) to the walking strip (maximum 4 mph) and in turn to the center of the domestic area (crawling speed or complete rest) should be translated into appropriate forms of design. The blank walls of parking lots, garages, and filling stations, broken only by signal pylons or directive signs, go well with the highest speed. Here each architectural form should be standardized to convey its function by its outline; repetition and absence of emphasis should characterize both planting and architecture on both sides of major traffic arteries. When one reaches the other extreme, however, a certain richness, variety, and even intricacy of detail, particularly in the treatment of landscape and garden, should characterize the neighborhood. The attempt to impose the aesthetics of the transportation artery upon residential neighborhoods, thus creating acres of formalized blankness, is none the better for being called modern architecture.

The only traditional images that at all suggest this new order of design are those of certain college campuses in the United States or the ancient Inns of Court in London. But in any case the architectural result of divorcing buildings from through-traffic streets should be noted: the two-dimensional façade disappears as the major element in planning, and the three-dimensional building—conceived in depth and showing a silhouette as well as a façade—again becomes possible as an urban form. Even when such buildings are organized in rows, as in Baldwin Hills Village in Los Angeles, their third dimension remains an essential architectural feature, preserved by the diverse angles of approach. With such neighborhood planning in complete units, the natural setting and the buildings can be treated as a unified whole.

The unit principle of urban design carries through every part of the new city. Instead of stretching out indefinitely along the traffic street or highway in typical ribbon development, the modern market center —first concretely embodied in the drive-in markets of California and in the Sears, Roebuck suburban retail stores—is a compact unit, off the highway, with a special parking space for cars. When the original proposals for a collective shopping precinct in Coventry were vetoed by the shortsighted merchants of that city, who wanted their center bisected by a through-traffic artery, these businessmen were in fact acting to restrain trade rather than to promote it. Good marketing practice demands access to the shopping area but not passage through it; for shopping is done on foot, and even in the old-fashioned type of city narrow shopping streets like Bond Street and Madison Avenue and others in Amsterdam or Buenos Aires remain the most efficient and prosperous districts. The compact alignment of shops around an elongated narrow plaza at right angles to a main traffic artery and with parking facilities on the outer rim is a correlate of modern design—a form that lends itself to possible variations by arrangement in the shape of a fret or a succession of scallops. [Patrick] Abercrombie's proposals for such marketing centers in his report on Greater London are not the least brilliant features of that great overall design. In one of the first British New Towns, Stevenage, such a center has, in fact, been designed.

In replanning the old towns as well as in developing the new, certain further results follow from a recognition of the fact that the neighborhood and not the avenue or the building is the true unit of planning. Piecemeal construction or readaptation is a wasteful and unsatisfactory process. To make an effective reconstruction in accordance with modern principles of design, a whole quarter must be built from the ground up. Whatever merit there is in Rockefeller Center, New York, or in Lansbury Neighborhood, London, springs in part from this unified operation. Once such unity is established aesthetically over a considerable urban area, as in Bloomsbury in London, the structures tend to resist degrading urban changes; where, on the other hand, it has been absent from the beginning, blight easily enters and spreads.

When a city is planned and created by quarters, it preserves the virtue of visual coherence and unity and avoids the baroque vice of denying time and change and rival points of view. Even in a relatively small city of twenty thousand people one should not look for a single building form or tradition; rather, it is a mark of architectural vitality that each age should choose its own symbols and its own expression. Indeed, the preservation of the best of these expressions gives a link of continuity in time, and the most comprehensive scheme of demolition and reconstruction should go out of its way—even at the expense of superficial unity—to preserve such buildings when they are still service-able. An organic plan will always have a place for such departures, which, like the off-colored flower the French gardener wisely puts in the midst of his most harmonious bed, even serve to accentuate that very harmony. When a town is built by quarters, as modern Amsterdam has been planned, each quarter will have its own character—a unity in the diversity of the city as a whole.

One further point that relates to the nature of man remains to be dealt with. Part of man's nature is enchanced by association, participa-tion, and togetherness, and the city is pre-eminently the environment in which the functions men best perform in groups are housed and symbolized. But another aspect of man's nature must also be heeded if association is to be durable and fruitful: there must be a place for withdrawal, a refuge for privacy, solitary communion, innerness. One of the commonest mistakes of contemporary planning is to conceive of man as a purely extroverted creature who thrives on external stimuli, with never a moment when he seeks to be alone and never a place to be alone in. But the goldfish bowl is no more natural to man than the cave; in so far as men live well, they must alternate between the two —between light and darkness, between society and solitude, between participation and withdrawal. Part of the charm of a big city like Lon-don or Paris is that out of its slow organic growth it provides a place for both attitudes—witness Westminister with its broad walks and pleas-ances and public spaces where the collective architecture and the peo-ple make a maximum impression and, by contrast, the devious walks it offers through alleys, backways, and lanes which are as private as a cloister. Children show a demand for solitariness, and good nursery schools provide perches or cubbyholes into which a child may withdraw for solitary brooding. Where the need for seclusion is recognized, it can be translated into public forms, just as Olmsted laid out the Ramble in Central Park for this very purpose. A city without such secluded walks and retreats is no place for lovers or thinkers.

In short, if we respect the nature of man, the order established by urban planning must be an inclusive one: it must respect every side of man's nature and do equal justice to every need; it can no longer subordinate the major business of life to the profits of the ground land-lord or the desire of the transport corporation to promote more and more congested transportation. The modern planner will obey Emer-son's injunction to save on the low levels and to spend on the high ones, and, while rigorously standardizing, rationalizing, economizing, and at times eliminating the subordinate mechanical utilities, he will do this for the purpose of treating the positive functions of life with a noble largesse—the largesse of freedom, spontaneity, and art.

YESTERDAY'S CITY OF TOMORROW

. . . The major reaction against the misdemeanors of the city has been the escape to suburbia. For more than a century, families that were content to do without the social advantages of the city profited by the cheap land and the natural landscape to create a biologically more adequate environment, with full access to all the things now missing from the city: sunlight, untainted air, freedom from mechanical noises, ample lawns and gardens, accessible open country for walks and picnics; finally, individual houses, specially designed for family comfort, expressive of personal taste.

This impulse to have closer contact with the rural scene was fed by the literature of the Romantic movement, from Rousseau on to Thoreau; but it did not originate there. For the rich families of Florence, Rome, and Venice, in the fifteenth and sixteenth centuries, did not wait for either Romanticism or the railroad age to build their country villas in Fiesole, in Frascati, or on the Brenta. What marks the modern age is that both the impulse and the means of achieving it have become universal.

Though the ultimate outcome of this suburban retreat on a large scale has proved to be a non-city, if not an anti-city, just because of the very isolation and separation it proudly boasted, one must not underestimate its architectural results or its great human attraction; in fact, no adequate image of the emerging city will arise until these are both fully reckoned with. From William Morris's Red House to the shingle houses of H. H. Richardson, W. R. Emerson, and their colleagues, from Frank Lloyd Wright's prairie houses on to the work of Voysey, Parker, and Baillie-Scott, from Olmsted's Riverside and Roland Park to [Raymond] Unwin's Hampstead Garden Suburb, most of the fresh forms of domestic architecture and planning grew out of the suburb. This still holds true today: not merely in houses, but in shopping centers, school complexes, industrial parks. Apart from purely industrial architecture, like the cotton mills of Manchester or the early skyscrapers of Chicago, no other environment has proved so encouraging to positive architectural expression as the suburb.

Though the original values of the suburb have been fast disappearing in the welter of the ever-spreading conurbation, the image that was left behind has had an influence upon urban planning. This is the image of a new kind of city, the "City in a Park"; more open in texture than the more crowded cities of the past, with permanent access to gardens and parks for all the inhabitants of the city, not just for the dominant minority. That influence has expressed itself in three different conceptions of the contemporary city, advanced by three distinguished architects and planners, Raymond Unwin, Frank Lloyd Wright, and Le Corbusier. Though radically different in their human background and purpose, all three conceptions have a common denominator: an unqualified demand for more space. In this article I shall confine myself to the work of Le Corbusier. If space and speed, mass production and bureaucratic regimentation, were all that is necessary to form a new image of the modern metropolis, Le Corbusier would already have provided an adequate solution.

Most architects, during the last thirty years, and certainly most architectural and planning schools, have been dominated by the powerful propaganda and experimental achievement of this singular man of genius, Le Corbusier. If anyone put forward what seemed a fresh and original conception of the City of Tomorrow, it was this redoubtable leader. Though that conception has gone through a series of changes, corresponding to changes that have taken place likewise in his architecture, certain main features stand out, and will probably for a while continue to have influence, even if the master should abandon them. And though no one city, except Chandigarh, shows the full range of his influence, his thought has run so closely along the grain of our age that fragments of it are scattered everywhere.

The chief reason for Le Corbusier's immediate impact lies in the fact that he brought together the two architectural conceptions that separately have dominated the modern movement in architecture and city planning: the machine-made environment, standardized, bureaucratized, "processed," technically perfected to the last degree; and to offset this, the natural environment, treated as so much visual open space, providing sunlight, pure air, green foliage, and views.

Not the least attraction of Le Corbusier's thought to his contemporaries was that in bringing these two together, he paid no more attention to the nature of the city and to the orderly arrangements of its constantly proliferating groups, societies, clubs, organizations, institutions, than did the real-estate broker or the municipal engineer. In short, he embraced every feature of the contemporary city except its essential social and civic character. . . .

In his first presentation of the City of the Future, Le Corbusier overemphasized its new mechanical facilities, and equated urban progress with geometrical order, rectilinear planning, and mechanized bureaucratic organization. Enchanted by the possibilities of modern steel and concrete construction, Le Corbusier first presented a picture of a modern city like Paris, transformed into his new image: an image of free-standing, sixty-story office buildings, set in open spaces, as the central feature, with multiple high-speed transportation routes at many levels, feeding into this center, and long series of apartment houses, uniform in height, forming an undifferentiated residential district outside the bureaucratic core. This new unit would hold three million inhabitants, the equivalent of Paris. Le Corbusier's Voisin plan (1922–25) was superimposed on the center of Paris: he proposed to tear down the historic core of Paris, as confused, unsanitary, pestilent, preserving only a few ancient monuments, and packing all its multifarious activities into uniform structures.

In his readiness to demolish the historic quarter of Paris and replace it with these towering isolated buildings, Le Corbusier's imagination worked like a bulldozer on an urban renewal project. In the name of efficiency, he paid no attention to the actual functions and purposes of the structures he proposed to rehouse, or to historic buildings that by their individual character give form and continuity to the life that goes on within them. In short, he ignored the main office of the city, which is to enrich the future by maintaining in the midst of change visible structural links with the past in all its cultural richness and variety. In proposing prudently to preserve a handful of historic buildings as isolated monuments, Le Corbusier overlooked the fact that no small part of their value and meaning would disappear, once they were cut off from the multitudinous activities and associations that surrounded them; that, in fact, it was people, not space, that they needed if they were even properly to be seen.

In placing his emphasis on the vertical, rather than the horizontal, elements of city design, Le Corbusier was fascinated, not only by the general possibilities of technology, but also by the desire to give a more rigorous, Cartesian expression to the American skyscraper. He had returned, most probably without any consciousness of it, to the form of the early Chicago skyscrapers, and had removed, not merely the romantic pinnacles and setback towers that had followed, but also the visual jumble and congestion. His novel proposal was to combine the new order of height with something that had never been seriously suggested before, a palatial increase of open space, in the form of a park, between the buildings.

In that simple act, Le Corbusier wiped out the complex tissue of a thousand little and not so little urban activities that cannot be economically placed in tall structures or function efficiently except at points where they are encountered at street level and utilized by a multitude of people going about their business at all times of the day.

The extravagant heights of Le Corbusier's skyscrapers had no reason for existence apart from the fact that they had become technological possibilities; the open spaces in his central areas had no reason for existence either, since on the scale he imagined there was no motive during the business day for pedestrian circulation in the office quarter. By mating the utilitarian and financial image of the skyscraper city to the romantic image of the organic environment, Le Corbusier had, in fact, produced a sterile hybrid.

But perhaps the very sterility of Le Corbusier's conception was what has made it so attractive to our age. In American cities tall buildings came into existence not simply as a convenience for business enterprise, but as a mode of increasing land values and the opportunities for highly profitable large-scale building and speculation; and even when the business towers provided too little floor space in proportion to elevator space to be profitable, they served by their very extravagance as a form of commercially valuable advertisement. The tall building was accepted in America as a standardized substitute, with convertible units of space, for more functional plans and elevations that might require a more generous—that is, expensive—allotment of land along with a more exacting design.

By stressing the visual openness between tall buildings, offsetting the low coverage with ever-higher structures, Le Corbusier seemed to have satisfied two hitherto irreconcilable conditions: higher densities with higher rents on one hand, and greater exposure to light and air, along with a greater sense of open space, however unusable except to the eye. This pattern could be reduced to a mechanical formula and repeated anywhere precisely because it paid so little attention to the variety of human needs and the complexities of human association. That failing largely accounts for the present success of Le Corbusier's formula. But applied to urban renewal projects it has proved a disastrous success. . . .

. . .

Le Corbusier's early images of the city were supplemented by later designs that could be carried out on a more modest scale: his plan in the 1930s for the little town of Nemours in North Africa, with its geometric grouping of domino structures, set the fashion for high-rise slabs. Both images in turn have had a massive impact upon the minds of today's architect–city planners. The postwar housing estates of the London County Council record that influence at its best, sometimes in more ingratiating forms than he had pictured—as in the Alton estate at Roehampton, on land already richly landscaped by the original suburban owners—but also at its worst, as in their overemphatic repetitions of his Unity House slab in another area.

In the United States the standard urban renewal projects fostered by the federal government have been designed in a similar socially heedless fashion. Le Corbusier meanwhile has kept on modifying his original proposals, which were exclusively metropolitan and bureaucratic. In more recent statements since 1945 he has envisaged small, better-balanced, more self-contained communities, as complementary members of the metropolis; and in Chandigarh he even took over from Albert Mayer and Matthew Nowicki, the first planners, the outlines of the Radburn plan, with its series of neighborhood superblocks and its inner green walkways.

But the gigantic scale of that city demands a completely motorized population: that is the mischief of excessive openness. Though Le Corbusier's buildings are low, his walks are long, and the central public buildings swim in space under a torrid summer sun whose heat further penalizes pedestrian circulation. The misplaced openness of Le Corbusier's new capital turns the great buildings and monuments into isolated works of sculpture, exhibited as in a high outdoor museum. They are meant to be visited piously or admired occasionally at a distance: not to serve as intimate architectural companions in the daily traffic of the city, visible at all times, with sufficient detail to hold the eye and refresh the spirit even under intimate inspection. In its excessive, official openness this plan vies with Walter Burley Griffin's purely suburban conception of the Australian capital of Canberra: but already it is plain that Griffin's plan is the better one.

Le Corbusier was, of course, right in thinking that the functions of business and transportation could be more efficiently handled in structures specially designed to fit modern needs; he was right, too, in thinking that a basic pattern of order is essential to the full enjoyment of the city, particularly in our own age, in which a multitude of sensual and symbolic stimuli—print, sound, images—at every hour of the day, would produce overwhelming confusion if the general background were equally confused. So, too, he was correct in thinking that the skyscrapers of New York or Chicago should be thinned out, if they were to be visible from street level, or if the traffic avenues were to remain usable; and further, that sunlight, pure air, vegetation, along with order and measure, were essential components of any sound environment, whether urban or rural.

But in his contempt for historic and traditional forms, Le Corbusier lost not merely continuity with the past but likewise any sense of how much of the present he was also losing. His new conception of the City in a Park misconceived the nature and functions of both city and park.

The monotony of Le Corbusier's favored forms has expressed the dominant forces of our age, the facts of bureaucratic control and mechanical organization, equally visible in business, in industry, in government, in education. That fact itself constituted one of its meretricious attractions. But until Le Corbusier theoretically destroyed the historic tissue of the city, with its great complexity of form and its innumerable variations even within the fixed geometry of the gridiron plan, the prevailing bureaucratic pattern had been modified by many human, sometimes all-too-human, departures. The old skyscrapers of Wall Street or the Loop may have been anarchic in their efforts to pre-empt space or claim attention, but they did not present the faceless conformist image of present-day Park Avenue. As for urban compositions that have been more directly influenced by Le Corbusier's idea of the City in a Park—the collection of office buildings in the Pittsburgh Triangle, for example—they might as well be in a suburb as in the city itself. Even the open space around these buildings has become meaningless in terms of light and air, for all-day fluorescent lighting and air conditioning flout the one benefit that would justify this type of plan.

Unmodified by any realistic conception of urban functions and urban purposes, apart from the bureaucratic process itself, Le Corbusier's City in a Park turns out in fact to be a suburban conception. By its very isolation of functions that should be closely connected to every other aspect of city life, and by its magnification of the forces that govern metropolitan life today, it can be detached from the organic structure of the city and planted anywhere. Even the space around Le Corbusier's skyscrapers has an ambivalent function, for the City in a Park has now taken a more acceptable, commercially attractive form, and has become a City in a Parking Lot.

When we follow this whole process through, we discover that the freedom of movement, the change of pace, the choice of alternative destinations, the spontaneous encounters, the range of social choices and the proliferation of marketing opportunities, in fact, the multifarious life of a city, have been traded away for expressways, parking space, and vertical circulation. It is not for nothing that so many of the new urban housing projects, filled with twenty-story skyscrapers, are called villages: the conformities they demand, the social opportunities they offer, are as limited as those of a village. These islands of habitation in the midst of a sea of parking lots might have densities of five hundred inhabitants a residential acre, and be part of a megalopolitan complex holding tens of millions of inhabitants, but the total mass still would lack the complex character of a city.

In short, the City in a Park does nothing to foster the constant give and take, the interchange of goods and ideas, the expression of life as a constant dialogue with other men in the midst of a collective setting that itself contributes to the animation and intensity of that dialogue. The architectural blankness of such a city mirrors the only kind of life possible under it: overall control at the top, docile conformity at the bottom.

While Le Corbusier's image of the city is still often regarded as the last word in modern design, it combines, in fact, the three chief mistakes of the nineteenth century. These misconceptions destroyed the classic form of the city, as it had existed almost from the beginning, and replaced it with a succession of urban and suburban wastelands: anticities.

The first mistake was the overvaluation of mechanization and standardization as ends in themselves, without respect to the human purpose to be served. The second was the theoretical destruction of every vestige of the past, without preserving any links in form or visible structure between past and future, thereby overmagnifying the importance of the present and at the same time threatening with destruction whatever permanent values the present might in turn create, and nullifying any lessons that might be learned from its errors. This is the error of the "disposable urban container." Finally, Le Corbusier's concept carried to its extreme the necessary reaction against urban overcrowding: the mistake of separating and extravagantly overspacing facilities whose topographic concentration is essential for their daily use.

Now that a sufficient number of adaptations of Le Corbusier's leading concepts are in existence, we begin to have an insight into both their social and their aesthetic limitations; for the two are, in fact, closely connected. The visual open space that this planning produces has no relation to the functional open space, space as used for non-visual purposes, for meeting and conversation, for the play of children, for gardening, for games, for promenades, for the courting of lovers, for outdoor relaxation. At the high density of 250 to 500 people per acre, what seems by the trick of low coverage an ample provision of open space turns out to be miserly.

The aesthetic monotony of these high-rise dominoes is, in fact, a reflection of their social regimentation: they do not represent, in architectural form, the variety that actually exists in a mixed human community; uniformity and conformity are written all over them. Such freedom, such family intimacy, such spontaneous utilization of the natural environment, and such architectural identity as even the old-fashioned railroad suburb offered have been forfeited without any equivalent return.

The City in a Park, as so far conceived by Le Corbusier and his followers, is a blind alley. Yet its basic ingredients, the more adroit use of present-day mechanical facilities and the constant respect for the natural conditions for health and child nurture, must play a part in any better image of the future city. Neither high-rise structures, vertical transportation, spatial separation, multiple expressways and subways, nor wholesale parking space will serve to produce a community that can take advantage of all the facilities modern civilization offers and work them into an integrated urban form. Even when assembled together in orderly fashion, they still do not constitute a city. Before the architect can make his contribution to this new form, his private services to his client must be combined with a better understanding of the nature and functions of the city as a device for achieving the maximum amount of human cooperation and crystallizing in more durable and visible form the whole creative process.

HOME REMEDIES
FOR
URBAN CANCER

Ever since 1948, when the national Urban Renewal Act was passed, the cities of this country have been assaulted by a series of vast federally aided building operations. These large-scale operations have brought only small-scale benefits to the city. The people who gain by the government's handouts are not the displaced slum dwellers but the new investors and occupants. In the name of slum clearance, many quarters of Greater New York that would still have been decently habitable with a modest expenditure of capital have been razed, and their inhabitants, along with the shopkeepers and tavern keepers who served them, have been booted out, to resettle in even slummier quarters.

Even in municipal projects designed to rehouse the displaced slum dwellers or people of equivalent low income, the physical improvements have been only partial and the social conditions of the inhabitants have been worsened through further social stratification—segregation, actually—of people by their income levels. The standard form of housing favored by the federal government and big-city administrators is high-rise slabs—bleak structures of ten to twenty stories. Superficially, these new buildings are an immense improvement over both the foul Old Law Tenements of New York and the New Law (1901) Tenements that covered the newer sections of the Bronx and the Upper West Side up to 1930. The latest model buildings are only two rooms deep; all the flats have outside exposure; the structures are widely spaced around small play areas and patches of fenced grass spotted with benches. Not merely are the buildings open to the sun and air on all sides but they are also as bugproof and verminproof as concrete floors and brick walls can make them; they have steam heat, hot and cold water, standard bathroom equipment, and practically everything a

184

well-to-do family could demand except large rooms and doors for their closets; the absence of the latter is an idiotic economy achieved at the expense of the tenants, who must provide curtains.

These buildings, with all their palpable hygienic virtues, are the response to a whole century of investigation of the conditions of housing among the lower-income groups in big cities, particularly New York. Shortly after 1835, when the city's first deliberately congested slum tenement was built, on Cherry Street, the health commissioner of New York noted the appallingly high incidence of infant mortality and infectious diseases among the poor, and he correlated this with overcrowding of rooms, overcrowding of building plots, poor ventilation, and lack of running water and indoor toilet facilities. For a large part of the nineteenth century, in all big cities, housing conditions worsened, even for the upper classes, despite the common boast that this was "the Century of Progress." It was only because of the most massive effort by physicians, sanitarians, housing reformers, and architects that legislation established minimum standards for light, air, constructional soundness, and human decency.

Unfortunately, it turned out that better housing was more expensive housing, and at the rents the lower-income groups could afford no landlord could be tempted to invest. The most profitable rentals came from congested slum housing. So pressing were the economic and sanitary problems in urban housing that when finally government aid on a large scale was secured, the dominant conception of good lower-income housing was naturally centered on physical improvements. Our current high-rise housing projects find their sanction in the need to wipe out more than a century of vile housing and provide space for people who have been living in slums holding three hundred to seven hundred people an acre. On sound hygienic terms, this demand can be met within the limited areas provided only by tall buildings whose grim walls are overshadowing ever-larger sections of Manhattan.

There is nothing wrong with these buildings except that, humanly speaking, they stink. What is worse, after a few years of occupancy, some of them stink in an olfactory sense, for children, out of mischief or embarrassment, often use the elevators as toilets. And the young have found the automatic elevators marvelous instruments for annoying adults; putting them out of order or stalling them has become a universal form of play. London County Council administrators have told me the same story about the conflict between high-rise urban aesthetics and the spirit of youth in city elevator shafts. By the very nature of the high-rise slab, its inhabitants are cut off from the surveillance and protection of neighbors and passers-by, particularly when in elevators. In some housing projects, the possibility of casual violence,

186 THE URBAN PROSPECT

rape, even murder, a rising menace in all our big cities, is conspicuously present. The daily life of the inhabitants, besides being subject to the insistent bureaucratic regulation of the management, labors under a further handicap. Because of a long-standing rule, only lately removed, urban renewal projects could not provide marketing facilities to replace those they had wiped out; often the housewife had to trundle her heavy shopping bags many blocks and was denied the convenience of sending a small member of the family to the corner store.

In short, though the hygiene of these new structures was incomparably superior to anything the market had offered in the past—and in sunlight, air, and open view definitely superior to the congested superslums of the rich on Park Avenue—most of the other desirable facilities and opportunities had descended to a lower level.

From time to time in *The New Yorker* I have pointed out these deficiencies in public housing in New York; as far back as 1942, when one of the first high-rise projects opened in the Navy Yard area of Brooklyn, I foretold that it would become the slum that it now notoriously is. But the person who has lately followed through on all the dismal results of current public housing and has stirringly presented them is Jane Jacobs, whose book *The Death and Life of Great American Cities* has been an exciting theme for dinner-table conversation all over the country this past year. Though her examples of desirable urban quarters are drawn chiefly from New York—indeed, largely from a few tiny pockets of New York—the bad fashionable patterns she points to are universal.

A few years ago, Mrs. Jacobs stepped into prominence at a planners' conference at Harvard. Into the foggy atmosphere of professional jargon that usually envelops such meetings, she blew like a fresh, offshore breeze to present a picture, dramatic but not distorted, of the results of displacing large neighborhood populations to facilitate largescale rebuilding. She pointed out a fact to which many planners and administrators had been indifferent—that a neighborhood is not just a collection of buildings but a tissue of social relations and a cluster of warm personal sentiments, associated with the familiar faces of the doctor and the priest, the butcher and the baker and the candlestick maker, not least with the idea of "home." Sanitary, steam-heated apartments, she observed, are no substitute for warmhearted neighbors, even if they live in verminous cold-water flats. The chat across the air shaft, the little changes of scene as a woman walks her baby or tells her troubles with her husband to the druggist, the little flirtations that often attend the purchase of a few oranges or potatoes, all season the housewife's day and mean more than mere physical shelter. It is no real gain to supplant the sustaining intimacies of long neighborhood association with the professional advice of a social worker or a psychiatrist, attempting by a wholly inadequate therapy to combat the trauma of social dislocation.

Mrs. Jacobs gave firm shape to a misgiving that many people had begun to express. But she saw more deeply into the plight of both those who were evicted and those who came back to living in homogenized and sterilized barracks. These barracks had been conceived in terms of bureaucratic regimentation, financial finagling, and administrative convenience, without sufficient thought for the diverse needs of personal and family life, thus producing a human void that matched the new architectural void. In this process, even valuable buildings, though cherished landmarks in the life of the community, are often destroyed, so that the operation may "start clean," without any encumbrances.

Mrs. Jacobs's criticism established her as a person to be reckoned with. Here was a new kind of "expert," very refreshing in current planning circles, where minds unduly fascinated by computers carefully confine themselves to asking only the kinds of questions that computers can answer and are completely negligent of the human contents or the human results. This able woman had used her eyes and, even more admirably, her heart to assay the human result of large-scale housing, and she was saying, in effect, that these toplofty barracks that now crowd the city's skyline and overshadow its streets were not fit for human habitation. . . .

From a mind so big with fresh insights and pertinent ideas, one naturally expected a book of equally large dimensions. But whereas "Sense and Sensibility" could have been the title of her Harvard discourse, what she sets forth in *The Death and Life of Great American Cities* comes close to deserving the secondary title of "Pride and Prejudice." The shrewd critic of dehumanized housing and faulty design is still evident, and has applied some of her sharp observations and her political experience to the analysis of urban activities as a whole. But this excellent clinical analyst has been joined by a more dubious character who has patched together out of the bits and pieces of her personal observation nothing less than a universal theory about the life and death of our great—by "great," Mrs. Jacobs seems always to mean "big"— American cities. This new costume of theory, though not quite as airy as the emperor's clothes, exposes such large areas of naked unawareness that it undermines many of Mrs. Jacobs's sound statements. Some of her boldest planning proposals, indeed, rest on faulty data, inadequate evidence, and startling miscomprehensions of views contrary to hers. This does not make her book easy to appraise.

Before seeking to do justice to Mrs. Jacobs's work as a whole, I must say a word about her first chapter, in which she does not do justice to herself. Ironically, this doughty opponent of urban renewal projects turns out to have a huge private urban renewal project of her own. Like a construction gang bulldozing a site clean of all habitations, good or bad, she bulldozes out of existence every desirable innovation in urban planning during the last century, and every competing idea, without even a pretense of critical evaluation. She is sensibly opposed to sterile high-rise projects, but she is even more opposed to the best present examples of urban residential planning, such as Chatham Village, in Pittsburgh, and she seems wholly to misunderstand their nature, their purpose, and their achievement. Her misapprehension of any plans she regards as subversive of her own private concepts of urban planning leads her to astounding statements, and she even attempts to liquidate possible opponents by treating anyone who has attempted to improve the design of cities by another method as if such people were determined enemies of the city. To wipe out her most dangerous rival, she concentrates her attack on Sir Ebenezer Howard, the founder of the New Towns (Garden City) movement in England. Her handling of him is, for those who know anything of his biography, comic. Howard, it happens, devoted the last quarter century of his life to the improvement of cities, seeking to find by actual experiment the right form and size, and the right balance between urban needs and purposes and those of the rural environment. Under the rubric of the "garden city," he reintroduced into city building two important ideas: the notion that there was a functional limit to the area and population of a city; and the notion of providing for continued population growth by founding more towns, which would form "town clusters," to perform the more complex functions of a metropolis without wiping out the open recreational spaces and the rural activities of the intervening countryside. . . .

Ebenezer Howard, Mrs. Jacobs insists, "set spinning powerful and city-destroying ideas. He conceived that the way to deal with the city's functions was to sort and sift out of the whole certain simple uses, and to arrange each of these in relative self-containment. He focused on the provision of wholesome housing as the central problem to which everything else was subsidiary." No statement could be further from the truth. Mrs. Jacobs's wild characterization contradicts Howard's clearly formulated idea of the garden city as a balanced, many-sided, urban community. In the same vein, Mrs. Jacobs's acute dislike of nearly every improvement in town planning is concentrated in one omnibus epithet expressive of her utmost contempt: "Radiant Garden City Beautiful." Obviously, neither radiance (sunlight), nor gardens, nor spaciousness, nor beauty can have any place in Mrs. Jacobs's picture of a great city.

I shall say no more of Mrs. Jacobs's lack of historical knowledge and scholarly scruple except that her disregard of easily ascertainable facts is all too frequent. An English reviewer has charitably called her an enfant terrible; terrible or not, she has become a rampant public figure in the cities movement, and she has a sufficiently large uncritical following even among supposedly knowledgeable professors of planning like Charles Abrams to require a rigorous appraisal of her work lest all of it be accepted as holy writ.

"This book is an attack on current city planning and rebuilding." With these words Mrs. Jacobs introduces herself. An exhaustive critical analysis and appraisal of the torrent of urban renewal that has been reducing areas of New York and other cities to gargantuan nonentities of high-rise buildings has been long overdue. To have someone look over the situation with her rude fresh eye seemed almost a gift from heaven. Unfortunately, her assault on current planning rests on an odd view of the nature and function and structure of big cities. Underneath her thesis—that the sidewalk, the street, and the neighborhood, in all their higgledy-piggledy unplanned casualness, are the very core of a dynamic urban life—lies a preoccupation that is almost an obsession, the prevention of criminal violence in big cities.

Despite the grandiloquent title of her book, Mrs. Jacobs's obsession prevents her from presenting a total view of the great metropolis, in life or in death: she beholds it just in fragments, especially the rundown fragment of Greenwich Village she has lived in and sentimentally over-values. While she exults in the mere size of New York and the immense diversity of its activities, she overlooks even the most obvious price of that size in millions of dismal man-hours of daily bus and subway transportation and even longer commuter journeys by rail and car, just as she overlooks the endless rows and blocks and square miles of almost identical houses, spreading from Brooklyn to Queens, from Queens over Long Island, that have not the least touch of the diversity she finds so valuable in her own familiar Village quarters.

When the inhabitants of Greenwich Village go to work each day, they have the unique grace, in Mrs. Jacobs's rose-spectacled eyes, of performers in a ballet. But she has no epithet and no image for the daily walk to the subway station, or for the tense scrimmage and grim incarceration of the subway ride. She recognizes the existence of "gray areas," with their overpowering monotony. But she dogmatically attributes this to the low density of population, even though the post-1904 Bronx, one of the grayest of gray areas, is a high-density borough. And she ignores the appalling prison routine that most of the inhabitants of a great city have to follow, a state that in some measure accounts for some of the aggressive reactions that are now visible. Her great American city has as its sole background the humble life of a very special, almost unique historic quarter, Greenwich Village: for long a backwater whose lack of dynamism accounts for such pleasant features as it has successfully retained.

With Greenpoint and East New York, with the Erie Basin and Harlem, with Flatbush and Canarsie, Mrs. Jacobs's analysis has nothing to do. She does not even trace to its turbid source the violence overflowing into the area around Columbia University. Had Mrs. Jacobs been more aware of urban realities that long antedated high-rise housing, she would have admitted that the crime rate on Morningside Heights is not, as she suggests, the result of recently planning superblocks or segregating urban functions. What is more, one solitary walk through Harlem should have made Mrs. Jacobs revise her notions of the benefits of high density, pedestrian-filled streets, crosslines of circulation, and a mixture of primary economic activities on every residence block, for all these "ideal" conditions are fulfilled in Harlem—without achieving the favorable results she expects of her prescription.

Mrs. Jacobs gives the show away on the first page, in introducing her new principles of town planning. "I shall mainly be writing about common ordinary things: for instance, what kinds of city streets are safe and what kinds are not; why some city parks are marvellous and others are vice traps and death traps," Mrs. Jacobs says. This sentence reveals an overruling fear of living in the big city she so openly adores, and, as all New Yorkers know, she has considerable reason for fear. Her underlying animus fosters some of her most sensitive interpretations of the quality of life in a genuine neighborhood, but it also fosters a series of amateurish planning proposals that will not stand up under the most forbearing examination.

From her point of view, one of the chief mischiefs of contemporary planning is that it reduces the number of streets by creating superblocks reserved almost exclusively for pedestrian movement, free from through wheeled traffic, with the space once pre-empted by unnecessary paved streets turned into open areas for play or provided with benches and plantations for the sedentary enjoyment of adults. Such a separation of automobile and pedestrian walks runs counter to her private directives for a safe and animated neighborhood; namely, to multiply the number of cross streets, to greatly widen the sidewalks, to reduce all other open spaces, and to place many types of shops and services on streets now devoted solely to residences. The street is her patent substitute for the more adequate meeting places which traditional cities have always boasted.

What is behind Mrs. Jacobs's idea of assigning exclusively to the street the mixed functions and diverse activities of a well-balanced neighborhood unit? The answer, I repeat, is simple: her ideal city is mainly an organization for the prevention of crime. To her, the best way to overcome criminal violence is such a mixture of economic and social activities at every hour of the day that the streets will never be empty of pedestrians, and that each shopkeeper, each householder, compelled to find both his main occupations and his recreations on the street, will serve as watchman and policeman, each knowing who is to be trusted and who not, who is defiant of the law and who upholds it, who can be taken in for a cup of coffee and who must be kept at bay. . . .

In judging Mrs. Jacobs's interpretations and her planning prescriptions, I speak as a born and bred New Yorker, who in his time has walked over almost every street in Manhattan, and who has lived in every kind of neighborhood and in every type of housing, from a private row house on the West Side to an Old Law dumbbell railroad flat, from a grim walkup apartment off Washington Square to the thirtieth floor of an East Side hotel, from a block of row houses with no shops on Hicks Street in Brooklyn Heights to a two-room flat over a lunchroom in the same general neighborhood, with the odor of stale fat filtering through the windows, and with a tailor, a laundry, a florist, grocery stores, and restaurants—Mrs. Jacobs's favorite constellation for "urban liveliness"—immediately at hand. Like a majority of my fellow citizens, I am still unregenerate enough to prefer the quiet flat with a back garden and a handsome church beyond it on Hicks Street to all the dingy "liveliness" of Clinton Street as it was back in the twenties. Finally, for ten years I lived in Sunnyside Gardens, the kind of well-planned neighborhood Mrs. Jacobs despises: modestly conceived for people with low incomes, but composed of one-, two-, and three-family houses and flats, with private gardens and public open spaces, plus playgrounds, meeting rooms, and an infants' school. Not utopia, but better than any existing New York neighborhood, even Mrs. Jacobs's backwater in Greenwich Village.

As one who has spent more than fifty years in New York, speaking to a native of Scranton who has not, I must remind Mrs. Jacobs that many parts of the city she denounces because they do not conform to her peculiar standards—and therefore, she reasons, are a prey to violence—were for over the better part of a century both economically quite sound and humanly secure. In the urban range of my boyhood, there were occasional rowdy gangs even half a century ago—we always ran for cover when the West Ninety-eighth Street gang invaded our street—but their more lethal activities were confined largely to their own little ghettos and nearby territory, like Hell's Kitchen or the Gas House District. With the policeman on his beat, a woman could go home alone at any hour of the night on a purely residential street without apprehension. (She could even, astonishingly, trust the police-man.) As for the great parks that Mrs. Jacobs fears as an invitation to crime, and disparages as a recreation space on the strange ground that no one any longer can safely use them, she treats as a chronic ailment a state that would have seemed incredible as late as 1935. Until the Age of Extermination widened the area of violence, one could walk the eight hundred acres of Central Park at any time of the day without fear of molestation.

Certainly it was not any mistake of Frederick Law Olmsted's in laying out Riverside Drive, Morningside Park, and St. Nicholas Park that has made these large parks unusable shambles today. What is re-sponsible for their present emptiness is something Mrs. Jacobs disre-gards—the increasing pathology of the whole mode of life in the great metropolis, a pathology that is directly proportionate to its overgrowth, its purposeless materialism, its congestion, and its insensate disorder—the very conditions she vehemently upholds as marks of urban vitality. That sinister state manifests itself not merely in the statistics of crime and mental disorder but in the enormous sums spent on narcotics, sedatives, stimulants, hypnotics, and tranquilizers to keep the popula-tion of our "great" cities from coming to terms with the vacuous desper-ation of their daily lives and with the even more vacuous horrors that their more lunatic rulers and scientific advisers seem to regard as a reasonable terminus for the human race. Lacking any sense of an intelli-gible purpose or a desirable goal, the inhabitants of our "great Ameri-can cities" are simply "waiting for Godot."

Mrs. Jacobs is at her best in dealing with small, intimate urban areas. She understands that the very life of a neighborhood depends upon the maintenance of the human scale, for it fosters relations be-tween visible people sharing a common environment, who meet face to face without intermediaries, who are aware of their personal identity and their common interests even though they may not exchange a word. This sense of belonging rests, however, not on a metropolitan dynamism but on continuity and stability, the special virtues of the village. These virtues remain conspicuous features of Greenwich Vil-lage, the area in New York Mrs. Jacobs favors as a model of healthy urban activity. By the beginning of the nineteenth century this part of the city, the old Ninth Ward, was so well defined, so individualized, that the city-planning commissioners of 1811 did not dare to make it con-form to the gridiron pattern they imposed with geometric rigor on the rest of the city.

The larger part of this homogeneous area consisted of two- and three-story red brick houses with white porticoes, some of the best of which, those on Varick and King Streets, were destroyed to make way for the Seventh Avenue extension. For long, a loyal population clung to these quarters partly because—as an old friend of mine who lived there remembers—though the residents of the oldest houses had to draw their supply of water from a common pump in the backyard, they were far cheaper than more up-to-date accommodations. This historic enclave, a weedy backwater left behind in the tide of urban growth, would have lost most of the very features Mrs. Jacobs admires, including its short streets, if it had been sufficiently "dynamic." The Village's two special characteristics, indeed, make mock of her "new" principles—its original low density of population and its well-defined architectural character, which graciously set it off from the up-and-coming brown-stone-front city that leaped beyond it. In short, old Greenwich Village was almost as much a coherent, concrete entity, with definite boundary lines, as a planned neighborhood unit in a British New Town.

The contradiction between Mrs. Jacobs's perceptions of the intimate values of neighborhood life and her unqualified adoration of metropolitan bigness and activism remains unreconciled, largely because she rejects the principles of urban design that would unite these complementary qualities. Her ultimate criteria of sound metropolitan planning are dynamism, density, and diversity, but she never allows herself to contemplate the unfortunate last term in the present series—disintegration. Yet her concern for local habits and conventions points her in the right direction for overcoming this ultimate disintegration: the recognition of the neighborhood as a vital urban entity, with an inner balance and an inner life whose stability and continuity are necessary for rebuilding the kind of community that the metropolis, in all its cataclysmic economic voracity—"cataclysmic" is Mrs. Jacobs's happy epithet—has destroyed.

She recognizes that a city is more than buildings, but she fails to perceive that a neighborhood is more than its streets and street activities. The new street system she proposes, with twice the number of intersecting north-and-south streets, would do nothing to give visible reality to the social functions of a neighborhood—those performed by school, church, market, clinic, park, library, tavern, eating house, theater. Mrs. Jacobs has no use for the orderly distribution of these activities or the handsome design of their necessary structures; she prefers the hit-and-miss distribution of the present city. No wonder she opposes the admirable work of Clarence Stein and Henry Wright. These pioneer planners have repeatedly demonstrated—in Sunnyside Gardens, on Long Island; in Radburn, New Jersey; in Chatham Village, Pittsburgh —how much superior a well-planned, visibly homogeneous neighborhood can be to the sort of random community she advocates.

In the multidimensional order of the city Mrs. Jacobs favors, beauty does not have a place. Yet it is the beauty of great urban cathedrals and palaces, the order of great monastic structures or the university precincts of Oxford and Cambridge, the serenity and spaciousness of the great squares of Paris, London, Rome, Edinburgh, that have preserved intact the urban cores of truly great cities over many centuries. Meanwhile, the sordid dynamism of the dingier parts of these same cities has constantly proved uneconomic, inefficient, and self-destructive.

Instead of asking what are the best possible urban patterns today for renovating our disordered cities, Mrs. Jacobs asks only under what conditions can existing slums and blighted areas preserve their congenial humane features without any serious improvements in their physical structure or their mode of life. Her simple formula does not suggest that her eyes have ever been hurt by ugliness, sordor, confusion, or her ears offended by the roar of trucks smashing through a once quiet residential neighborhood, or her nose assaulted by the chronic odors of ill-ventilated, unsunned housing at the slum standards of congestion that alone meet her ideal standards for residential density. If people are housed in sufficiently congested quarters—provided only that the buildings are not set within superblocks—and if there is a sufficiently haphazard mixture of functions and activities, her social and aesthetic demands are both satisfied. She has exposed these convictions in a flat statement: "A city cannot be a work of art." The citizens of Florence, Siena, Venice, and Turin will please take note! But of course Mrs. Jacobs would have her own smug answer to this: if these places are beautiful, they are not and never were cities.

What has happened is that Mrs. Jacobs has jumped from the quite defensible position that good physical structures and handsome design are not everything in city planning to the callow notion that they do not matter at all. That beauty, order, spaciousness, clarity of purpose may be worth having for their direct effect on the human spirit even if they do not promote dynamism, increase the turnover of goods, or reduce criminal violence seems not to occur to Mrs. Jacobs. This is aesthetic philistinism with a vengeance.

Mrs. Jacobs's most original proposal, then, as a theorist of metropolitan development, is to turn its chronic symptom of disorganization—excessive congestion—into a remedy, by deliberately enlarging the scope of the disease. It is her belief, unshaken by irrefutable counter-evidence, that congestion and disorder are the normal, indeed the most desirable, conditions of life in cities. But it is now a well-established fact in biology that overcrowded quarters produce conditions of stress even in animals, a state marked by anxiety and hostility. Elbow room is a general condi-

tion for even animal health. Since her obstinate belief in high population density underlies Mrs. Jacobs's entire argument, it gratuitously
vitiates even her valid contributions.

Yet despite blind spots and omissions, this book at times offers
valuable insights into the complex activities of the city—especially
those urban functions that flourish precisely because of all the inter-
changes that take place, by chance no less than by plan, most frequently
in cities that have reached a certain order of bigness and complexity.
Mrs. Jacobs recognizes how much of value they will leave behind, unlike the big corporations and research laboratories that are stampeding
into suburbia, in exchange for temporary access to a golf course, a
private airfield, or a few domestic acres. She also recognizes, by observation and experience, the communal nucleus of the city—the spontaneous "primary" association of families and neighbors, upon which all
the later complexities of urban life are based. And though she dislikes
the notion of a planned "neighborhood unit," she chooses for her normal neighborhood the size that Clarence Perry, in his studies for the
Regional Plan of New York back in the twenties, hit upon as roughly
the proper size for such a unit—about five thousand people. "We shall
have something solid to chew on," she observes, "if we think of city
neighborhoods as mundane organs of self-government. Our failures
with city neighborhoods are, ultimately, failures in localized self-government. And our successes are successes at localized self-government.
I am using self-government in its broadest sense, meaning both the
informal and formal self-management of society." . . .

. . . About the long-term remoralization of this demoralized metropolitan community, she is emphatically right: the stabilities of the family and the neighborhood are the basic sources of all higher forms of
morality, and when they are lacking, the whole edifice of civilization is
threatened. When no one cares for anyone else, because we have all
become mere computer digits or Social Security numbers, the elaborate
fabric of urban life breaks down. Out of this rejection and isolation and
emptiness comes, probably, the boiling hostility of both juvenile and
adult delinquent.

Mrs. Jacobs's concern for the smallest unit of urban life is, then,
pertinent and well directed. . . . She has had enough political experience
to recognize that the city, by its very size, has got out of hand, particularly out of the hands of its own citizens, and that its hugeness causes
it to be misplanned and maladministered. Because they lack any integral organs for formulating policies or making decisions, or even con-
testing the proposals of the mayor, the city-planning commissioners, the
borough presidents, or Mr. Moses, the political pressure exerted by local
areas is feeble and sporadic, and achieved only with great effort through

ad hoc organizations. The result has been a docile conformity by our governing agencies to other more powerful financial influences, unconcerned with the common good.

Mrs. Jacobs realizes that if public officials are to be made more responsive to public opinion and to be prevented from making wanton changes in neighborhoods to favor lending institutions, big contractors, and rich tenants instead of the old residents, politics must be organized on a local basis. So, too, her proposed new neighborhood organ of government, like the English borough and unlike the purely formal area of an assembly district, must have some coherence and integrity as an economic and social unit. Functions that were once pushed to the periphery of the city, or packed into specialized enclaves, like the Seventh Avenue garment district, should be distributed over wider areas in these local-government units. For smaller metropolises like Pittsburgh, she suggests that thirty thousand would be the right population for such units, while for cities as big as Chicago and New York, she chooses a hundred thousand, and she recognizes that to form these boroughs into active municipal entities industry and business must be established in these sub-centers. . . .

I take a certain mischievous delight in pointing out that the 30,000 she has hit on for a self-governing "district" is precisely the . . . number Ebenezer Howard—the arch-villain in Mrs. Jacobs's private urban melodrama—tentatively chose for his original Garden City. Nor do I think less of her proposals because . . . the wise Howard got there before Mrs. Jacobs. But the recent Royal Commission in Great Britain on the government of London, which included such a masterly interpreter of urban government as Professor William Robson, concluded that 100,-000 to 250,000 was the desirable population for the boroughs of Metropolitan London. If Mrs. Jacobs errs in laying down the ideal number for a borough, she errs in favor of the smaller unit. I salute her as a reluctant ally of old Ebenezer Howard.

Mrs. Jacobs innocently believes that complexity and diversity are impossible without the kind of intense congestion that has in fact been emptying out the big city, hurling masses of people into the vast, curdled Milky Ways of suburbia. In the desire to enjoy amenities impossible at even a quarter of the density of population she considers desirable, millions of people are giving up the delights and stimulations of genuine city life. It is millions of quite ordinary people who cherish such suburban desires, not a few fanatical haters of the city, sunk in bucolic dreams. Now, it is this massive century-old drift to suburbia, not the building of superblocks or garden cities, that is mainly responsible for the dilapidation and the near-death of big cities. How could Mrs. Jacobs ignore this staring historic fact?

This movement toward the rural periphery in search of things that were the proud possession of every premechanized city has been helped by the most active enemies of the city—the overbudgeted highway programs that have riddled metropolitan areas with their gaping expressways and transformed civic cores into parking lots. Those who leave the city wish to escape its snarling violence and its sickening perversions of life, its traffic in narcotics and its gangster-organized lewdness, which break into the lives even of children. Not least, the suburban exiles seek to find at least nightly surcease from constant bureaucratic regimentation: Punch the time clock! Watch your step! Curb your dog! Do not spit! No parking! Get in line for a ticket! Move on! Keep off the grass! Follow the green line! Wait for the next train! Buy now, pay later! Don't buck the system! Take what you get! The refugees who leave the metropolis may not keep even the fleeting illusion of freedom and security and a normal family life for long: all too soon rising land values and high rents bring high-rise housing, asphalted parking lots, and asphyxiating traffic jams. But their reaction is evidence of their own spontaneous vitality and a quickened desire for autonomy, which most of the rest of their existence as members of a gigantic, overcongested, necessarily impersonal hive defeats. Strangely, the city that so insistently drives its population into the suburbs is the very same city that Mrs. Jacobs quaintly describes as "vital." She forgets that in organisms there is no tissue quite so "vital" or "dynamic" as cancer growths.

But if *The Death and Life of Great American Cities*, taken as a critique of modern city planning, is a mingling of sense and sentimentality, of mature judgments and schoolgirl howlers, how does it stand as an interpretation of the larger issues of urban development and urban renewal, which the title itself so boldly points to? Here again Mrs. Jacobs heads her argument in the right direction, toward matters that have been insufficiently appreciated or misinterpreted. No one has surpassed her in understanding the reasons for the great metropolis's complexity and the effect of this complexity, with its divisions of labor, its differentiations of occupations and interests, its valuable racial, national, and cultural variety, upon its daily activities. She recognizes that one cannot handle such a multidimensional social organization as one might handle a simple machine, designed for a single function. "A growing number of people have begun, gradually," she notes, "to think of cities as problems in organized complexity—organisms that are replete with unexamined, but obviously intricately interconnected, and surely understandable, relationships."

That is an admirable observation, but the author has forgotten the most essential characteristic of all organic growth—to maintain diversity and balance the organism must not exceed the norm of its species. Any ecological association eventually reaches the "climax stage," beyond which growth without deterioration is not possible.

Despite Mrs. Jacobs's recognition of organic complexity in the abstract, she has a very inadequate appreciation of the ecological setting of cities and neighborhoods; she brusquely turns her back to all but the segregated local environment. Yet the overgrowth of our big cities has destroyed those special environmental qualities that made their setting desirable and fostered their growth in the first place. The obvious result of the large-scale metropolitan congestion she advocates she flatly ignores—the poisoning of the human system with carbon monoxide and the two hundred known cancer-producing substances usually in the air, the muffling of the vital ultraviolet rays by smog, the befouling of streams and oceanside (once used for fishing and bathing) with human and industrial waste. This is something worse than an oversight; it is willful blindness.

Mrs. Jacobs approvingly quotes Dr. Karl Menninger's observation that the best remedies for delinquency are "plentiful contacts with other people, work, including even drudgery, and violent play." But the kind of congested conglomeration she advocates would provide no room for violent play, and no sufficient opportunity to find relief from the monotonous and depressing regimentation of the big city. From the days of Ur onward, city dwellers have always had the countryside close at hand. There their homicidal impulses could be exorcised by digging and delving, or by shooting at destructive animals, and there their need for spontaneous muscular exercise could be satisfied by swimming and boating and climbing rather than by knives, brass knuckles, and rumbles. (Emerson long ago prescribed a pasture and a wood lot as the best cure for juvenile village mischief; they didn't call it "juvenile delinquency" in his day.)

When they have reached a point long ago overpassed by New York, Chicago, London, Tokyo, and Moscow, big cities are under the necessity to expand their operations to a more capacious container—the region. The forces that have formed our cities in the past are now almost automatically, by their insensate dynamism, wrecking them and threatening to destroy whole countries and continents. Against this background, the problem of policing public thoroughfares against violence is minor; violence and vice are symptoms of those far graver forms of disorder that Mrs. Jacobs rules out of consideration because they challenge her rosily sentimental picture of the "great American city."

To blame the conditions in the congested, overgrown metropolis of today on the monumental scale and human hollowness of its urban renewal projects is preposterous, for this draws attention from the grim, enveloping realities that our whole metropolitan civilization confronts. The prevailing economic and technological forces in the big city have broken away from the ecological pattern, as well as from the moral inhibitions and the social codes and the religious ideals that once, however imperfectly, kept them under some sort of control, and reduced their destructive potentialities.

Just as there is no limit to the power assigned to those who build nuclear weapons and rockets, who plan space shots and lunatic-cool mass exterminations, so there is no limit to those who multiply motor roads for the sake of selling more motorcars and gasoline and road-building machinery, who push on the market every variety of drug, narcotic, chemical, and biotic agent, without regard to their ultimate effect on the landscape or upon any form of organic life. Under this "cataclysmic" eruption of power, with its lack of any goal but its own expansion, as Henry Adams presciently predicted half a century ago, "law disappears as a priori principle and gives place to force: morality becomes police: disintegration overcomes integration." The present metropolitan explosion is both the symbol and agent of this uncontrolled power. . . .

. . . No planning proposal now makes sense unless it is conceived in terms of truly human purposes—self-chosen, self-limited, and self-directed. The command of this unlimited, automatically expanding power is, again as Henry Adams wisely pointed out half a century ago, the central problem of our civilization. For Mrs. Jacobs to imagine that the horrifying human by-products of the city's disordered life can be eliminated by a few tricks of planning is as foolish as for her to imagine that a too generous supply of open spaces and superblocks fostered these symptoms.

If our urban civilization is to escape progressive dissolution, we shall have to rebuild it from the ground up. Certainly we shall have to do far more than alter street plans, humanize housing projects, or give wider geographic distribution to economic activities. Since such a general transformation will affect every aspect of life, urban politics and planning must of course play an active and significant part. But it is the formative, stabilizing, coherent, order-making forces, not the overdynamic ones, that now need special encouragement.

One cannot control destructive automatisms at the top unless one begins with the smallest units and restores life and initiative to them—to the person as a responsible human being, to the neighborhood as the primary organ not merely of social life but of moral behavior, and finally to the city, as an organic embodiment of the common life, in ecological balance with other cities, big and little, within the larger region in which they lie. A quick, purely local answer to these problems is no better than applying a homemade poultice for the cure of a cancer. And that, I am afraid, is what the more "original" Jacobsean proposals in *The Death and Life of Great American Cities* comes to.

RESTORED
CIRCULATION,
RENEWED LIFE

Most of the fancy cures that the experts have offered for New York's congestion are based on the innocent notion that the problem can be solved by increasing the capacity of the existing traffic routes, multiplying the number of ways of getting in and out of town, or providing more parking space for cars that should not have been lured into the city in the first place. Like the tailor's remedy for obesity—letting out the seams of the trousers and loosening the belt—this does nothing to curb the greedy appetites that have caused the fat to accumulate. . . .

Before we cut any more chunks out of our parks to make room for more automobiles or let another highway cloverleaf unfold, we should look at the transformation that has taken place during the last thirty years in Manhattan—a city that is steadily growing higher, denser, more complex, more clotted, more confused, its chaos solidifying into an insane mess of high buildings placed within a rigid urban framework that is hopelessly out of date. Our mild legal limits on the height of midtown buildings merely encourage tall structures in the very areas where traffic congestion is already close to paralysis, and we demolish crowded slums only to replace them with public-housing developments whose population densities, as high as 450 people an acre, are twice the average residential density of the city. We have consistently acted as if there were no relation between the number of people we dump on the land and the amount of congestion on the streets and arterial traffic routes.

Instead of maximizing facilities for motorcars, we should maximize the advantages of urban life. Parks, playgrounds, and schools, theaters, universities, and concert halls, to say nothing of a quiet night's sleep and a sunny outlook when one wakes up, are more important than any

201

benefits to be derived from the constant use of the automobile. To accomplish this improvement, we must devise a fundamental change in the city's whole pattern. The plain fact is that the high-density city is obsolete. If the city is to become livable again, and if its traffic is to be reduced to dimensions that can be handled, the city will have to bring all its powers to bear upon the problem of creating a new metropolitan pattern, not just unintegrated segments of such a pattern, like the dubious public-housing projects of the Lower East Side.

A large part of the present difficulty (as visible, by the way, in London, a city of low buildings, as it is in New York) is caused by the overemployment of one method of transportation, the private motorcar—a method that happens to be, on the basis of the number of people it transports, by far the most wasteful of urban space. Because we have apparently decided that the private motorcar has a sacred right to go anywhere, halt anywhere, and remain anywhere as long as its owner chooses, we have neglected other means of transportation, and have even permitted some public mass-transportation facilities to lapse while our municipalities and states spend public moneys in astronomical amounts to provide additional facilities for private transportation. The major corrective for this crippling overspecialization is to redevelop now despised modes of circulation—public vehicles and private feet, both of which are essential for mass movement. An effective modern city plan would use each kind in its proper place and to its proper extent —the walker, the vertical elevator, the private car, public surface and subway transportation, and (for longer distances) the railroad, to mention them in the order of increasing speed and capacity. Only when all five are made use of and planned in relation to one another can an efficient circulation of traffic be maintained. When, for example, the vertical elevator is used to excess, it produces a mass of buildings so high that no feat of horizontal mass transportation can handle the resulting human traffic without insufferable rush-hour jams. On the other hand, if the jumble of enterprises that now clutter the great midtown and downtown areas of the city were more generally dispersed—in the way that Macy's has established a branch in Flatbush, Bloomingdale's has set up one in Fresh Meadows, and so on—this would take some of the burden off the congested central district, and many people who are now long-distance shoppers by car might become pedestrians again.

I have suggested earlier the possibility that private vehicles may eventually be excluded from whole urban areas. Do not fancy that this is a mere whimsy. It has already happened in the Wall Street district, and through traffic has for a long time been barred from Manhattan's "play streets." . . . Fifth Avenue, during the hours when its traffic is stalled, is for all practical purposes now a pedestrian mall between Thirty-fourth and Fifty-ninth Streets. Removing the cars from it might make it as pleasant a place to shop in as Amsterdam's Kalverstraat or Buenos Aires's Calle Florida, both of which are sacred to pedestrians. The replanning of New York so that the pedestrian may again have a real place in the urban economy would have seemed fantastic only a generation ago. But if the pedestrian is to come back, it is necessary, for both his safety and his health, to insulate his promenades from the traffic thoroughfare, just as it is necessary to keep motorcars from entering areas where they do not belong and to provide for their swift movement through areas where they do belong. . . .

The principle of separating walkers from drivers, which involves planning whole neighborhoods at a time, is known to planners as the Radburn idea, after the planned town of Radburn, New Jersey, . . . but as a matter of fact it was first embodied in the plan of medieval Venice, whose canals carried the swift-moving traffic of another age. Until Radburn was designed, in 1928, no professional planner seemed able to understand that the extraordinary charm of Venice, which persists despite its overcrowding and decay, is due partly to the fact that each neighborhood was planned as a unit, for the benefit of the foot walker, and is not menaced by the rumble and roar of wheeled traffic, and that to go from one part of the city to a distant part one uses an entirely different transportation system, which never suffers any interruption by the pedestrian and does not interrupt his progress, either. Leonardo da Vinci proposed to overcome the congestion of Milan by a similar separation of wheeled traffic from pedestrian walks. The first modern planners to effect such separation were Olmsted and Vaux, in their brilliant plan for Central Park. Their scheme provided separate ways for the pedestrian, the horseback rider, and the carriage driver—to say nothing of confining commercial traffic to the "expressway" transverses—and it minimized the number of intersections by using overpasses and underpasses. If you examine the original plan of Central Park, you are examining a modern city plan, and if you walk through the Mall, noting how the traffic circulates around it, you have only to imagine buildings spaced at intervals along it, in related groups, to understand the principle of the superblock, which should be the minimum unit of land subdivision for the ideal big city, as against the standard New York block, whose inadequate size is one of the chief handicaps to a sensible redevelopment of our metropolis. Harvard Yard, in Cambridge, is a superblock; indeed, Cambridge is full of mid-nineteenth-century superblocks, with economical cul-de-sacs (rather than the conventional space-wasting gridiron of streets) and spacious gardens that have proved a happy barrier to overcrowding. And Rockefeller Center, too, is a quasi-superblock, though by no means a perfect example, since the unifying pedestrian feature is underground. While it maintains the gridiron street pattern, and has, in fact, even added a north-and-south street in its middle, it has at least demonstrated that a related group of office buildings, with plenty of room for pedestrian traffic, has vast advantages over the average helter-skelter city block.

The superblock—a unified campus, or precinct, as the British call it—is now the fundamental unit of modern urban planning. Instead of fronting buildings on streets and stringing stores and offices along avenues, modern planning insulates wheeled traffic and groups related buildings into campuses and unified working quarters, scaled to the pedestrian, with every necessary utility or facility concentrated close at hand. . . .

. . . The system of planning cities as a group of neighborhoods and precincts, with internal traffic minimized and outside traffic excluded, can be applied to old cities, too.

[But], no private agent, not even a wealthy life-insurance corporation, can undertake the task of regrouping the business, the industrial, and the residential areas of New York so as to facilitate their activities and reduce the amount of long-distance traffic in the city, for such a project requires not only immense sums of capital but the full use of public powers. At present, the municipality has no legal authorization to acquire by condemnation land for such large-scale redevelopment. The only agency that has public powers on a regional scale sufficient to deal with even the traffic aspect of the problem is the Port Authority. Unfortunately, this body has taken its privileges as a profit-making corporation more seriously than its public obligations as a planner of interstate industrial and civic enterprises, so instead of helping to solve our traffic problems, it is now one of the major interests fostering congestion, and it levies tolls on that congestion in every new tunnel or bridge it builds. To replace our present bungling palliatives for congestion with a plan for building a permanently attractive and livable city, the municipality needs legal powers to acquire and redevelop land for a variety of purposes. It should also be legally enabled to plan residential neighborhoods for more than merely the lower-income groups, and to plan business quarters on a far greater scale than Rockefeller Center.

In a city already as deeply committed to congestion as New York, with its property values, its system of taxation, its budgetary needs all geared to the policy of furthering congestion, genuine planning can make headway only gradually, and after much public education. In redesigning New York, we would, by the way, do well to heed the precedent, ignored by our planners, that was set long ago by Superintendent John Tildsley, who sited the public high schools erected in the city during his tenure so that the students would mainly travel against the prevalent streams of traffic morning and afternoon. Shopping centers and business quarters should be planned in the same fashion, to disperse some of the institutions of the city not to distant suburbs but to its own peripheral sections, instead of so concentrating them that it is necessary to pump almost four million people daily into the area south of Fifty-ninth Street.

If Manhattan were replanned in this new fashion, what would it look like? For another thirty years, it would hardly be possible to note the difference merely by gazing at the silhouette of the city; from a distance it would still be the same hilarious upheaval of steel and stone, romantic beyond words when viewed against the sunset from the approach to the Triborough Bridge or from the Brooklyn Bridge. But in time the great volcanic palisade of buildings in downtown and midtown Manhattan would give way to whole quarters in which the tall structures—none of them, even the office buildings, over fifteen stories high —would be widely spaced and placed near the mass-transportation routes and stops, while the trees and the grass-lined walks within these quarters would have the charm of a Paris boulevard, without the stench and noise that now make the café terraces of that city a humbug and an ordeal, as far as aesthetic pleasure goes. Each of these new quarters would have its own form and character, with its own social core of shops, markets, restaurants, churches, and schools, no longer scattered at random on through streets and avenues. Perhaps as many people as now enter the city from a distance by car would be able to take a salubrious walk to their work, just as the residents of the more fortunate areas of the East Side now do in the midtown area, though the salubrity of *their* walk is sadly tinctured by carbon monoxide. The great tides of traffic, instead of sluggishly moving in congested streams, would flow rapidly along new traffic routes, including crosstown expressways, and only vehicles that had business there would filter through the smaller capillaries into the unified neighborhoods. The daytime population of Manhattan would decrease, but as the city became more livable and the decayed neighborhoods above Fifty-ninth Street and below Twenty-third Street were restored to life, the living-in population might go up a little. One might again think of raising children in such a city without worrying about dope peddlers, juvenile delinquents, psychotics, and the dangers the young now encounter even on an afternoon walk in the public parks.

I do not suggest that the municipality can effect such a change

while the whole force of government highway aid and business enterprise is addressed to promoting the growing congestion in the area both
in and outside the city of New York. No internal corrective for congestion will work unless the principle of decentralization is applied to a
much wider area. The kind of planning that stops at the limits of the
metropolitan zone is as useless as that which stops at the legal limits of
the municipality. Such planning forgets that there is a new, modern
scale of distances, and that problems that were once soluble within a
city now involve public control and development of enormously larger
areas. We must not merely think of planning satellite communities
around New York; we must overcome the highway engineers' itch to
congeal into a solid urban mass towns and rural areas that should retain
their individuality and their comparative independence. If this kind of
long-range thinking gives anyone a headache, he is at liberty to exchange it for our present headache—a New York inhabited by a shifting, overcrowded, demoralized population, and a superhighway system
jammed with people fleeing not from disaster but from the very city
that is supposed to offer all the benefits that make life desirable.

THE REGIONAL
FRAMEWORK OF
CIVILIZATION

Regions—To Live In

The hope of the city lies outside itself. Focus your attention on the cities
—in which more than half of us live—and the future is dismal. But lay
aside the magnifying glass which reveals, for example, the hopelessness
of Broadway and Forty-second Street, take up a reducing glass, and look
at the entire region in which New York lies. The city falls into focus.
Forests in the hill counties, waterpower in the mid-state valleys, farm-
land in Connecticut, cranberry bogs in New Jersey, enter the picture.
To think of all these acres as merely tributary to New York, to trace and
strengthen the lines of the web in which the spider city sits unchal-
lenged, is again to miss the clue. But to think of the region as a whole
and the city merely as one of its parts—that may hold promise.

Not merely a wistful hope of a better environment, but sheer necessity, leads us thus to change our approach to the problem. For cities
. . . are becoming too big; as they grow they fall behind in the barest
decencies of housing; they become more expensive to operate, more
difficult to police, more burdensome to work in, and more impossible
to escape from even in the hours of leisure that we achieve. The forces
that have created the great cities make permanent improvement
within them hopeless; our efforts to plan them lag pitifully behind the
need when indeed they do not foster the very growth that is becoming
insupportable. We are providing, in Professor Geddes's sardonic
phrase, more and more of worse and worse.

Not so with regional planning. Regional planning asks not how
wide an area can be brought under the aegis of the metropolis, but how

This selection is composed of excerpts from two essays, "Regions—To Live In" and
"Regional Planning." *(Editor's note)*

207

the population and civic facilities can be distributed so as to promote and stimulate a vivid, creative life throughout a whole region—a region being any geographic area that possesses a certain unity of climate, soil, vegetation, industry, and culture. The regionalist attempts to plan such an area so that all its sites and resources, from forest to city, from highland to water level, may be soundly developed, and so that the population will be distributed so as to utilize, rather than to nullify or destroy, its natural advantages. It sees people, industry, and the land as a single unit. Instead of trying, by one desperate dodge or another, to make life a little more tolerable in the congested centers, it attempts to determine what sort of equipment will be needed for the new centers. It does not aim at urbanizing automatically the whole available countryside; it aims equally at ruralizing the stony wastes of our cities. . . . The civic objective of the regional planning movement is summed up with peculiar accuracy in the concept of the garden city.

There are a hundred approaches to regional planning. . . . But each approach has this in common with the others: it attempts to promote a fuller kind of life, at every point in the region. No form of industry and no type of city is tolerable that takes the joy out of life. Communities in which courtship is furtive, in which babies are an unwelcome handicap, in which education, lacking the touch of nature and of real occupations, hardens into a blank routine, in which people achieve adventure only on wheels and happiness only by having their minds "taken off" their daily lives—communities like these do not sufficiently justify our modern advances in science and invention.

Now, the impulse that makes the prosperous minority build country estates, that causes the well-to-do professional man to move out into the suburbs, the impulse that is driving the family of small means out upon the open road, there to build primitive bungalows regardless of discomfort and dangers to health, seems . . . to be a pretty common one. These people are in the vanguard of a general effort to get a little joy back into life. At present this exodus is undertaken blindly and, . . . all its promises are illusory, since a helter-skelter development such as is now going on in the countryside around our big cities promises only to spoil the landscape without permanently satisfying the hungry urbanites. The community-planning movement in America and the garden-cities movement in England are definite attempts to build up a more exhilarating kind of environment—not as a temporary haven of refuge but as a permanent seat of life and culture, urban in its advantages, permanently rural in its situation. This movement toward garden cities is a movement toward a higher type of civilization than that which has created our present congested centers. It involves a change in aim as well as a change of place. Our present congested districts are the results of the crude applications of the mechanical and mathematical sciences to social development; our garden cities represent fuller development of the more humane arts and sciences—biology and medicine and psychiatry and education and architecture. As modern engineering has made Chicago or New York physically superior to Athens, whilst the labyrinth of subways and high buildings is more deficient for complete living than a Stone Age cave, so we may expect that the cities of tomorrow will not merely embody all that is good in our modern mechanical developments, but also all that was left out in this one-sided existence, all the things that fifth-century Athens or thirteenth-century Florence, for all their physical crudity, possessed. . . .

Regional planning is the New Conservation—the conservation of human values hand in hand with natural resources. Regional planning sees that the depopulated countryside and the congested city are intimately related; it sees that we waste vast quantities of time and energy by ignoring the potential resources of a region, that is, by forgetting all that lies between the terminal points and junctions of our great railroads. Permanent agriculture instead of land skinning, permanent forestry instead of timber mining, permanent human communities, dedicated to life, liberty, and the pursuit of happiness, instead of camps and squatter settlements, and to stable building, instead of the scantling and falsework of our "go-ahead" communities—all this is embodied in regional planning.

It follows pretty plainly from this summary that, unlike city planning, regional planning is not merely the concern of a profession: it is a mode of thinking and a method of procedure, and the regional plan itself is only a minor technical instrument in carrying out its aims. . . .

Regional Planning

. . . Perhaps the best way to define regional planning is to establish what is meant today by the "region."

The eighteenth century saw the decay and the final destruction of many types of corporate organization that had flourished in the Middle Ages. To the progressive minds of the eighteenth century, humanity was an undifferentiated mass of individuals: if they had any special historical and political identity in groups, it was that which they achieved as members of the state. The city and the region ceased to have, politically, their separate identity; they became in theory creatures of the state; and for purposes of state these natural groupings were often completely ignored. As a result of the revolution of 1789 in France, for example, the historic regions were broken up arbitrarily into a series of administrative departments, which ignored the historic boundaries and affiliations.

In the colonization of America beyond the eastern seaboard this habit of creating artificial boundaries, drawn on the map with the aid of the ruler, without regard for the actual possibilities of settlement and development, was driven to absurd lengths, partly by sheer haste, partly by ignorance of actual resources, and partly by political theories which sought to override the facts of nature. The new states, with their subdivisions defined by the section and the quarter-section, were drawn up without the slightest respect for actualities. Many of our states are even "defined" by river boundaries despite the fact, which the geographers of the nineteenth century were to establish, that the river is a highway and a means of intercourse, not a barrier; so that, except for temporary military purposes—an exception which the airplane has wiped out—it is the worst of all possible boundaries.

The great states of the world, still more their minor administrative districts, are the products of political forces and events which have only accidental relations to the underlying geographic, economic, and social realities. Their boundaries, their subdivisions, antedate for the most part our present scientific knowledge; they also antedate and ignore the instruments of communication and traffic that have made the world as a whole, for many fundamental purposes, a single unit.

Now, the human region existed as a fact, long before the political state as we know it came into existence. The region continued to exist, even though it was ignored and to no small degree frustrated by the prevailing theories of politics. But it needed the development of human geography to establish the region on a scientific basis. This was something that has taken place in almost less than a hundred years, thanks to a succession of able minds, Humboldt in Germany, Buyot in France, George Perkins Marsh in the United States, followed by Ritter, Reclus, Vidal de la Blache, Le Play, Herbertson, and Geddes—to say nothing of our own contemporaries in America like Fenneman, Mark Jefferson, and J. Russell Smith.

The geographer points out that mankind has not spread out in a formless undifferentiated mass, if only for the reason that the surface of the globe prevents this kind of diffusion. The major land masses divide naturally into smaller units, with special characteristics in the underlying geological structure, in the climate, and consequently in the soils and the vegetation and animal life and available mineral deposits. In each of these natural regions, certain modes of life have arisen in adaptation to the fundamental conditions: these modes have been modified by previous cultural accumulations and by contacts with other peoples, since no region is completely isolated from even distant neighbors, nor can it be, even in the most primitive stages of culture, self-sufficient: did not flint and jade and salt, even in the earliest dawn of history, travel thousands of miles and pass through many hands before they were finally used?

But the geographic environment sets a limit to the types of work that can be economically done, and predisposes favorably certain lines of activity; and this in turn profoundly modifies the social habits and institutions of the inhabitants. There may be mines without miners, just as there may be mulberry trees without the culture of silkworms; hunters may attempt to get a meager living out of an area that will yield a handsome living only to a high state of culture by irrigation and social effort: all these facts, which the ethnologist is quick to point out, are indisputable; but in regions that have been settled over a considerable period, the underlying possibilities of the environment have been explored, and its uses are more fully exploited. Apart from its selective influence upon occupations, the region provides a common background: the air we breathe, the water we drink, the food we eat, the landscape we see, the accumulation of experience and custom peculiar to the setting, tend to unify the inhabitants and to differentiate them from the members of other regions.

These regional differentiations do not deny the facts . . . of universality. . . . The lanes of international travel and trade, the spread of a universal religion like Mohammedanism or Christianity, or of a universal technique, like that of Western science and mechanical invention, the existence of a common fund of ideas and interests, tends to break down regional differentiations and to establish a universal basis for the common life. A regionalism that affected to ignore these forces would be absurd and stultifying, for the presence of universal agencies does not wipe out the realities of regional life: it merely unites them to a greater whole. One must create an identity, a center of one's own, before one can have fruitful intercourse with other personalities. This holds true, too, for the relations between regions. It is only in the dangerous theory of the all-powerful and all-sufficing national state that self-sufficiency within political boundaries can be treated, as it now is, as a possibility; and it is only in wartime that this mischievous notion can be even momentarily effectuated—albeit with great suffering to the underlying population.

The region, then, . . . has a natural basis, and is a social fact. The term cannot . . . be applied to any large area. A city is not just a city when it is bounded by a circle with a five-mile radius, and a region when it is bounded by another circle with a fifty-mile radius. We obviously need some name to cover our large urban agglomerations, actual or possible; but "region" is not a happy one. . . . Until a better one can be coined, it would be as well to call such a collection a metropolitan area. Planning such an area, though its radius were twice as great, would still be metropolitan planning, not regional planning: it would be city planning on a large scale, and not regional development. Does this suggest that there are factors in regional planning which do not exist in metropolitan planning? That is exactly what I mean. Let us examine these factors.

The first different factor in regional planning is that it includes cities, villages, and permanent rural areas, considered as part of the regional complex. While metropolitan planning regards the surrounding open country as doomed to be swallowed up in the inevitable spread and increase of population, the regional planner seeks to preserve the balance between the agricultural and primeval background and the urban environment. Easy access on the part of the city resident to the country, equally easy access on the part of the country dweller to the city, are necessary to their culture and education. A type of metropolitan development which makes such intercourse difficult, tiresome, unfruitful, must, the regionalist thinks, be deliberately overcome. Metropolitanism is in fact another form of land skinning. In the interests of urban growth, rising land values, opportunities for financial killings, it ignores the natural capacities of site and soil, and continues to spread a uniform urban layer over the countryside.

This urban layer lacks for the most part the cultural and commercial advantages of the central district of the metropolis quite as much as would a destitute rural area the same distance from the center: but the massing of population it creates tends to increase and bolster up financial values at the center. Regional planning, on the other hand, begins not with the city as a unit in itself: it begins with the region as a whole and it seeks to bring every capacity of the region up to its fullest state of cultivation or use. This does not mean filling up the land with an undifferentiated urban mass; nor does it necessarily mean, on the other hand, decentralization. But it may mean weeding out, by transplanting to more favorably situated centers, part of the population of the congested metropolises of today; since the assumption that they are bound to grow continually on the lines they have followed in the past is fundamentally an assumption that planning is impotent, except to facilitate results which would take place anyway without planning.

The second important factor in regional planning is its respect of balanced environment and a settled mode of life. The city growth and land colonization of the last century ignored both these factors of balance and settlement. We created the coal agglomeration and the financial metropolis, seeking quickly to extract coal and iron from the soil, and to organize industry so as to produce a maximum profit to the investors; in the act of paying attention only to these limited ends, we forgot to create orderly, healthy, hygienic, and aesthetically decent environments. While our cities produced pig iron, textiles, coal, chemicals, money in quantities the world had never seen before, they also produced an appalling amount of human misery, degradation, sordidness, which mocked all our fine pretensions to progress and enlightenment.

We produced an environment that in part—its inefficiencies were so great that one must stress this phrase—in part was good for machines and money-making: but it was not good for men. It was not a lively and educative and recreative environment. Art, culture, education, recreation—all these things came as an afterthought if they came at all, after our one-sided preoccupation with industry had ruined a great many of their potentialities, both in the life of the individual, whose health and intelligence had been sacrificed to material gain, and in the life of the community. When the pioneer had skinned the soil, he moved on; when the miner had exhausted his mine, he moved on; when the timber cutter had gutted out the forests of the Appalachians, he moved on. All these social types left rack and ruin behind them. The regional planner points out that no civilization can exist on this unstable and nomadic basis: it requires a settled life, based on the possibility of continuously cultivating the environment, replacing in one form what one takes away in another. Regional planning is concerned with provisions for the settlement of the country; and this settlement in turn implies a balanced use of resources and a balanced social life. Both these conditions are impossible in an unbalanced environment.

This brings us to the next important conception of the new regionalism: namely, the regional city. What is the proper size of the city? . . . We have not yet sufficient knowledge to say how many different types of city and satellite and village are appropriate to our life today, and what the limits of population in those various types are: but we can at least put the question to ourselves and suggest in what direction an answer lies.

The size of a city cannot, plainly, be defined by its actual or potential boundary lines; for anyone, with sufficient hardihood and a sufficiently large compass, could merely carry the method of metropolitan planning to a logical conclusion by describing a circle with a radius a thousand miles around Chicago and say that this was all potential Chicago territory, to be filled up by continuous growth from the Loop outward within, say, a thousand years. No: the size of a city cannot be determined by a superficial area to be filled: it is related to the institutions and functions to be served. Primarily, the city differentiates itself from the rural area, from the market center by itself, and from the industrial unit, by the institutions which serve the cultural and educational life of the inhabitants. Farms, markets, and industries are the basis of its existence: but its end, as Aristotle would have said, is the cultivation of the good life. A definite relationship can be established between the population and its civic institutions. Twelve hundred families, for example, can support a modern public school: if one doubles the number of families, one must double the number of schools. A still larger population is necessary for a high school, and one must draw on something beyond the immediate local area for a college or university. Similarly with other functions: fifty thousand people might support a well-equipped maternity hospital; but it would require many times this number to supply a sufficient number of cases for a cancer hospital. There is no reason whatever that, with modern transportation and communication, any one city should attempt to provide for every possible human function. Even New York does not succeed in doing that: there are certain types of operations for which one must go to Rochester, Minnesota, or to Johns Hopkins, if one wants the highest degree of skill, just as there are certain works of art for which one must still go to Florence or Madrid or Amsterdam.

Now, the major common functions of a community can plainly be taken care of in towns of from five thousand to a hundred thousand population quite as well—frequently much better—than they can in a vast megalopolis. But there are special institutions which require a large basis of population, and it would be futile to duplicate these in small communities and unfortunate to do without them: they must be produced on a regional scale. This suggests that the new regional pattern will be a constellation of related cities, separated by parks and permanent agricultural areas, and united for common projects by a regional authority. Each city would have all the local institutions necessary to its own effective life, local shops, schools, auditoriums, theaters, churches, clubs; and in addition each center would perhaps tend to specialize on some one institution of culture or social life, a museum of natural history in one center, a radio broadcasting station in another, a university in a third. Modern transportation and communication remove the necessity for the continuous urban agglomeration; they make this new pattern of cities possible. Each city would perhaps be a regional center for at least one function; but no city would attempt to be the regional center for everything. Without such a pattern as this, it is impossible to do away with the congestion of the central districts and our present waste of resources in providing temporary palliatives for this congestion—palliatives whose effect is speedily ruined by the further congestion that must follow in order to pay for the costs. The undoubted advantages that come with the massing of a great population in the metropolis would be even more available in a well-wrought network of regional cities. In contrast to the metropolitan planner, the regional planner seeks to establish new norms of city growth and to create a fresh pattern of regional and civic activities. To discover these various norms, to relate them to civic functions, and to embody them in communities is one of the major functions of the regional planner.

Finally, regional planning differentiates itself from metropolitan planning by its respect for new and emergent elements in our civilization. The metropolis is a large and unwieldy unit: it represents an enormous vested interest of capital, and it necessarily will take no steps that are likely to displace the real and imaginary values that have been created. As the metropolis increases in magnitude, it becomes more and more committed to the mistakes of the past, and these mistakes are more and more costly to rectify, even when they have become unbearable. This reason alone would be sufficient, if no others were important, to justify the regional planner's interest in small-scale communities: flexibility, ease of adjustment to a new situation, the speedy utilization of new mechanical and scientific advantages—all these things are more easy in a small community than a great one, provided that the intelligence is there to take command. Do we need to widen an avenue? It is easier if the buildings are four stories high than forty. Do we need an aviation field? In New York the distance of the landing field from the center of the city nullifies the greater speed of the airplane over the railroad train on short journeys. Do we wish to take advantage of the auto or the autogiro? Once we have escaped the congestion of the metropolis, it is far easier. The small industrial town may have its housing congestions, its slum area, as well as the metropolis: on a small scale, conditions may be even worse, for lack of any public conscience or remedial measures. But in the small town there are not, as in the metropolis, tremendous physical and financial obstacles to solving it.

The radio, the moving picture, the airplane, the telephone, electric power, the automobile—all these modern utilities have only increased the potential advantages of the region-as-a-whole over the congested metropolis: for with these instruments, the unique superiority of the more congested areas is removed and their benefits are equalized and distributed. Regional planning can help to realize positively all the important achievements of the new age: metropolitan planning exhausts itself in temporarily alleviating the disastrous results of its own elephantine and unregulated growth. Once the region becomes again the center of organized intelligence, as it was in the Middle Ages, as it is today in certain parts of Germany and France and Spain, the superiorities of region over the merely metropolitan area will become manifest. The region as a natural and human grouping is a fact. Regional cities and regional development are possibilities: regional planning itself is an attempt not to ignore these possibilities, in the interest of finance or abstract growth of population, but to make the fullest use of them. Regionalism is only an instrument: its aim is the best life possible.

THE
FOUNDATIONS
OF EUTOPIA

The sort of thinking that has created our utopias has placed desire above reality; and so their chief fulfillment has been in the realm of fantasy. This is true of the classic utopias . . . and it is true—though not perhaps quite so apparent—of the partial utopias that were formulated by the various reconstruction movements during the last century.

While the classic utopias have so far been nearer to reality [in] that they have projected a whole community, living and working and mating and spanning the gamut of man's activity, their projections have nevertheless been literally up in the air, since they did not usually arise out of any real environment or attempt to meet the conditions that this environment presented. This defect has been suggested by the very name of Utopia, for as Professor Patrick Geddes points out, Sir Thomas More was an inveterate punster, and Utopia is a mock name for either Outopia, which means noplace, or Eutopia—the good place.

It is time to bring our utopian idola* and our everyday world into contact; indeed, it is high time, for the idola that have so far served us are now disintegrating so rapidly that our mental world will soon be as empty of useful furniture as a deserted house, while wholesale dilapidation and ruin threaten the institutions that once seemed permanent. Unless we can weave a new pattern for our lives, the outlook for our civilization is almost as dismal as Herr Spengler finds it in *Der Untergang des Abendlandes* [*The Decline of the West*]. Our choice is not between eutopia and the world as it is, but between eutopia and noth-

This essay consists of excerpts from chapter 12 of *The Story of Utopias*. *(Editor's note)*
*Mumford uses the term "idola" or "idolum" to describe "the world of ideas." *(Editor's note)*

ing—or rather, nothingness. Other civilizations have proved inimical to the good life and have failed and passed away; and there is nothing but our own will-to-eutopia to prevent us from following them.

If this dissipation of Western civilization is to cease, the first step in reconstruction is to make over our inner world, and to give our knowledge and our projections a new foundation. The problem of real-izing the potential powers of the community—which is the fundamen-tal problem of eutopian reconstruction—is not simply a matter of economics or eugenics or ethics as the various specialist thinkers and their political followers have emphasized. Max Beer, in his *History of British Socialism,* points out that Bacon looked for the happiness of mankind chiefly in the application of science and industry. But by now it is plain that if this alone were sufficient, we could all live in heaven tomorrow. Beer points out that More, on the other hand, looked to social reform and religious ethics to transform society; and it is equally plain that if the souls of men could be transformed without altering their material and institutional activities, Christianity, Mohammedan-ism, and Buddhism might have created an earthly paradise almost any-time this last two thousand years. The truth is, as Beer sees, that these two conceptions are still at war with each other: idealism and science continue to function in separate compartments; and yet "the happiness of man on earth" depends upon their combination. . . .

There was a time when the world of knowledge and the world of dreams were not separated; when the artist and the scientist, for all practical purposes, saw the "outside world" through the same kind of spectacles.

What we call "science" today was in its primitive state part and parcel of that common stock of knowledge and belief which makes up a community's literature. . . . The departure of science from this main body of literature begins for the Western world, probably, with the death of Plato and the institution of Aristotle's collections in natural history; and from that point onwards the separate sciences increasingly isolate themselves from the general body of knowledge, and utilize methods which had been unknown to the earlier philosophers and sages; so that by the time the twentieth century dawns the process of differentiation has been completed, and philosophy, once the compen-dium of the sciences, has disappeared except as a sort of impalpable, viscous residue.

When Aristotle divided his writing into the exoteric and esoteric groups, into the popular and the scientific, he definitely recognized the existence of two separate branches of literature, two different ways of taking account of the world, two disparate methods of approaching its problems. The first branch was that of the philosophers, the prophets, the poets, and the plain people. Its background was the generality of human experience: its methods were those of discussion and conference: its criteria were those of formal dialectics: its interests were specifically those of the community, and nothing human was foreign to it. With the petrification of Greek thought that followed the collapse of the Alexandrian school, the second branch was slow in coming into its own. As late as the eighteenth century its adherents were called natural philosophers, to distinguish them from the more humane variety; and it is only with the nineteenth century that the subject became universally known as science and its practitioners as scientists.

In the *Phaedrus* Socrates had expressed the humanist outlook of literature by saying: "Trees and fields, you know, cannot teach me anything, but men in the city can." The shortest way of describing the attitude of science is to say that it resolutely turned its back on men in the city and devoted itself to the trees and fields and stars and the rest of brute nature. If it paid attention to men at all it saw them—if we may abuse an old quotation—as trees walking. Socrates had said: Know thyself. The scientist said: Know the world that lies outside man's dominion. As science progressed these attitudes became more rigid, unfortunately, and a conflict grew up between literature and science, between the humanities and natural philosophy. . . .

Science has provided the factual data by means of which the industrialist, the inventor, and the engineer have transformed the physical world; and without doubt the physical world has been transformed. Unfortunately, when science has furnished the data its work is at an end: whether one uses the knowledge of chemicals to cure a patient or to poison one's grandmother is, from the standpoint of science, an extraneous and uninteresting question. So it follows that while science has given us the means of making over the world, the ends to which the world has been made over have had, essentially, nothing to do with science. . . .

. . . Indeed scientific knowledge has not merely heightened the possibilities of life in the modern world: it has lowered the depths. When science is not touched by a sense of values it works—as it fairly consistently has worked during the past century—toward a complete dehumanization of the social order. The plea that each of the sciences must be permitted to go its own way without control should be immediately rebutted by pointing out that they obviously need a little guidance when their applications in war and industry are so plainly disastrous. . . .

. . .

If the sciences are to be cultivated anew with respect for a definite hierarchy of human values, it seems to me that the sciences must be focused again upon particular local communities, and the problems which they offer for solution. Just as geometry in Egypt arose out of the need for annually surveying the boundaries that the Nile wiped out, and as astronomy developed in Chaldea in order to determine the shift of the seasons for the planting of crops, . . . so may the sciences which are today incomplete and partial develop along the necessary lines by a survey of existing conditions and intellectual resources in a particular community. . . .

Apart from its great function as a plaything, science is valuable only to the extent that its researches can be brought to bear upon the conditions in a particular community, in a definite region. . . . If science is to play the significant part that Bacon and Andreae and Plato and the other great humanists desired it to, it must be definitely brought home and realized in our here and now.

The need for this humanization of science has already been perceived in Great Britain. During the last decade a movement has gathered headway in the schools and extended itself to associations outside the schools. The title of this movement is "Regional Survey," and its point of origin is, I believe, the Outlook Tower in Edinburgh, which was well described more than two decades ago as the "world's first sociological laboratory."

The aim of the Regional Survey is to take a geographic region and explore it in every aspect. It differs from the social survey with which we are acquainted in America in that it is not chiefly a survey of evils; it is, rather, a survey of the existing conditions in all their aspects; and it emphasizes to a much greater extent than the social survey the natural characteristics of the environment, as they are discovered by the geologist, the zoologist, the ecologist—in addition to the development of natural and human conditions in the historical past, as presented by the anthropologist, the archaeologist, and the historian. In short, the Regional Survey attempts a local synthesis of all the specialist "knowledges." . . .

The knowledge embodied in the Regional Survey has a coherence and pithiness which no isolated study of science can possibly possess. It is presented in such a form that it can be assimilated by every member of the community who has the rudiments of an education, and it thus differs from the isolated discipline which necessarily remains the heritage of the specialist. Above all, this knowledge is not that of "subjects," taken as so many watertight and unrelated compartments: it is a knowledge of a whole region, seen in all its aspects; so that the relations between the work aspect and the soil aspect, between the play aspect and the work aspect, become fairly simple and intelligible. This common tissue of definite, verifiable, localized knowledge is what all our . . . utopias and reconstruction programs have lacked; and, lacking it, have been one-sided and ignorant and abstract—devising paper programs for the reconstruction of a paper world.

Regional survey, then, is the bridge by which the specialist whose face is turned toward the library and the laboratory, and the active worker in the field, whose face is turned toward the city and region in which he lives, may come into contact; and out of this contact our plans and our eutopias may be founded on such a permanent foundation of facts as the scientist can build for us, while the sciences themselves will be cultivated with some regard for the human values and standards, as embodied in the needs and the ideals of the local community. This is the first step out of the present impasse: we must return to the real world, and face it, and survey it in its complicated totality. Our castles-in-air must have their foundations in solid ground.

The needed reorientation of science is important; but by itself it is not enough. Knowledge is a tool rather than a motor; and if we know the world without being able to react upon it, we are guilty of that aimless pragmatism which consists of devising all sorts of ingenious machines and being quite incapable of subordinating them to any coherent and attractive pattern.

Now, men are moved by their instinctive impulses and by such emotionally colored pattern-ideas or idola as the dreamer is capable of projecting. When we create these pattern-ideas, we enlarge the environment, so that our behavior is guided by the conditions which we seek to establish and enjoy in an imaginary world. However crude the Marxian analysis of society may have been, it at least had the merit of presenting a great dream—the dream of a titanic struggle between the possessors and the dispossessed in which every worker had a definite part to play. Without these dreams, the advances in social science will be just as disorderly and fusty as the applications of physical science have been in our material affairs, where in the absence of any genuine scale of values, a patent collar button is regarded as equally important as a tungsten filament if the button happens to bring the inventor as great a financial reward. . . .

. . .

222 · THE URBAN PROSPECT

There is no genuine logical basis, as far as I can see, in the dissociation of science and art, of knowing and dreaming, of intellectual activities and emotional activities. The division between the two is simply one of convenience; for both these activities are simply different modes in which human beings create order out of the chaos in which they find themselves. Such is the humanist view. . . .

We must now consider the development of the arts in the modern community. At the height of the Middle Age, as in fifth-century Athens, the arts formed together a living unity. A citizen did not go into a concert hall to hear music, to a church to say his prayers, to a theater to see a play, to a picture gallery to view pictures: it was a mean town, indeed, that could not boast a cathedral and a couple of churches; and in these buildings, drama and music and architecture and painting and sculpture were united for the purpose of ringing changes on the emotional nature of men and converting them to accept the theological vision of otherworldly utopia.

The splitting up of these arts into a number of separate boxes was part of that movement toward individualism and protestantism whose effects most people are familiar with in the field of religion alone. Henceforward, music, drama, painting, and the other arts developed largely in isolation; and each of them was forced to build up a separate world. The greater part of the gains that were made in these worlds was not carried over into the community at large, but remained the possession of the artists themselves or their private patrons and critics. . . .

The divorce of the art of the cultivated classes from that of the whole community tended to deprive it of any other standards than the artist himself was content to erect. Here again the comparison with science is curiously pertinent. The world of art is in a sense a separate world, and it can be cultivated for a time without reference to the desires and emotions of the community out of which it has sprung. But the motto "Art for art's sake" turns out in practice to be something quite different—namely, art for the artist's sake. . . . Divorced from his community, the artist was driven back upon himself: instead of seeking to create a beauty which all men might share, he devoted himself to projecting a poignant angle of his personal vision—an angle which I shall call the picturesque. . . .

Now, I would not . . . underrate the gains which have been achieved by the divorce of art from the whole life of the community. In their isolation from the social group that produced them, the modern artists have been able to pursue their solitary way to limits which the common man is probably incapable of reaching: they have widened the field of aesthetic delight and have introduced new values into the world of painting, values which will remain even though the disease which created them disappears, just as one can salvage a pearl from an oyster whose sickness is healed. The view from the mountain top is none the worse because many people are afflicted with dizziness and nausea before they have reached the summit; and, like the pursuit of truth, the pursuit of aesthetic values is a good in itself apart from any values which may be realized in the community. On these terms, Cézanne and van Gogh and Ryder, to mention a few of the dead, will hold their own, and keep the boundaries of art from ever shrinking again, I trust, to its academic limits.

Nevertheless, the effects of focusing on the picturesque can no more be overlooked in art than the dangers of specialization in science. It is almost a banality to point out how, historically, as the picturesque developed in art, beauty has tended to disappear from life. Whilst the cultivated few have become gloriously alive to more exquisite sensations than their ancestors had probably ever experienced, the "mutilated many" have been forced to live in great cities and in abject country towns of a blackness and ugliness such as the world, if we are to judge by the records that exist, has never seen before. In other words, we have become more sensitive to the experiences—to the contents of our inner worlds—only to become more callous to things, to the brash surfaces of the world without. . . .

The divorce of the artist from the community . . . has scarcely been compensated by the advances that have been made in the separate world of art. The result has been that work which should have been done by artists of great capacity has been done by people of minor or degraded ability. Anonymous jerry-builders have erected the greater number of our houses, absurd engineers have laid out our towns with no thought for anything but sewers and paving contracts; rapacious and illiterate men who have achieved success in business discourse to the multitude on what constitutes the good life—and so on. There is really no end to the number of things which we do badly in the modern community, for want of the artist to do them at all.

This generalization applies to the whole range of the arts. The greater part of the creative dreaming and planning which constitutes literature and art has had very little bearing upon the community in which we live, and has done little to equip us with patterns, with images and ideals, by means of which we might react creatively upon our environment. Yet it should be obvious that if the inspiration for the good life is to come from anywhere, it must come from no other people than the great artists. . . . The common man, when he is in love, has a little glimpse of the way in which the drudgery of the daily world may be transmuted through emotional stimulus; it is the business of the artist to make the transmutation permanent, for the only difference between the artist and the common man is that the artist is, so to say, in love all the while. It is out of the vivid patterns of the artist's ecstasy that he draws men together and gives them the vision to shape their lives and the destiny of their community anew. . . .

It comes to this, then: our plans for a new social order have been as dull as mud because, in the first place, they have been abstract . . . and have not taken into account the immense diversity and complexity of man's environment; and in the second place, they have not created any vivid patterns that would move men to great things. . . .

Through the paralysis of the arts and sciences our contemporary programs for revolution and reform have done very little to lift our heads over the disorderly and bedraggled environments in which we conduct our daily business. This failure to create a common pattern for the good life in each region has made such excellent efforts as the garden-city movement seem weak and ineffectual when we place them alongside the towns that medieval civilization, which had such a common pattern, created. Without the common background of eutopian idola, all our efforts at rehabilitation . . . are spotty and inconsecutive and incomplete. It was not, let us remember, by any legislative device that the cities of the industrial age were monotonously patterned in the image of [Dickens's] Coketown. It was rather because everyone within these horrid centers accepted the same values and pursued the same ends—as they were projected by economists like Ricardo, industrialists like Stephenson, and lyric poets like Samuel Smiles—that the plans of the jerry-builder and the engineer expressed to perfection the brutality and social disharmony of the community. The same process that gave us Coketown can, when our world of ideas is transformed, give us something better than Coketown.

. . . The same methods which are used by the utopian thinkers to project an ideal community on paper may be employed, in a practical way, to develop a better community on earth. The weakness of the utopian thinkers consisted in the assumption that the dreams and projects of any single man might be realized in society at large. From the bitter frustration of Fourier, Cabet, Hertzka, and even John Ruskin, those who are in search of the beloved community may well take a warning. Where the critics of the utopian method were, I believe, wrong was in holding that the business of projecting prouder worlds was a futile . . . pastime. These anti-utopian critics overlooked the fact that one of the main factors that condition any future are the attitudes and beliefs which people have in relation to that future—that, as Mr. John Dewey would say, in any judgment of practice one's belief in a hypothesis is one of the things that affect its realization.

When we have projected the pattern of an ideal community and tend to warp our conduct in conformity with that pattern, we overcome the momentum of actual institutions. In feeling free to project new patterns, in holding that human beings can will a change in their institutions and habits of life, the utopians were, I believe, on solid ground; and the utopian philosophies were a great improvement over the more nebulous religious and ethical systems of the past in that they saw the necessity for giving their ideals form and life. . . .

What, then, is the first step out of the present disorder? The first step, it seems to me, is to ignore all the fake utopias and social myths that have proved either so sterile or so disastrous during the last few centuries. There is perhaps no logical reason why the myth of the national state should not be preserved; but it is a myth which has done very little, on the whole, to promote the good life, and has on the contrary done a great deal to make the good life impossible; and to continue to cling to it in the face of perpetual wars, pestilences, and spiritual devastations is the sort of fanaticism which will probably seem as blind and cruel to future generations as persecutions for Christian heresy do to the present one. On the same grounds, there are a number of other social myths, like the proletarian myth, which run so badly against the grain of reality that they cannot be preserved without ignoring a great many values which are essential to a humane existence; and on pragmatic grounds it would be fine and beneficial to drop them quickly into limbo. . . .

. . . In turning away from obsolete and disastrous social mythis I do not suggest that we give up the habit of making myths; for that habit, for good or bad, seems to be ingrained in the human psyche. The nearest we can get to rationality is not to efface our myths but to attempt to infuse them with right reason, and to alter them or exchange them for other myths when they appear to work badly.

Here is where we reap the full benefit of the great utopian tradition. In turning away from the social myths that hamper us, we do not jump blindly into a blankness: we rather ally ourselves with a different order of social myth which has always been vivified and enriched by the arts and sciences.

The idolum of eutopia which we may seek to project in this or that region is not a carte blanche which any one may fill in at his will and caprice; certain lines have already been fixed; certain spaces have already been filled. There is a consensus among all utopian writers, to begin with, that the land and natural resources belong undividedly to the community; and even when it is worked by separate people or associations, as in Utopia . . . the increment of the land—the economic rent—belongs to the community as a whole. There is also a pretty common notion among the utopians that, as land is a common possession, so is work a common function; and no one is let off from some sort of labor of body or mind because of any inherited privileges or dignities that he can point to. Finally, . . . from Ebenezer Howard we can learn the importance of converting the idolum of eutopia into plans and layouts and detailed projections, such as a town planner might utilize; and we may suspect that a eutopia which cannot be converted into such specific plans will continue, as the saying is, to remain up in the air. . . .

. . . I conceive that we shall not attempt to envisage a single utopia for a single unit called humanity; that is the sort of thin and tepid abstraction which the discipline of the Regional Survey will tend to kill off even in people who are now inured by education to dealing only in verbal things. . . .

As far as extent or character of territory goes, we will remember that the planet is not as smooth as a billiard ball, and that the limits of any genuine community rest within fairly ascertainable geographic regions in which a certain complex of soil, climate, industry, institutional life, and historic heritage has prevailed. We shall not attempt to legislate for all these communities at one stroke; for we shall respect William Blake's dictum that one law for the lion and the ox is tyranny. There are some fifteen million local communities in the world, the postal directory tells us; and our eutopia will necessarily take root in one of these real communities, and include within its cooperations as many other communities as have similar interests and identities. It may be that our eutopia will embrace a population as great as that in the metropolis of London or New York; but it is needless to say that the land which lies beyond the limits of the metropolis will no longer be regarded as a sort of subterranean factory for the production of agricultural goods. In sum, as Patrick Geddes has finely said, in the kingdom of Eutopia—the world Eutopia—there will be many mansions.

The inhabitants of our eutopias will have a familiarity with their local environment and its resources, and a sense of historical continuity, which those who dwell within the paper world of Megalopolis and who touch their environment mainly through the newspaper and the printed book, have completely lost. The people of Newcastle will no longer go to London for coals, as the people in the provinces have in a sense been doing this last century and more: there will be a more direct utilization of local resources than would have seemed profitable or seemly to the metropolitan world which now has command of the market. In these varied eutopias, it is safe to say, there will be a new realization of the fact that a cultivated life is essentially a settled life. . . .

If the inhabitants of our eutopias will conduct their daily affairs in a possibly more limited environment than that of the great metropolitan centers, their mental environment will not be localized or nationalized. For the first time perhaps in the history of the planet our advance in science and invention has made it possible for every age and every community to contribute to the spiritual heritage of the local group; and the citizen of eutopia will not stultify himself by being, let us say, a hundred percent Frenchman when Greece, China, England, Scandinavia, and Russia can give sustenance to his spiritual life. Our eutopians will necessarily draw from this wider environment whatever can be assimilated by the local community; and they will thus add any elements that may be lacking in the natural situation.

The chief business of eutopians was summed up by Voltaire in the final injunction of Candide: Let us cultivate our garden. The aim of the real eutopian is the culture of his environment, most distinctly not the culture, and above all not the exploitation, of some other person's environment. Hence the size of our eutopia may be big or little; it may begin in a single village; it may embrace a whole region. A little leaven will leaven the whole loaf; and if a genuine pattern for the eutopian life plants itself in any particular locality it may ramify over a whole continent as easily as Coketown duplicated itself throughout the Western world. The notion that no effective change can be brought about in society until millions of people have deliberated upon it and willed it is one of the rationalizations which are dear to the lazy and the ineffectual. Since the first step toward eutopia is the reconstruction of our idola, the foundations for eutopia can be laid, wherever we are, without further ado.

Our most important task at the present moment is to build castles in the air. We need not fear, as Thoreau reminds us, that the work will be lost. If our eutopias spring out of the realities of our environment, it will be easy enough to place foundations under them. Without a common design, without a grand design, all our little bricks of reconstruction might just as well remain in the brickyard; for the disharmony between men's minds betokens, in the end, the speedy dilapidation of whatever they may build. Our final word is a counsel of perfection. When that which is perfect has come, that which is imperfect will pass away.

THE CHOICES
AHEAD

. . . Ever since the 1830s the effects of bad urban planning and bad housing in accentuating all the miseries of inhuman economic exploitation have been recognized. But the attempts to cope with these evils, even in the provision of elementary sanitary facilities, were feeble, superficial, halting, maddeningly slow; and this was especially true in the more congested urban centers, whose very congestion raised land values, and made the vilest slum tenements far more profitable to their landlords than decent houses for the middle classes.

In [the 1920s], when the Regional Planning [Association of American was formed] . . . , only a few people realized that there was something fundamentally wrong with the quality of life in our "great" and growing American cities, and that far bolder measures than any so far taken were necessary, if these cities were to remain socially well-balanced and attractive places to work and live in. What then seemed to many people healthy evidences of buzzing social activity and economic dynamism were too often, like kiting land values and congested streets, symptoms of social malfunction or organic defects in planning. Most of the evils now so portentously evident in urban communities today were already visible half a century ago—chronic poverty, blighted areas, filthy slums, gangsterism, race riots, police corruption and brutality (the "third degree"), and a persistent deficiency in medical, social, and educational services.

But the chief proof that something was radically at fault with the whole pattern of life in our metropolitan centers is that those who could afford to leave the city were deserting it—indeed, they had begun to desert long before, seeking in the residential suburb, with its pleasant gardens, its nearby woods and fields, its quiet and safe residential quar-

228

ters, its neighborly social life, qualities that were steadily disappearing in the more affluent metropolises. And instead of taking this desertion as an instruction to rehabilitate the central city, the leaders of urban society took it as an invitation to invest profitably in multiplying the means of escape, first by railroads, subways, and trolleys, then by motor-cars, bridges, tunnels. Automatic congestion was counterbalanced by an equally automatic decongestion and dispersal; and between then, the notion of the city as a socially concentrated, varied, and stimulating and rewarding human environment vanished.

As living conditions worsened in the overcrowded central districts, the area of suburban dispersal widened, until the overflow of one metropolis mingled with the overflow of another metropolis to form the disorganized mass of formless, low-grade urban tissue that is now nicknamed Megalopolis. Like the suburban flight itself, this megalopolitan conglomeration has been treated, often by urban sociologists who should know better, as a recent phenomenon brought about by equally recent technological developments. But Patrick Geddes identified a similar random massing of sub-urban populations more than half a century ago on the British coalfields, and called it, with nicer accuracy, a conurbation—though it turns out that anti-city would be a still better name for it. Observers who now regard this urbanoid massing as the new form of the city, or praise it as a more complex, though unplannable and uncontrollable, substitute for the city, demonstrate that they have never grasped what the historic functions and purposes of the city actually are.

The ultimate mode of this physical dispersal was presciently foretold by H. G. Wells at the beginning of this century in his *Anticipations of the Reaction of Mechanical and Scientific Progress upon Human Life*: but he had, unfortunately, no premonition of the kind of social disintegration that it would bring about. These results are taking form under our eyes, with the result that the residential quarters of our "great American cities" now tend to separate out into two kinds of ghettos: an upper-class ghetto of high-rise apartments designed, with or without governmental assistance, as status symbols for the super-affluent, and another, lower-class ghetto, scarcely distinguishable from the first on the exterior, for the lowest-income groups. The latter is the home of the new urban proletariat, mainly Negro and Puerto Rican, seeking to escape even worse conditions in San Juan or the Deep South. Those who do not qualify for either ghetto now swell the mass migration to suburbia.

When one translates into concrete terms the current talk about the increasing urbanization of the United States today, one must understand that sociologists are speaking loosely of people who are, in fact, dis-urbanized, who no longer live in cities, or enjoy, except as visitors or part-time occupants, the concentrated social advantages of the city: the face-to-face meetings, the cultural mixtures, the human challenges. For the growing majority of the nonagricultural population of the United States now lives for better or worse in suburbia: indeed, even many rural areas, where farming is still practiced, are in social content suburban. Meanwhile those who hold fast as residents in the big urban centers—or even in small towns that harbor resentful racial minorities —do so at the peril of their lives. No Berlin walls separate the Gilded Ghetto from the tarnished, oxidized ghettos that spread around them —except in ominously prophetic enclosures like [New York's] Stuyvesant Town. But even daylight is not a safeguard against robbery, rape, and murder, as any metropolitan taxi driver will testify. . . .

Meanwhile, during the last three decades, the racial composition of American cities has changed. Into the great vacuum produced by the suburban exodus has rushed a new army of "internal immigrants." Faced with this influx of two depressed minorities, ill-educated, impoverished, usually untrained for work except in agriculture, tens of thousands unable to speak English, American municipalities experienced, in even more acute form, the same difficulties that mass migration from Europe had caused between 1870 and 1920. Though the United States Congress had belatedly sought to ease these difficulties by limiting the number of foreign immigrants admitted in any one year, no attempt was made to direct this internal migration, or limit it to proportions that could be absorbed and assimilated in any one community—still less to spread it over many communities by providing jobs, housing, schools.

The problems raised by these newcomers would have been difficult to handle even if the municipalities concerned had not themselves already been hopelessly in arrears in providing out of their own budgets the necessary schools and hospitals, to say nothing of new housing, for the population already established. Even if state and federal funds had been available in sufficient amounts to provide both housing and rent subsidies—and under the terms of our Cold War economy they were not available—the very volume of this sudden influx would have condemned most of the newcomers to the same verminous, insanitary, congested quarters that, in cities like New York and Boston, they were forced to occupy.

With respect to basic deficiencies—lack of light, air, space, privacy, sanitary services, schools—the grievances of the minorities, both new migrants and those long established, were well justified. But the slowness of municipal authorities in coming to terms with these grievances only reflected an earlier unreadiness to take any measures for improving the city that did not win the approval of real-estate operators, banks, and insurance companies. What was different between this situation and that which had existed in the 1890s is that the new immigrants had higher expectations and made new demands.

. . . These negative aspects of modern city development, the rising rate of crime, delinquency, drug addiction, and random violence, . . . could not be treated by purely temporizing local remedies, since they were symptomatic of deeper organic defects in our civilization. Until now, this point of view has been dismissed as "unrealistic" or "pessimistic," even "apocalyptic," by those planners, administrators, and social-service workers who sought only to achieve such piecemeal urban improvements as were acceptable and feasible without any critical assessment and renovation of current institutions.

This refusal to look any deeper into the causes of urban deterioration, at a time when the vast surplus of energy, wealth, and knowledge available should have produced a marked improvement of urban life, came out clearly in a common reaction to my book *The Culture of Cities,* when it was published in 1938. This study of city development was, on the whole, sufficiently hopeful and constructive to be well received. But one section was singled out by certain critics as a dark subjective fantasy, inapplicable to our contemporary urban culture. The offending section, "A Brief Outline of Hell," was one in which I had summed up the current disintegration of urban life and the probable fate of the city, *if these tendencies continued.* This summary was the restatement of a diagram devised by my old master, Patrick Geddes.

In this diagram Geddes traced the city's evolution through an upward curve, beginning with the polis and reaching a climax in the metropolis, or mother city: then through a downward curve, from Megalopolis, handicapped by its own overgrowth, to Parasitopolis and Patholopolis, till it reached a terminal point: Necropolis, the city of the dead. Those who were eager to discredit Geddes's historical scheme apparently never read to the end of my chapter, where I dealt with "Possibilities of Renewal" and "Signs of Salvage." For had they done so they could not so easily have charged me with holding that Geddes's purely theoretical terminal stage of megalopolitan overgrowth was either necessary or inevitable, still less irreparable.

On the contrary, I had pointed out that cities, not being biological organisms, have often shown signs of senile decrepitude at an early stage, or had undergone processes of renewal at a late moment of their existence, and thus got a new lease on life. And, so far from denying the value of large urban concentrations, I had said that as many as thirty great metropolitan centers might prove necessary to serve as a medium for world intercourse, and as containers of world culture. But the fact that I was aware of the pathological conditions undermining urban life caused many critics to regard me, by some quaint logic of their own, as a sworn enemy of the city.

At the end of *The Culture of Cities* I had written, with a confidence that had somehow survived the First World War and the economic depression of the thirties: "Already, in the architecture and layout of the new community, one sees the knowledge and discipline that the machine has provided turned to more vital conquests, more human consummations. Already, in imagination and plan, we have transcended the sinister limitations of the existing metropolitan environment. We have much to unbuild, and much more to build: but the foundations are ready. . . ."

The rhetoric now sounds hollow, yet what it suggested seemed possible, even at that late moment. But the Second World War blasted these naïve hopes. At the end of that war, instead of laying the foundations for a cooperative civilization, the citizens of the United States put themselves by passive consent in the hands of a "military-scientific-industrial elite," to use President Eisenhower's accurate characterization. By imposing a permanent state of war, this "elite" . . . placed the mass production of extermination weapons above human welfare, and so laid the foundations, not for a life economy, but for an anti-life economy, every part of which is elaborately oriented . . . toward death. Witness a regime that spends 57 percent of its budget every year for military purposes, and has only 6 percent available for education, health, and other social services.

But if my hopes for effective urban renovation in America were soon buried, my grimmest apprehensions about the urban future came true more swiftly than I could have anticipated. Only two years after *The Culture of Cities* came out, the central area of one city after another in Europe was reduced to rubble by aerial bombardments: first Warsaw and Rotterdam, then London and Berlin, then minor cities in an ever-spreading carnage. Not surprisingly, the harried survivors of this destruction and massacre, as first instituted by the Nazis, did not find my analysis unduly pessimistic: Necropolis lay all around them. Though my work may have had little visible influence in the United States, the Nazi Luftwaffe and its later Allied Air Force imitators had at least given authority to my most ominous predictions, though the invisible moral debacle proved worse—and more permanent—than the visible physical destruction.

Since all my thought about the city had been toward laying the social foundations for urban rebuilding on a regional scale in both old cities and new communities, by stimulating the regenerative and constructive processes already active in our civilization, those who had followed my work were not unprepared for this challenge. This explains

why in Europe *The Culture of Cities* had a far-reaching influence out
of proportion, perhaps, to its immediate usefulness; for it was not
merely eagerly studied and discussed in England, even while the bombs
were dropping, but was used, I have been told, in the Underground
architectural schools set up by planners in Poland, the Netherlands, and
Greece, to teach the rising generation of planners a new conception of
urban development. This situation, at once so menacing and yet so
promising, was an incentive to further thinking on my own part.

In 1945, accordingly, in a critique of Abercrombie and Forshaw's
plan for Greater London, I outlined specifically the further steps that
should be taken—apart from the needed building of New Towns—to
prevent the further congestion of London, and to make possible its
rebuilding on a more human scale. One of these steps was the local
decentralization of governmental and business offices into the constituent boroughs of London, in order to lessen the daily commuter traffic
to Central London and restore the metropolis itself as a place of residence, with amenities equal or superior to those of any suburb, and with
greater facilities for human association, unpenalized by time-wasting,
energy-depleting travel.

These specific proposals—the building of a series of New Towns,
with the removal of suitable industries and bureaux from congested
areas to relatively empty ones, the planning of neighborhoods to facilitate family life and autonomous communal activity, the creation of
regional authorities to direct the work of urban development over a
wider area—were, in fact, all carried on vigorously in Britain after 1947,
with the exception of the last item; and even this necessary extension
of urban authority, from the metropolis to the region, is now under
active discussion. Whatever further initiatives and modifications may
be needed, these measures have all proved practical; and in the case of
the most disputed and disparaged proposal, that for a large-scale building of New Towns to provide both industrial and social advantages that
no congested metropolis can offer, these towns have proved immensely
successful—so successful, in fact, that canny speculators even attempted a "take-over" of the oldest New Town, Letchworth, lured by
the prospective increase in values. However modest my own contributions have been to this program, they at least antedated the postwar
legislation and building.

But I have an arresting objective reason rather than a personal one
for dwelling on these details. And this is to point out that despite Britain's immense constructive achievements in housing and planning and
the industrial replenishment of underdeveloped areas, the same general disintegration and demoralization that has been going on in other
parts of Western civilization has gone on there. This can no longer be

attributed to postwar exhaustion. Three centuries of brutal exploitation, enslavement, destruction, and extermination have left their mark on civilized society. In England now, no less than in the United States, the same marks of urban disintegration have nevertheless appeared in massive quantities—police corruption, marital promiscuity, random reproduction, overt racial and class antagonism, narcotic addiction, cultivated sadism, defiant criminality. The cult of anti-life, symbolically prefigured in much of the avant-garde art and music and drama of our time, is now spreading actively into every part of megalopolitan routine. Patholopolis and Parasitopolis, in fact, are fast establishing themselves as normal forms of the city, or, rather, as negative heavens: ideal environments for the psychotic, the criminal, the feckless, and the demoralized. The terminal stage in city development would seem nearer than ever.

Now, in all societies, the upbuilding and the breaking-down processes go on side by side, as they do in living organisms. As long as the constructive processes are dominant, the organism survives, and to the extent that it has a margin of free energy and maintains its powers of self-direction and self-replication, the organism may flourish. What makes the present situation so singular and so threatening is that the extra energies available, when not claimed by the production of lethal weapons and space rockets, are absorbed by the centralized bureaucratic and technological processes that are scattering the specialized parts of the city over the landscape. These individual urban groups and communities no longer have effective control over their own destinies. As a result, if anything goes wrong, locally, the defective part, so to say, can no longer be repaired on the spot, but must be "sent back to the factory."

These facts have convinced me, and I think should convince any unbiased observer, that the underlying causes for the recurrent outbreaks of violence among the disturbed minorities are not to be found solely in the sordid physical conditions of the cities themselves. While the recent demonstrations and revolts are partly accountable as a long-delayed reaction to poverty, slum housing, unemployment, social discrimination, police animosity, and segregation, the cities that have taken the most vigorous measures to deal with these evils, like Detroit and New Haven, have proved no more immune to attack than those that have been inert and indifferent. So, though the continued effort to turn the city into a comely, life-fulfilling environment is still one of the great collective tasks of our day, it is not a panacea. Such efforts will enhance the goodness of the city's goods; but they will not abate the evil of its real evils, since the latter are not under local control, nor have they only a local origin.

Those who now impatiently demand, or confidently prescribe, a heavy national investment in good housing or a "model cities program" as an antidote for demonstrative mass violence or as a curb to juvenile delinquency and adult criminality have not looked carefully enough at the evidence. If juvenile delinquency, for example, were mainly the result of poverty and alienation, why should it break out equally in spacious upper-class, white American suburbs? Certainly the common denominator here is not a bad physical environment. To ask the legislator or the planner to apply such immediate remedial measures to restore order is to ask for quackery. It is not just the city but the whole body politic that demands our attention. The advertiser's mirage of the Affluent Society may tease and torment the depressed minorities that are denied a full share of this affluence, but the reality itself appalls the overfed, overstimulated, overcoddled young who are bored by its smooth lubricity.

These outbreaks are but local incidents in the vast eruptions and lava flows of collective violence that mark the last half century as the most violent age in history, with a record of wholesale destruction and merciless extermination that makes the most savage conquests of the Assyrians, the Tartars, and the Aztecs seem the work of diffident amateurs. What has been happening in our cities can be neither understood nor controlled except in the light of this larger example of insensate destruction. The progressive technology that the Victorian exponents of industrialism looked upon as a certain means of assuring peace and plenty has been increasingly corrupted by its commitment to organized nihilism and aggression. Its greatest achievements—nuclear bombs, computers, radar, rockets, supersonic planes—are all by-products of war. Constant indoctrination in violence is the main office of our ubiquitous agents of mass communication and mass education. To believe that a single organ of the body politic, the city, can be cured of this disease while the same deadly cells flow through the entire bloodstream is to betray an ignorance of elementary physiology.

One thing should at least be obvious by now. Neither the past diagnoses of urban defects nor the positive regimens offered for urban health have proved competent or effective. So, though the kind of constructive planning I have advocated . . . is still viable, and indeed more urgent now than ever, it would be foolish to put forth these proposals as a means of averting future gang rumbles, "race riots," or Negro–Puerto Rican revolts. That situation has another dimension. . . .

. . . To suppose that a fresh start can be made merely by pouring millions of dollars into the same public housing and urban renewal projects that have already proved so futile would be to nourish further illusions. This is like prescribing massive doses of penicillin to a patient in the terminal stages of a chronic disease—though, at an earlier moment, diet and surgery might have cured him. No quick miraculous recovery can now be hoped for; or, rather, the one conceivable miracle that might yet occur is that a sufficient number of people should recognize that every part of our life must be overhauled, including "the technology of Megalopolis" and the supporting ideology of an affluent society under an ever-expanding economy.

This larger theme is not one that I can handle even sketchily in [this essay]. Many contemporary thinkers have at least made a beginning in diagnosing our present situation, from Spengler, Toynbee, and Schweitzer onward; and I have made an extensive contribution in a series of books, most recently in *The City in History* and *The Myth of the Machine.* In this final comment I shall only pose some of the difficult immediate problems that neither the dissident minorities, justifiably outraged and impatient, nor the once blindly complacent majority have so far been willing to face. . . .

To go deeper into [our] immediate situation we must, I suggest, distinguish between three aspects, only one of which is open to immediate rectification. We must first separate out the problems that are soluble with the means we have at hand: this includes such immediate measures as vermin control, improved garbage collection, cheap public transportation, new schools and hospitals, and health clinics. Second, those that require a new approach, new agencies, new methods, whose assemblage will require time, even though the earliest possible action is urgent. And finally, there are those that require a reorientation in the purposes and ultimate ideals of our whole civilization—solutions that hinge on a change of mind, as far-reaching as that which characterized the change from the medieval religious mind to the modern scientific mind. Ultimately, the success of the first two changes will hinge upon this larger—and, necessarily, later—transformation. So, far from looking to a scientifically oriented technology to solve our problems, we must realize that this highly sophisticated dehumanized technology itself now produces some of our most vexatious problems, including the unemployment of the unskilled.

Let me touch on the hardest aspect first, for though the goal indicated is remote, a beginning should be made at once. In the most general terms, this basic problem is the control of power, quantification, automatism, aimless dynamism. That problem has become acute in our age, because scientific technology has colossally magnified the amount of energy that advanced industrial societies command. But even more,

it has become difficult because in our overreliance upon purely intellectual enlightenment we have allowed earlier systems of moral, political,
and social control to break down, and have transferred systematic discipline and order to the very corporate organizations that must be
brought once more under human direction, if they are to pursue human
ends.

Once the traditional system of moral restraints and personal inhibitions has dissolved in any society, as completely as has happened during
the last half century throughout the Western world, the warfare of each
against all, which Thomas Hobbes falsely pictured as the original state
of primitive man, becomes more than a theoretical possibility: it has, in
fact, become a demonstrable reality. And unfortunately, the very institution that Hobbes relied upon to put down this internecine strife, the
Leviathan state, is now the chief offender in flouting law and order, in
extending the sphere of violence and magnifying all the possibilities of
destruction and extermination. In effect, the policeman is the chief
criminal, and his bad example has proved infectious.

There is not a single human problem posed in our cities, as between
White Power and Black Power, that was not prefigured in the last three
centuries of conquest, colonization, enslavement, exploitation, and extermination; and there is not a difficulty faced by the United Nations,
seeking to achieve a balance between tribalism and universalism, between nationalism and cosmopolitanism, that will not have to be
worked out in the smallest neighborhood.

The forces that have violated the elemental moralities and that
now threaten all life on this planet will not be easily or quickly brought
under control. But in so far as command of these menacing forces
means imposing salutary inhibitions, restraints, prudences, it is open to
every sane, responsible person to make a beginning in his own life. Only
those who have lost respect for the principle of autonomy may either
"go with" the forces of disintegration or express their disillusioned
dissent merely by "dropping out."

With regard to the immediate urban situation, one must qualify the
boldest measures by a realization that they must overcome a massive
inertia: indeed, they must go against the dominant forces in our civilization, even those forces in science and technology which, if we eventually emerge from this Age of Violence, may be at last put to more
admirable human uses. But our first duty here is to recognize the symptoms of decay, and not to cooperate further with the forces of disintegration. If the Romans had learned that lesson, at the moment when
they boasted of their unchallengeable power and affluence under the
Pax Romana, they might not so soon have lost their grip.

Unfortunately, even some of the urban problems that would seem to be immediately soluble, once we accepted the high price of a solution, are not quite so simple as reformers have hitherto believed. To begin with, consider desegregation. The mass migration of Negroes and Puerto Ricans into Northern communities has turned once-diffused minorities into concentrated metropolitan enclaves that will soon, if present tendencies continue, constitute a hapless proletarian majority. No open housing or school busing can overcome the isolation and resultant self-segregation that sheer numbers have produced. Before any urban renewal program can be instituted for the benefit of given racial or cultural groups, the first question that must be answered, by the minorities themselves, is whether they are willing to move out of their present neighborhoods, even if this means scattering widely in a mixed community, and losing some of their present identity and cohesion.

If they choose to remain in numbers where they are, they commit themselves to continued segregation: not merely to segregation but also to congestion, and, along with congestion, to insufficient recreation areas and overcrowded health and hospital services, too. But if they choose to move far enough away to invite the provision for good housing, new industrial or agricultural opportunities, and stable neighborhood facilities, they will become a part of New Towns, suburbs, or growing rural communities; and they will, like any other newcomers, perhaps need a generation before they are fully integrated, no matter how faithfully their legal status as citizens is secured.

This decision cannot be made in local city halls, still less in Washington; for only those concerned have the right to make it, after the way has been sufficiently opened by experimental planning and building to make a genuine choice possible. Yet no intelligent program of urban renewal can be framed until this alternative has been built into the program itself. Only one thing can be predicted: if the immigration to big cities and the metropolitan birthrate continues at the past high levels, there will be no alternative to organizing dispersal and relocation, both regionally and nationally, into smaller communities. Fortunately, a rational program for resettlement . . . is still an open option, more open now than ever, because so many industries and business organizations have been, during the last two decades, sporadically moving away from the metropolis.

But the underlying human factors are still too delicate and uncertain to admit quick decisions. The policy of dispersal now quietly favored by educated middle-class Negroes in professions and businesses . . . would leave the metropolitan ghettos without leadership; and so, worse off socially than before. Dispersal would also have the effect of undermining the subculture that has developed in Harlem and other major metropolitan centers: yet this subculture, through its expression in music, the dance, and the theater, is one of the chief sources of the Negro's and the Puerto Rican's individuality and self-respect. (Certainly, something was lost to the once-thriving Yiddish subculture by its voluntary removal to improved living quarters away from the Lower East Side.) By now there is an activist Negro minority—how large is anyone's guess—that would resist such assimilation. Neither choice is clear and easy: so both must be kept open.

But if the slums and the blighted areas where the minorities now live were to be rehabilitated for the existing overcrowded population, this would mean continuing to build superslums, whether on the open high-rise pattern favored by municipal authorities, or the dense housing on crowded lots, without provisions for sunlight, open air, or visual amenity, favored by Jane Jacobs, in which streets would remain the chief play areas, though filled, as now, with dangerous traffic. Neither the frying pan nor the fire is attractive; for housing designed at three hundred to four hundred people to the acre—to say nothing of the greater number some favor—is not conducive to health, neighborly cooperation, or adequate child care. The slum dweller's justifiable resentment against arbitrary uprooting and his unwillingness to return to the kind of inhuman high-rise apartments offered has now been fully demonstrated; and to go on building in this fashion would be foolish.

The core of any adequate neighborhood housing program should be, above all, the provision for the health, security, education, and adult care of young children; and except perhaps in health, all high-rise projects are, by their very scale and impersonality, an alien and even hostile environment for the young, since, apart from organized playground games, it leaves the majority of children such little scope for their own activities. In these new quarters, even the mildest outbreak of juvenile adventure or wanton mischief becomes all too quickly labeled as juvenile delinquency—on which terms, Robert Frost once confessed to me, he probably would have spent his own boyhood in San Francisco in a reformatory.

Lacking both normal parental disciplines and normal outlets for defiance of adults, something worse now takes place. One of the most sinister features of the recent urban riots has been the presence of roaming bands of children, armed with bottles and stones, taunting and defying the police, smashing windows and looting stores. But this was only an intensification of the window breakings, knifings, and murders that have for the past twenty years characterized "the spirit of youth in the city streets."

. . . Juvenile delinquency is not confined to a depressed minority living in slums: it is also an upper- or middle-class white, suburban phenomenon. But in both cases it seems to point to two underlying conditions: an idle, empty, purposeless existence, and a total breakdown of parental guidance and communal discipline. In both groups we find, among the younger adults, that marital promiscuity and parental irresponsibility have undermined the basic unit of all stable societies—the family. The fact that, according to current estimates, in the Negro metropolitan community half the children cannot identify their fathers, not merely deprives them of the supervision and example of the male parent, but probably also undermines their own sense of personal loyalty and identity.

This family disintegration can only in part be attributed to bad housing. Unfortunately, it has been worsened by what was, by intention, a humane achievement in legislation: the provision of welfare relief to mothers solely responsible for their children's support. This legislation turns out, in the case of husbandless mothers, too often to be a subsidy to sexual irresponsibility and an invitation to chronic idleness. The demoralizing effects of this remedy come out in the disturbing, if perhaps apocryphal, story of the little girl brought up under such conditions who, when asked what work she intended to do when she grew up, replied that she wanted to draw. Inquiry revealed that what she wanted to "draw" was not pictures, but a welfare check, as her mother did.

Obviously, the high rate of unemployment among Negroes and Puerto Ricans, and the lower wages and poorer conditions offered needier groups, both colored and white, discourages stable marriages, and perhaps vitiates male parental feeling as well. But to think of correcting this condition solely by rent subsidies, that is, in effect, more welfare checks, or by better physical housing, is to overlook the equal need for active responsive cooperation by those concerned. Promiscuity cannot be legally suppressed: but marital stability and parental prudence could be honorably rewarded, not only by year-round employment, but by family wages to the fathers of families, as in France; financed in the United States as Social Security is financed —with bonuses that would cease after the third child. This lies outside the scope of urban renewal; but no adequate renewal program will be possible until the restoration of the basic family constellation is taken as one of the essential goals of adequate housing.

On this matter, if one can safely accept a recent report, the example of Hong Kong is pertinent, for it would seem to show that moral factors count for more than purely physical ones, as soon as a certain minimum standard of sanitation has been achieved. In that oppressively congested metropolis, high-rise housing has been provided for the lowest-income groups at much higher densities than any housing authority has dared to establish in America. About the best that can be said for these quarters is that they are ratproof, fireproof, sanitary. Since the parents and the older children must work, the very young are habitually locked in their flats all day. On the surface, these grim conditions would seem to intensify all the domestic difficulties and juvenile disturbances that characterize high-rise housing for lower-income groups in America.

But however far from ideal the conditions for family life are in the municipal tenements of Hong Kong, they are partly redeemed, it would seem, by two factors not present in contemporary American communities: one is that the Chinese cult of the family still prevails, with the young conditioned to respect their elders and accept their authority, while the parents shoulder their responsibility; and the other is that, under bitter pressure of necessity, every member of the family, old and young, has daily work to do. Thus the young are demoralized neither by the breakdown of the family nor by the absence of active duties and serious tasks; nor yet are their parents haunted by such dreams of effortless affluence as would make their present poverty harder to bear. Even Hong Kong's sweatshop labor seems less demoralizing than total idleness. To protect the young from overidleness has now become as important as it was once to protect them from overwork. To this end both child labor legislation and trade union regulations need to be judiciously overhauled.

One would have reservations about this Hong Kong report, but for the fact that it is confirmed by earlier American experience. Much the same conditions for stability prevailed in American cities among the older immigrant groups; for they were held together by Old World village loyalties, by family closeness, by religious precept and ritual: such hopes as they cherished for a better future were based upon their own foresight, thrift, and self-education. The physical conditions of life in the nineteenth-century slums were often as bad as those in Harlem today and much worse than those in Watts: but there were strong moral counterweights that have now been lost through the more general dissolution of human values.

I have said enough to indicate that neither public housing, slum clearance, nor neighborhood rehabilitation, even when done along more human lines than those now in evidence in urban renewal areas, will suffice by themselves to overcome the internal disorders of the city. Those disorders are symptoms of a wider moral breakdown in our whole civilization; and though good planning, like pure water, is essential to urban health, it is not any more than water a prescription for curing disease. Anything worthy to be called urban renewal today must recapture in concrete form many of the values that our affluent, remote-controlled, electronically massaged society has lost. And there is no urban program that one might offer to minority groups that is not just as imperatively applicable to the rest of society. In that sense, there is no Negro problem and no Puerto Rican problem: there is only a human problem.

On this subject we should do well to heed Dr. C. G. Jung's observations about his own life. In his autobiography, *Memories, Dreams, Reflections,* Jung recalled a difficult period when he was in a psychotic state, at the mercy of his unconscious. What kept him from going completely to pieces was his consciousness that he was an identifiable person, with a family to support, that he was a member of a respected profession, living in a particular house, in an equally familiar and recognizable city, where he had daily duties to perform. By clinging to these reassuring evidences of stability, he was able to resist the internal forces of disintegration.

All of these vital conditions for social continuity and personal integrity have been breaking down in both the central metropolis and its outlying areas; and they have most completely broken down among the lowest-income groups. This unfortunate minority lacks regular work and the self-respect that comes from performing such work: their immediate neighborhood and city have undergone and are still undergoing abrupt structural changes, for both bad and good, that erase their familiar social patterns and destroy their sense of belonging, so that their own selves become so much scattered debris in the larger demolition process. Neither family nor property nor vocational respect nor an earned income nor an identifiable home helps the segregated or displaced minority to resist further internal disintegration.

In analyzing the conditions that saved him from disruption, Jung demonstrated the unique advantage of the historic city over the unstable, incoherent, haphazardly dispersed megalopolis. In that act, he put his finger likewise on the essential requisites for overcoming the forces that have been disintegrating and dehumanizing both our cities and our civilization.

V

VISIONS OF
AMERICA

Wherever a man comes, there comes revolution.
—Ralph Waldo Emerson

Introduction

In *The Story of Utopias* Mumford developed a theme that runs strong in all of his later work—the idea of the creative artist as prophet and revolutionary. In this vividly written book, he presented a program for a new kind of revolution, inspired and led not by insurgent politicians or aroused proletarians but by "creators and originators" in the mold of Emerson, Whitman, and Thoreau. "To the artist has been given the command to go forth into all the world and preach the gospel of beauty. The perfect man is the perfect artist."[1] These words from Walt Whitman describe the spirit in which Mumford began his wide-ranging career as a writer and a self-proclaimed revolutionary.

The cultural awakening Mumford called for in his earliest work would appear first, he was convinced, in America, a nation of unlimited promise; and he and other young writers would prepare the soil for this New World risorgimento. For this, they would need a sustaining cultural tradition to identify with and draw support from. But it must be America's own tradition, Mumford insisted in some of his first published essays of the 1920s.[2] It was time for American intellectuals to stop looking to Europe for guidance, and to take a fresh look at their own culture, for there they would find a vigor and a creative promise that had not been sufficiently appreciated. In association with Van Wyck Brooks, Waldo Frank, Paul Rosenfeld, Constance Rourke, and other "scouts and prospectors," Mumford dedicated himself in the 1920s to uncovering what he called America's buried cultural past. This was his first contribution to the creation of the modern humanist synthesis he called for in *The Story of Utopias.*

At about the same time, Mumford took on a project that would take him nearly a lifetime to complete—to describe "what has happened to the Western European mind since the breakdown of the medieval synthesis, and to trace out the effects of this in America."[3] In the Middle Ages he knew from his reading of John Ruskin, William Morris, and Henry Adams, he found an ideal balance between man's emotional and rational sides, his spiritual and material concerns—a balance he felt had disappeared, for the most part, in the one-sided age of science and rationalism that followed.

He called his first book on this theme *The Golden Day*. The Golden Day he evoked, however, was not Europe in the age of walled towns and soaring cathedrals but America in the period of Whitman, Emerson, and Melville. In the work of these writers he found a living link between the Middle Ages and the immediate concerns of his own time. In three boldly original books, written one after the other—*The Golden Day*, *Herman Melville*, and *The Brown Decades*—Mumford did more than chart the rise and decline of the organic outlook in America; he located in the work of the literary giants of mid-nineteenth-century America a rich native tradition in the arts. He hoped that this would serve as a creative source and inspiration for the regional movement he was simultaneously encouraging in his work for the Regional Planning Association of America. Mumford's writings on regionalism and American cultural history form an interconnected program for the renewal of American culture, with insurgent artists like himself in the vanguard.

In the opening chapter of *The Golden Day*, "The Origins of the American Mind," Mumford describes the settlement of America as the concluding moment of one process, the breakdown of the medieval synthesis and the start of another, the new age of time-keeping, science, Protestantism, and capitalism. When the Europeans settled in America, they brought with them the seeds of this new culture, with its preoccupation with practical utility, material advancement, and the conquest of nature. From the beginning, the besetting problem of the American writer, as he saw it, was how to survive and create in his one-sided utilitarian society. Most American writers, he argued in *The Golden Day*, were in one way or another "curbed and crippled" by the culture of the quick buck and the easy answer.[4]

In developing his argument, Mumford drew freely on the work of Van Wyck Brooks, one of his first mentors and sponsors. Yet *The Golden Day* differs in an important way from Brooks's earliest assessments of the American literary imagination. Mumford found in the procession of American development an outstanding period of achievement and integration, whereas at this point in his career Brooks found only failure and incompletely developed genius.

In the age of the young Herman Melville, American culture had what Mumford called its Golden Day. The five commanding figures of this New World renaissance—Emerson, Thoreau, Whitman, Hawthorne, and Melville—represented for Mumford a new kind of American personality, combining intellectual insight with emotional openness and embodying all the promise and potential of their country. Each possessed what Mumford called complete vision, the quality he most admired in the thought of the Middle Ages. And while they drew upon the wider cultural inheritance of Europe, they did not return to the past for their model of culture. They welcomed the new forces of exploration, science, steam power, and democracy, absorbing them into their work to create a fresh outlook and orientation, just as Mumford hoped the young writers and builders of his own time would do.

Mumford's is undeniably an idealized account of the Golden Day, but we must remember that for him, as for Van Wyck Brooks, the past had no "objective reality."[5] It was the responsibility of each generation to recover and reshape history to its own purposes, to rewrite it in behalf of a better future. It is no coincidence, then, that the creative artists who were to head Mumford's regional movement were also the formative figures in his histories of American development. In their lives and in their work, they personified what he saw disappearing in the current age of specialization and mechanization. Creative, balanced, self-directed, they knew what it meant to live a fully rounded life.

This was the New Man Emerson had celebrated; and of all of the writers of the Golden Day, Emerson had the largest continuing influence on Mumford's life. Emerson is clearly a figure such as young Mumford wanted to be—a moral reformer concerned primarily with values, not with the fine details of political or econmic readjustment; a prophet and a preacher, not a planner or a politician. Like Emerson, Mumford would fearlessly speak out against the injustices of his day, but he never joined any political movements or sects. This isolated him and made him less effective in the short term; but it allowed him to keep his inner integrity intact and his ideas remarkably consistent throughout an obstinate, lifelong struggle for a reconstructed world. Nowhere is this more apparent than in the concluding essay of this section, "The New World Promise," the summation address on American culture he gave at the age of seventy, when he was still "waging contention," in Shelley's words, "with the times' decay," no matter how impossible the odds.

Notes

1. Quoted in Justin Kaplan, *Walt Whitman: A Life* (New York: Simon and Schuster, 1980), 168–69.

2. Mumford, "The Collapse of Tomorrow," *The Freeman* 3 (July 13, 1921): 414–15; Mumford, "Abandoned Roads," *The Freeman* 5 (April 12, 1922), 101–2.

3. Mumford to Dorothy Cecilia Loch, December 8, 1925, LM MSS.

4. Mumford, "The Ordeal of Mark Twain," *Saturday Review of Literature* 9 (May 6, 1933): 473–75.

5. Van Wyck Brooks, "On Creating a Usable Past," *The Dial,* April 11, 1918, 338.

THE ORIGINS
OF THE
AMERICAN MIND

The settlement of America had its origins in the unsettlement of Europe. America came into existence when the European was already so distant in mind from the ancient ideas and ways of his birthplace that the whole span of the Atlantic did not materially widen the gulf. The dissociation, the displacement, and finally the disintegration of European culture became most apparent in the New World: but the process itself began in Europe, and the interests that eventually dominated the American scene all had their origin in the Old World.

The Protestant, the inventor, the politician, the explorer, the restless delocalized man—all these types appeared in Europe before they rallied together to form the composite American. If we can understand the forces that produced them, we shall fathom the origins of the American mind. The settlement of the Atlantic seaboard was the culmination of one process, the breakup of medieval culture, and the beginning of another. If the disintegration went farthest in America, the processes of renewal have, at intervals, been most active in the new country; and it is for the beginnings of a genuine culture, rather than for its relentless exploitation of materials, that the American adventure has been significant. To mark the points at which the culture of the Old World broke down, and to discover in what places a new one has arisen are the two poles of this study. Something of value disappeared with the colonization of America. Why did it disappear? Something of value was created. How did that come about? If I do not fully answer these questions, I propose, at least, to put them a little more sharply, by tracing them to their historical beginnings, and by putting them in their social context.

. . .

In the thirteenth century the European heritage of medieval culture was still intact. By the end of the seventeenth it had become only a heap of fragments, and men showed, in their actions if not by their professions, that it no longer had a hold over their minds. What had happened?

If one tries to sum up the world as it appeared to the contemporaries of Thomas Aquinas or Dante one is conscious of two main facts. The physical earth was bounded by a narrow strip of seas: it was limited: while above and beyond it stretched the golden canopy of heaven, infinite in all its invitations and promises. The medieval culture lived in the dream of eternity: within that dream, the visible world of cities and castles and caravans was little more than the forestage on which the prologue was spoken. The drama itself did not properly open until the curtains of Death rang down, to destroy the illusion of life and to introduce the main scene of the drama, in heaven itself. During the Middle Ages the visible world was definite and secure. The occupations of men were defined, their degree of excellence described, and their privileges and duties, though not without struggle, were set down. Over the daily life lay a whole tissue of meanings, derived from the Christian belief in eternity: the notion that existence was not a biological activity but a period of moral probation, the notion of an intermediate hierarchy of human beings that connected the lowest sinner with the august Ruler of Heaven, the idea that life was significant only on condition that it was prolonged, in beatitude or in despair, into the next world. The beliefs and symbols of the Christian Church had guided men, and partly modified their activities, for roughly a thousand years. Then, one by one, they began to crack; one by one they ceased to be "real" or interesting; and gradually the dream that held them all together started to dissolve. When the process ceased, the united order of Christendom had become an array of independent and sovereign states, and the Church itself had divided up into a host of repellent sects.

At what point did medieval culture begin to break down? The current answer to this, "With the Renaissance," is merely an evasion. When did it finally cease to exist? The answer is that a good part of it is still operative and has mingled with the customs and ideas that have succeeded it. But one can, perhaps, give an arbitrary beginning and an arbitrary end to the whole process. One may say that the first hint of change came in the thirteenth century, with the ringing of the bells, and that medieval culture ceased to dominate and direct the European community when it turned its back upon contemporary experience and failed at last to absorb the meanings of that experience, or to modify its nature. The Church's inability to control usury; its failure to reckon in time with the Protestant criticism of its internal administration; the unreadiness of the scholastics to adapt their methods to the new interests and criteria of science; the failure to prevent the absorption of the free cities, the feudal estates, and the monasteries by the central government—these are some of the stigmata of the decline. It is impossible to give a date to all of them; but it is pretty clear that by the end of the seventeenth century one or another had come to pass in every part of Europe. In countries like England, which were therefore "advanced," all of them had come to pass.

It is fairly easy to follow the general succession of events. First, the bells tolled, and the idea of time, or rather, temporality, resumed its hold over men's minds. All over Europe, beginning in the thirteenth century, the townsman erected campaniles and belfries, to record the passing hour. Immersed in traffic or handicraft, proud of his city or his guild, the citizen began to forget his awful fate in eternity; instead, he noted the succession of the minutes, and planned to make what he could of them. It was an innocent enjoyment, this regular tolling of the hour, but it had important consequences. Ingenious workmen in Italy and southern Germany invented clocks, rigorous mechanical clocks: they adapted the principle of the woodman's lathe and applied it to metal. Here was the beginning of the exact arts. The craftsman began by measuring time; presently he could measure millimeters, too, and with the knowledge and technique introduced by the clockmaker, he was ready to make the telescope, the microscope, the theodolite—all of them instruments of a new order of spatial exploration and measurement.

The interests in time and space advanced side by side. In the fifteenth century the mapmakers devised new means of measuring and charting the earth's surface, and scarcely a generation before Columbus's voyages they began to cover their maps with imaginary lines of latitude and longitude. As soon as the mariner could calculate his position in time and space, the whole ocean was open to him; and henceforward even ordinary men, without the special skill and courage of a Marco Polo or a Leif Ericsson, could travel to distant lands. So time and space took possession of the European's mind. Why dream of heaven or eternity, while the world was still so wide, and each new tract that was opened up promised, if not riches, novelty, and if not novelty, well, a new place to breathe in? So the bells tolled, and the ships set sail. Secure in his newly acquired knowledge, the European traveled outward in space, and, losing that sense of the immediate present which went with his old belief in eternity, he traveled backward and forward in time. An interest in archaeology and utopias characterized the Renaissance. They provided images of purely earthly realizations in past and future: ancient Syracuse and the City of the Sun were equally credible.

The fall of Constantinople and the diffusion of Greek literature had not, perhaps, such a formative influence on this change as the historian once thought. But they accompanied it, and the image of historic Greece and Rome gave the mind a temporary dwelling place. Plainly, the knowledge which once held it so firmly, the convictions that the good Christian once bought so cheaply and cheerfully, no longer sufficed: if they were not altogether thrown aside, the humanists began, with the aid of classic literature, to fill up the spaces they had left open. The European turned aside from his traditional cathedrals and began to build according to Vitruvius. He took a pagan interest in the human body, too, and Leonardo's Saint John was so lost to Christianity that he became Bacchus without changing a feature. The Virgin herself lost her old sanctity. Presto! the Child disappeared, the responsibilities of motherhood were gone, and she was now Venus. What had Saint Thomas Aquinas to say about theology? One could read the *Phaedo*. What had Aristotle to say about natural history? Leonardo, unaided, discovered fossils in the Tuscan hills and inferred that the ocean was once there. Simple peasants might cling to the Virgin, ask for the intercession of the saints, and kneel before the cross; but these images and ideas had lost their hold upon the more acute minds of Europe. They had broken, these intellectual adventurers, outside the tight little world of Here and Eternity: they were interested in Yonder and Yesterday; and since eternity was a long way off and we'll "be damnably moldy a hundred years hence," they accepted tomorrow as a substitute.

There were some who found it hard to shake off the medieval dream in its entirety; so they retained the dream and abandoned all the gracious practices that enthroned it in the daily life. As Protestants, they rejected the outcome of historical Christianity, but not its inception. They believed in the Eucharist, but they did not enjoy paintings of the Last Supper. They believed in the Virgin Mary, but they were not softened by the humanity of Her motherhood. They read, voraciously, the literature of the ancient Jews, and the legends of that sect which grew up by the shores of Galilee, but, using their private judgment and taking the bare words as the sum and substance of their religion, they forgot the interpretations from the early Fathers to Thomas Aquinas which refined that literature and melted it into a comprehensible whole. When the Protestant renounced justification by works, he included under works all the arts which had flourished in the medieval church and created an independent realm of beauty and magnificence. What remained of the faith was perhaps intensified during the first few generations of the Protestant espousal—one cannot doubt the original intensity and vitality of the protest—but alas! so little remained!

In the bareness of the Protestant cathedral of Geneva one has the beginnings of that hard barracks architecture which formed the stone tenements of seventeenth-century Edinburgh, set a pattern for the austere meetinghouses of New England, and finally deteriorated into the miserable shanties that line Main Street. The meagerness of the Protestant ritual began that general starvation of the spirit which finally breaks out, after long repression, in the absurd jamborees of Odd Fellows, Elks, Woodmen, and kindred fraternities. In short, all that was once made manifest in a Chartres, a Strasbourg, or a Durham minster, and in the mass, the pageant, the art gallery, the theater—all this the Protestant bleached out into the bare abstraction of the printed word. Did he suffer any hardship in moving to the New World? None at all. All that he wanted of the Old World he carried within the covers of a book. Fortunately for the original Protestants, that book was a whole literature; in this, at least, it differed from the later protestant canons, perpetrated by Joseph Smith or Mary Baker Eddy. Unfortunately, however, the practices of a civilized society cannot be put between two black covers. So, in some respects, Protestant society ceased to be civilized.

Our critical eyes are usually a little dimmed by the great release of energy during the early Renaissance: we forget that it quickly spent itself. For a little while the great humanists, such as More, Erasmus, Scaliger, and Rabelais, created a new home for the spirit out of the fragments of the past, and the new thoughts were cemented together by the old habits of medieval civilization, which persisted among the peasants and the craftsmen long after they had been undermined in the Church and the palace.

The revival of classic culture, however, did not give men any new power of command over the workaday routine of life, for the very ability to re-enter the past and have commerce with its great minds implied leisure and scholarship. Thus the great bulk of the community had no direct part in the revival, and if the tailor or the tinker abandoned the established Church, it was only to espouse that segment called Protestantism. Tailors and tinkers, almost by definition, could *not* be humanists. Moreover, beyond a certain point, humanism did not make connections with the new experience of the Columbuses and the Newtons any better than did the medieval culture. If the criticism of the pagan scholars released a good many minds from Catholic theology, it did not orient them toward what was "new" and "practical" and "coming." The Renaissance was not, therefore, the launching out of a new epoch: it simply witnessed the breakdown and disruption of the existing science, myth, and fable. When the Royal Society was founded in London in the middle of the seventeenth century the humanities were deliberately excluded. "Science" was indifferent to them.

Once the European, indeed, had abandoned the dream of medieval theology, he could not live very long on the memory of a classic culture: that, too, lost its meaning; that, too, failed to make connections with his new experiences in time and space. Leaving both behind him, he turned to what seemed to him a hard and patent reality: the external world. The old symbols, the old ways of living, had become a blank. Instead of them, he took refuge in abstractions, and reduced the rich actuality of things to a bare description of matter and motion. Along this path went the early scientists, or natural philosophers. By mathematical analysis and experiment, they extracted from the complicated totality of every day experience just those phenomena which could be observed, measured, generalized, and, if necessary, repeated. Applying this exact methodology, they learned to predict more accurately the movements of the heavenly bodies, to describe more precisely the fall of a stone and the flight of a bullet, to determine the carrying load of a bridge, or the composition of a fragment of "matter." Rule, authority, precedent, general consent—these things were all subordinate in scientific procedure to the methods of observation and mathematical analysis: weighing, measuring, timing, decomposing, isolating—all operations that led to results.

At last knowledge could be tested and practice reformed; and if the scientists themselves were usually too busy to see the upshot of their investigations, one who stood on the sidelines, Francis Bacon, was quick to announce their conclusion: science tended to the relief of man's estate.

With the aid of this new procedure, the external world was quickly reduced to a semblance of order. But the meanings created by science did not lead into the core of human life: they applied only to "matter," and if they touched upon life at all, it was through a post-mortem analysis, or by following Descartes and arbitrarily treating the human organism as if it were automatic and externally determined under all conditions. For the scientists, these new abstractions were full of meaning and very helpful; they tunneled through whole continents of knowledge. For the great run of men, however, science had no meaning for itself; it transferred meaning from the creature proper to his estate, considered as an independent and external realm. In short, except to the scientist, the only consequences of science were practical ones. A new view of the universe developed, naturally, but it was accepted less because of any innate credibility than because it was accompanied by so many cogent proofs of science's power. Philosophy, religion, art, none of these activities had ever baked any bread: science was ready, not merely to bake the bread, but to increase the yield of the wheat, grind the flour, and eliminate the baker. Even the plain man would appreciate consequences of this order. Seeing was believing. By the middle of the seventeenth century all the implications of the process had been imaginatively grasped. In 1661 Joseph Glanvill wrote:

> I doubt not posterity will find many things that are now but rumors, verified into practical realities. It may be that, some ages hence, a voyage to the Southern tracts, yea, possibly to the moon, will not be more strange than one to America. To them that come after us, it may be as ordinary to buy a pair of wings to fly to remotest regions, as now a pair of boots to ride a journey; and to confer at the distance of the Indies by sympathetic conveyances may be as usual in future times as by literary correspondence. The restoration of gray hairs to juvenility, and renewing the exhausted marrow, may at length be effected without a miracle; and the turning of the now comparatively desert world into a Paradise may not improbably be effected from late agriculture.

The process of abstraction began in the theology of Protestantism as an attempt to isolate, deform, and remove historic connections; it became habitual in the mental operations of the physical scientist; and it was carried over into other departments.

The extended use of money, to replace barter and service, likewise began during this same period of disintegration. Need I emphasize that in their origin Protestantism, physical science, and finance were all liberating influences? They took the place of habits and institutions which, plainly, were moribund, being incapable of renewal from within. Need I also emphasize the close historic interconnection of the three things? We must not raise our eyebrows when we discover that a scientist like Newton in seventeenth-century England, or Rittenhouse in eighteenth-century America, became master of the mint, nor must we pass by, as a quaint coincidence, the fact that Geneva is celebrated both as the home of Jean Calvin and as the great center of watches and clocks. These connections are not mystical or factitious. The new financial order was a direct outgrowth of the new theological and scientific views. First came a mechanical method of measuring time: then a method of measuring space: finally, in money, men began more widely to apply an abstract way of measuring power, and in money they achieved a calculus for all human activity.

This financial system of measurement released the European from his old sense of social and economic limitations. No glutton can eat a hundred pheasants; no drunkard can drink a hundred bottles of wine at a sitting; and if anyone schemed to have so much food and wine brought to his table daily, he would be made. Once he could exchange the potential pheasants and Burgundy for marks or thalers, he could direct the labor of his neighbors, and achieve the place of an aristocrat without being to the manor born. Economic activity ceased to deal with the tangible realities of the medieval world—land and corn and houses and universities and cities. It was transformed into the pursuit of an abstraction—money. Tangible goods were only a means to this supreme end. When some incipient Rotarian finally coined the phrase "Time is money," he expressed philosophically the equivalence of two ideas which could not possibly be combined, even in thought, so long as money meant houses, food, pictures, and time meant only what it does in Bergson's *durée*, that is, the succession of organic experiences.

Does all this seem very remote from the common life? On the contrary, it goes to the roots of every activity. The difference between historical periods, as the late T. E. Hulme pointed out, is a difference between the categories of their thought. If we have got on the trail of their essential categories, we have a thread which will lead outward into even remote departments of life. The fact is that from the seventeenth century onward, almost every field was invaded by this process of abstraction. The people not affected were either survivals from an older epoch, like the orthodox Jews and Roman Catholics in theology, or the humanists in literature, or they were initiators, working through to a new order—men like Lamarck, Wordsworth, Goethe, Comte.

Last and most plainly of all, the disintegration of medieval culture became apparent in politics. Just as "matter," when examined by the physicist, is abstracted from the aesthetic matrix of our experience, so the "individual" was abstracted by the political philosopher of the new order from the bosom of human society. He ceased, this individual, to maintain his omnipresent relations with city, family, household, club, college, guild, and office: he became the new unit of political society. Having abstracted this purely conceptual person in thought—he had, of course, no more actual existence than an angel or a cherub—the great problem of political thinking in the eighteenth century became: How shall we restore him to society?—for somehow we always find man, as Rousseau grimly said, in chains, that is, in relations with other human beings. The solution that Rousseau and the dominant schools of the time offered was ingenious: each individual is endowed with natural rights, and he votes these political rights into society, as the shareholder votes his economic rights into a trading corporation. This principle of consent was necessary to the well-being of a civil society; and assent was achieved, in free political states, through the operation of the ballot, and the delivery of the general will by a parliament.

The doctrine broke the weakening chain of historical continuity in Europe. It challenged the vested interests; it was ready to declare the existing corporations bankrupt; it was prepared to wipe away the traditional associations and nests of privileges which maintained the clergy, the nobility, the guilds. On its destructive side, the movement for political liberty, like that for free contract, free association, and free investigation, was sane and reasonable; for the abuses of the past were genuine and the grievances usually had more than a small touch of justice. We must not, however, be blind to the consequences of all these displacements and dissociations. Perhaps the briefest way of characterizing them is to say that they made America inevitable. To those who were engaged in political criticism, it seemed that a genuine political order had been created in the setting up of free institutions; but we can see now that the process was an inevitable bit of surgery, rather than the beginning of a more organic form of political association. By 1852 Henry James, Sr., was keen enough to see what had happened: "Democracy," he observed, "is not so much a new form of political life as a dissolution and disorganization of the old forms. It is simply a resolution of government into the hands of the people, a taking down of that which has before existed, and a recommitment of it to its original sources, but it is by no means the substitution of anything else in its place."

Now we begin to see a little more clearly the state of mind out of which the great migrations to the New World became possible. The physical causes have been dwelt on often enough; it is important to recognize that a cultural necessity was at work at the same time. The old culture of the Middle Ages had broken down; the old heritage lingered on only in the "backward" and "unprogressive" countries like Italy and Spain, which drifted outside the main currents of the European mind. Men's interests became externalized and abstract. They fixed their attention on some narrow aspect of experience, and they pushed that to the limit. Intelligent people were forced to choose between the fossilized shell of an old and complete culture, and the new culture, which in origin was thin, partial, abstract, and deliberately indifferent to man's proper interests. Choosing the second, our Europeans already had one foot in America. Let them suffer persecution, let the times get hard, let them fall out with their governments, let them dream of worldly success— and they will come swarming over the ocean. The groups that had most completely shaken off the old symbolisms were those that were most ready for the American adventure: they turned themselves easily to the mastery of the external environment. To them matter alone mattered.

The ultimate results of this disintegration of European culture did not come out, in America, until the nineteenth century. But its immediate consequence became visible, step by step, in the first 150 years or so of the American settlement. Between the landing of the first colonists in Massachusetts, the New Netherlands, Virginia, and Maryland, and the first thin trickle of hunters that passed over the Alleghenies, beginning figuratively with Daniel Boone in 1775, the communities of the Atlantic seaboard were outposts of Europe: they carried their own moral and intellectual climate with them.

During this period, the limitations in the thought of the intellectual classes had not yet wrought themselves out into defects and malformations in the community itself: the house, the town, the farm were still modeled after patterns formed in Europe. It was not a great age, perhaps, but it had found its form. Walking through the lanes of Boston, or passing over the wide lawns to a manor house in Maryland, one would have had no sense of a great wilderness beckoning in the beyond. To tell the truth, the wilderness did not beckon: these solid townsmen, these freeholders, these planters, were content with their civil habits; and if they thought of expansion, it was only over the ocean, in search of Palladian designs for their houses, or of tea and sperm-oil for their personal comfort. On the surface, people lived as they had lived in Europe for many a year.

In the first century of colonization, this life left scarcely any deposit in the mind. There was no literature but a handful of verses, no music except the hymn or some surviving Elizabethan ballad, no ideas except those that circled around the dogmas of Protestantism. But, with the eighteenth century, these American communities stepped fully into the sphere of European ideas, and there was an American equivalent for every new European type. It is amusing to follow the leading biographies of the time. Distinguished American figures step onto the stage, in turn, as if the Muse of History had prepared their entrances and exits. Their arrangement is almost diagrammatic: they form a résumé of the European mind. In fact, these Edwardses and Franklins seem scarcely living characters: they were Protestantism, Science, Finance, Politics.

The first on the stage was Jonathan Edwards: he figured in American thought as the last great expositor of Calvinism. Edwards wrote like a man in a trance, who at bottom is aware that he is talking nonsense; for he was in love with beauty of the soul, like Plato before him, and it was only because he was caught in the premises of determinism that, with a heavy conscience, he followed his dire train of thought to its destination. After Edwards, Protestantism lost its intellectual backbone. It developed into the bloodless Unitarianism of the early nineteenth century, which is a sort of humanism without courage, or it got caught in orgies of revivalism and, under the name of evangelical Christianity, threw itself under the hoofs of more than one muddy satyr. There were great Protestant preachers after Edwards, no doubt: but the triumph of a Channing or a Beecher rested upon personal qualities; and they no longer drew their thoughts from any deep well of conviction.

All the habits that Protestantism developed, its emphasis upon industry, upon self-help, upon thrift, upon the evils of "idleness" and "pleasure," upon the worldliness and wickedness of the arts, were so many gratuitous contributions to the Industrial Revolution. When Professor Morse, the inventor of the telegraph, was still a painter, traveling in Italy, he recorded in one of his letters the animus that pervaded his religious creed: the testimony loses nothing by being a little belated. "I looked around the church," he wrote, "to ascertain what was the effect upon the multitude, assembled. . . . Everything around them, instead of aiding devotion, was entirely calculated to destroy it. The imagination was addressed by every avenue; music and painting pressed into the service of—not religion but the contrary—led the mind away from the contemplation of all that is practical in religion to the charms of mere sense. No instruction was imparted; none ever seems to be intended."

It is but a short step from this attitude to hiring revivalist mountebanks to promote factory morale; nor are these thoughts far from that fine combination of commercial zeal and pious effort which characterize such auxiliaries as the Y.M.C.A. The fictions of poetry and the delusions of feeling were the bugbears of Gradgrind, Bounderby, and M'Choakumchild in Dickens's classic picture of industrialism: for the shapes and images they called forth made those which were familiar to the Protestant mind a little dreary and futile. It was not merely that Protestantism and science had killed the old symbols: they must prevent new ones from developing: they must abolish the contemplative attitude in which art and myth grow up, and create new forms for man's activities. Hence the fury of effort by which the leaders of the new day diverted energies to quantitative production. The capacity to do work, which the new methods in industry had so enormously increased, gave utilitarian objects an importance they had not hitherto possessed. Did not God's Word say "Increase and multiply"? If babies, why not goods: if goods, why not dollars? Success was the Protestant miracle that justified man's ways to God.

The next figure that dominated the American scene stood even more completely for these new forces. He was, according to the pale lights of his time, a thoroughly cultivated man, and in his maturity he was welcomed in London and Paris as the equal of scientists like Priestley and Erasmus Darwin, and of scholars like d'Alembert and d'Holbach. As a citizen, by choice, of Philadelphia, Benjamin Franklin adopted the plain manners and simple thrifty ways of the Quakers. He went into business as a publisher, and with a sort of sweet acuteness in the pursuit of money, he imparted the secrets of his success in the collection of timely saws for which he became famous. The line from Franklin through Samuel Smiles to the latest advertisements for improving one's position and doubling one's income, in the paper that dates back to Franklin's ownership, is a pretty direct one. If one prefers Franklin's bourgeois qualities to those of his successors, it is only perhaps because his life was more fully rounded. If he was not without the usurious habits of the financier, he had also the dignity and freedom of the true scientist.

For Franklin was equally the money-maker, the scientist, the inventor, and the politician, and in science his fair boast was that he had not gained a penny by any of his discoveries. He experimented with electricity; he invented the lightning rod; he improved the draft of chimneys; in fact, on his last voyage home to America, shortly before his death, he was still improving the draft of chimneys. Finally he was a Deist: he had gotten rid of all the "gothick phantoms" that seemed so puerile and unworthy to the quick minds of the eighteenth century —which meant that he was completely absorbed in the dominant abstractions and myths of his own time, namely, matter, money, and political rights. He accepted the mechanical concept of time: time is money; the importance of space: space must be conquered; the desirability of money: money must be made; and he did not see that these, too, are phantoms, in preoccupation with which a man may lose most of the advantages of a civilized life. As a young man, Franklin even invented an elaborate system of moral bookkeeping: utilitarianism can go no further.

Although Franklin's sagacity as a statesman can hardly be overrated, for he had both patience and principle, the political side of the American thought of his time is best summed up in the doctrines of a new immigrant, that excellent friend of humanity, Thomas Paine. Paine's name has served so many purposes in polemics that scarcely anyone seems to take the trouble to read his books: and so more than one shallow judgment has found its way into our histories of literature, written by worthy men who were incapable of enjoying a sound English style, or of following, with any pleasure, an honest system of thought, clearly expressed. *The Rights of Man* is as simple as a geometrical theorem; it contains, I think, most of what is valid in political libertarianism. I know of no other thinker who saw more clearly through the moral humbug that surrounds a good many theories of government. Said Paine:

> Almost everything appertaining to the circumstances of a nation has been absorbed and confounded under the general and mysterious word government. Though it avoids taking to its account the errors it commits and the mischiefs it occasions, it fails not to arrogate to itself whatever has the appearance of prosperity. It robs industry of its honors by pedantically making itself the cause of its effects; and purloins from the general character of man the merits that appertain to him as a social being.

Passage after passage in *The Rights of Man* and *The Age of Reason* is written with the same pithiness. Paine came to America as an adult, and saw the advantages of a fresh start. He believed that if first principles could be enunciated, here, and here alone, was a genuine opportunity to apply them. He summed up the hope in reason and in human contrivance that swelled through the eighteenth century. Without love for any particular country, and without that living sense of history which makes one accept the community's past, as one accepts the totality of one's own life, with all its lapses and mistakes, he was the vocal immigrant, justifying in his political and religious philosophy the complete break he had made with old ties, affections, allegiances.

Unfortunately, a man without a background is not more truly a man: he has merely lost the scenes and institutions which gave him his proper shape. If one studies him closely, one will find that he has secretly arranged another background, made up of shadows that linger in the memory, or he is uneasy and restless, settles down, moves on, comes home again, lives on hopeless tomorrows, or sinks back into mournful yesterdays. The immigrants who came to America after the War of Independence gave up their fatherland in exchange for a Constitution and a Bill of Rights: they forfeited all the habits and institutions which had made them men without getting anything in exchange except freedom from arbitrary misrule. That they made the exchange willingly, proves that the conditions behind them were intolerable; but that the balance was entirely in favor of the new country, is something that we may well doubt. When the new settlers migrated in bodies, like the Moravians, they sometimes managed to maintain an effective cultural life; when they came alone, as "free individuals," they gained little more than cheap land and the privileges of the ballot box. The land itself was all to the good; and no one minded the change, or felt any lack, so long as he did not stop to compare the platitudes of Fourth of July orations with the actualities of the slave trade, the constitutional conventions, Alien and Sedition Acts, and Fugitive Slave Laws.

It was possible for Paine, in the eighteenth century, to believe that culture was served merely by the absence of a church, a state, a social order such as those under which Europe labored. That was the error of his school, for the absence of these harmful or obsolete institutions left a vacancy in society, and that vacancy was filled by work, or more accurately speaking, by busywork, which fatigued the body and diverted the mind from the things which should have enriched it. Republican politics aided this externalism. People sought to live by politics alone; the national state became their religion. The flag, as Professor Carleton Hayes has shown, supplanted the cross, and the Fathers of the Constitution the Fathers of the Church.

The interaction of the dominant interests of industry and politics is illustrated in Paine's life as well as Franklin's. Paine was the inventor of the take-down iron bridge. Indeed, politics and invention recurred rhythmically in his life, and he turned aside from his experiments on the iron bridge to answer Edmund Burke's attack on the French Revolution. "The War of Independence," as he himself said, "energized invention and lessened the catalogue of impossibilities. . . . As one among thousands who had borne a share in that memorable revolution, I returned with them to the enjoyment of a quiet life, and that I might not be idle, undertook to construct a bridge of a single arch for this river [the Schuylkill]."

That I might not be idle! What a tale those words tell! While the aristocracy was in the ascendant, patient hirelings used to apply their knowledge of hydraulics to the working of fountains, as in Versailles, or they devised automatic chess players, or they contrived elaborate clocks which struck the hour, jetted water, caused little birds to sing and wag their tails, and played selections from the operas. It was to such inane and harmless performances that the new skills in the exact arts were first put. The bored patron was amused; life plodded on; nothing was altered. But in the freedom of the new day, the common man, as indifferent to the symbols of the older culture as the great lords and ladies, innocent of anything to occupy his mind, except the notion of controlling matter and mastering the external world—the common man turned to inventions. Stupid folk drank heavily, ate gluttonously, and became libertines; intelligent, industrious men like Franklin and Paine turned their minds to increasing the comforts and conveniences of existence. Justification by faith: that was politics: the belief in a new heaven and a new earth to be established by regular elections and parliamentary debate. Justification by works: that was invention. No frivolities entered this new religion. The new devices all saved labor, decreased distances, and in one way or another multi-plied riches.

With these inventors, the American, like his contemporary in Europe, began the utilitarian conquest of his environment. From this time on, men with an imaginative bias like Morse, the pupil of Benjamin West, men like Whitney, the schoolteacher, like Fulton, the miniature painter, turned to invention or at least the commercial exploitation of inventions without a qualm of distrust: to abandon the imaginative arts seemed natural and inevitable, and they no longer faced the situation, as the painters of the Renaissance had done, with a divided mind. Not that America began or monopolized the developments of the Industrial Revolution: the great outbreak of technical patents began, in fact, in England about 1760, and the first inklings of the movement were al-ready jotted down in Leonardo da Vinci's notebooks. The point is that in Europe heavy layers of the old culture kept large sections of the directing classes in the old ways. Scholars, literary men, historians, art-ists still felt no need of justifying themselves by exclusive devotion to practical activities. In America, however, the old culture had worn thin, and in the rougher parts of the country it did not exist. No one in America was unaffected by the progress of invention; each improve-ment was quickly cashed in. When Stendhal wrote *L'Amour* the Ameri-can love of comfort had already become a by-word: he refers to it with contempt.

Given an old culture in ruins, and a new culture in vacuo, this externalizing of interest, this ruthless exploitation of the physical envi-ronment, was, it would seem, inevitable. Protestantism, science, inven-tion, political democracy—all of these institutions denied the old values; all of them, by denial or by precept or by actual absorption, furthered the new activities. Thus in America the new order of Europe came quickly into being. If the nineteenth century found us more raw and rude, it was not because we had settled in a new territory; it was rather because our minds were not buoyed up by all those memorials of a great past that floated over the surface of Europe. The American was thus a stripped European; and the colonization of America can, with justice, be called the dispersion of Europe—a movement carried on by people incapable of sharing or continuing its past. It was to America that the outcast Europeans turned, without a Moses to guide them, to wander in the wilderness; and here they have remained in exile, not without an occasional glimpse, perhaps, of the promised land.

THE
GOLDEN DAY

No one who was awake in the early part of the nineteenth century was unaware that in the practical arrangements of life men were on the brink of a great change. The rumble of the Industrial Revolution was heard in the distance long before the storm actually broke; and before American society was completely transformed through the work of the land pioneer and the industrial pioneer, there arose here and there over the land groups of people who anticipated the effects of this revolution and were in revolt against all its preoccupations. Some of these groups reverted to an archaic theocracy, like that of the Mormons, in which a grotesque body of beliefs was combined with an extraordinary amount of economic sagacity and statesmanship; some of them became disciples of Fourier and sought to live in cooperative colonies, which would foster men's various capacities more fully than the utilitarian community.

The air quivered with both hope and trepidation. In the new industrial cities, the slum made its appearance; great bodies of depauperate immigrants with strange traditions altered the balance of power; politics became the business of clever rapscallions who looted the public treasury; by the end of the fifties an editorial writer in *Harper's Weekly* prayed for professional administrators who might bring a public conscience into the corrupt democracy of the big cities. In general, all the forces that blighted America after the Civil War existed in embryonic form between 1830 and 1860. At the same time, the older regions began to reap the fruits of two centuries of contact with the new soil and new customs. It is at the hour when the old ways are breaking up that men step outside them sufficiently to feel their beauty and significance: lovers are often closest at the moment of parting. In New England, the inherited medieval civilization had become a shell; but, drying up, it left behind a sweet acrid aroma, and for a brief day it had a more intense existence in the spirit. Before the life itself collapsed, men felt the full weight of it in their imagination. In the act of passing away, the Puritan begot the Transcendentalist, and the will-to-power, which had made him what he was, with his firm but forbidding character and his conscientious but narrow activity, gave way to the will-to-perfection.

The period from 1830 to 1860 was in America one of disintegration and fulfillment: the new and the old, the crude and the complete, the base and the noble, mingled together. Puritan fanatics like Goodyear brought to the vulcanization of rubber the same intense passion that Thoreau brought to Nature: sharp mountebanks like Barnum grew out of the same sort of Connecticut village that nourished an inspired schoolmaster like Bronson Alcott: genuine statesmen like Brigham Young organized the colonization of Utah whilst nonentities like Pierce and Buchanan governed the whole country. During this period, the old culture of the seaboard settlement had its Golden Day in the mind; the America of the migrations, on the other hand, partly because of weaknesses developed in the pioneer, partly because of the one-sided interests of the industrialist, and partly because of the volcanic eruption of the Civil War, had up to 1890 little more than the boomtown optimism of the Gilded Age to justify its existence.

Despite the foreboding that every intelligent mind felt when it contemplated the barbarism of the industrial age, inimical to any culture except that which grew out of its own inhuman absorption in abstract matter and abstract power, the dominant note of the period was one of hope. Before the Civil War the promise of the westward march expanded the sense of achievement that came over the Eastern states; and men faced the world with a confidence that went beyond the complacent optimism of the British Utilitarians—tainted as that was by Carlyle's dire reminders of the palpable wreckage and jetsam that had been washed into the slums of London, Manchester, and Birmingham on the wave of "industrial prosperity."

There were no Carlyles or Ruskins in America during this period; they were almost unthinkable. One might live in this atmosphere, or one might grapple with the White Whale and die; but if one lived, one lived without distrust, without inner complaint, and even if one scorned the ways of one's fellows, as Thoreau did, one remained among them, and sought to remedy in oneself the abuses that existed in society. Transcendentalism might criticize a fossilized past; but no one imagined that the future could be equally fossilized. The testimony is unqualified. One breathed hope, as one might breathe the heady air of early autumn, pungent with the smell of hickory fires and baking bread, as one walked through the village street.

"One cannot look on the freedom of this country, in connection with its youth," wrote Emerson in "The Young American," "without a presentment that here shall laws and institutions exist in some proportion to the majesty of Nature. . . . It is a country of beginnings, of projects, of vast designs and expectations. It has no past: all has an onward and prospective look." The voice of Whitman echoed Emerson through a trumpet: but that of Melville, writing in 1850, was no less sanguine and full-pulsed: "God has predestinated, mankind expects, great things from our race; and great things we feel in our souls. The rest of the nations must soon be in our rear. We are the pioneers of the world; the advance guard, sent on through the wilderness of untried things, to break a new path in the New World that is ours. In our youth is our strength; in our inexperience, our wisdom."

"Every institution is the lengthened shadow of a man." Here and there in America during its Golden Day grew up a man who cast a shadow over the landscape. They left no labor-saving machines, no discoveries, and no wealthy bequests to found a library or a hospital: what they left was something much less and much more than that—an heroic conception of life. They peopled the landscape with their own shapes. This period nourished men, as no other has done in America before or since. Up to that time, the American communities were provincial; when it was over, they had lost their base, and spreading all over the landscape, deluged with newcomers speaking strange languages and carrying on Old World customs, they lost that essential likeness which is a necessary basis for intimate communication. The first settlement was complete: agricultural and industrial life were still in balance in the older parts of the country; and on the seas trade opened up activities for the adventurous. When [George] Ticknor was preparing to go to Germany, in the first decade of the century, there was one German dictionary, apparently, in New England. Within a generation, Goethe was translated, selections from the European classics were published; and importations of the Indian, Chinese, and Persian classics widened the horizon of people who had known India only by its shawls, China only by its tea.

The traffic of the American merchantmen across the seas brought ideas with every load of goods. Living lustily in all these new experiences, the pushing back of the frontier, the intercourse with the ancient East, the promises of science and invention—steamboats; railroads; telegraphs; rubber raincoats; reapers; Von Baer; Faraday; Darwin—living in these things, and believing in them, the capacity for philosophic exploration increased, too; and when an Emerson went into retreat, he retired with an armful of experiences and ideas comparable only to the treasuries that the Elizabethans grandly looted. Within the circle of the daily fact, the Transcendentalists might protest against the dull materialism which was beginning to dominate the period: but it needed only a little boldness to convert the materialism itself into a source of new potencies.

An imaginative New World came to birth during this period, a new hemisphere in the geography of the mind. That world was the climax of American experience. What preceded led up to it: what followed dwindled away from it; and we who think and write today are either continuing the first exploration, or we are disheartened, and relapse into some stale formula, or console ourselves with empty gestures of frivolity.

The American scene was a challenge; and men rose to it. The writers of this period were not alone; if they were outcasts in the company of the usual run of merchants, manufacturers, and politicians, they were at all events attended by a company of people who had shared their experience and moved on eagerly with it. When all is reckoned, however, there is nothing in the minor writers that is not pretty fully recorded by Emerson, Thoreau, Whitman, Melville, and Hawthorne. These men, as D. H. Lawrence has well said, reached a verge. They stood between two worlds. Part of their experience enabled them to bring the Protestant movement to its conclusion: the critical examination of men, creeds, and institutions, which is the vital core of Protestantism, could not go much further. But already, out of another part of their experience, that which arose out of free institutions planted in an unpre-empted soil, molded by fresh contact with forest and sea and the more ingenious works of man, already this experience pushed them beyond the pit Melville fell into, and led them toward new institutions, a new art, a new philosophy, formed on the basis of a wider past than the European, caught by his Mediterranean or Palestinian cultures, was capable of seizing.

It was the organic break with Europe's past that enabled the American to go on; just as the immigration of people to America came to include specimens from almost all the folk of the world, so the American past widened sufficiently to bring Eastern and Western cultures into a common focus. The American went on. Whereas, in their search for a new basis for culture, Nietzsche went back to pre-Socratic Greece, Carlyle to Abbot Samson, Tolstoy and Dostoevski to primitive Christianity, and Wagner to the early Germanic fables, Emerson, Thoreau, and Whitman went forward leaning on the experiences about them, using the past as the logger uses the corduroy road, to push further into the wilderness and still have a sound bottom under him.

They fathomed the possibilities, these Americans, of a modern basis for culture, and fathoming it, were nearer to the sources of culture, nearer to the formative thinkers and poets of the past, than those who sought to restore the past. What is vital in the American writers of the Golden Day grew out of a life which opened up to them every part of their social heritage. And a thousand more experiences and fifty million more people have made us no wiser. The spiritual fact remains unalterable, as Emerson said, by many or few particulars. It is the spiritual fact of American experience that we shall examine during the period of its clearest expression. . . .

All the important thinkers who shared in this large experience were born between 1800 and 1820; their best work was done by the time the Civil War came; if not beyond the reach of its hurt, they at all events could not be completely overthrown or warped by it. The leader of these minds, the central figure of them all, was Ralph Waldo Emerson. He was the first American philosopher with a fresh doctrine: he was the first American poet with a fresh theme: he was the first American prose writer to escape, by way of the Elizabethan dramatists and the seventeenth-century preachers, from the smooth prose of Addison or the stilted periods of Johnson. He was an original, in the sense that he was a source: he was the glacier that became the white mountain torrent of Thoreau, and expanded into the serene, ample-bosomed lake of Whitman. He loses a little by this icy centrality: he must be climbed, and there is so much of him that people become satisfied with a brief glimpse, and forget that they have not reached the summit which dominates the lower peaks and platforms. His very coldness seems familiar to academic minds; and for too long they appropriated him, as one of them: they forgot that his coldness is not that of an impotence, but of an inner intensity: it burns! The outward manner of his life was mild: there are summer afternoons when from the distance Mont Blanc itself seems little more than a cone of ice cream; and his contemporaries forgot that this sweet man carried a lash, a lash that would not merely drive the money changers from the temple but the priests.

Emerson was a sort of living essence. The preacher, the farmer, the scholar, the sturdy New England freeholder, yes, and the shrewd Yankee peddler or mechanic, were all encompassed by him; but what they meant in actual life had fallen away from him: he represented what they stood for in eternity. With Emerson's works one might reconstruct the landscape and society of New England: a few things would be left out from Nature which Thoreau would have to supply for us—a handful of flora and fauna, and the new Irish immigrants who were already building the railroads and who finally were to take possession of Boston —but what remained would still be everything of importance in the New England scheme of things. The weaknesses of New England are there, too: its bookishness, its failure, as Margaret Fuller said of Emerson, to kiss the earth sufficiently, its impatience to assume too quickly an upright position, its too-tidy moral housekeeping. Strong or weak, Emerson was complete: in his thought the potentialities of New England were finally expressed.

It is almost impossible to sum up Emerson's doctrine, for he touched life on many sides, and what is more, he touched it freshly, so though he is a Platonist, one will not find Plato's doctrines of Art in his essay on Art; and though he was in a very derivative way a Kantian, one will not find Kant's principles at the bottom of his ethics. With most of the resources of the past at his command, Emerson achieved nakedness: his central doctrine is the virtue of this intellectual, or cultural, nakedness: the virtue of getting beyond the institution, the habit, the ritual, and finding out what it means afresh in one's own consciousness. Protestantism had dared to go this far with respect to certain minor aspects of the Catholic cult: Emerson applied the same method in a more sweeping way, and buoyed up by his faith in the future of America— a country endowed with perhaps every advantage except venerability —he asked not merely what Catholic ritual means but all ritual, not merely what dynastic politics means but all politics; and so with every other important aspect of life. Emerson divested everything of its associations, and seized it afresh, to make what associations it could with the life he had lived and the experience he had assimilated. As a result, each part of the past came to him on equal terms: Buddha had perhaps as much to give as Christ: Hafiz could teach him as much as Shakespeare or Dante. Moreover, every fragment of present experience lost its associated values, too: toward the established hierarchy of experiences, with vested interests that no longer, perhaps, could exhibit the original power of sword or spade, he extended the democratic challenge: perhaps new experiences belonged to the summit of aristocracy, and old lines were dying out, or were already dead, leaving only empty venerated names.

Emerson saw the implications of this attempt to rethink life, and to accept only what was his. He did not shrink from them. "Nothing is at last sacred but the integrity of your own mind. . . . I remember an answer which when quite young I was prompted to make to a valued adviser, who was wont to importune me with the dear old doctrines of the church. On my saying, 'What have I to do with the sacredness of traditions, if I live wholly from within?' my friend suggested,—'But these impulses may be from below, not from above.' I replied, 'They do not seem to me to be such; but if I am the Devil's child, I will live then from the Devil.' No law can be sacred to me but that of my Nature."

"Life only avails, not the having lived." There is the kernel of the Emersonian doctrine of self-reliance: it is the answer which the American, in the day of his confidence and achievement, flung back into the face of Europe, where the "having lived" has always been so conspicuous and formidable. In a certain sense, this doctrine was a barbarism; but it was a creative barbarism, a barbarism that aimed to use the old buildings not as a shell, but as a quarry; neither casting them aside altogether, nor attempting wretchedly to fit a new and lush existence into the old forms. The transcendental young photographer in Hawthorne's *House of the Seven Gables* suggested that houses should be built afresh every generation, instead of lingering on in dingy security, never really fitting the needs of any family, but that which originally conceived and built it. An uncreative age is aghast at this suggestion: for the new building may be cruder than the old, the new problem may not awaken sufficient creative capacities, equal to the previous one: these are the necessary counsels of prudence, impotence.

In the heyday of the American adventure, neither Emerson nor Hawthorne was afraid. Emerson rethought life, and in the mind he coined new shapes and images and institutions, ready to take the place of those he discarded. A building was perishable; a custom might fall into disuse; but what of it? The mind was inexhaustible; and it was only the unawakened and unimaginative practical people who did not feel that these dearly purchased trinkets might all be thrown into the melting pot and shaped over again, without a penny lost. It was not that nakedness itself was so desirable: but clothes were cheap! Why keep on piecing together and patching the old doctrines, when the supply never could run out, so long as life nourished Emersons? "We shall not always set so great a price," he exclaimed, "on a few texts, a few lives. We are like children who repeat by rote the sentences of grandames and tutors, and, as they grow older, of the men of talents and character they chance to see,—painfully recollecting the exact words they spoke; afterwards, when they come into the point of view which these had who uttered these sayings, they understand them, and are willing to let the words go; for at any time, they can use words as good when the occasion comes. . . . When we have new perceptions, we shall gladly disburden the memory of its hoarded treasures, as of old rubbish."

The Platonism of Emerson's mind has been overemphasized; or rather, it has been misconstrued to mean that he lived in a perpetual cloud world. The truth is, however, that Emerson's Platonism was not a matter simply of following Plato: it was a matter of living like Plato, and achieving a similar mode of thought. Critics have too often spoken of Plato's forms as if they were merely a weak escape from the urgent problems of fifth-century Athens; and of Emerson's, as if they were a neurotic withdrawal from the hurly-burly of American life. They were both, in a sense, a withdrawal; but it was a withdrawal of water into a reservoir, or of grain into a bin, so that they might be available later, if they could not be effectively distributed at once. Both Plato and Emerson had mixed with the life about them and knew its concrete details: both were conscious of the purely makeshift character of existing institutions; both were aware that they were in a period of transition. Instead of busying himself with the little details of political or economic readjustment, each sought to achieve a pattern which would permit the details to fall into place, and to make possible a creative renovation. Emerson wrote about Man the Reformer; but he never belonged to any political sect or cult. The blight of Negro slavery awakened his honest anger, and his essay on the Know-nothings is an excellent diatribe: but even this great issue did not cause him to lose his perspective: he sought to abolish the white slaves who maintained that institution.

In coupling Emerson's name with Plato's I have hinted that Emerson was a philosopher; I see no reason to qualify this hint, or to apologize for the juxtaposition. He has been more or less grudgingly given such a place by current philosophic commentators, because on a superficial examination there is no originality in his metaphysics: both Plato and Kant had given an independent reality to the world of ideas, and the habit of treating existing facts as symbols is so ancient it became a shocking novelty when re-employed in our own time by Dr. Sigmund Freud. The bare metaphysical outlines of Emerson's work give no insight, however, into the body of his thought as a whole. The content of Emerson's philosophy is much richer, I think, than that of any of his contemporaries; and he is denied a high place in philosophy largely because the content is so rich that it cannot be recognized, in the attenuated twilight of academic groves, as philosophy. Hegel and Comte and Spencer, Emerson's contemporaries, had all found formulae which led them into relations with a vast mass of concrete facts: the weakness of their several philosophies was due to severe defects of personality—they were sexually neurotic, like Comte, with his pathetic apotheosis of Clothilde, or they were querulous invalids, like Spencer, who had never been able to correct by a wider experience the original bias given to his mind by his early training as a railroad engineer. Emerson had the good fortune to live a healthy and symmetrical life: he answered Tolstoy's demand for essential greatness—he had no kinks.

In him, philosophy resumed the full gamut of human experience it had known in Pythagoras and Plato.

Emerson's uniqueness, for his time, consists in the fact that he appreciated not merely the factual data of science, and the instrumental truth of scientific investigation: he also recognized the formative role of ideas, and he saw the importance of "dialectic" in placing new patterns before the mind which did not exist, ready-made, in the order of Nature. "All the facts of the animal economy, sex, nutriment, gestation, birth, growth, are symbols of the passage of the world into the soul of man, to suffer there a change, and reappear a new and higher fact." The occasion for, or the efficacy of, this passage into the soul of man was denied by the externalism of nineteenth-century empiricism; obscurely, it was the ground for contention between religion and science, a quarrel which religion lost by holding fast to a purely superstitious empiricism. If instrumental truths are the only order of truth, all religion is a superstition, all poetry a puerility, and all art itself is a weak anticipation of photography and mechanical drawing.

Emerson's affirmation of both physics and dialectic, of both science and myth, an affirmation which justified the existence of the artists, the poet, the saint, was of prime importance; for he did not make the mistake of disdaining the order and power that science had achieved within its proper department. Emerson was a Darwinist before the *Origin of Species* was published, because he was familiar with the investigations which were linking together the chain of organic continuity, and he was ready to follow the facts wherever they would lead him. Agassiz, Cambridge's great man of science, accepted the facts, too; but he was afraid of them; insulated in his evangelical Christianity, he insisted that the facts did not exist in Nature but in the mind of God. Emerson was untroubled by Agassiz's reluctance: the function of "God" was perpetually being performed for him in the passage of the world into the soul of man; and there was nothing in his philosophy to make him deny an orderly sequence in Nature. For Emerson, matter and spirit were not enemies in conflict: they were phases of man's experience: matter passed into spirit and became a symbol: spirit passed into matter and gave it a form; and symbols and forms were the essences through which man lived and fulfilled his proper being. Who was there among Emerson's contemporaries in the nineteenth century that was gifted with such a complete vision? To withhold the name of philosopher from the man who saw and expressed this integral vision of life so clearly is to deny the central office of philosophy.

Emerson's thought does not seal the world up into a few packets, tied with a formula, and place them in a pigeonhole. In the past, it was not limited to a phase of Christianity, nor a phase of classic culture: it roamed over a much wider area, and as he himself suggested, used Plato and Proclus, not for what they were, but as so many added colors for his palette. The past for Emerson was neither a prescription nor a burden: it was rather an aesthetic experience. Being no longer inevitable in America, that is, no longer something handed down with a fellowship at Oxford or a place at court, the past could be entertained freely and experimentally. It could be revalued; and the paradox of Brahma became as acceptable as the paradox that the meek shall inherit the earth.

The poet, for Emerson, was the liberator; and in that sense, he was a great poet. With him one does not feel that our "civilization nears its meridan, but rather that we are yet only at the cock-crowing and the morning star." The promise of America, of an unspotted Nature and a fresh start, had seeped into every pore of Emerson's mind. "Do not set the least value on what I do," he warns, "nor the least discredit on what I do not, as if I pretended to settle anything as true or false. I unsettle all things. No facts to me are sacred; none are profane; I simply experiment, an endless seeker, with no Past at my back. . . . Why should we import rags and relics into the new hour? . . . Nothing is secure but life, transition, the energizing spirit. No love can be bound by oath or covenant to secure it against a higher love. No truth so sublime but it may be trivial tomorrow in the light of new thoughts. People wish to be settled: only as far as they are unsettled is there any hope for them."

The vigor of this challenge, the challenge of the American wilderness, the challenge of the new American society, where the European lost the security of his past in order to gain a better stake in the future —who can but feel that this is what was distinguished and interesting in our American experience, and what was salutary, for all its incidental defects, in the dumb physical bravado of the pioneer? Two men met the challenge and carried it further: Thoreau and Whitman. They completed the Emersonian circle, carrying the potted flower of the scholar's study out into the spring sunshine, the upturned earth, and the keen air.

The pioneer who broke the trail westward left scarcely a trace of his adventure in the mind: what remains are the tags of pioneer customs, and mere souvenirs of the past, like the Pittsburgh stogy, which is our living connection today with the Conestoga wagon, whose drivers used to roll cigars as the first covered wagons plodded over the Alleghenies.

What the pioneer felt, if he felt anything, in the midst of these new solitudes; what he dreamt, if he dreamt anything; all these things we must surmise from a few snatches of song, from the commonplace reports issued as the trail was nearing its end, by the generation of Mark Twain and Hamlin Garland, or by the reflections of their sons and daughters, romantically eager, like John G. Neihardt's, critically reflective, like Susan Glaspell's, or wistfully sordid, like Edgar Lee Masters's *Anthology.* Those who really faced the wilderness, and sought to make something out of it, remained in the East; in their reflection, one sees the reality that might have been. Henry David Thoreau was perhaps the only man who paused to give a report of the full experience. In a period when men were on the move, he remained still; when men were on the make, he remained poor; when civil disobedience broke out in the lawlessness of the cattle thief and the mining-town rowdy, by sheer neglect, Thoreau practiced civil disobedience as a principle, in protest against the Mexican War, the Fugitive Slave Law, and slavery itself. Thoreau in his life and letters shows what the pioneer movement might have come to if this great migration had sought culture rather than material conquest, and an intensity of life, rather than mere extension over the continent.

Born in Concord about half a generation after Emerson, Thoreau found himself without the preliminary searchings and reachings of the young clergyman. He started from the point that his fellow townsman Emerson had reached; and where the first cleared out of his mind every idea that made no direct connections with his personal experience, Thoreau cleared out of his life itself every custom or physical apparatus, to boot, which could not stand up and justify its existence. "A native of the United States," de Tocqueville had observed, "clings to the world's goods as if he were certain never to die; and he is so hasty at grasping at all within his reach, that one would suppose he was constantly afraid of not living long enough to enjoy them. He clutches everything, he holds nothing fast, but soon loosens his grasp to pursue fresh gratifications." Thoreau completely reversed this process: it was because he wanted to live fully that he turned away from everything that did not serve toward this end. He prized the minutes for what they brought, and would not exercise his citizenship at the town meeting if a spring day by Walden Pond had greater promise; nor would he fill his hours with gainful practices, as a maker of pencils or a surveyor, beyond what was needed for the bare business of keeping his bodily self warm and active.

Thoreau seized the opportunity to consider what in its essentials a truly human life was; he sought, in Walden, to find out what degree of food, clothing, shelter, labor, was necessary to sustain it. It was not animal hardihood or a merely tough physical regimen he was after; nor did he fancy, for all that he wrote in contempt of current civilization, that the condition of the woodcutter, the hunter, or the American

Indian was in itself to be preferred. What he discovered was that people are so eager to get the ostentatious "necessaries" of a civil life that they lose the opportunity to profit by civilization itself: while their physical wants are complicated, their lives, culturally, are not enriched in proportion, but are rather pauperized and bleached.

Thoreau was completely oblivious to the dominant myths that had been bequeathed by the seventeenth century. Indifferent to the illusion of magnitude, he felt that Walden Pond, rightly viewed, was as vast as the ocean, and the woods and fields and swamps of Concord were as inexhaustible as the Dark Continent. In his study of Nature, he had recourse on occasion to the scientific botanists and zoologists; but he himself had possession of a method that they were slow to arrive at; and it is easier for us today to understand the metaphysical distinction of Thoreau's kind of nature study than it would have been for Gray or Agassiz. Like Wordsworth before him, like Bergson after him, he realized that in current science "we murder to dissect," and he passed beyond the artful dismemberments of contemporary science to the flower and the bird and the habitat themselves. "Not a single scientific term or distinction," he wrote once in his notebook, "is the least to the purpose. You would fain perceive something and you must approach the object totally unprejudiced. You must be aware that nothing is what you take it to be. . . . Your greatest success will be simply to perceive that such things are, and you will have no communication to make to the Royal Society." In other words. Thoreau sought in Nature all the manifold qualities of being; he was not merely in search of those likenesses or distinctions which help to create classified indexes and build up a system. The aesthetic qualities of a fern were as important for his mode of apprehension as the number of spores on a frond; it was not that he disdained science, but that, like the old herbalists and naturalists he admired, he would not let the practical offices of science, its classification, its measurements, its numerations, take precedence over other forms of understanding. Science, practiced in this fashion, is truly part of a humane life, and a Darwin dancing for joy over a slide in his microscope, or a Pupin, finding the path to physics through his contemplation of the stars he watched as a herd boy through the night, are not poorer scientists but richer ones for these joys and delights: they merely bow to the bias of utilitarianism when they leave these things out of their reports. In his attitude toward scientific truth Thoreau was perhaps a prophetic figure; and a new age may do honor to his metaphysics as well as to his humanity.

The resolute acceptance of his immediate milieu as equal to the utmost that the earth could offer stood by Thoreau in his other activities, too. He captained huckleberry parties as he might have led a battle, and was just as much the leader in one as he would have been in the other. His courage he reserved for better occasions than the battlefield, for he was ready to go to jail for his principles, and to mock Emerson for remaining outside. As for his country, he loved the land too well to confuse it with the shifting territorial boundaries of the national state. In this, he had that vital regional consciousness which every New Englander shared: Hawthorne himself had said that New England was as large a piece of territory as could claim his allegiance. Thoreau was not deceived by the rascality of politicians, who were ready to wage war for a coveted patch of Mexico's land; nor did he side with those who, for the sake of the Union, were ready to give up the principles that alone had made the Union valuable. What he loved was the landscape, his friends, and his companions in the spirit: when the political state presumed to exercise a brass counterclaim on these loyalties it might go to the devil.

Thoreau's attitude toward the State, one must note, was just the opposite to that of the progressive pioneer. The latter did not care what sort of landscape he "located" in, so long as he could salute the flag of his country and cast his vote: Thoreau, on the contrary, was far too religious a man to commit the idolatry of saluting a symbol of secular power; and he realized that the affairs controlled by the vote represented only a small fraction of an interesting life, while so far from being indifferent to the land itself, he absorbed it, as men have absorbed legends, and guarded it, as men preserve ceremonies. The things which his contemporaries took for the supreme realities of life, matter, money, and political rights, had only an instrumental use for Thoreau: they might contribute a little to the arrangement of a good life, but the good life itself was not contained, was not even implied, in them. One might spend one's life pursuing them without having lived. "There is not one of my readers," he exclaimed, "who has yet lived a whole human life."

In Thoreau's time, industrialism had begun to puff itself up over its multiplication of goods and the increase of wants that it fostered, in order to provide the machine with an outlet for its ever-too-plentiful supply. Thoreau simply asked: "Shall we always study to obtain more of these things, and not sometimes be content with less?" "If we do not get our sleepers and forge rails and devote long days and nights to work," he observed ironically, "but go tinkering with our lives to improve *them*, who will build the railroads?" Thoreau was not a penurious fanatic, who sought to practice bare living merely as a moral exercise: he wanted to obey Emerson's dictum to save on the low levels and spend on the high ones. It is this that distinguishes him from the tedious people whose whole existence is absorbed in the practice of living on beans, or breathing deeply, or wearing clothes of a vegetable origin:

simplification did not lead in Thoreau to the cult of simplicity: it led to a higher civilization.

What drove Thoreau to the solitude of the woods was no cynical contempt for the things beyond his reach. "Before we can adorn our houses with beautiful objects, the walls must be stripped, and our lives must be stripped, and beautiful housekeeping and beautiful living be laid for a foundation: now, a taste for the beautiful is most cultivated out of doors, where there is no house, and no housekeeper." The primeval woods were a favorable beginning for the search; but Thoreau did not think they could be the end of it. The land itself, however, did stir his imagination; he wrote:

> All things invite this earth's inhabitants
> To rear their lives to an unheard of height,
> And meet the expectation of the land.

"The expectation of the land!" One comes upon that phrase, or its equivalent, in almost every valid piece of early American thought. One thinks of moorland pastures by the sea, dark with bayberries and sweet fern, breaking out among the lichened rocks; and the tidal rivers bringing their weedy tang to the low meadows, wide and open in the sun; the purple pine groves, where the needles, bedded deep, hum to the wind, or the knotted New England hills, where the mountain laurel in June seems like upland snow, left over, or where the marble breaks through into clusters of perpetual laurel and everlasting; one sees mountain lakes, giant aquamarines, sapphires, topazes, and upland pastures where the blue, purple, lavender, and green of the huckleberry bushes give way in autumn to the fringe of sumach by the roadside, volcanoes of reds and crimsons; the yellow of September cornfields, with intenser pumpkins lying between the shocks, or the naked breasts and flanks of the autumn landscape, quivering in uneasy sleep before the white blanket puts it to rest. To smell this, taste this, and feel and climb and walk over this landscape, once untouched, like an unopened letter or a lover unkissed—who would not rise to meet the expectation of the land? Partly, it was the challenge of babyhood: how will it grow up and what will become of it? Partly, it was the charm of innocence; or again, it was the sense of the mighty variety that the whole continent gives, as if between the two oceans every possible human habitat might be built, and every conceivable variety of experience fathomed.

What the aboriginal Indian had absorbed from the young earth, Thoreau absorbed; what the new settlers had given her, the combing of the plow, the cincture of the stone fence or the row of planted elms, these things he absorbed too; for Thoreau, having tasted the settled life of Concord, knew that the wilderness was not a permanent home for man: one might go there for fortification, for a quickening of the senses, for a tightening of all the muscles; but that, like any retreat, is a special exercise and wants a special occasion: one returned to Nature in order to become, in a deeper sense, more cultivated and civilized, not in order to return to crudities that men had already discarded. Looking ahead, Thoreau saw what was needed to preserve the valuable heritage of the American wilderness. He wrote:

> The kings of England formerly had their forests to hold the king's game, for sport or food, sometimes destroying villages to create and extend them; and I think that they were impelled by a true instinct. Why should not we, who have renounced the king's authority, have our national preserves, where no villages need be destroyed, in which the bear and panther, and some even of the hunter race, may still exist, and not be "civilized off the face of the earth,"—our own forests, not to hold the king's game merely, but to hold and preserve the king himself also, the lord of creation,—and not in idle sport of food, but for inspiration and our own true recreation? or shall we, like the villains, grub them all up, poaching on our own national domain?

These pregnant suggestions of Thoreau, which were to be embodied only after two generations in our national and state parks, and in projects like Mr. Benton MacKaye's great conception of the Appalachian Trail, make the comments of those who see in him only an arch-individualist, half Diogenes, half Rousseau, seem a little beside the point. The individualism of an Emerson or a Thoreau was the necessary complement of the thoroughly socialized existence of the New England town; it was what prevented these towns from becoming collections of yes-men, with never an opinion or an emotion that differed from their neighbors. He wrote for his fellow townsmen; and his notion of the good life was one that should carry to a higher pitch the existing polity and culture of Concord itself. "As the nobleman of cultivated taste surrounds himself with whatever conduces to his culture—genius—learning—wit—books—paintings—statuary—music—philosophical instruments, and the like; so let the village do—not stop short at a pedagogue, a parson, a sexton, a parish library, and three selectmen, because our Pilgrim forefathers got through a cold winter once on a bleak rock with these. To act collectively is according to the spirit of our institutions; and I am confident that, as our circumstances are more flourishing, our means are greater than the nobleman's." Do not those sentences alter a little our stereotype of homespun New England, of Individualistic America?

Just as Thoreau sought Nature, in order to arrive at a higher state of culture, so he practiced individualism, in order to create a better order of society. Taking America as it was, Thoreau conceived a form, a habitat, which would retain what was unique in the American contact with the virgin forest, the cultivated soil, and the renewed institutions of the New England town. He understood the precise thing that the pioneer lacked. The pioneer had exhausted himself in a senseless external activity, which answered no inner demands except those for oblivion. In his experiment at Walden Pond, Thoreau "learned this, at least . . . that if one advances confidently in the direction of his dreams, and endeavors to live the life which he has imagined, he will meet with success unexpected in the common hours. . . . In proportion as he simplifies his life, the laws of the universe will appear less complex, and solitude will not be solitude, nor poverty poverty, nor weakness weakness. If you have built castles in the air, your work need not be lost; that is where they should be. Now put the foundations under them."

In short, Thoreau lived in his desires; in rational and beautiful things that he imagined worth doing, and did. The pioneer lived only in extraneous necessities; and he vanished with their satisfaction: filling all the conditions of his environment, he never fulfilled himself. With the same common ground between them in their initial feeling toward Nature, Thoreau and the pioneer stood at opposite corners of the field. What Thoreau left behind is still precious; men may still go out and make over America in the image of Thoreau. What the pioneer left behind, alas! was only the burden of a vacant life.

"He that by me spreads a wider breast than my own proves the width of my own." So Walt Whitman chanted in the "Song of Myself"; and in the greatness of Whitman the genius of Emerson was justified. Walt Whitman was a cosmos: he was inclusive where Emerson and Thoreau were restrictive: he was sensual and jolly where they were refined and taut: he identified himself with the mere bulk and vastness of the American continent, and, with a tremendous appetite for the actual, entered into the experience of the pioneer, the roadhand, the mechanic, the woodman, the soldier, the farmer. In some remote Dutch ancestor of Whitman's one figures the men and women of Franz Hals's portraiture, people large, lusty, loving, men who like their sweetheart and their steak, women who give themselves to love as the flower bows to the weight of the bee. With Emerson, to repeat the obvious, one surveys the world from a glacial summit: the air is rarefied, and at the distance even the treacherous places in the landscape seem orderly and innocent. With Whitman one sees the heights from the bosom of the valley: the "unseen is proved by the seen, till that becomes unseen, and receives proofs of its own."

Whitman absorbed so much of the America about him that he is more than a single writer: he is almost a literature. Pushing his way like some larval creature through one husk after another, through the hard shell of Puritanism, in which he wrote temperance tracts, through the shell of republicanism in which he glorified all the new political institutions, through the flimsy casement of Romantic poetry, iridescent with cheap colors and empty rhymes, Whitman finally achieved his own metamorphosis, and emerged, with dripping wings, into the untempered midday of the American scene. The stages of this metamorphosis have created contradictions in Whitman's work; and if we are to appreciate his full achievement, we must be ready to throw aside the vestiges of his larval state.

First, there was in Whitman a certain measure of the political religiosity of Joel Barlow and Philip Freneau. Political nationalism, in certain aspects of Whitman's thought, assumed a mystical beauty and centrality: he wrote about the United States as if they were the tissue of men's eternal desires—as if the robbery of Mexican territory, for example, could be justified to the Mexicans as well as the Americans by the inevitable drag of our Manifest Destiny. Here Whitman was confusing spiritual with temporal dominion. He had conceived new spiritual patterns, appropriate to the modern, which were to be fulfilled in the America of his dreams; and it was hard to resist identifying this hope of a wider America with the expansionist activities of political bandits. In this mood, to speak frankly, Whitman ranted.

Nevertheless, when one sums up Whitman's observations upon the Union and upon the political state of the country, no one surely ever ranted with so many reservations; and it is unfair to take the bombastic lines out of the context that perpetually qualifies them. The political reality that was so precious to Whitman was only a means of permitting the growth of "superb persons," and a life, "copious, vehement, spiritual, bold." Moreover, between the Walt Whitman who wrote the original *Leaves of Grass*, and the defeated and paralyzed man who lingered on through the Gilded Age, there is a difference; and by 1879 Whitman had come to realize that his democracy was one that had been based on free land and equal opportunity to use it, and that failure was beginning to threaten the political structure. "If the United States," he wrote, "like the countries of the Old World, are also to grow vast crops of poor, desperate, dissatisfied, nomadic, miserably waged populations, such as we see looming upon us of late years—steadily, even if slowly, eating into them like a cancer of lungs or stomach—then our republican experiment, notwithstanding all its surface-successes, is at heart an unhealthy failure. . . ." That was not all. "By the unprecedented open-up of humanity enmasse in the United States in the last hundred years, under our institutions, not only the good qualities of the race, but just as much the bad ones, are prominently brought forward. Man is about the same, in the main, whether with despotism or whether with freedom."

That saving and irrefragable common sense was what ballasted all of Whitman's hopes and expectations. He lived to see the America he dreamed of undermined and rotten: he saw the Kings of Iron and Oil and Cotton supplant not merely the older ones who ruled by divine right but the new one elected quadrennially by the people: he saw the diverse but well-mixed America of his youth give way to the America of the melting pot, which neither welded the old nationalities nor had the spiritual power to create a new one: he saw the sickly barbers and perfumers of the New York literary schools of the forties turn into the gentlemanly tailors who cut their stories and their thoughts to fit the fat paunches of the middle classes in the seventies: he saw all this, and denied nothing. No critic ferreted out the weaknesses and pettinesses of America with a surer nose than Whitman tracked them down in his *Democratic Vistas*: what could be said against his dream, Whitman said, with the staunch candor of a friend. But his thought and his vision were unshaken; the promise of America had not disappeared. If it was absent from the immediate scene, it had nevertheless taken form in his poems; and his poems were still waiting to shape a new America.

In *Leaves of Grass* Whitman had fulfilled Emerson in more ways than either of them suspected. There are passages of Emerson's prose which have, potentially, the prosody of Whitman; but whereas Emerson's poems, at their best, remain fragmentary and broken, because the meaning was somehow always warping the metes and measures Emerson respected and clung to, in Whitman, at his best, these new thoughts find their own beat, and become poetry of the first rank. Whitman had discovered Emerson's inner form in creating his own. He himself had stammered and stuttered so long as he kept to the old meters: his early work was weak and sentimental because he had nothing to say within the bounds of those previous culture molds which Whitman tagged as "feudal." New streams of thought and experience were confluent in Whitman: the *Weltanschauung* of Hegel, precursor of the evolutionists, who saw the world as a continual becoming, and both the bad and the good as part of the total meaning of the universe; the electric doctrine of Emerson, which bade every man find his own center and every institution to answer up for its results in one's own life; the unstratified society of America, where the bus driver was as good as the next man, and the private soldier as great as the statesman whose policies reduced him to a pawn; the cleansing operations of science, which confronted every variety in thought, and made no more distinction between the clean and the unclean, the minute and the immense, than some indifferent deity, for whom the fall of a gnat and the fall of an empire are of precisely the same importance. Out of the discussions of the Fourierists, and the societies of Free Lovers, and women who pressed for the political and social emancipation of their sex, as well as out of his own capacious adventures, Whitman got the courage to deal with the varieties of sexual experience, too: in the "Children of Adam" and "Calamus" he brushed past the nice restraints of Emerson—who "held his nose" at its passages—and Thoreau, who, like Natty Bumpo and Paul Bunyan, averted himself from any passion more intense than friendship.

Whitman took in the Quaker, the Puritan, the cosmopolitan, the pioneer, the republican; and what came out in his poems was none of these things: it was a new essence; none of the ordinary labels described it. It had the smell of reality which was science; it had the largeness of comprehension which was philosophy; and it had the doubts, searchings, quests, achievements, and consummations which are the stuff of life itself. Whitman found no need to add an extra dimension to his experience: to transcribe for him was in the highest sense to *translate*. Whatever tended to create full-bodied and full-minded men and women tended toward enlarging the significance of every single activity, no matter how base or minute. The veil of appearance was as mysterious and beautiful as anything behind the veil. Perhaps it was all Maya, all illusion; or perhaps life was like a set of Chinese boxes: one removed the outer box of appearance, and discovered another box— appearance. What of it? A single blade of grass was enough to confound all the atheists; and whatever else the universe might hold, he reckoned that there was no sweeter meat than that which clung to his own bones. Such faith does not need external props and certitudes: it mocks at the testimony of bibles, for it is itself the source of such testimony.

People have hesitated to call Whitman's poems poetry; it is useless to deny that they belong to sacred literature. If the *Leaves of Grass* are not poetry, it is only because not every generation endows us with such a poet.

Literature may be evocative or formative: one plays upon sentiments, emotions, ideas, that already exist: the other changes the very attitude of the audience, and calls new ones forth. The common American of the Golden Day responded to Longfellow and Whittier; for these men caught his ordinary mood, measured off and rhymed; and even when Whittier and Lowell wrote on abolition themes, they were only touching strings which a Garrison or a Wendell Phillips had already set in motion. It is amusing to note the way in which ante-bellum America responded to Whitman. Emerson and Thoreau were quick to see his genius, even to proclaim it. Lesser people, however, like Moncure Conway, were a little disappointed in him: they expected to find in Whitman the common workman, grown vocal, someone who could be taken into society and patronized; someone who would bolster up their notion of a poet who had risen from the lowly ranks.

Whitman was not a democrat, in the sense of being a popular mediocrity; he was a man of genius; who, mid all his school teaching, editing, carpentering, typesetting, and whatnot, remained consecrated to the profession of letters: Jesus Son of Sirach was no more certain of his vocation. Whitman was Pygmalion to his own Galatea: he had formed himself, so that he might give a new model to America. The imperturbable landscape, the satisfaction and aplomb of animals, the ecstasy of hearty lovers, the meditations of one who sits withdrawn in the crowd, or on a mountaintop—Whitman extracted from these things a new shape, which was himself. Every poem of Whitman's is the man; every part of the man threw forth tendrils which clung to the objects of poems. One could not become a sympathetic reader of Whitman without re-forming oneself into an approximation of this new shape. Only commonplace works of art reflect the everyday personality of the reader: the supreme works always show or hint of the new shape the reader may become: they are prophetic, formative. One might remove Longfellow without changing a single possibility of American life; had Whitman died in the cradle, however, the possibilities of American life would have been definitely impoverished. He created a new pattern of experience and character. The work he conceived still remains to be done: the America he evoked does not as yet exist.

Whitman was a poet in the braid [broad] Scots sense of "makkar": a maker or creator. He was conscious of the fact that the accumulated culture of Europe had lost a good part of its original meaning, through lack of direct contact with the new forces of discovery, science, democracy: the work of the old makkars was crumbling away; at best, it was repeated by rote, as in the churches, without any sense of the living reality, or the finer passages were rolled on the tongue, for sensation's sake, by an aristocratic minority. "Note to-day," Whitman observed in *Democratic Vistas,* "a curious spectacle and conflict. . . . Science, testing absolutely all thoughts, all works, has already burst well upon the world —a sun, mounting, most illuminating, most glorious, surely never again to set. But against it, deeply entrenched, holding possession, yet remains (not only through the churches and schools but by imaginative literature and unregenerate poetry) the fossil theology of the mythic-

materialistic superstitious, untaught and credulous, fable-loving primitive ages of humanity."

Whitman saw that the office of sacred literature was no longer
being performed; or at all events, that those who were pursuing it were
not fully conscious of either the need or the opportunity. Vulgar literature was, indeed, growing hugely. "To-day, in books, in the rivalry of
writers, especially novelists, success (so-called) is for him or her who
strikes the mean flat average, the sensational appetite for stimulus,
incident, persiflage, etc., and depicts to the common caliber, sensual,
exterior life." What remained of sacred literature was insufficient to
offset this. It was to establish a central point in literature, in terms of
science and the modern, that Whitman created: American poetry was
to do in our day what the Vedas, the Nackas, the Talmud, the Old
Testament, the Gospel, Plato's works, had done for their time: it was to
crystallize our most precious experience and in turn to modify, by that
act of crystallization, the daily routine.

What, in fact, were the active formative literatures when Whitman
wrote? In the Western world the principle one was, without doubt, that
great miscellany called the Old Testament, supplemented by the Gos-
pels; and among the cultivated classes, Homer, Horace, Plutarch,
Dante, Shakespeare, Corneille, played a lively but minor part. The
Romantic movement, which went back to the ballads and the folk
literature of the various regions of Europe, was a recognition of the fact
that something was lacking in both the Hebrew and the classic traditions, and in the literature which was directly founded upon them.
What was lacking was the direct historic connection with a people, a
place, and a special way of life. It is true that all literature has certain
common characters, and no great works of the spirit are foreign and
remote; but, as Whitman pointed out, "something is rooted in the invisible roots, the profoundest meanings, of a place, race, or nationality,"
and the Romantic movement had cut loose from classic and Hebraic
influences in order to absorb this more intimate order of meaning and
find a nearer and fresher source of spiritual activity. Blake, Keats, Shelley, had partly achieved this; Wordsworth alone, however, had created
new forms without relying on a mythic-materialistic past.

With what was universal in all these efforts, Whitman could sympa-
thize; Homer and Shakespeare and the Bible had been his daily food.
He sought to do for common men and women, for the contemporary
and the ordinary-heroic, what Shakespeare had achieved in his great
images of the aristocratic life. In America, in modern life, on the farm
and in the laboratory, in the progress of souls along the grand roads of
the Universe, in company with the Great Companions, the swift and
majestic men, the capacious and broad-bosomed women—here was the

stuff for new Vedas, Cycles, and Testaments. Whitman overvalued, if anything, the contrivances of political democracy; but that was only a first step; he overcountenanced, if anything, the absorption of America in materialistic effort; that, however, was only the second step. Neither political democracy nor industrial progress was for him anything but a prelude to the third stage, rising out of the two previous ones, and creating a "native expression spirit" and an abundance of rich personalities.

In his effort to keep ballasted and always find a landing place in contemporary existence, Whitman was perhaps too receptive and undiscriminating in his acknowledgment of current values and aims; in his old age, he accepted with childlike delight the evidences of material prosperity he found on his Western trip. His Hegelianism was dangerous stuff: it led him to identify the Real and the Ideal, instead of seeing, as William James put it, that they were dynamically continuous. But at the core, Whitman was never deceived: he knew that the meaning of all current activity lay only in the forms or symbols it created and the rational purposes it embodied; and so far from believing that the work of the poet or artist would be supplanted by science, he believed that "the highest and subtlest and broadest truths of modern science wait for their true assignment and last vivid flashes of light—as Democracy waits for its—through first-class metaphysicians and speculative philosophs—laying the basements and foundations for these new, more expanded, more harmonious, more melodious, freer American poems." To indicate these new meanings, to open up these new relationships, Whitman wrote his poems. I can think of no one in whom the unconscious and the conscious process worked more in harmony: the life and the doctrine were one. So far as Whitman went, he achieved his end.

So far as he went! Most people are unaware that the *Leaves of Grass*, "Calamus," the "Children of Adam," are only a part of the vast canvas he projected; they do not realize that he was diverted from his original intention and never lived to complete it. The *Leaves of Grass* were to deal chiefly with the palpable and the material; there was to be a complementary volume which would center mainly on the spiritual and the inactual—upon death and immortality and final meanings—for he was the poet of the body and he was the poet of the soul. Alas! The Civil War came. He threw himself into it as a hospital visitor, giving his personality and his radiant health to the sick and the wounded, as these men had given themselves in the camp and on the battlefield. Within a few years this ordeal exacted its revenge: he became paralyzed, and as he never fully recovered his physical powers, his mental powers diminished, too: if they are still at their summit in *Drum-Taps*, they recurred only fitfully in the later poems: and though he could outline his aspiration with a firm hand in *Democratic Vistas*, published in 1871, he could no longer model it and round it out. What he meant to create is implied in all his poems; the whole of it was never, perhaps, expressed.

Whitman himself had felt that the War for the American Union was the Odyssey of his generation; but except for himself and Herman Melville, no one lived to write about it in those terms; the stories of Ambrose Bierce, Stephen Crane, and Upton Sinclair did not treat it in this vein. Whitman did not see that the great conflict might have a Punic ending. As it turned out, the war was a struggle between two forms of servitude, the slave and the machine. The machine won, and the human spirit was almost as much paralyzed by the victory as it would have been by the defeat. An industrial transformation took place overnight: machines were applied to agriculture; they produced new guns and armaments; the factory regime, growing tumultuously in the Eastern cities, steadily undermined the balanced regimen of agriculture and industry which characterized the East before the war.

The machines won; and the war kept on. Its casualties were not always buried at Antietam or Gettysburg; they moldered, too, in libraries, studies, offices. The justifiable ante-bellum optimism of Emerson turned into a waxen smile. Whitman lost his full powers in what should have been his prime. Among the young men, many a corpse was left, to go through the routine of living. . . .

We have seen American culture as formed largely by two events: the breakdown of the medieval synthesis, in the centuries that preceded America's settlement and by the transferral to the new soil of an abstract and fragmentary culture, given definitive form by the Protestants of the sixteenth century, by the philosophers and scientists of the seventeenth, and by the political thinkers of the eighteenth century. Faced with the experience of the American wilderness, we sought, in the capacity of pioneers, to find a new basis for culture in the primitive ways of forest and field, in the occupations of hunter, woodman, miner, and pastoral nomad: but these occupations, practiced by people who were as much influenced by the idola of utilitarianism as by the deeper effort of the Romantic movement, did not lead toward a durable culture: the pioneer environment became favorable to an even bleaker preoccupation with the abstractions of matter, money, and political rights. In this situation, the notion of a complete society, carrying on a complete and symmetrical life, tended to disappear from the minds of everyone except the disciples of Fourier; with the result that business, technology, and science not merely occupied their legitimate place but took to themselves all that had hitherto belonged to art, religion, and poetry. Positive knowledge and practical action, which are indispensable elements in every culture, became the only living sources of our own; and as the nineteenth century wore on, we moved within an ever-narrower circle of experience, living mean and illiberal lives.

The moving out of Europe was not merely due to the lure of free land and a multitude of succulent foods: it pointed to cultural vacancy. For three centuries the best minds in Europe had either been trying to get nourishment from the leftovers of classic culture or the Middle Ages, or they had been trying to reach some older source of experience, in order to supplement their bare spiritual fare. Science built up a new conception of the universe, and it endowed its disciples with the power to understand—and frequently to control—external events; but it achieved these results by treating men's central interests and desires as negligible, ignoring the fact that science itself was but a mode of man's activity as a living creature, and that its effort to cancel out the human element was only a very ingenious human expedient. In America, it was easy for an Emerson or a Whitman to see the importance of welding together the interests which science represented, and those which, through the accidents of its historical development, science denied. Turning from a limited European past to a wider heritage, guiding themselves by all the reports of their own day, these poets continued the old voyages of exploration on the plane of the mind, and, seeking passage to India, found themselves coasting along strange shores. None of the fine minds of the Golden Day was afraid to welcome the new forces that were at large in the world. Need I recall that Whitman wrote an apostrophe to the locomotive, that Emerson said a steamship sailing promptly between America and Europe might be as beautiful as a star, and that Thoreau, who loved to hear the wind in the pine needles, listened with equal pleasure to the music of the telegraph wires? . . .

We cannot return to the America of the Golden Day, nor keep it fixed in the postures it once naturally assumed; and we should be far from the spirit of Emerson or Whitman if we attempted to do this. But the principal writers of that time are essential links between our own lives and that earlier, that basic, America. In their work, we can see in pristine state the essential characteristics that still lie under the surface: and from their example, we can more readily find our own foundations, and make our own particular point of departure. . . .

THE NEW
WORLD PROMISE

It has been explained that the "Cities of the New World" theme refers to the geographic New World, the Western Hemisphere, and not to the New World of science and technics which was opened up at the same moment in history. With due respect to those who have properly sought to emphasize our territorial and historic unities, I find, as a historian, that it is impossible to separate these New Worlds. The archetypal models for our mechanical New World were already in existence when Columbus set sail, and long before the massive industrial changes produced by steam, coal, and iron, they had wrought a far greater change, not just in the physical environment but in the human mind.

In the very decade that the New World was officially discovered and claimed by European governments, the leading spirits of the time saw in both New Worlds the beginning of a great human transformation. It was in those terms that Poliziano, the great Florentine humanist, characterized the coming age and a little later Campanella, the author of an early utopia full of prophetic inventions, observed in a letter to Galileo: "The novelties of ancient truths, of new worlds, new systems, new nations, are the beginning of a new era."

There were both positive and negative reasons for these New World hopes; and as to the latter, it was plain that Old World civilization had once more reached a terminus. That civilization, if viewed in the light of its actual performances—not its ideals or its pretensions—has proved incapable of further development on its original terms. All the magnificent achievements of Old World culture, in law and order, in art and architecture, in religion and abstract thought, had been fatally undermined and repeatedly destroyed by having been set from the beginning upon treacherous human foundations. From the Pyramid

Age on, every historic civilization had been based on a monopoly of power and authority by a self-appointed minority, who treated war, slavery, regimented labor, and class exploitation as the necessary price of man's higher development.

Despite repeated attempts to correct these chronic defects, the original pattern of the Old World order remained in essentials unchanged. Even the moral authority of the high religions after the seventh century B.C.—Buddhism, Judaism, Confucianism, Mazdaism, Christianity, Islam—had failed to re-establish civilization on a sounder basis. But at the close of the Middle Ages in Europe a new remedy suggested itself, one that physicians have often turned to in desperation when their usual treatments have failed: namely, a long ocean voyage and a complete change of scene. And in one mind after another, among both dreamers and practical men, the notion arose that a fresh start might be made by migrating to the Western Hemisphere and beginning life all over again, exploring new habitats, making new choices, following new paths.

Looking backward, we can now see that the proposal to wipe the slate clean and begin afresh in the New World was based on an illusion, or rather a series of illusions. As in the typical myth of Robinson Crusoe, survival in the New World was possible only if valuable lumber and tools could be salvaged from the European wreckage and used to shape the raw materials that here lay so abundantly at hand. But willy-nilly, the new settlers brought with them the very practices that for five thousand years had hampered human development—only to find that the same Old World institutions, slavery and war, were already entrenched here among the more civilized peoples: the Maya, the Aztecs, and the Peruvians. In the act of conquering the Americas, the invaders imposed their Old World vices, and in turn disdained and cast aside many precious cultural gifts that the New World actually offered. When Albrecht Dürer beheld the marvelous works of art sent by Montezuma to Charles V, he wrote: "Never . . . have I seen anything that warmed my heart so much as these things." But as you know, it took four centuries before Dürer's feelings about the indigenous art were generally shared.

The hostility that the European displayed toward the native cultures was carried over, at first, into his relation to the land: the immense open spaces of our continent and all its unexploited resources were treated as a challenge to unrelenting war and conquest. In the act of conquering nature, our ancestors treated the land as contemptuously and brutally as they treated its original inhabitants, wiping out great animal species like the bison and the passenger pigeon, mining the soils instead of replenishing them, cutting down the primeval forests, even the great sequoias, and breaking open the prairie, instead of setting part of this primeval landscape aside as a special New World gift that could never be replaced. We did not learn how precious that gift really was.

Yet the hope first expressed in the sixteenth century was not without a genuine foundation. The New World expanded the human imagination. In its vastness and geographic variety, in its range of climates and physiographic profiles, in both its wildlife and in the treasure hoard of cultivated food plants and flowers that we owe solely to the original neolithic cultures, the New World was a land of promise, indeed a land of many promises, for both body and mind. Here was a natural abundance which promised to lift the curse of both slavery and poverty, even before the machine lightened the burden of purely physical toil. The belief that a better society would be possible in the New World stirred company after company of immigrants, from the Jesuits of Paraguay to the Pilgrims of Massachusetts. Thus, until almost the end of the nineteenth century, the secret name of the New World was Utopia.

This sense of continually unfolding human possibilities, which was evoked by the landscape of the New World, gave a special lift to Thoreau's line: "Who would not rise to meet the expectation of the land?" That New World utopia took many forms, but by the nineteenth century it had come to rest on three implicit assumptions. The first was the biological premise that man's life is closely attached to nature and can be lived fully only by entering into an understanding and loving partnership with nature. The second was the mechanical premise that the exploitation of nonhuman sources of energy, through science and invention, is essential toward increasing man's mastery over his physical environment and breaking down the purely physical barriers to further human cooperation and communication on a planetary scale. Finally, it rested on the human premise that the goods of every culture, both spiritual and material, must be offered freely to all its members, and eventually to all mankind.

All three of these assumptions, at least when taken together, were sound; and though we are still far from achieving them, they constitute what we may honestly call the New World promise. These three underlying beliefs were not explicitly formulated and did not come fully into consciousness until the nineteenth century. In the end, though they modified Old World beliefs and institutions at many points, they never fully displaced them. Yet there was a moment, at least in my own country, and particularly in one region of that country, New England, when it seemed that the potentialities of the New World would actually be realized in every area of life, as one by one the Old World barriers between peoples and between economic classes were breaking down and a new aristocracy of the spirit, open to all men, was arising.

What Van Wyck Brooks called "the flowering" of New England took place between 1820 and 1860; and it was then that the fresh experience of the New World at last took shape in the mind. This was a period when a Harvard graduate named Thoreau, who gained a living as a pencil maker and a surveyor, found the leisure to write his classic *Walden;* when a youthful sailor and farmer, Herman Melville, wrote the tragic epic of *Moby Dick;* when an unschooled woodchopper and country lawyer could become a national president whose moral insights and humanity were as profound as those of Marcus Aurelius. In an Emerson, a Whitman, a Lincoln, the New World north of the Rio Grande—I regret that I cannot speak with authority of the southern parallels—produced its fruit, a New World personality.

Almost all that is truly original and humane in architecture and planning in the United States derives directly or indirectly from this brief period of integration. From Thoreau and Olmsted came our national parks and our wildlife reservations; from George Perkins Marsh, the author of *Man and Nature,* and Major Wesley Powell, came our conservation movement and our insights into natural and social ecology; from this common fund of ideas came the fresh forms of parks, parkways, and parklike settings for cities, beginning in 1869 with Olmsted's Riverside and culminating in 1929 in the Radburn plan of Henry Wright and Clarence Stein, with its equal respect for communal, mechanical, and biological needs. And from the same sources came the domestic architecture of H. H. Richardson, Frank Lloyd Wright, and Bernard Maybeck. A fresh feeling for nature and for man's intercourse with nature characterized these achievements.

What we have to explain to ourselves now, as we look around our New World cities and regions, is why, in spite of many brilliant single works, we have made such a mess and a muddle of our opportunities. Why, with our increasing power to exploit natural resources and technological inventions, has there been such a loss of individuality and character in our urban environment, such a failure to conserve and utilize all the dazzling variety that nature, to begin with, offered us? Why were the old New England towns, even Greater Boston itself up to 1895, better urban forms than the latest Back Bay urban renewal projects? Why are those Latin-American cities that were built according to the laws of the Indies, with their open plaza in the middle, still a more humane environment than, say, Brasília? Did we promise too much for the future or did we forget too much of the past?

One naturally hesitates to give too simple an answer to these questions; but surely one of the obvious reasons for our failure is that we have been overweighing the very component of the New World promise that the framers of this program sought to eliminate from this discussion: the New World of science and technics. Our leaders have been trying to create a substitute life out of the machine, and have subordinated the character of the landscape and the needs of its inhabitants to the dynamics of mass production and the exploitation of technological power, treated as if this were a valid human end in itself.

Now, among North American scholars it is customary to smile patronizingly at the romantic idea of believing that both wild nature and the cultivated countryside are essential backgrounds for human development. This bucolic idyll, as the apologists for Megalopolis like to call it, is supposed to contrast unfavorably with their own inverted romanticism of living, not according to nature but according to the machine; and the machine worshipers show their hatred of nature by turning every landscape into an urbanoid wasteland paved with multilaned motorways, parking lots, and cloverleafs, with rubbish dumps and motorcar cemeteries, in which buildings, low and high, are thrown almost at random without respect to any human purpose except to absorb the products of an expanding economy, whose affluence so largely takes the form of organized waste.

Yet even these inverted romanticists cannot entirely ignore the older passion for nature which still survives as an essential part of our New World heritage; for they have invented a prefabricated substitute for the wilderness, or at least an equivalent for the hunter's campfire. That ancient paleolithic hearth has become a backyard picnic grill, where, surrounded by plastic vegetation, factory-processed frankfurters are broiled on an open fire, made with pressed-charcoal eggs, brought to combustion point by an electric torch connected by wire to a distant socket, while the assembled company views, either on television or on a domestic motion picture screen, a travelogue through Yosemite or Yellowstone. Ah, wilderness! For many of my countrymen, I fear, this is the ultimate terminus of the New World dream.

Against such a defective vision of life, a more organic view of man's place in nature, based on historic and prehistoric realities, has no need to bow respectfully, still less to blush in embarrassment. Those who belittle the importance of the natural landscape and the regional habitat overlook the fact that the discovery of the complex interrelationship of organisms, functions, and environments is one of the masterly achievements of modern biology: more significant for man's further development than the most spectacular flights of nuclear physics or computer technology. For the first time since the neolithic period, man has made a beginning of understanding the biological properties of a life-sustaining environment.

This insight into the realities of organic existence has opened up a true New World. One of the most important discoveries of biological science is that man's creativity is only a minute, specialized fraction of nature's immense creativity, and yet man's own ever-increasing consciousness of nature's processes adds a fresh dimension to all natural events and makes his own cultural development a so-far ultimate term in a process that began many billions of years ago. The humblest living organism, we now know, is far more wonderful in its potentialities for growth and self-transformation than the most complex machine, since whatever seems lifelike in our mechanisms is a mere by-product of organic life and human culture.

But what, you may ask impatiently, has all this to do with our New World cities? And I answer: Just to the extent that this consciousness of natural functions and human purposes is absent from their design, they are not yet New World cities, in any hopeful sense of the word. When an invading species upsets the ecological balance of a habitat, as the Canada thistle did when it invaded the Argentine pampas, it often grows to gigantic proportions and curbs all other forms of growth. This is what is happening in our cities, now that one component of the New World promise, the machine, has become dominant, replacing human choice, variety, autonomy, and cultural complexity with its own kind of uniformity and automatism. The result is an urban environment that is both biologically and culturally deficient.

If we are to produce humanly adequate cities, we must critically appraise the results of this one-sided technical domination. What kind of half-baked science has gone into the design of motorcars, which bring into our cities lethal concentrations of the very chemicals that cause heart disease and cancer? What kind of half-baked planning has deliberately broken down our efficient many-sided transportation network, based on the pedestrian, the railroad, the motorbus, and the private motorcar, in favor of a space-wasting, city-destroying system of monotransportation, based on the private motorcar alone? These and many other features of our urban architecture are both technological and social absurdities. Only one thing need be said about such cities: those who have a free economic choice are constantly moving out of them— though they must sacrifice the social facilities of the city in order to ensure all too temporarily a better biological environment.

But a worse fate is in store if we continue to let technological expansion curb human purposes and flout essential human traditions. Anyone who wishes to know what lies ahead if the present tendencies continue need only examine the mechanical labyrinths that the so-called advance guard of planners have been presenting as the "cities of the future." A few years ago, the Museum of Modern Art in New York held an exhibition of such work, and if the designs shown there had been called "Prisons and Penal Colonies of the Future," they would still have been monstrous. These ideal plans showed cities built underwater, cities suspended in the air, cities burrowed underground, or cities covered by immense geodesic domes—all of them using the most extravagant kind of mechanical and electronic apparatus to achieve the smallest possible human benefit, under a system so tightly controlled that no individual alteration would be possible.

Is it not time that we asked ourselves whether total mechanical control and total uniformity are in any sense human ideals? Whether they are not in fact just the opposite of the original dream that lured daring men to the New World in order to recapture some of the wild freedom of movement and choice that Old World civilization had harshly smothered? More than fifteen years ago, in an essay entitled "Social Effects of the Atom Bomb," I predicted that such dehumanized urban projects would be the inevitable response to the threat of nuclear extermination, unless the United States enlisted the help of all the nations of the world to protect mankind against the premature exploitation of nuclear power before we had rebuilt the moral and political safeguards our own country had demolished. But I was not sufficiently foresighted to suppose that anyone would be so insane as to think underground cities were desirable, and would put them forth, even in fantasy, as the last word in urban progress. If this is all that is left of the New World dream, I would propose to head a movement back to the Stone Age, to begin all over again. There is still more promise of life in the images on the walls of the Altamira or Lascaux caves than in these immature avant-garde designs, for all their semblance of scientific sophistication.

Now, I cannot console you with the thought that this is just a fashionable aberration, which, like all fashions, will soon pass. For the fact is that cities designed to fit no human needs except those that conform to the machine are precisely the kind that are favored by our financial, industrial, scientific, military, and educational experts—the new Pentagon of power—whose underdimensioned ideology now increasingly dominates our society. All that the planners who conform to these requirements are doing is to blow up into vast urbanoid mechanisms a variety of small-scale models that are already in existence. Witness our underground rocket centers, our battery-chicken farms, our stratoliners, and, increasingly, our motorcars: they are all variations on the archetypal space capsule. And by necessity, a space capsule—a minimal environment permitting only a minimal life—is the precise antithesis of a rich, many-sided, exuberant, life-sustaining habitat, teeming with biological fulfillments and cultural possibilities.

Thus the mechanical New World to which we have increasingly committed ourselves turns out, when taken as our ultimate goal, to be the chief enemy of the territorial and utopian New World that raised men's hopes to such a high pitch four centuries ago. And yet so deeply has the myth of the machine taken hold of our age, so close does it come to being the only religion for which we are prepared to make sacrifices, that [Frank Lloyd Wright,] the most imaginative architect of our time finally succumbed to it. He whose early work marvelously wrought into a unity the three aspects of the New World dream—the culture of the landscape, the free use of the machine, the full expression of the human personality—ended his life by designing the Machine Age equivalent of an Egyptian pyramid: a building a mile high, a kind of static space rocket. That design demolished in a single stroke all that was most deeply creative in his philosophy and his art. Thus mechanical triumphs that once seemed like an advancing wave of the future now turn out to be a deadly undertow.

But we are not doomed to sleep this nightmare out till its end; we have only to open our eyes to make it vanish. Life is real, life is earnest, and the space capsule is not its goal. In taking possession of the Western Hemisphere, our ancestors mistakenly thought that they could trade time for space. All too eagerly, they turned their backs on the past, so that they might make a fresh start; and too many thought not only that mechanical progress would be a positive aid to human improvement, which is true, but that the mechanical progress is the equivalent of human improvement, which turns out to be sheer nonsense. The time has come to restore man himself, once more, in all his cumulative historic richness, his regional individuality, his cultural complexity, to the center of the picture, so that he may play his part once more as dramatist, scenic designer, actor, and spectator in the unfolding drama of life. And the cities we build must give all of their citizens, at every stage in their development, a role to play and a dialogue in which to participate.

To achieve such cities, we must reverse the present order of our thinking, and restore those components of nature and culture that we have neglected in our one-sided preoccupation with financial profits, national aggrandizement, and mechanical power. In nature, we must safeguard what is left of our primeval inheritance; in our culture, we must emphasize continuity as essential to all rational change; and in the depths of the individual soul, we must attempt to transcend the limitations of our time and our place by seeking what is eternal and divine —addressing ourselves to possibilities still unplumbed and to ideals that have still to emerge. There, and not through rocket trips into outer space, lies the New World that has still to be discovered and domesticated by the spirit of man.

VI

TECHNOLOGY AND CULTURE

However far modern science and
technics have fallen short of their
inherent possibilities, they have taught
mankind at least one lesson: Nothing is
impossible.
—Lewis Mumford

Introduction

With the publication of *The Brown Decades,* his fourth and final book on American culture, Mumford secured his reputation as a writer of the first rank, an all-around man of letters, not just an architecture critic. At age thirty-five, he took on a major work he had been preparing to write for almost a decade—a sweeping survey of the development of the machine, the city, and Western thought from the Middle Ages to the present. This became the four-volume Renewal of Life series, one of the great intellectual undertakings of our time. "To produce a mighty volume," Mumford had observed in his biography of Melville, "you must choose a mighty theme."[1] His theme, he decided, would be nothing less than the making of the modern world and the modern mind. It would take him twenty years to complete this enormous project.

Technics and Civilization, the opening volume of the series, is a pioneering work in the history of technology. It is both the first full-scale study in the English language of the rise of the machine in the modern world and one of the first scholarly studies in any language to emphasize the interplay of technology and the surrounding culture. Mumford described not simply the work of inventors and scientists but also the cultural sources and moral consequences of the breakthroughs in technology and science. He placed technology squarely within the context of what he called the social ecology.

Drawing on the latest German scholarship, Mumford analyzed the process of ideological preparation for full mechanization, arguing that the Industrial Revolution began as far back as the Middle Ages, when a number of cultural transformations occurred that prepared the ground for the larger technical revolution that altered all of Western culture. "Men became mechanical," in Mumford's words, "before they perfected complicated machines to express their new bent and interest."[2] The passion for order, regularity, and regimentation appeared first in the routinized world of the medieval monastery, then spread to the army and the countinghouse before it finally entered the factory. In this mental transformation, the clock, Mumford claimed, played a crucial role, an interpretation now widely accepted by historians of science and technology.

With the new concern with time came a closely related concern with exact measurement; together, these developments led to the emergence of what Mumford called a new scientific picture of the world. In its urge to comprehend and control the physical world, the new science, he argued, defined as "real" only those aspects of experience that were external and repeatable, that could be studied and verified by careful experimentation. Existence was separated into units that could be "weighed, measured or counted"; all else was judged "unreal." Subjectivity, intuition, and feeling had no place in a framework of ideas emphasizing organization, regularity, standardization, and control.[3] This denial of the organic, in Mumford's view, allowed the West to surrender to the machine, to turn inventions and mechanical contrivances that other cultures, such as the Chinese, possessed in abundance into what he called "the machine." By this term he meant not only mechanical devices but a mode of life geared to the pace of high-speed technology and committed to the technological ideals of specialization, automation, and rationality.

For Mumford, then, the emergence of the machine was fundamentally a change of mind, a movement from organic to mechanical thinking. This refusal to see the machine as a force independent of human will and purpose explains the underlying optimism of *Technics and Civilization.* Rejecting all forms of technological or economic determinism, Mumford insisted that human desires, decisions, and dreams influenced the course of modern invention fully as much as invention influenced the modern sensibility. Our modern machine world was a creation of human effort and will; and any thoroughgoing change would involve first of all a change in values and social priorities. Mumford had said this before. But from this point forward this theme became *the* theme of his life and art.

Written during a period of rapid social disintegration—of economic depression, spreading totalitarianism, and a world war that became, in the end, an atomic war—the next three volumes of the Renewal of Life series *(The Culture of Cities, The Condition of Man,* and *The Conduct of Life)* record a profound change in Mumford's social outlook. They reflect a growing disenchantment with modern life and a gathering pessimism, but not despair, about the possibilities of human renewal. Like John Ruskin, Mumford began to see "thunder on the horizon as well as dawn."[4]

Mumford's pessimism deepened in the years after World War II. The invention and deployment of the atomic bomb had a large and lasting effect on his outlook. "It showed me," he wrote a friend three decades after the war, that "Hitler had . . . conquered the minds of the most democratic governments."[5] But in his fervent postwar essays in favor of nuclear disarmament, Mumford argued that America's slide into "moral barbarism" began midway in the war, when the Air Force adopted the policy of obliteration bombing against German cities like Dresden and Cologne, abandoning centuries-old restraints against the wanton killing of noncombatants. It was this "moral reversal" that he was most concerned about, for it vastly widened the destructive capabilities of nuclear weapons. America had shown that if pressed or pushed too hard it would not be bound by previous moral restraints against random killing. Cosmic power and moral nihilism, Mumford agreed with Henry Adams, was truly a deadly combination.[6]

Mumford had lived through what he considered the worst twenty years in mankind's history, the age of Hitler and Hiroshima, and his work in the postwar years is an effort to discover and explain what had gone wrong. Was the modern association of power and productivity with mass violence and destructiveness merely coincidental? This was the old Frankenstein problem of man's misuse of his technology, but in *The Myth of the Machine,* the two-volume work Mumford completed in 1970, he put this problem into the widest possible historical context. The modern "religion" of technology, he argued, was based upon a gross misconception of human origins and human nature. Furthermore, our modern doctrine of progress, with its association of technological advance with human advance, was merely a "scientifically dressed-up justification" for practices the ruling classes had used since the time of the Pharaohs to gain and hold power.[7]

In the first four selections in this section, three of which are taken from *The Myth of the Machine,* Mumford unfolds his complex, radically speculative theory of human origins and technological advance, concluding with what is perhaps his most controversial thesis: that the modern power state is merely an updated and vastly magnified version of an ancient bureaucratic-military system he calls the megamachine, a labor machine composed entirely of human parts, assembled by the Egyptian Pharaohs to build the great pyramids. In both the ancient and the modern megamachine the key functional figure was the Organization Man, the supinely loyal bureaucrat willing to surrender his soul to the system he served. With the invention of nuclear weapons, however, the Organization Man becomes a menace to global survival; surely, Mumford notes, there are Eichmanns in every missile center, ready to obey any orders, no matter how horrific.

The Myth of the Machine is a world removed, in temper and tone, from *Technics and Civilization.* Yet, for all his premonitions of chaos and catastrophe, Mumford ends it with the reminder that the megamachine, at least in the United States, is based on little more than an enticing "bribe"—if the individual gives the system his unquestioning allegiance, he will have a chance to enjoy the privileges and pleasures of "megatechnic" affluence—and that this bribe, in turn, is based upon the myth that power and economic growth are the main aims of life. Once we reject this bribe and cast off this myth, the modern megamachine will, Mumford predicts, crumble and collapse, the ironical victim of those it claimed to serve.[8]

Historically, the revolutionary movements that have been most successful, Mumford points out in the final essay of this section, were those started by individuals and small groups who nibbled at the edges of the power system "by breaking routines and defying regulations."[9] Such a line of attack seeks not to capture the power center but to withdraw from it and thereby paralyze it. In this view, Thoreau, not Marx, is the more dangerous revolutionary, for Thoreau recognized that disobedience is the first step toward autonomy.

It is not, then, as a prophet of doom but as a rising voice of renewal, an Isaiah for his age, that Mumford hoped to be remembered. Mumford always liked to claim that he was temperamentally an optimist; yet though he continued to be an optimist about possibilities, he became in advanced age a pessimist about probabilities. Certainly the optimism of the concluding pages of *The Myth of the Machine* is not altogether convincing, coming as it does after a grimly gray portrayal of the "megatechnical wasteland." Still, Mumford refused to give up hope.

His slender yet stubborn faith in the future comes through in a letter he wrote late in his life to his Italian friend Bruno Zevi. "I have not the heart to tell [people] . . . what I actually think about our human prospects," he noted, "unless something approaching a miracle takes place." He then went on to tell Zevi a story he had heard about a famous palmist in Berlin in the 1920s. Writers and artists flocked to this man. He told them things about their character and lives he could have known only by intuition. He also made predictions that turned out to be frighteningly accurate. He prophesied early death, divorces, financial catastrophes. His predictions became so dismal that people hesitated to go back to him. Eventually he became so tortured and dispirited by his own readings that he committed suicide. "I can understand his predicament!" Mumford confided to Zevi, "though I have no intention of committing suicide. For I still believe in miracles."[10]

Notes

1. Mumford, *Herman Melville* (New York: Harcourt, Brace, 1929), 151.
2. Mumford, *Technics and Civilization* (New York: Harcourt, Brace, 1934), 12–22.

3. Ibid., 212–15, 265–67.

4. Quoted in Mumford, *Values for Survival: Essays, Addresses, and Letters on Politics and Education* (New York: Harcourt, Brace, 1946), iii.

5. Mumford to Bruno Zevi, October 12, 1973, LM MSS.

6. Mumford, "The Morals of Extermination," *Atlantic Monthly*, October 1959, 38–44; Mumford, "Anticipations and Social Consequences of Atomic Energy," *Proceedings of the American Philosophical Society* 98, no. 2 (1954): 149–52; Mumford, "Apology to Henry Adams," *Virginia Quarterly Review*, 38 (Spring 1962): 196–217.

7. Mumford, "Prologue to Our Time," *The New Yorker*, March 10, 1975, 45; Mumford, *The Myth of the Machine*, vol. 1, *Technics and Human Development* (New York: Harcourt, Brace and World, 1967).

8. Mumford, *The Myth of the Machine*, vol. 2, *The Pentagon of Power* (New York: Harcourt Brace Jovanovich, 1970), 330–34, 430.

9. Ibid., 243–330.

10. Mumford to Bruno Zevi, October 12, 1973, LM MSS.

TECHNICS
AND HUMAN
DEVELOPMENT

The last century, we all realize, has witnessed a radical transformation in the entire human environment, largely as a result of the impact of the mathematical and physical sciences upon technology. This shift from an empirical, tradition-bound technics to an experimental mode has opened up such new realms as those of nuclear energy, supersonic transportation, cybernetic intelligence, and instantaneous distant communication. Never since the Pyramid Age have such vast physical changes been consummated in so short a time. All these changes have, in turn, produced alterations in the human personality, while still more radical transformations, if this process continues unabated and uncorrected, loom ahead.

In terms of the currently accepted picture of the relation of man to technics, our age is passing from the primeval state of man, marked by his invention of tools and weapons for the purpose of achieving mastery over the forces of nature, to a radically different condition, in which he will have not only conquered nature, but detached himself as far as possible from the organic habitat.

With this new "megatechnics" the dominant minority will create a uniform, all-enveloping, super-planetary structure, designed for automatic operation. Instead of functioning actively as an autonomous personality, man will become a passive, purposeless, machine-conditioned animal whose proper functions, as technicians now interpret man's role, will either be fed into the machine or strictly limited and controlled for the benefit of depersonalized, collective organizations.

My purpose [here] is to question both the assumptions and the predictions upon which our commitment to the present forms of technical and scientific progress, treated as if ends in themselves, have been based. I shall bring forward evidence that casts doubts upon the current theories of man's basic nature which overrate the part that tools once played—and machines now play—in human development. I shall suggest not only that Karl Marx was in error in giving the material instruments of production the central place and directive function in human development, but that even the seemingly benign interpretation of Teilhard de Chardin reads back into the whole story of man the narrow technological rationalism of our own age, and projects into the future a final state in which all the possibilities of human development would come to an end. At that "omega-point" nothing would be left of man's autonomous original nature, except organized intelligence: a universal and omnipotent layer of abstract mind, loveless and lifeless.

Now, we cannot understand the role that technics has played in human development without a deeper insight into the historic nature of man. Yet that insight has been blurred during the last century because it has been conditioned by a social environment in which a mass of new mechanical inventions had suddenly proliferated, sweeping away ancient processes and institutions, and altering the traditional conception of both human limitations and technical possibilities.

Our predecessors mistakenly coupled their particular mode of mechanical progress with an unjustifiable sense of increasing moral superiority. But our own contemporaries, who have reason to reject this smug Victorian belief in the inevitable improvement of all other human institutions through command of the machine, nevertheless concentrate, with manic fervor, upon the continued expansion of science and technology, as if they alone magically would provide the only means of human salvation. Since our present overcommitment to technics is in part due to a radical misinterpretation of the whole course of human development, the first step toward recovering our balance is to bring under review the main stages of man's emergence from its primal beginnings onward.

Just because man's need for tools is so obvious, we must guard ourselves against overstressing the role of stone tools hundreds of thousands of years before they became functionally differentiated and efficient. In treating tool-making as central to early man's survival, biologists and anthropologists for long underplayed, or neglected, a mass of activities in which many other species were for long more knowledgeable than man. Despite the contrary evidence put forward by R. U. Sayce, Daryll Forde, and André Leroi-Gourhan, there is still a tendency to identify tools and machines with technology: to substitute the part for the whole.

Even in describing only the material components of technics, this practice overlooks the equally vital role of containers: first hearths, pits, traps, cordage; later baskets, bins, byres, houses, to say nothing of still later collective containers like reservoirs, canals, cities. These static components play an important part in every technology, not least in our own day, with its high-tension transformers, its giant chemical retorts, its atomic reactors.

In any adequate definition of technics, it should be plain that many insects, birds, and mammals had made far more radical innovations in the fabrication of containers, with their intricate nests and bowers, their geometric beehives, their urbanoid anthills and termitaries, their beaver lodges, than man's ancestors had achieved in the making of tools until the emergence of *Homo sapiens*. In short, if technical proficiency alone were sufficient to identify and foster intelligence, man was for long a laggard, compared with many other species. The consequences of this perception should be plain: namely, that there was nothing uniquely human in tool-making until it was modified by linguistic symbols, aesthetic designs, and socially transmitted knowledge. At that point, the human brain, not just the hand, was what made a profound difference; and that brain could not possibly have been just a hand-made product, since it was already well developed in four-footed creatures like rats, which have no free-fingered hands.

More than a century ago Thomas Carlyle described man as a "tool-using animal," as if this were the one trait that elevated him above the rest of brute creation. This overweighting of tools, weapons, physical apparatus, and machines has obscured the actual path of human development. The definition of man as a tool-using animal, even when corrected to read "tool-making," would have seemed strange to Plato, who attributed man's emergence from a primitive state as much to Marsyas and Orpheus, the makers of music, as to fire-stealing Prometheus, or to Hephaestus, the blacksmith-god, the sole manual worker in the Olympic pantheon.

Yet the description of man as essentially a tool-making animal has become so firmly embedded that the mere finding of the fragments of little primate skulls in the neighborhood of chipped pebbles, as with the Australopithecines of Africa, was deemed sufficient by their finder, Dr. L. S. B. Leakey, to identify the creature as in the direct line of human ascent, despite marked physical divergences from both apes and later men. Since Leakey's subhominids had a brain capacity about a third of *Homo sapiens*—less indeed than some apes—the ability to chip and use crude stone tools plainly neither called for nor by itself generated man's rich cerebral equipment.

If the Australopithecines lacked the beginning of other human characteristics, their possession of tools would only prove that at least one other species outside the true genus *Homo* boasted this trait, just as parrots and magpies share the distinctly human achievement of speech, and the bower bird that for colorful decorative embellishment. No single trait, not even tool-making, is sufficient to identify man. What is specially and uniquely human is man's capacity to combine a wide variety of animal propensities into an emergent cultural entity: a human personality.

If the exact functional equivalence of tool-making with utensil-making had been appreciated by earlier investigators, it would have been plain that there was nothing notable about man's hand-made stone artifacts until far along in his development. Even a distant relative of man, the gorilla, puts together a nest of leaves for comfort in sleeping, and will throw a bridge of great fern stalks across a shallow stream, presumably to keep from wetting or scraping his feet. Five-year-old children, who can talk and read and reason, show little aptitude in using tools and still less in making them: so if tool-making were what counted, they could not yet be identified as human.

In early man we have reason to suspect the same kind of facility and the same ineptitude. When we seek for proof of man's genuine superiority to his fellow creatures, we should do well to look for a different kind of evidence than his poor stone tools alone; or rather, we should ask ourselves what activities preoccupied him during those countless years when with the same materials and the same muscular movements he later used so skillfully he might have fashioned better tools.

. . . There was nothing specifically human in primitive technics, apart from the use and preservation of fire, until man had reconstituted his own physical organs by employing them for functions and purposes quite different from those they had originally served. Probably the first major displacement was the transformation of the quadruped's fore-limbs from specialized organs of locomotion to all-purpose tools for climbing, grasping, striking, tearing, pounding, digging, holding. Early man's hands and pebble tools played a significant part in his development, mainly because, as Du Brul has pointed out, they facilitated the preparatory functions of picking, carrying, and macerating food, and *thus liberated the mouth for speech*.

If man was indeed a tool-maker, he possessed at the beginning one primary, all-purpose tool, more important than any later assemblage: his own mind-activated body, every part of it, including those members that made clubs, hand-axes, or wooden spears. To compensate for his extremely primitive working gear, early man had a much more impor-tant asset that extended his whole technical horizon: he had a far richer biological equipment than any other animal, a body not specialized for any single activity, and a brain capable of scanning a wider environ-ment and holding all the different parts of his experience together.

Precisely because of his extraordinary plasticity and sensitivity, he was able to use a larger portion of both his external environment and his internal, psychosomatic resources.

Through man's overdeveloped and incessantly active brain, he had more mental energy to tap than he needed for survival at a purely animal level; and he was accordingly under the necessity of canalizing that energy, not just into food-getting and sexual reproduction, but into modes of living that would convert this energy more directly and constructively into appropriate cultural—that is, symbolic—forms. Only by creating cultural outlets could he tap and control and fully utilize his own nature.

Cultural "work" by necessity took precedence over manual work. These new activities involved far more than the discipline of hand, muscle, and eye in making and using tools, greatly though they aided man: they likewise demanded a control over all man's natural functions, including his organs of excretion, his upsurging emotions, his promiscuous sexual activities, his tormenting and tempting dreams.

With man's persistent exploration of his own organic capabilities, nose, eyes, ears, tongue, lips, and sexual organs were given new roles to play. Even the hand was no mere horny specialized work-tool: it stroked a lover's body, held a baby close to the breast, made significant gestures, or expressed in shared ritual and ordered dance some otherwise inexpressible sentiment about life or death, a remembered past, or an anxious future. Tool-technics, in fact, is but a fragment of biotechnics: man's total equipment for life.

This gift of free neural energy already showed itself in man's primate ancestors. Dr. Alison Jolly has recently shown that brain growth in lemurs derived from their athletic playfulness, their mutual grooming, and their enhanced sociability, rather than from tool-using or food-getting habits; while man's exploratory curiosity, his imitativeness, and his idle manipulativeness, with no thought of ulterior reward, were already visible in his simian relatives. In American usage, "monkeyshines" and "monkeying" are popular identifications of that playfulness and nonutilitarian handling of objects. I shall show that there is even reason to ask whether the standardized patterns observable in early tool-making are not in part derivable from the strictly repetitive motions of ritual, song, and dance, forms that have long existed in a state of perfection among primitive peoples, usually in far more finished style than their tools.

Only a little while ago the Dutch historian J. Huizinga in *Homo Ludens* brought forth a mass of evidence to suggest that play, rather than work, was the formative element in human culture: that man's most serious activity belonged to the realm of make-believe. On this showing, ritual and mimesis, sports and games and dramas, released man from his insistent animal attachments; and nothing could demonstrate this better, I would add, than those primitive ceremonies in which he played at being another kind of animal. Long before he had achieved the power to transform the natural environment, man had created a miniature environment, the symbolic field of play, in which every function of life might be refashioned in a strictly human style, as in a game.

So startling was the thesis of *Homo Ludens* that his shocked translator deliberately altered Huizinga's express statement, that all culture was a form of play, into the more obvious conventional notion that play is an element in culture. But the notion that man is neither *Homo sapiens* nor *Homo ludens,* but above all *Homo faber,* man the maker, had taken such firm possession of present-day Western thinkers that even Henri Bergson held it. So certain were nineteenth-century archaeologists about the primacy of stone tools and weapons in the "struggle for existence" that when the first paleolithic cave paintings were discovered in Spain, in 1879, they were denounced, out of hand, as an outrageous hoax, by "competent authorities," on the ground that Ice Age hunters could not have had the leisure or the mind to produce the elegant art of Altamira.

But mind was exactly what *Homo sapiens* possessed in a singular degree: mind based on the fullest use of all his bodily organs, not just his hands. In this revision of obsolete technological stereotypes, I would go even further: for I submit that at every stage man's inventions and transformations were less for the purpose of increasing the food supply or controlling nature than for utilizing his own immense organic resources and expressing his latent potentialities, in order to fulfill more adequately his superorganic demands and aspirations.

When not curbed by hostile environmental pressures, man's elaboration of symbolic culture answered a more imperative need than that for control over the environment—and, one must infer, largely predated it and for long outpaced it. Among sociologists, Leslie White deserves credit for giving due weight to this fact by his emphasis on "minding" and "symboling," though he has but recovered for the present generation the original insights of the father of anthropology, Edward Tylor.

On this reading, the evolution of language—a culmination of man's more elementary forms of expressing and transmitting meaning—was incomparably more important to further human development than the chipping of a mountain of hand-axes. Besides the relatively simple coordinations required for tool-using, the delicate interplay of the many organs needed for the creation of articulate speech was a far more striking advance. This effort must have occupied a greater part of early man's time, energy, and mental activity, since the ultimate collective product, spoken language, was infinitely more complex and sophisticated at the dawn of civilization than the Egyptian or Mesopotamian kit of tools.

To consider man, then, as primarily a tool-using animal, is to overlook the main chapters of human history. Opposed to this petrified notion, I shall develop the view that man is pre-eminently a mind-making, self-mastering, and self-designing animal; and the primary locus of all his activities lies first in his own organism, and in the social organization through which it finds fuller expression. Until man had made something of himself he could make little of the world around him.

In this process of self-discovery and self-transformation, tools, in the narrow sense, served well as subsidiary instruments, but not as the main operative agent in man's development; for technics has never till our own age dissociated itself from the larger cultural whole in which man, as man, has always functioned. The classic Greek term *tekhne* characteristically makes no distinction between industrial production and "fine" or symbolic art; and for the greater part of human history these aspects were inseparable, one side respecting the objective conditions and functions, the other responding to subjective needs.

At its point of origin, technics was related to the whole nature of man, and that nature played a part in every aspect of industry: thus technics, at the beginning, was broadly life-centered, not work-centered or power-centered. As in any other ecological complex, varied human interests and purposes, different organic needs, restrained the overgrowth of any single component. Though language was man's most potent symbolic expression, it flowed, I shall attempt to show, from the same common source that finally produced the machine: the primeval repetitive order of ritual, a mode of order man was forced to develop, in self-protection, so as to control the tremendous overcharge of psychal energy that his large brain placed at his disposal.

So far from disparaging the role of technics, however, I shall rather demonstrate that once this basic internal organization was established, technics supported and enlarged the capacities for human expression. The discipline of tool-making and tool-using served as a timely correction, on this hypothesis, to the inordinate powers of invention that spoken language gave to man—powers that otherwise unduly inflated the ego and tempted man to substitute magical verbal formulae for efficacious work.

On this interpretation, the specific human achievement, which set man apart from even his nearest anthropoid relatives, was the shaping of a new self, visibly different in appearance, in behavior, and in plan of life from his primitive animal forebears. As this differentiation widened and the number of definitely human "identification marks" increased, man speeded the process of his own evolution, achieving through culture in a relatively short span of years changes that other species accomplished laboriously through organic processes, whose results, in contrast to man's cultural modes, could not be easily corrected, improved, or effaced.

Henceforth the main business of man was his own self-transformation, group by group, region by region, culture by culture. This self-transformation not merely rescued man from permanent fixation in his original animal condition, but freed his best-developed organ, his brain, for other tasks than those of ensuring physical survival. The dominant human trait, central to all other traits, is this capacity for conscious, purposeful self-identification, self-transformation, and ultimately for self-understanding.

Every manifestation of human culture, from ritual and speech to costume and social organization, is directed ultimately to the remodeling of the human organism and the expression of the human personality. If it is only now that we belatedly recognize this distinctive feature, it is perhaps because there are widespread indications in contemporary art and politics and technics that man may be on the point of losing it —becoming not a lower animal, but a shapeless, amoeboid nonentity.

In recasting the stereotyped representations of human development, I have fortunately been able to draw upon a growing body of biological and anthropological evidence, which has not until now been correlated or fully interpreted. Yet I am aware, of course, that despite this substantial support the large themes I am about to develop, and even more their speculative subsidiary hypotheses, may well meet with justifiable skepticism; for they have still to undergo competent critical scrutiny. Need I say that so far from starting with a desire to dispute the prevailing orthodox views, I at first respectfully accepted them, since I knew no others? It was only because I could find no clue to modern man's overwhelming commitment to his technology, even at the expense of his health, his physical safety, his mental balance, and his possible future development, that I was driven to re-examine the nature of man and the whole course of technological change.

In addition to discovering the aboriginal field of man's inventiveness, not in his making of external tools, but primarily in the refashioning of his own bodily organs, I have undertaken to follow another freshly blazed trail: to examine the broad streak of irrationality that runs all through human history, counter to man's sensible, functionally rational animal inheritance. As compared even with other anthropoids, one might refer without irony to man's superior irrationality. Certainly human development exhibits a chronic disposition to error, mischief, disordered fantasy, hallucination, "original sin," and even socially organized and sanctified misbehavior, such as the practice of human sacrifice and legalized torture. In escaping organic fixations, man forfeited the innate humility and mental stability of less adventurous species. Yet some of his most erratic departures have opened up valuable areas that purely organic evolution, over billions of years, had never explored.

The mischances that followed man's quitting mere animalhood were many, but the rewards were great. Man's proneness to mix his fantasies and projections, his desires and designs, his abstractions and his ideologies, with the commonplaces of daily experience were, we can now see, an important source of his immense creativity. There is no clean dividing line between the irrational and the super-rational; and the handling of these ambivalent gifts has always been a major human problem. One of the reasons that the current utilitarian interpretations of technics and science have been so shallow is that they ignore the fact that this aspect of human culture has been as open to both transcendental aspirations and demonic compulsions as any other part of man's existence—and has never been so open and so vulnerable as today.

The irrational factors that have sometimes constructively prompted, yet too often distorted, man's further development became plain at the moment when the formative elements in paleolithic and neolithic cultures united in the great cultural implosion that took place around the fourth millennium B.C.: what is usually called "the rise of civilization." The remarkable fact about this transformation technically is that it was the result, not of mechanical inventions, but of a radically new type of social organization: a product of myth, magic, religion, and the nascent science of astronomy. This implosion of sacred political powers and technological facilities cannot be accounted for by any inventory of the tools, the simple machines, and the technical processes then available. Neither the wheeled wagon, the plow, the potter's wheel, nor the military chariot could of themselves have accomplished the mighty transformations that took place in the great valleys of Egypt, Mesopotamia, and India, and eventually passed, in ripples and waves, to other parts of the planet.

The study of the Pyramid Age I made in preparation for writing *The City in History* unexpectedly revealed that a close parallel existed between the first authoritarian civilizations in the Near East and our own, though most of our contemporaries still regard modern technics, not only as the highest point in man's intellectual development, but as an entirely new phenomenon. On the contrary, I found that what economists lately termed the Machine Age or the Power Age, had its origin, not in the so-called Industrial Revolution of the eighteenth century, but at the very outset in the organization of an archetypal machine composed of human parts.

Two things must be noted about this new mechanism, because they identify it throughout its historical course down to the present. The first is that the organizers of the machine derived their power and authority from a heavenly source. Cosmic order was the basis of this new human order. The exactitude in measurement, the abstract mechanical system, the compulsive regularity of this "megamachine," as I shall call it, sprang directly from astronomical observations and scientific calculations. This inflexible, predictable order, incorporated later in the calendar, was transferred to the regimentation of the human components. As against earlier forms of ritualized order, this mechanized order was external to man. By a combination of divine command and ruthless military coercion, a large population was made to endure grinding poverty and forced labor at mind-dulling repetitive tasks in order to ensure "Life, Prosperity, and Health" for the divine or semi-divine ruler and his entourage.

The second point is that the grave social defects of the human machine were partly offset by its superb achievements in flood control and grain production, which laid the ground for an enlarged achievement in every area of human culture: in monumental art, in codified law, in systematically pursued and permanently recorded thought, in the augmentation of all the potentialities of the mind by the assemblage of a varied population, with diverse regional and vocational backgrounds in urban ceremonial centers. Such order, such collective security and abundance, such stimulating cultural mixtures, were first achieved in Mesopotamia and Egypt, and later in India, China, Persia, and in the Andean and Mayan cultures: and they were never surpassed until the megamachine was reconstituted in a new form in our own time. Unfortunately these cultural advances were largely offset by equally great social regressions.

Conceptually the instruments of mechanization five thousand years ago were already detached from other human functions and purposes than the constant increase of order, power, predictability, and, above all, control. With this proto-scientific ideology went a corresponding regimentation and degradation of once-autonomous human activities: "mass culture" and "mass control" made their first appearance. With mordant symbolism, the ultimate products of the megamachine in Egypt were colossal tombs, inhabited by mummified corpses; while later in Assyria, as repeatedly in every other expanding empire, the chief testimony to its technical efficiency was a waste of destroyed villages and cities, and poisoned soils: the prototype of similar "civilized" atrocities today. As for the great Egyptian pyramids, what are they but the precise static equivalents of our own space rockets? Both devices for securing, at an extravagant cost, a passage to heaven for the favored few.

These colossal miscarriages of a dehumanized power-centered culture monotonously soil the pages of history from the rape of Sumer to the blasting of Warsaw and Rotterdam, Tokyo and Hiroshima. Sooner or later, this analysis suggests, we must have the courage to ask ourselves: Is this association of inordinate power and productivity with equally inordinate violence and destruction a purely accidental one?

In the working out of this parallel and in the tracing of the archetypal machine through later Western history, I found that many obscure irrational manifestations in our own highly mechanized and supposedly rational culture became strangely clarified. For in both cases, immense gains in valuable knowledge and usable productivity were canceled out by equally great increases in ostentatious waste, paranoid hostility, insensate destructiveness, hideous random extermination.

. . . This widened interpretation of the past is a necessary move toward escaping the dire insufficiencies of current one-generation knowledge. If we do not take the time to review the past, we shall not have sufficient insight to understand the present or command the future: for the past never leaves us, and the future is already here.

THE FIRST
MEGAMACHINE

Though the [megamachine] came into existence roughly during the same period as the first industrial use of copper, it was an independent innovation, and did not at first utilize any new mechanical aids. But . . . once conceived, [it] was assembled within a short period; and it spread rapidly, not by being imitated, but by being forcefully imposed by kings, acting as only gods or the anointed representatives of gods could act. Wherever it was successfully put together the new machine commanded power and performed labor on a scale that was never even conceivable before. With this ability to concentrate immense mechanical forces, a new dynamism came into play, which overcame, by the magic of success, the sluggish routines, the petty inhibitions, the dull repetitive routines of the basic neolithic village culture. . . .

With the energies available through . . . the megamachine, the very dimensions of space and time were enlarged. Operations that once could hardly be finished in centuries were now accomplished in less than a generation. If whole mountains were not moved, large portions of them were, sometimes in blocks far bigger than any ordinary motor truck could now handle; while, on the level plains, man-made mountains of stone or baked clay, pyramids and ziggurats, arose in response to royal command. No power machines at all comparable to this mechanism were utilized on any scale until watermills and windmills swept over western Europe from the fourteenth century of our era.

From the beginning, this human machine presented two aspects: one negative and coercive, the other positive and constructive. In fact, the second factors could not function unless the first were present. Though the military machine probably came before the labor machine, it was the latter that first achieved an incomparable perfection of performance, not alone in quantity of work done, but in quality. To call these collective entities machines is no idle play on words. If a machine be defined more or less in accord with the classic definition of Reuleaux, as a combination of resistant parts, each specialized in function, operating under human control, to transmit motion and to perform work, then the labor machine was a real machine: all the more because its component parts, though composed of human bone, nerve, and muscle, were reduced to their bare mechanical elements and rigidly restricted to the performance of their mechanical tasks.

Such machines, of immense power and practical utility, had already been invented by kings in the early part of the Pyramid Age, from the end of the fourth millennium on. Just because of their detachment from any external structure, they had paradoxically much fuller capacities for change and adaptation than the more rigid metallic counterparts of a modern assembly line. In fact, it is in the building of the pyramids that we find the first indubitable evidence of the machine's existence, and the first proof of its astonishing efficiency. Wherever kingship spread, the human machine, in its destructive if not its constructive form, always went with it. This holds as true for Mesopotamia, India, China, Cambodia, Mexico, Yucatán, or Peru, as for Egypt.

Let us examine the human machine in its archetypal original form. . . .The pyramid took form as a tomb to hold the embalmed body of the Pharaoh and secure his safe passage into the after-life: though he alone, at first, had the prospect of such a godlike extension of his existence, the very idea of being able to fabricate personal immortality shows an alteration in all the dimension of existence.

Between the first small pyramid, built in the step form we find later in Central America, and the mighty pyramid of Cheops at Giza, the first and the most enduring of the Seven Wonders of the Ancient World, lies the short span of three hundred years. On the ancient time scale for inventions the most primitive form and the final one, never again to be equaled, were practically contemporary. The swiftness of this development indicates a concentration of physical power and technical imagination: for it took far more than faith to move the mountain of stone that composed this ultimate monument. That transformation is all the more striking because the Pharaohs' tombs did not stand alone: they were part of a whole city of the dead, with buildings that housed the priests who conducted the elaborate rituals deemed necessary to ensure a happy fate for the departed divinity.

The Great Pyramid is one of the most colossal and perfect examples of the engineer's art at any period or in any culture. Considering the state of all the other arts in the third millennium, no construction of our own day surpasses this in either technical virtuosity or human audacity.

This great enterprise was undertaken by a culture that was just emerging from the Stone Age, and was long to continue using stone tools, though copper was available for the chisels and saws that shaped building stones for the new monuments.

The actual operations were performed by specialized handicraft workers, aided by an army of unskilled or semiskilled laborers, drafted at quarterly intervals from agriculture. The whole job was done with no other material aids than the "simple machines" of classical mechanics: the inclined plane and the lever, for neither wheel nor pulley nor screw had yet been invented. We know from graphic representations that large stones were hauled on sledges, by battalions of men, across the desert sands. Yet the single stone slab that covers the inner chamber of the Great Pyramid where the Pharaoh lies weighed fifty tons. An architect today would think twice before calling for such a mechanical exploit.

Now, the Great Pyramid is more than a formidable mountain of stone, 755 feet square at the base, rising to a height of 481.4 feet. It is a structure with a complex interior, consisting of a series of passages at different levels that lead into the final burial chamber. Yet every part of it was built with a kind of precision that, as J. H. Breasted emphasized, belongs to the optician's art rather than that of the modern bridge builder or skyscraper constructor. Blocks of stone were set together with seams of considerable length, showing joints of one-ten-thousandth of an inch; while the dimensions of the sides at the base differ by only 7.9 inches, in a structure that covers acres. In short, what we now characterize as flawless machine precision and machine perfection first manifested itself in the building of this great tomb: at once a symbol of the mountain of creation that emerged out of the primeval waters and a visible effort, so far remarkably successful, by purely human measure, to solidify both time and the human body in an eternal form. No ordinary human hands, no ordinary human effort, no ordinary kind of human collaboration such as was available in the building of village huts and the planting of fields, could muster such a superhuman force, or achieve an almost supernatural result. Only a divine king could accomplish such an act of the human will and such a large-scale material transformation.

Was it possible to create such a structure without the aid of a machine? Emphatically not. I repeat, the product itself showed that it was not only the work of a machine, but of an instrument of precision. Though the material equipment of dynastic Egypt was still crude, the patient workmanship and disciplined method made good these shortcomings. The social organization had leaped ahead five thousand years to create the first large-scale power machine: a machine of a hundred thousand manpower, that is, the equivalent, roughly, of ten thousand horsepower: a machine composed of a multitude of uniform, specialized, interchangeable, but functionally differentiated parts, rigorously marshaled together and coordinated in a process centrally organized and centrally directed: each part behaving as a mechanical component of the mechanized whole: unmoved by an internal impulse that would interfere with the working of the mechanism.

In less than three centuries, this collective human machine was perfected. Once organized and set in motion by the Pharaoh through his chief architect, *the technical competence* and imagination that envisaged the entire design was passed on, by word of mouth, and written instruction, to the component parts: the skilled workers, the overseers and taskmasters, the dumb hands. The kind of mind that designed the pyramid was a new human type, capable of abstraction of a high order, using astronomical observations for the siting of the structure, so that each side was oriented exactly in line with true points of the compass: since at inundation the pyramid site is only one quarter of a mile from the river, a rock foundation—which demanded the removal of sand— was needed. In the Great Pyramid the perimeter of that bed deviates from true level by little more than one-half an inch.

But the workers who carried out the design also had minds of a new order: trained in obedience to the letter, limited in response to the word of command descending from the king through a bureaucratic hierarchy, forfeiting during the period of service any trace of autonomy or initiative; slavishly undeviating in performance. Their leaders could read written orders; for the men employed left their names in red ocher, Edwards tells us, on the blocks of the Meidum pyramid: "Boat Gang," "Vigorous Gang." They themselves would have felt at home today on an assembly line. Only the naked pin-up girl was lacking.

Alike in organization, in mode of work, and in product, there is no doubt that the machines that built the pyramids, and that performed all the other great constructive works of "civilization" in other provinces and cultures, were true machines. In their basic operations, they collectively performed the equivalent of a whole corps of power shovels, bulldozers, tractors, mechanical saws, and pneumatic drills, with an exactitude of measurement, a refinement of skill, and even an output of work that would still be a theme for boasting today.

This extension of magnitude in every direction, this raising of the ceiling of human effort, this subordination of individual aptitudes and interests to the mechanical job in hand, and this unification of a multitude of subordinates to a single end that derived from the divine power exercised by the king, in turn, by the success of the result, confirmed that power.

For note: it was the king who uttered the original commands: it was the king who demanded absolute obedience and punished disobedience with torture, mutilation, or death: it was the king who alone had the godlike power of turning live men into dead mechanical objects: and finally it was the king who assembled the parts to form the machine and imposed the new discipline of mechanical organization, with the same regularity that moved the heavenly bodies on their undeviating course.

No vegetation god, no fertility myth, could produce this kind of cold abstract order, this detachment of power from life. Only one empowered by the Sun God could remove all hitherto respected norms or limits of human endeavor. The king figures, in early accounts, as a being of heroic mold: he alone slays lions singlehanded, builds great city walls, or like Menes turns the course of rivers. That straining ambition, that defiant effort belongs only to the king and the machine that he set in motion.

To understand the structure or the performance of the human machine, one must do more than center attention upon the point where it materializes. Even our present technology, with its vast reticulation of visible machines, cannot be understood on those terms alone. In order to put together a collective machine composed solely of human parts, one needed a complex transmission mechanism, to ensure that commands issued at the top would be swiftly and accurately conveyed to every member of the unit, so that the parts would interlock to form a single operating whole.

Two collective devices were essential, to make the machine work: a reliable organization of knowledge, natural and supernatural: and an elaborate structure for giving and carrying out orders. The first was incorporated in the priesthood, without whose active aid divine kingship could not have come into existence: the second in a bureaucracy: both hierarchical organizations at whose apex stood the temple and the palace. Without them the power complex could not operate. This condition remains true today, even though the existence of automated factories and computer-regulated units conceals the human components essential even to automation.

What would now be called science was an integral part of the new machine system from the beginning. This science, based on cosmic regularities, flourished with the cult of the sun: record-keeping, time-keeping, star-watching, calendar-making, coincide with and support the institution of kingship, even though no small part of the efforts of the priesthood were, in addition, devoted to interpreting the meaning of singular events, such as the appearance of comets or eclipses of the sun or moon, or natural irregularities, such as the flight of birds or the state of a sacrificed animal's entrails.

No king could move safely or effectively without the support of such organized higher knowledge, any more than the Pentagon can move today without consulting scientists, "games theorists," and computers, a new hierarchy supposedly less fallible than entrail-diviners, but to judge by their repeated miscalculations, not notably so. To be effective, this kind of knowledge must remain a priestly monopoly: if everyone had equal access to the sources of knowledge and to the system of interpretation, no one would believe in infallibility, since its errors could not be concealed. Hence the shocked protest of Ipu-wer against the revolutionaries who overthrew the Old Kingdom was that the "secrets of the temple lay unbared"; that is, they had made "classified information" public. Secret knowledge belongs to any system of total control. Until printing was invented, this remained a class monopoly.

Not the least affiliation of kingship with the worship of the sun is the fact that the king, like the sun, exerts force at a distance. For the first time in history, power became effective outside the immediate range of hearing and vision and the arm's reach. No military weapon by itself sufficed to convey such power: what was needed was a special form of transmission gear: an army of scribes, messengers, stewards, superintendents, gang bosses, and major and minor executives, whose very existence depended upon their carrying out the king's orders, or those of his powerful ministers and generals, to the letter. In other words, a bureaucracy: a group of men, capable of transmitting and executing a command, with the ritualistic punctilio of a priest, the mindless obedience of a soldier.

To fancy that bureaucracy is a relatively recent institution is to ignore the annals of ancient history. The first documents that attest the existence of bureaucracy belong to the Pyramid Age. In a cenotaph description at Abydos, a career official under Pepi I, in the Sixth Dynasty, c. 2375 B.C., reported: "His majesty sent me at the head of this army, while the counts, while the Seal-bearers of the King of Lower Egypt, while the sole companions of the Palace, while the nomarchs (governors) and *mayors* of Upper and Lower Egypt, the companions and chief dragomans, the chief prophets of Upper and Lower Egypt, and the Chief bureaucrats were (each) at the head of a troop of Upper or Lower Egypt, or of the villages and towns which they might rule."

Not merely does this text establish a bureaucracy: it shows that the division of labor and specialization of functions necessary for efficient mechanical operation had already taken place in the organization that, as executors of the sovereign's will, already controlled the operations of both the military and the labor machine. This development had begun at least three dynasties before, not by accident, with the building of the great stone pyramid of Djoser at Sakkara. [John A.] Wilson observes, in *City Invincible*, that "we credit Djoser, not only with the beginnings of monumental architecture in stone in Egypt, but also with the setting up of a new monster, the bureaucracy." This was no mere coincidence. And W. F. Albright, commenting upon this, pointed out that "the greater number of titles found in sealings of the First Dynasty . . . certainly pre-supposes an elaborate officialdom of some kind."

Once the hierarchic structure of the human machine was established, there was no limit to the number of hands it might control or the power it might exert. The removal of human dimensions and organic limits is indeed the chief boast of the authoritarian machine. Part of its productivity is due to its use of unstinted physical coercion to overcome human laziness or bodily fatigue. Occupational specialization was a necessary step in the assemblage of the human machine: only by intense specialization at every part of the process could the superhuman accuracy and perfection of the product have been achieved. The large-scale division of labor throughout industrial society begins at this point.

The Roman maxim that the law does not concern itself with trifles applies likewise to the human machine. The great forces that were set in motion by the king demanded collective enterprises of a commensurate order. These human machines were by nature impersonal, if not deliberately dehumanized; they had to operate on a big scale or they could not work at all; for no bureaucracy, however well organized, could govern a thousand little workshops, each with its own traditions, its own craft skills, its own willful personal pride and sense of responsibility. So the form of control imposed by kingship was confined to great collective enterprises.

The importance of this bureaucratic link between the source of power, the divine king, and the actual human machines that performed the works of construction or destruction can hardly be exaggerated: all the more because it was the bureaucracy that collected the annual taxes and tributes that supported the new social pyramid and forcibly assembled the manpower that formed the new mechanical fabric. The bureaucracy was, in fact, the third type of "invisible machine," co-existing with the military and labor machines, and an integral part of the total structure.

Now the important part about the functioning of a classic bureaucracy is that it originates nothing: its function is to transmit, without alteration or deviation, the orders that come from above. No merely local information or human considerations may alter this inflexible transmission process—except by corruption. This administrative method ideally requires a studious repression of all the autonomous functions of the personality, and a readiness to perform the daily task with ritual exactitude. Not for the first time does such ritual exactitude enter into the process of work: indeed, it is highly unlikely that submission to colorless repetition would have been possible without the millennial discipline of religious ritual.

Bureaucratic regimentation was in fact part of the larger regimentation of life, introduced by this power-centered culture. Nothing emerges more clearly from the Pyramid texts themselves, with their wearisome repetitions of formulae, than a colossal capacity for enduring monotony: a capacity that anticipates the universal boredom achieved in our own day. Even the poetry of both early Egypt and Babylonia reveals this iterative hypnosis: the same words, in the same order, with no gain in meaning, repeated a dozen times—or a hundred times. This verbal compulsiveness is the psychical side of the systematic compulsion that brought the labor machine into existence. Only those who were sufficiently docile to endure this regimen at every stage from command to execution could become an effective unit in the human machine.

Though the human machine was powerful, it was likewise extremely fragile: once the royal power was switched off, it "went dead." The royal machine reached the limit of its capabilities, without doubt, in the construction of the Great Pyramid. Soon after this came a revolt so shattering, so profound, that centuries passed before the severed regions of Egypt could be assembled once more under a single divine ruler. Never was power to be raised to such heights of absolute command again until our own day. But the institutional forces set in motion by this first effort continued to operate. Wherever the army, the bureaucracy, and the priesthood worked together under unified royal command, the technics of unqualified power would resume operation. . . .

In short, none of the destructive fantasies that have taken possession of leaders in our own age, from Hitler to Stalin, from the khans of the Kremlin to the Kahns of the Pentagon, were foreign to the souls of the divinely appointed founders of the first machine civilization. With every increase of effective power, extravagantly sadistic and murderous impulses emerged out of the unconscious: not radically different from those sanctioned, not only by Hitler's extermination of six million Jews and uncounted millions of other people, but by the extermination by the United States Air Force of [approximately] 180,000 civilians in Tokyo in a single night by roasting alive. When a distinguished Mesopotamian scholar proclaimed that "civilization begins at Sumer" he innocently overlooked how much must be forgotten before this can be looked upon as a laudable achievement. Mass production and mass destruction are the positive and negative poles, historically, of the myth of the megamachine. . . .

THE MONASTERY
AND THE CLOCK

Where did the "Machine" first take form in modern civilization? There was plainly more than one point of origin. Our mechanical civilization represents the convergence of numerous habits, ideas, and modes of living, as well as technical instruments; and some of these were, in the beginning, directly opposed to the civilization they helped to create. But the first manifestation of the new order took place in the general picture of the world: during the first seven centuries of the machine's existence the categories of time and space underwent an extraordinary change, and no aspect of life was left untouched by this transformation. The application of quantitative methods of thought to the study of nature had its first manifestation in the regular measurement of time; and the new mechanical conception of time arose in part out of the routine of the monastery. Alfred [North] Whitehead has emphasized the importance of the scholastic belief in a universe ordered by God as one of the foundations of modern physics: but behind that belief was the presence of order in the institutions of the Church itself.

The technics of the ancient world were still carried on from Constantinople and Baghdad to Sicily and Cordova: hence the early lead taken by Salerno in the scientific and medical advances of the Middle Ages. It was, however, in the monasteries of the West that the desire for order and power, other than that expressed in the military domination of weaker men, first manifested itself after the long uncertainty and bloody confusion that attended the breakdown of the Roman Empire. Within the walls of the monastery was sanctuary: under the rule of the order surprise and doubt and caprice and irregularity were put at bay. Opposed to the erratic fluctuations and pulsations of the worldly life was the iron discipline of the rule. Benedict added a seventh period

324

to the devotions of the day, and in the seventh century, by a bull of Pope Sabinianus, it was decreed that the bells of the monastery be rung seven times in the twenty-four hours. These punctuation marks in the day were known as the canonical hours, and some means of keeping count of them and ensuring their regular repetition became necessary.

According to a now discredited legend, the first modern mechanical clock, worked by falling weights, was invented by the monk named Gerbert who afterwards became Pope Sylvester II, near the close of the tenth century. This clock was probably only a water clock, one of those bequests of the ancient world either left over directly from the days of the Romans, like the waterwheel itself, or coming back again into the West through the Arabs. But the legend, as so often happens, is accurate in its implications if not in its facts. The monastery was the seat of a regular life, and an instrument for striking the hours at intervals or for reminding the bell-ringer that it was time to strike the bells was an almost inevitable product of this life. If the mechanical clock did not appear until the cities of the thirteenth century demanded an orderly routine, the habit of order itself and the earnest regulation of time sequences had become almost second nature in the monastery. [George Gordon] Coulton agrees with [Werner] Sombart in looking upon the Benedictines, the great working order, as perhaps the original founders of modern capitalism: their rule certainly took the curse off work and their vigorous engineering enterprises may even have robbed warfare of some of its glamour. So one is not straining the facts when one suggests that the monasteries—at one time there were forty thousand under the Benedictine rule—helped to give human enterprise the regular collective beat and rhythm of the machine; for the clock is not merely a means of keeping track of the hours, but of synchronizing the actions of men.

Was it by reason of the collective Christian desire to provide for the welfare of souls in eternity by regular prayers and devotions that time-keeping and the habits of temporal order took hold of men's minds: habits that capitalist civilization presently turned to good account? One must perhaps accept the irony of this paradox. At all events, by the thirteenth century there are definite records of mechanical clocks, and by 1370 a well-designed "modern" clock had been built by Heinrich von Wyck at Paris. Meanwhile, bell towers had come into existence, and the new clocks, if they did not have, till the fourteenth century, a dial and a hand that translated the movement of time into a movement through space, at all events struck the hours. The clouds that could paralyze the sundial, the freezing that could stop the water clock on a winter night, were no longer obstacles to time-keeping: summer or winter, day or night, one was aware of the measured clank of the clock.

The instrument presently spread outside the monastery; and the regular striking of the bells brought a new regularity into the life of the workman and the merchant. The bells of the clock tower almost defined urban existence. Time-keeping passed into time-serving and time-accounting and time-rationing. As this took place, Eternity ceased gradually to serve as the measure and focus of human actions.

The clock, not the steam engine, is the key machine of the modern industrial age. For every phase of its development the clock is both the outstanding fact and the typical symbol of the machine: even today no other machine is so ubiquitous. Here, at the very beginning of modern technics, appeared prophetically the accurate automatic machine which, only after centuries of further effort, was also to prove the final consummation of this technic in every department of industrial activity. There had been power-machines, such as the water mill, before the clock; and there had also been various kinds of automata, to awaken the wonder of the populace in the temple, or to please the idle fancy of some Moslem caliph: machines one finds illustrated in Hero and Al-Jazari. But here was a new kind of power-machine, in which the source of power and the transmission were of such a nature as to ensure the even flow of energy throughout the works and to make possible regular production and a standardized product. In its relationship to determinable quantities of energy, to standardization, to automatic action, and finally to its own special product, accurate timing, the clock has been the foremost machine in modern technics: and at each period it has remained in the lead: it marks a perfection toward which other machines aspire. The clock, moreover, served as a model for many other kinds of mechanical works, and the analysis of motion that accompanied the perfection of the clock, with the various types of gearing and transmission that were elaborated, contributed to the success of quite different kinds of machine. Smiths could have hammered thousands of suits of armor or thousands of iron cannon, wheelwrights could have shaped thousands of great waterwheels or crude gears, without inventing any of the special types of movement developed in clockwork, and without any of the accuracy of measurement and fineness of articulation that finally produced the accurate eighteenth-century chronometer.

The clock, moreover, is a piece of power-machinery whose "product" is seconds and minutes: by its essential nature it dissociated time from human events and helped create the belief in an independent world of mathematically measurable sequences: the special world of science. There is relatively little foundation for this belief in common human experience: throughout the year the days are of uneven duration, and not merely does the relation between day and night steadily change, but a slight journey from East to West alters astronomical time by a certain number of minutes. In terms of the human organism itself, mechanical time is even more foreign: while human life has regularities of its own, the beat of the pulse, the breathing of the lungs, these change from hour to hour with mood and action, and in the longer span of days, time is measured not by the calendar but by the events that occupy it. The shepherd measures from the time the ewes lambed; the farmer measures back to the day of sowing or forward to the harvest: if growth has its own duration and regularities, behind it arc not simply matter and motion but the facts of development: in short, history. And while mechanical time is strung out in a succession of mathematically isolated instants, organic time—what Bergson calls duration—is cumulative in its effects. Though mechanical time can, in a sense, be speeded up or run backward, like the hands of a clock or the images of a moving picture, organic time moves in only one direction—through the cycle of birth, growth, development, decay, and death—and the past that is already dead remains present in the future that has still to be born.

Around 1345, according to [Lynn] Thorndike, the division of hours into sixty minutes and of minutes into sixty seconds became common: it was this abstract framework of divided time that became more and more the point of reference for both action and thought, and in the effort to arrive at accuracy in this department, the astronomical exploration of the sky focused attention further upon the regular, implacable movements of the heavenly bodies through space. Early in the sixteenth century a young Nürnberg mechanic, Peter Henlein, is supposed to have created "many-wheeled watches out of small bits of iron" and by the end of the century the small domestic clock had been introduced in England and Holland. As with the motorcar and the airplane, the richer classes first took over the new mechanism and popularized it: partly because they alone could afford it, partly because the new bourgeoisie were the first to discover that, as Franklin later put it, "time is money." To become "as regular as clockwork" was the bourgeois ideal, and to own a watch was for long a definite symbol of success. The increasing tempo of civilization led to a demand for greater power: and in turn power quickened the tempo.

Now, the orderly punctual life that first took shape in the monasteries is not native to mankind, although by now Western peoples are so thoroughly regimented by the clock that it is "second nature" and they look upon its observance as a fact of nature. Many Eastern civilizations have flourished on a loose basis in time: the Hindus have in fact been so indifferent to time that they lack even an authentic chronology of the years. Only yesterday, in the midst of the industrialization of Soviet Russia, did a society come into existence to further the carrying of watches there and to propagandize the benefits of punctuality. The popularization of time-keeping, which followed the production of the cheap standardized watch, first in Geneva, then in America around the middle of the last century, was essential to a well-articulated system of transportation and production.

To keep time was once a peculiar attribute of music: it gave industrial value to the workshop song or the tattoo or the chantey of the sailors tugging at a rope. But the effect of the mechanical clock is more pervasive and strict: it presides over the day from the hour of rising to the hour of rest. When one thinks of the day as an abstract span of time, one does not go to bed with the chickens on a winter's night: one invents wicks, chimneys, lamps, gaslights, electric lamps, so as to use all the hours belonging to the day. When one thinks of time, not as a sequence of experiences, but as a collection of hours, minutes, and seconds, the habits of adding time and saving time come into existence. Time took on the character of an enclosed space: it could be divided, it could be filled up, it could even be expanded by the invention of labor-saving instruments.

Abstract time became the new medium of existence. Organic functions themselves were regulated by it: one ate, not upon feeling hungry, but when prompted by the clock: one slept, not when one was tired, but when the clock sanctioned it. A generalized time-consciousness accompanied the wider use of clocks: dissociating time from organic sequences, it became easier for the men of the Renaissance to indulge the fantasy of reviving the classic past or of reliving the splendors of antique Roman civilization: the cult of history, appearing first in daily ritual, finally abstracted itself as a special discipline. In the seventeenth century journalism and periodic literature made their appearance: even in dress, following the lead of Venice as fashion center, people altered styles every year rather than every generation.

The gain in mechanical efficiency through coordination and through the closer articulation of the day's events cannot be overestimated: while this increase cannot be measured in mere horsepower, one has only to imagine its absence today to foresee the speedy disruption and eventual collapse of our entire society. The modern industrial regime could do without coal and iron and steam easier than it could do without the clock.

"A child and an adult, an Australian primitive and a European, a man of the Middle Ages and a contemporary, are distinguished not only by a difference in degree, but by a difference in kind by their methods of pictorial representation."

Dagobert Frey, whose words I have just quoted, has made a penetrating study of the difference in spatial conceptions between the early Middle Ages and the Renaissance: he has reinforced, by a wealth of specific detail, the generalization that no two cultures live conceptually in the same kind of time and space. Space and time, like language itself, are works of art, and like language they help condition and direct practical action. Long before Kant announced that time and space were categories of the mind, long before the mathematicians discovered that there were conceivable and rational forms of space other than the form described by Euclid, mankind at large had acted on this premise. Like the Englishman in France who thought that bread was the right name for *le pain,* each culture believes that every other kind of space and time is an approximation to or a perversion of the real space and time in which *it* lives.

During the Middle Ages spatial relations tended to be organized as symbols and values. The highest object in the city was the church spire, which pointed toward heaven and dominated all the lesser buildings, as the church dominated their hopes and fears. Space was divided arbitrarily to represent the seven virtues or the twelve apostles or the Ten Commandments or the Trinity. Without constant symbolic reference to the fables and myths of Christianity the rationale of medieval space would collapse. Even the most rational minds were not exempt: Roger Bacon was a careful student of optics, but after he had described the seven coverings of the eye he added that by such means God had willed to express in our bodies an image of the seven gifts of the spirit.

Size signified importance: to represent human beings of entirely different sizes on the same plane of vision and at the same distance from the observer was entirely possible for the medieval artist. This same habit applies not only to the representation of real objects but to the organization of terrestrial experience by means of the map. In medieval cartography the water and the land masses of the earth, even when approximately known, may be represented in an arbitrary figure like a tree, with no regard for the actual relations as experienced by a traveler, and with no interest in anything except the allegorical correspondence.

One further characteristic of medieval space must be noted: space and time form two relatively independent systems. First: the medieval artist introduced other times within his own spatial world, as when he projected the events of Christ's life within a contemporary Italian city, without the slightest feeling that the passage of time has made a difference, just as in Chaucer the classical legend of Troilus and Cressida is related as if it were a contemporary story. When a medieval chronicler mentions the king, as [Helen Waddell,] the author of *The Wandering Scholars,* remarks, it is sometimes a little difficult to find out whether he is talking about Caesar or Alexander the Great or his own monarch: each is equally near to him. Indeed, the word "anachronism" is meaningless when applied to medieval art: it is only when one related events to a coordinated frame of time and space that being out of time or being untrue to time became disconcerting. Similarly, in Botticelli's *The Three Miracles of Saint Zenobius,* three different times are presented upon a single stage.

Because of this separation of time and space, things could appear and disappear suddenly, unaccountably: the dropping of a ship below the horizon no more needed an explanation than the dropping of a demon down the chimney. There was no mystery about the past from which they had emerged, no speculation as to the future toward which they were bound: objects swam into vision and sank out of it with something of the same mystery in which the coming and going of adults affects the experience of young children, whose first graphic efforts so much resemble in their organization the world of the medieval artist. In this symbolic world of space and time everything was either a mystery or a miracle. The connecting link between events was the cosmic and religious order: the true order of space was heaven, even as the true order of time was eternity.

Between the fourteenth and the seventeenth century a revolutionary change in the conception of space took place in western Europe. Space as a hierarchy of values was replaced by space as a system of magnitudes. One of the indications of this new orientation was the closer study of the relations of objects in space and the discovery of the laws of perspective and the systematic organization of pictures within the new frame fixed by the foreground, the horizon, and the vanishing point. Perspective turned the symbolic relation of objects into a visual relation: the visual in turn became a quantitative relation. In the new picture of the world, size meant not human or divine importance, but distance. Bodies did not exist separately as absolute magnitudes: they were coordinated with other bodies within the same frame of vision and must be in scale. To achieve this scale, there must be an accurate representation of the object itself, a point for point correspondence between the picture and the image: hence a fresh interest in external nature and in questions of fact. The division of the canvas into squares and the accurate observation of the world through this abstract checkerboard marked the new technique of the painter, from Paolo Uccello onward.

The new interests in perspective brought depth into the picture and distance into the mind. In the older pictures, one's eye jumped from one part to another, picking up symbolic crumbs as taste and fancy dictated: in the new pictures, one's eye followed the lines of linear perspective along streets, buildings, tessellated pavements whose parallel lines the painter purposely introduced in order to make the eye itself travel. Even the objects in the foreground were sometimes grotesquely placed and foreshortened in order to create the same illusion. Movement became a new source of value: movement for its own sake. The measured space of the picture reinforced the measured time of the clock.

Within this new ideal network of space and time all events now took place; and the most satisfactory event within this system was uniform motion in a straight line, for such motion lent itself to accurate representation within the system of spatial and temporal coordinates. One further consequence of this spatial order must be noted: to place a thing and to time it became essential to one's understanding of it. In Renaissance space, the existence of objects must be accounted for: their passage through time and space is a clue to their appearance at any particular moment in any particular place. The unknown is therefore no less determinate than the known: given the roundness of the globe, the position of the Indies could be assumed and the time-distance calculated. The very existence of such an order was an incentive to explore it and to fill up the parts that were unknown.

What the painters demonstrated in their application of perspective, the cartographers established in the same century in their new maps. The Hereford Map of 1314 might have been done by a child: it was practically worthless for navigation. That of Uccello's contemporary Andrea Banco, 1436, was conceived on rational lines, and represented a gain in conception as well as in practical accuracy. By laying down the invisible lines of latitude and longitude, the cartographers paved the way for later explorers, like Columbus: as with the later scientific method, the abstract system gave rational expectations, even if on the basis of inaccurate knowledge. No longer was it necessary for the navigator to hug the shoreline: he could launch out into the unknown, set his course toward an arbitrary point, and return approximately to the place of departure. Both Eden and Heaven were outside the new space; and though they lingered on as the ostensible subjects of painting, the real subjects were Time and Space and Nature and Man.

Presently, on the basis laid down by the painter and the cartographer, an interest in space as such, in movement as such, in locomotion as such, arose. Back of this interest were of course more concrete alterations: roads had become more secure; vessels were being built more soundly; above all, new inventions—the magnetic needle, the astrolabe, the rudder—had made it possible to chart and to hold a more accurate course at sea. The gold of the Indies and the fabled fountains of youth and the happy isles of endless sensual delight doubtless beckoned too:

but the presence of these tangible goals does not lessen the importance of the new schemata. The categories of time and space, once practically dissociated, had become united: and the abstractions of measured time and measured space undermined the earlier conceptions of infinity and eternity, since measurement must begin with an arbitrary here and now even if space and time be empty. The itch to *use* space and time had broken out: and once they were coordinated with movement, they could be contracted or expanded: the conquest of space and time had begun. (It is interesting, however, to note that the very concept of acceleration, which is part of our daily mechanical experience, was not formulated till the seventeenth century.)

The signs of this conquest are many; they came forth in rapid succession. In military arts the crossbow and the ballista were revived and extended, and on their heels came more powerful weapons for annihilating distance—the cannon and later the musket. Leonardo conceived an airplane and built one. Fantastic projects for flight were canvassed. In 1420 Fontana described a velocipede: in 1589 Gilles de Bom of Antwerp apparently built a man-propelled wagon: restless preludes to the vast efforts and initiatives of the nineteenth century. As with so many elements in our culture, the original impulse was imparted to this movement by the Arabs: as early as 880 Abû il-Qâsim had attempted flight; and in 1065 Oliver of Malmesbury had killed himself in an attempt to soar from a high place; but from the fifteenth century on the desire to conquer the air became a recurrent preoccupation of inventive minds; and it was close enough to popular thought to make the report of a flight from Portugal to Vienna serve as a news hoax in 1709.

The new attitude toward time and space infected the workshop and the countinghouse, the army and the city. The tempo became faster; the magnitudes became greater; conceptually, modern culture launched itself into space and gave itself over to movement. What Max Weber called the "romanticism of numbers" grew naturally out of this interest. In time-keeping, in trading, in fighting, men counted numbers; and finally, as the habit grew, only numbers counted.

THE REINVENTION
OF THE
MEGAMACHINE

The reinvention and expansion of the megamachine was in no sense an inevitable outcome of historical forces; indeed, until the end of the nineteenth century it seemed to many able thinkers that the major changes in Western civilization, even in technology, were favorable to freedom. A mind as detached as Ernest Renan's, echoing Comte's earlier dictums, could observe, in the 1890s, that belligerent nationalism was on the wane, and the animus against war was so widespread that the armed services could be maintained only by conscription. . . .

. . . Until the outbreak of the First World War, reason and compassion seemed to be gaining the upper hand, along with democratic understanding and cooperation. But the balance in favor of such constructive developments was shaken by that war, and the faith that had equated technological with human improvement was badly damaged by the realization that all the potentialities for evil had been augmented by the very energies technics had released. The first intimation that a new megamachine was being assembled came only after the war, with the rise of the totalitarian states, beginning with Russia and Italy. This reversed the trend toward representative government and popular participation that had been the dominant note even in the Russia of the previous century. The form of the Fascist and Communist dictatorships was a single-party organization, based on a self-appointed revolutionary junta and headed by a flesh-and-blood incarnation of the old-time "king by divine right"—one no longer anointed by God but, like Napoleon, self-crowned: a ruthless dictator (Lenin), a demonic *Führer* (Hitler), a bloody tyrant (Stalin) proclaiming the lawfulness of unqualified power unlawfully seized. That doctrine was as old as Thrasymachus's statement in Plato's *Republic,* while the example was, of course, thousands of years older.

The reassemblage of the ancient megamachine took place in three main stages. The first stage was that marked by the French Revolution of 1789. Though this revolution deposed and executed the traditional king, it reinstated with far greater power his abstract counterpart, the national state, upon which, in accord with Rousseau's pseudodemocratic theory of the general will, it bestowed absolute powers, like conscription—powers that kings would have envied. . . .

The second stage came with the First World War, though many of the preliminary steps had been taken by Napoleon I and carried further by the Prussian military autocracy under Bismarck after the Franco-Prussian War in 1870. This stage included the enlistment of scholars and scientists as an arm of the state, and the placating of the working classes by universal suffrage, social-welfare legislation, national elementary education, job insurance, and old-age pensions—measures that Napoleon, despite his high esteem for law and science and uniform education, had never carried so far. . . .

Before the First World War was over, the main features of the new megamachine had been roughed in. Even nations that had already achieved a large measure of political freedom, like England and the United States, introduced military conscription, and to meet the exorbitant demands for war matériel England established partial industrial conscription as well, . . . while the services of scientists were marshaled in every country to devise more destructive weapons, like TNT bombs and poison gases, to hasten "victory." Thus collective power on a scale never previously achieved heightened the pace of technical change, and the control of information by the government, which involved the feeding of officially selected and favorably colored information to its own people as a means of "maintaining morale" (that is, quieting disillusion and opposition), gave modern "democratic" governments their first taste of thought control on a more efficient, positive basis than antiquated organizations, such as the Russian autocracy, had employed. This provided the megamachine with a valuable supplement to physical coercion and military discipline.

The third stage in re-establishing the megamachine took place during the Second World War. It was facilitated by the resurrection of the original, Pyramid Age mechanism as an absolute military dictatorship. This came about, with every classic feature intact, in Russia and Germany, and in a more obsolete, though less formidable, form in the Fascist dictatorships of Italy, Turkey, Spain, and certain states in South America. Instead of a divine king with a mandate from heaven, there was now a vulgar counterpart—an image inflated and exalted by every kind of optical and aural illusion but commanding diabolic powers, turning torture, collective massacre, and total destruction into respectable professions. . . .

In its extreme Stalinist form, the Russian megamachine betrayed, even before Hitler, the most sinister defects of the ancient megamachine: its reliance upon physical coercion and terrorism, its systematic enslavement of the entire working population, including members of the dictatorial Party; its suppression of free personal intercourse, free travel, free access to the existing store of knowledge, free association; and the imposition of human sacrifice to appease the wrath and sustain the life of its blood-drinking god, Stalin. The result was to transform the whole country into a prison—part concentration camp, part extermination laboratory from which the only hope of escape was death. The "liberty, equality, and fraternity" of the French Revolution had turned, by a further revolution around the same axle, into enslavement, inequality, and alienation. By the time Stalin died, he had rehabilitated and magnified all the most repulsive features of the ancient megamachine, while his surviving scientific and technical collaborators, both voluntarily and under compulsion, had already begun to construct the principal components of the modern megamachine.

As it turned out, Hitler was destined to become, even more effectively than Stalin, the chief agent in the modernization of the megamachine. This is not because he was less psychotic, for delusions of grandeur and fantasies of absolute power are an essential motive power for this peculiar mechanism—as in America in its technically most advanced state. Hitler's model, assembled in a scientifically advanced country, was a base hybrid—partly archaic, on the Assyrian model, and partly improved, on the mechanized but still clumsy early model (Louis XIV–Napoleon), and partly modern, utilizing aspects of the available science, plus the latest behaviorist advertising techniques, to condition the entire population, but adding psychotic components derived from Hitler's own autistic fantasies. Albert Speer, the architect who was finally placed in charge of war production under Hitler, pointed out the singular merits of the Nazi megamachine in a speech at the Nürnberg trials. "Hitler's dictatorship," he noted, "differed in one fundamental point from all its predecessors in history. . . . Through technical devices like the radio and the loudspeaker, eighty million people were deprived of independent thought. . . . Earlier dictators needed highly qualified assistants, even at the lowest level—men who could think and act independently. The totalitarian system in the period of modern technical development can dispense with such men . . . it is possible to mechanize the lower leadership. As a result of this there has arisen the new type of the uncritical recipient of orders." One can take exception to Speer's analysis in only one respect: the uncritical acceptance began at the top, as he himself demonstrated.

The leaders of the Nazi Third Reich regarded war as the natural state of human society and extermination as a desirable way of establishing the dominance of their national organization and their ideology over rival systems. The enslavement or extermination of "inferior" groups and nations thus became the appointed duty of those who accepted the doctrine of "Aryan" superiority, and only in the atmosphere of constant war could totalitarian leaders command the absolute obedience and unqualified loyalty necessary for the smooth operation of the megamachine. . . .

But every totalitarian system brings its own enemies, to the very degree that the system is self-sealed—incapable of self-criticism and self-correction. With poetic justice, the first victims of the new system were the leaders themselves, whose control was undermined by self-induced phobias, hallucinations, and prefabricated lies that they themselves had come to believe. Witness Stalin's stubbornness in rejecting authentic information about Hitler's approaching attack on Russia—a calamitous misjudgment that caused incredible suffering and military humiliation—and, indeed, almost lost Russia the war. At the end of the conflict, the Nazi megamachine had become the victim of the ideological perversities and emotional aberrations of its leaders; they had wasted on the occupation and greedy exploitation of peripheral countries military forces that could have been concentrated in combat, they had undermined military and industrial effort by exterminating millions of noncombatant Russians and Poles for the mere gratification of their pathological hatred and contempt, and they had further deprived themselves—by starvation, torture, and death—of six million Jews, many of whom, until they faced their incredible fate, had remained patriotic Germans, whose labor might have been used to increase production.

What with all these screaming errors of judgment and miscarriages of military effort, one might think that the Russian and the Nazi megamachines would have passed completely out of existence, more discredited than the one that had flourished in the Pyramid Age. Unfortunately, the errors committed by the Nazis did not prevent them from at first achieving a series of astounding military successes, and these victories brought about a recrudescence of the megamachine in Britain and the United States. By the curious dialectic of history, Hitler's enlargement and refurbishment of the Nazi megamachine gave rise to the conditions for creating the counter-instruments that would conquer it and temporarily wreck it. Far, then, from being utterly discredited by the colossal errors of its ruling elite, the megamachine was rebuilt by the Western Allies on advanced scientific lines, with its defective human parts replaced by mechanical and electronic and chemical substitutes, and—eventually—coupled to the source of power that has made all other modes of power production as obsolete as Bronze Age missiles. Thus, in the very act of dying, the Nazis transmitted the germs of their disease to their American opponents—not only the methods of compulsive organization and physical destruction but the moral corruption that made it feasible to employ these methods without stirring effective opposition.

THE NUCLEAR COALITION

To effect the implosion of ideas and forces that finally produced the atomic reactor and the atom bomb, more than three centuries of preparation had been needed. But even so, no proposal of this magnitude could have been broached with sufficient authority to overcome the peacetime inertia of "business as usual" had there not been a direct military challenge from the refashioned megamachine: the vivid possibility that German physicists would soon place within Hitler's hands an "absolute" weapon, by means of which he might blackmail all other nations into submission. Such a threat of worldwide domination by the totalitarian Axis—Germany, Italy, Japan, and (prior to June 1941) Russia—brought about a similar concentration of physical power on the part of the "democracies," even before the United States had been dragged into war by its enemies. At that time, it was plain—though the memory of this reality has unfortunately faded—that no compromise with the victory-intoxicated Axis, still less any mode of passive or nonviolent resistance, such as that practiced by the natives against the British government in India, could halt their accelerating program of enslavement and extermination. If proof were still needed, the fate of the Jews and several national groups under the Nazis—a total of some twenty million massacred—supplied it.

Once the 1939 war enveloped the planet, the necessary components of the megamachine were not merely enlarged in scope but brought into close coordination and cooperation, and in every country involved they functioned increasingly as a single unit. Every part of the daily routine was placed directly or indirectly under governmental control—food rationing, fuel rationing, clothes production, building—in accordance with the regulations laid down by the central agency; the system of conscription applied in effect not only to the armed forces but to the entire country. Industry at first moved reluctantly into this new orbit. The growth of cartels, trusts, and monopolies during the previous century had, however, equipped these organizations for collaboration under government control, and they were lured, naturally, by a huge financial incentive for accepting such integration; namely, costs plus a large guaranteed profit. This ensured both maximum productive and maximum financial return. As the war progressed, this megatechnic assemblage functioned more and more effectively—despite corporate jealousies and local antagonisms—as a single unit.

One more component was needed to effect the transition to the new megamachine: an absolute ruler. As it happened, the President of the United States had been equipped with emergency wartime powers anticipated by the American Constitution, in direct imitation of Roman precedent. Under wartime conditions, the President had unlimited authority to take whatever steps were necessary to safeguard the nation; no absolute monarch could have exercised greater power. The mere threat that Hitler might possess a superweapon enabled President Roosevelt, with the budgetary consent of Congress, to draft the manpower and brain power that resulted in the invention of the nuclear reactor and the atom bomb. To produce this result, the classic components of the ancient megamachine were made over on a pattern that took full advantage of megatechnic organization and scientific research. No smaller concentration of the power complex could have produced the transformation of the military-industrial-scientific Establishment. Out of this union, between 1940 and 1961, the modern megamachine, commanding absolute powers of destruction, emerged.

. . . Only under the intense pressures of war could such a coalition of forces have taken place. The production of the atom bomb was essential to the new megamachine, little though anyone at the time had that larger objective in mind. For it was the success of this project that gave the scientists a central place in the new power complex and resulted eventually in the invention of many other instruments that have rounded out and universalized the system of control established to meet only the exigencies of war. Overnight, the civilian and military leaders of the United States were endowed with powers that hitherto had been claimed only by Bronze Age gods—powers that had never been exercised by any merely human ruler. Thereafter, the irreplaceable scientist-technician stood highest in the new hierarchy of power, and every part of the megamachine was made over in consonance with the peculiarly limited type of knowledge, deliberately sterilized of other human values and purposes, that its refined mathematical analysis and exact methods had been designed to further.

In view of the cataclysmic changes that followed, it is significant that the initiative in bringing about the release of nuclear energy, the major event in the recrudescence of the megamachine in modern form, was taken not by the central government but by a small group of physicists. No less significant is the fact that these advocates of nuclear power were themselves unusually humane and morally sensitive people—notably Albert Einstein, Enrico Fermi, Leo Szilard, Harold Urey. These were the last scientists one would accuse of seeking to establish a new priesthood capable of assuming autocratic authority and wielding satanic power. Those unpleasant characteristics, which have become all too evident in later collaborators and in their successors, were derived from the new instruments commanded by the megamachine and the dehumanized concepts that were rapidly incorporated in its whole program. As for the initiators of the atom bomb, their innocence concealed from them, at least in the beginning stages, the dreadful ultimate consequences of their effort.

The physicists who were alert to the immediate threat that the splitting of the atom held if this knowledge were in the hands of a totalitarian dictator came to unsound political and military conclusions, against those hasty applications their scientific training had given them no adequate safeguards. Fearful that the Nazis would gain an overwhelming advantage by manufacturing an atom bomb first, Einstein and his associates, without taking the prudent precautions of canvassing possible alternatives, placed before the chief executive the case for the United States's developing such a weapon. Their fears were well grounded, their alertness was admirable. Had they, in their corporate capacity, taken heed of warnings sounded a generation earlier, they might have addressed themselves in time to the critical underlying problems: how to mobilize the intelligence of mankind to prevent such potentially catastrophic energy from being prematurely released. Unhappily, their training had conditioned them to the idea that the continued increase of scientific knowledge, and its speediest possible translation into practice, without regard to social consequences, was nothing less than a categorical imperative.

While a concerned contemporary can understand the initiative taken by Einstein and ratified by President Roosevelt—quite possibly the present critic would under the same circumstances have made the same tragic mistake—it is now plain that this proposal was made within a far too limited historical context. It was a short-term decision to effect an immediately desired result, even though the consequences might undermine mankind's future. To propose creating a weapon of "cosmic violence" without at the same time requiring, as a condition for their scientific aid, the coordinate moral and political safety measures shows how unused these scientists were to considering the practical consequences of their vocational commitments. But preparations for the misuse of power preceded the explosion of the first atom bomb. Well before it was tested, the American Air Forces had adopted the hitherto "unthinkable" practice of the indiscriminate extermination bombing of civilian populations; this paralleled, except for the distance of the destroyers from the victims, the practices employed by Hitler's sub-men in extermination camps like Buchenwald and Auschwitz. Using napalm bombs, the American Air Forces had roasted alive eighty-four thousand civilians in Tokyo in a single night. Thus the descent to total demoralization and extermination was neatly plotted well before the supposedly "ultimate" weapon, the atom bomb, was invented.

Once the plan to make the bomb was sanctioned, the scientists who gave themselves to this project were trapped by their own erroneous ideological premises into accepting its military use. Their error could not easily be repaired, no matter how their consciences might pain them or how strenuous the efforts of their more sensitive and intelligent leaders to awaken mankind to its plight. For something worse than the invention of a deadly weapon had taken place. The act of making the bomb had hastened the assemblage and completion of the new megamachine, and to keep that megamachine in effective operation once the immediate military emergency was over, a permanent state of war became necessary. . . .

The parallels between the Pyramid Age achievements and those of the Nuclear Age force themselves upon one, however reluctant one may be to admit them. Once more, a divine king, embodying all the powers and prerogatives of the whole community, supported by a revered priesthood and a universal religion, positive science, began the assemblage of the megamachine in a technologically more adequate and impressive form. If one omits the part played by the king (wartime American President), by the priesthood (secret enclave of scientists), by the vast enlargement of the bureaucracy, the military forces, and the industrial Establishment, one will have no realistic conception of what took place. Only in terms of the Pyramid Age do all the seemingly dispersed and accidental events become coalesced into an orderly constellation. The construction of the modern totalitarian megamachine, fortified by the invention of mechanical and electronic agents that could not be fully utilized until this construction had taken place, proved to be Hitler's most sinister—if, in this instance, wholly unintended—contribution to the enslavement of mankind.

Thus, one of the supreme feats in modern man's understanding of the ultimate constituents of the "physical universe"—a fear that culminated in his unlocking of the very energies that the Sun God commands—came about under the pressure of a genocidal war and the threat of wholesale annihilation: a condition that paralyzed all life-conserving and life-promoting efforts. The continuation of that state of affairs, with the deepening and widening of the crisis in the ensuing Cold War, has greatly increased the malign possibilities that we face. . . .

. . . Though the Second World War was formally halted by the Axis surrender in 1945, the megamachine that had evolved by the end of it did not surrender its absolute weapons or the scheme for universal domination by threat of total destruction that had given the coalition of scientific and military agencies such inordinate power. Far from it. Though the older organs of industry and government nominally resumed their diverse activities, the military "elite" fortified themselves in an inner citadel—so beautifully symbolized by the architecturally archaic Pentagon—cut off from inspection and control by the rest of the community. With the consent of the Congress, they extended their tentacles throughout the industrial and the academic worlds by way of fat subsidies for "research and development"—that is, for weapons expansion—that made these once independent institutions willing accomplices in the whole totalitarian process.

Thus the area of this citadel has widened steadily, and the walls around it have grown thicker and less penetrable. By the simple expedient of creating new emergencies, fomenting new fears, visualizing new enemies, and magnifying, through free use of fantasy, the evil intentions of "the enemy," the megamachines of the United States and Russia, instead of being dismantled as a regrettable temporary wartime necessity, were elevated into permanent institutions in what has now become a permanent war—the so-called Cold War. As it has turned out, this form of war, with its ever-expanding demands for scientific ingenuity and technological innovations, has been up to now the most effective device for keeping the overproductive technology in full operation.

In the course of this development, the two dominant megamachines exchanged characteristics. The Russian machine departed from the obsolete original model by relying ever more heavily on its scientific and technological arm, while the American machine took over the most regressive features of the czarist-Stalinist system, vastly augmenting both its military force and its agents of centralized control: the Atomic Energy Commission, the Federal Bureau of Investigation, the Central Intelligence Agency, the National Security Agency—all secret organizations whose methods and policies have never been openly discussed or effectively challenged, still less curtailed by the national legislative authority. So well established are these agents that they dare to flout and disobey the authority of both the President and the Congress.

This enlarged Establishment has been as immune to public criticism, correction, and control as any dynastic Establishment of the Pyramid Age. And though, like every other machine, this contemporary megamachine is an agent for performing work, the work that has occupied the huge scientific and technical staff it has assembled, in both the United States and Russia—the work that supposedly justifies its existence and lightens the heavy sacrifices it calls for—is no less than an elaboration of the mechanism of total destruction. The only question the megamachine leaves open is whether this destruction shall be swift or slow; the negative goal is incorporated in the basic ideological assumptions that govern the system. The generation that has permitted the new megamachine to be installed as a permanent feature of national existence has been reluctant to confront the evidence of this radical miscarriage of human purpose. This generation accepted the goal of total extermination as a mere extension of war without perceiving that the prospective increase of quantity was a far more frightful aberration than war itself. Paralyzed like a monkey in the coils of a python, the immediate post-Hiroshima generation, unable to utter a rational sound, shut its eyes and waited for the end. . . .

ORGANIZATION MAN

Neither the ancient nor the modern megamachine, however automatic its separate mechanisms and operations, could have come into existence except through deliberate human invention, and the most of the attributes of this large collective unit were first incarnated in an ancient, archetypal figure—Organization Man. From the most primitive expression of tribal conformity to that of the highest political authority, the system is an extension of Organization Man—he who stands as at once the creator and the creature, the originator and the ultimate victim, of the megamachine. . . . We must begin our description of Organization Man at the point at which, through documents and symbolic evidence, he becomes visible. Since the first definite records, after the paleolithic caves, are temple accounts, tabulating the quantities of grain received and disbursed, it seems likely that the meticulous order that characterizes bureaucracy in every phase derives originally from the ritual observances of the temple, for this kind of order is incompatible with the hazardous events of the hunt or the chance happenings of organized war. Yet even for this last occupation we find remarkably early records, in definite figures, of prisoners captured, animals rounded up, loot taken. As far back as that early stage, Organization Man can be identified by his concern with quantitative accountancy.

Behind every process of organization and mechanization there are primordial aptitudes, deeply ingrained in the human organism—and shared with many other species—for ritualizing behavior and finding satisfaction in a repetitive order that establishes a human connection with organic rhythms and cosmic events. Out of this cluster of repetitive, standardized acts, increasingly isolated from other bodily and mental functions, Organization Man seems to have sprung. Or, to put it another way, when we have detached, one by one, the organs and functions of the human body, and—along with them—all the historical accretions of art and culture, what we are left with is its mechanical skeleton and muscle power, essential for vertebrate life but functionless and meaningless when treated as a separate entity. The present age has reinvented this "ideal" creature in the form of the robot, but it has always existed as a recognizable part of the human organism. . . . Organization Man is the link between the ancient and the modern types of megamachine; that is perhaps why, the specialized functionaries, with their supporting layers of slaves, conscripts, and subjects—that is, the controllers and the controlled—have changed so little in the last five thousand years. Like any other cultural type, Organization Man is a human artifact, though the materials out of which he has been fashioned belong to the system of animate nature. It is an anachronism to picture Organization Man as a purely modern product, or as solely the product of an advanced technology. He is, rather, an extremely primitive "ideal" type, carved out of the rich potentialities of the living organism, with most of the living organs either extracted or embalmed and desiccated, with the brain shrunken to meet the requirements of the megamachine.

William H. Whyte has given us, within the limited setting of large-scale corporate economic organizations in the United States, a classic picture of the selection, training, and discipline of Organization Man at the higher levels of command, and the transformation of the "fortunate"—or, at least, fortune-seeking—minority into smoothly working components of the bigger mechanism. But this is only a small part of the conditioning that begins with the infant's toilet training and, by means of the welfare state, covers every aspect of life through to death and organ transplantation. The degree of external pressure necessary to model Organization Man is probably no greater than that needed by any tribal society to secure conformity to ancient traditions and rituals; indeed, through compulsory elementary education, military conscription, and mass communication the same stamp can be imprinted on millions of individuals in modern society quite as easily as upon a few hundred who meet face to face. What the sociologist Max Weber called "the bureaucratic personality" was destined, he thought, to be the "ideal type" in the modern world. If the present constellation of forces continues to operate without abatement or change of direction, his prediction may easily be realized.

The virtues of Organization Man correspond as nearly as possible to the machine that he serves. The stamp of mechanical regularity lies on the face of every human unit. To follow the program, to obey instructions; to "pass the buck," to be uninvolved as a person in the needs of other persons, to limit responses to what lies immediately, so to say, on the desk; to heed no relevant human considerations, however vital; never to question the origin of an order or inquire as to its ultimate destination; to follow through on every command, however irrational; to make no judgements of value or relevance on the work in hand; finally, to eliminate feelings and emotions and rational moral misgivings that might interfere with the immediate dispatch of the work—these are the standard duties of the bureaucrat, and these are the conditions under which Organization Man flourishes, a virtual automaton within a collective system of automation. The model for Organization Man is the machine itself. And as the mechanism grows toward perfection, the residue of life needed to carry on the process grows smaller and eventually becomes meaningless.

Ultimately, Organization Man will have no reason for existence except as a depersonalized servo-mechanism in the megamachine. On those terms, Adolf Eichmann, the obedient exterminator, who carried out Hitler's policy and Himmler's orders with unswerving fidelity, should be hailed as the Hero of Our Time. Today, we can do with napalm and bombs what the exterminators of Belsen and Auschwitz had to do by old-fashioned handicraft methods. These were slower in execution but far more thrifty, for they carefully conserved the by-products—the gold from the teeth, the fat, the bone meal for fertilizers, even the skin for lampshades. In every country there are now many Eichmanns in administrative offices, in business corporations, in universities, in laboratories, in the armed forces—orderly, obedient people, ready to carry out any officially sanctioned fantasy, however dehumanized and debased.

The more power entrusted to Organization Man, the less qualms he has about using it. And what makes this "ideal" type even more menacing is his successful use of the human disguise. His robot mechanism simulates flesh and blood, and—except in a few troglodyte specimens—there is nothing to distinguish him outwardly from a reasonable human being, smooth-mannered, low-keyed, presumably amiable. Like Himmler, he may even be a "good family man." This type was not unknown in earlier cultures. Even within our own era, this sort of servo-mechanism arranged gladiatorial combats in the Roman arena and manipulated the bone-racking machines used by the Holy Inquisition. Before megatechnics invaded every aspect of existence, Organization Man had fewer opportunities; he was once a minority, largely confined to the bureaucracy and the army. But today he is legion. And since he beholds only his own image when he looks around him, he regards himself as a normal specimen of humanity. . . .

THE MEGAMACHINES COMPARED

We are now in a position to compare the ancient and modern forms of the megamachine. . . . These megamachines have similar technological capacities: they are mass organizations able to perform tasks that lie outside the range of small work collectives and loose tribal or territorial groups. Yet at every point the ancient machine, since it was composed mainly of human parts, was subject to human limitations, for even under the harshest taskmaster a slave cannot exert much more than a tenth of a horsepower, nor can he keep working indefinitely without lowering his output. The great contrast between the two machines is that the modern one has progressively multiplied the use of the more reliable mechanical components while not merely reducing the labor force needed for a colossal operation but, through electronics, facilitating instantaneous remote control. Though human servo-mechanisms are still necessary at nodal points in the system, the modern machine escapes spatial and temporal limitations; it can operate as a single, largely invisible unit over a wide area, its functioning parts operating as a unit through instant communication. Thus the new model commands whole regiments of diversified mechanical units, with superhuman power and superhuman mechanical reliability, and with lightning speed. . . .

Both these machines aim to ultimately exert control over the entire community at every point of human existence. But in the method of control there is a radical difference, largely in the modern machine's favor. Possibly because life in the neolithic villages, centering on food and sex, was sufficiently gratifying, demands for sacrificial effort, or even extra work, were reluctantly met. (Small, thrifty democratic communities do not tax themselves willingly even for their own palpable good.) At all events, it is clear that the human parts of the original megamachine were assembled only under severe military coercion and drilled into the perfect performance of their tasks under "army discipline." To ensure compliance with the tax collector and the draft organizer, merciless punishment was visited not only upon slaves but upon harmless villagers and temporary conscripts. For the mass of men, then, the ancient megamachine operated with only minimal rewards but with maximal punishments, and so pervasive was this practice that even the highest officers of the state were frequently subject to abasements and coercions. Exhausting labors were periodically performed by the whole community under threat of even worse treatment if the workers did not meet their quotas.

From such evidence, one has reason to infer that the megamachine was originally the creation of the weapons-bearing minority that invented organized warfare and imposed unconditional obedience and regular tribute upon the passive, nonaggressive, compliant neolithic peasants—peasants who have throughout all succeeding history, in fact, formed the larger part of the human population. Though the modern megamachine is equally the product of war, it has partly overcome the need for overt coercion with a more subtle kind, which substitutes rewards, or seeming rewards, for punishments, and with every show of reasonable consideration, as when the Nazi executioners persuaded their victims to dig their own graves. Yet up to a point, it must be confessed, the system of punishment worked. What is more, it produced results that, however harsh the conditions of work, sometimes benefited the whole community. On the other hand, this system not merely wasted manpower by requiring an excessive number of slave drivers and overseers—one for each squad of ten men—but produced friction, sullen resentment, lowered outputs, and tempered down the energies of superior minds that might have engaged in free invention and spontaneous creativity. . . .

The ideology that underlies and unites the ancient and the modern megamachine ignores the needs and purposes of life in order to fortify the power complex and extend its dominion. Both megamachines are oriented toward death, and the closer they approach unified planetary control, the less escapable does that result promise to become. Everyone is familiar with this constant historical drive in the gross form of war, for military violence—as distinguished from sporadic, minor forms of animal aggression—is the historical product of a special form of social organization, developed in certain ant societies sixty million years ago, and re-established, with all its sinister institutional accomplishments, in the Egyptian and Mesopotamian communities of the Pyramid Age. . . .

All these ancient features were restored during the nineteenth century—above all, the collective dedication to death. During the last half century alone, between fifty and a hundred million people—it is impossible to make precise calculations—have met premature death through violence and starvation, on the battlefield, in concentration camps, in bombed cities and agricultural areas that have been turned into mass-extermination camps. What is more, we have been repeatedly informed by authorities in the United States—indeed, they boast about it—that in the first nuclear strike launched by powers as well equipped as the United States and Russia, between a quarter and half of the inhabitants in each of those countries would be killed on the first day. With justifiable prudence, these official predictions refrain from estimating further losses by the other means of genocide they have perfected—during the second day, the second week, the second year, and even the second century, for this would involve factors of astronomical dimensions, whose unforeseeable consequences might be permanently irreparable. (Scientists so supremely vain as to suppose that they have the ability to foresee these effects are among the trusted advisers of the American government.)

Like all other modern technical performances, the mass infliction of death has been both expanded and speeded up. So far, nuclear explosions and rocket explorations, both directly deriving from plans for war, have been the most conspicuous manifestations of our lethal facilities, along with the communications systems upon which they depend. The fact that no *human* purpose, present or prospective, would be served by the new modes of extermination, no matter how successful in "overkill," only demonstrates the deep underlayers of psychotic irrationality upon which the fantasies of absolute weapons, of absolute power, and of absolute control have been set. Freud drew a parallel between the magic rituals of many so-called primitive peoples and the behavior of neurotic personalities in our time. But there is no practice in these arrested cultures—headhunting or cannibalism or voodoo murder— that is comparable in superstitious savagery and mental corruption to the plans of highly trained scientists, technologists, and military men to inflict collective death on the scale that modern technological agents have made possible. No wonder some of the best of our younger generation regard their acquiescent elders with unutterable horror and rage.

Compared with this pervasive dedication to death in our own culture, the Egyptian cult of the dead, developed during the Pyramid Age, with its magniloquent pyramids, its magic rituals, and its elaborate techniques of mummification, was a relatively innocent exhibition of irrationality. Actually, the destruction that accompanied the wars of the early military machines was so limited by the necessary reliance upon mere manpower and hand weapons and hand tools that even their most extravagant efforts were reparable. It is our present removal of all limits, made possible only by the advances of science and technics, that reveals the true nature of this culture and its chosen destiny.

Yes, the priests and warriors of the megamachine can exterminate mankind; so if [John] von Neumann is right, they will. No mere animal instinct of aggression accounts for this growing aberration. But something more than the animal instinct for self-preservation—an immense increase in emotional alertness, moral concern, and practical audacity —will be necessary on a worldwide scale if mankind is finally to save itself.

ART AND
TECHNICS

Art and the Symbol

At the beginning of a series of lectures, it is perhaps well to establish some common point of agreement between the lecturer and his audience; and to ensure this I shall begin by making a flat observation: *We live in an interesting age!* This is not quite so innocent a commonplace as you may fancy; for like the Chinese, who have lived through many periods of disorder and violence, similar to our own, I would use the word "interesting" in a somewhat acrid sense. We are told that when traditionally a Chinese scholar wished to utter a withering curse upon his enemy, he merely said: May you live in an interesting age! The Chinese knew that few of the good things of life could come to consummation in the midst of moral landslides and political earthquakes.

What makes our age so interesting, of course, is the number of shocking contradictions and tragic paradoxes that confront us at every turn, creating problems that tax our human capacities for understanding, releasing forces we lack the confidence to control. We have seen starvation in the midst of plenty, as millions of desolate people in India still see it: we have seen the heartfelt renunciation of war, which followed the First World War, leading to the enthronement of military dictatorship, . . . and so it has been with many other apparent blessings. . . .

Three and a half centuries ago Francis Bacon hailed the advancement of scientific learning and mechanical invention as the surest means of relieving man's estate: with a few expiatory gestures of piety, he turned his back upon religion and philosophy and art and pinned

This selection combines two essays, "Art and the Symbol" and "Art, Technics, and Cultural Integration," both from *Art and Technics*. (*Editor's note*)

348

every hope for human improvement on the development of mechanical invention. He met his death, indeed, not after writing a series of final aphorisms about the conduct of life, but after exposing himself to the elements in one of the first experiments in the use of ice for preserving food. Neither Bacon nor his eager followers in science and technics, the Newtons and Faradays, the Watts and the Whitneys, had any anticipation of the fact that all our hard-won mastery of the physical world might, in the twentieth century, threaten the very existence of the human race. If by some clairvoyance Bacon could have followed to their ultimate conclusions the developments he forecast with such unqualified optimism, he might easily have decided, instead of continuing his speculations in science, to write Shakespeare's plays, as at least a more innocent occupation. Bacon did not foresee that the humanization of the machine might have the paradoxical effect of mechanizing humanity; and that at this fatal moment the other arts, once so nourishing to man's humanity and spirituality, would become equally arid, and so incapable of acting as a counterpoise to this one-sided technical development. . . .

During the last two centuries there has been a vast expansion of the material means of living throughout the world. But instead of our thus producing a state of widely distributed leisure, favorable to the cultivation of the inner life and the production and enjoyment of the arts, we find ourselves more absorbed than ever in the process of mechanization. Even a large part of our fantasies are no longer self-begotten, they have no reality, no viability, until they are harnessed to the machine, and without the aid of the radio and television they would hardly have the energy to maintain their existence. Compare our present situation with that which accompanied the relatively technical primitive era of the seventeenth century. In that time a good London burgher, like Samuel Pepys, a practical man, a hard-working administrator, would select the servants in his household partly on the basis of their having a good voice, so that they might sit down with the family in the evening to take part in domestic singing. Such people not merely listened passively to music, but could produce it, or at least reproduce it, in their own right. Today, in contrast, we often see people wandering around with a portable radio set on Riverside Drive, listening to a radio musical program, with no thought that they might sing a song freely in the open air without invoking any mechanial aid.

Even worse, the very growth of mechanical facilities has given people a false ideal of technical perfectionism, so that unless they can compete with the products of the machine or with those whose professional training qualifies them for such a public appearance, they are all too ready to take a back seat. And, to complete this process, not in the least to offset it, in those special realms of art, above all, painting, that once recorded the greatest freedom and creativeness, we find that the symbols that most deeply express the emotions and feelings of our age are a succession of dehumanized nightmares, transposing into aesthetic form either the horror and violence or the vacuity and despair of our time. Undoubtedly one of the great paintings of our day is Picasso's *Guernica* mural, just as he himself is one of the great artists of our time, with a capacity for beautiful rhythmic expression like that of a dancer; a gift that the stroboscopic camera has recently revealed. But the fresh symbols that come forth from his masterly hand reveal chiefly the wounds and scars of our time, with not even the faintest hints of a new integration. At times, in the preliminary sketches for the *Guernica* mural, the emotion is so lacerating that the next step beyond would be either insanity or suicide.

Violence and nihilism: the death of the human personality. This is the message that modern art brings to us in its freest and purest moments; and that, obviously, is no counterpoise to the dehumanization wrought by technics.

Most of the great artists of the last two centuries—and this has been equally true, I think, in music and poetry and painting, even in some degree in architecture—have been in revolt against the machine and have proclaimed the autonomy of the human spirit: its autonomy, its spontaneity, its inexhaustible creativeness. Actually, the religious impulse, suppressed by the institutionalism of the churches, manifested itself during this period chiefly in the arts, so that the great saints of the last century were as often as not artists, like van Gogh or Ryder or Tolstoy. This strong reaction against a too-singleminded commitment to mechanical invention and practical effort helped produce great works of music and painting, perhaps as great as any other age could show. In the great symphonic music of the nineteenth century the human spirit utilized its characteristic division of labor, its specialization of functions, and its intricate organization of time and rhythm to express the tragic yearnings and joyful triumphs of this new epoch. Because of the traditional separation of art and technics we have yet sufficiently to realize that the symphony orchestra is a triumph of engineering, and that its products, such as the music of Mozart and Beethoven, etherealized into symbols, will probably outlast all our steel bridges and automatic machines.

But that protest was possible, those triumphs could be expressed, only so long as a belief in the human person, and particularly in the inner life, the creative moment, remained dominant, carried over from the older cultures that had nourished the human spirit. By the end of the nineteenth century, this evocative protest began to die away. In a mood of submission and self-abnegation, sensitively recorded by Henry Adams, people began to worship the machine and its masters. If anyone was *un*real, Adams wrote, it was the poet, not the businessman. We had created a topsy-turvy world in which machines had become autonomous and men had become servile and mechanical: that is, thing-conditioned, externalized, dehumanized—disconnected from their historic values and purposes. And so it has come about that one whole part of man's life, springing from his innermost nature, his deepest desires and impulses, his ability to enjoy and bestow love, to give life to and receive life from his fellow men, has been suppressed. Those deep organic impulses for which art is both the surrogate in immediate action and the ultimate expression of that action as transferred to the life of other men —all this part of man's nature has become progressively empty and meaningless. The maimed fantasies, the organized frustrations, that we see in every comprehensive exhibition of modern painting today are so many symptoms of this deep personal abdication. Pattern and purpose have progressively disappeared, along with the person who once, in his own right, embodied them. Man has become an exile in this mechanical world: or rather, even worse, he has become a displaced person.

On one hand, through the advance of technics, we have produced a new kind of environment and a highly organized routine of life, which satisfies, to a fabulous degree, man's need to live in an orderly and predictable world. There is something noble . . . in the fact that our railroads, our ocean steamships, our planes, run on a time schedule almost as regular as the movement of the heavenly bodies. Uniformity, regularity, mechanical accuracy, and reliability all have been advanced to a singular degree of perfection. And just as the autonomic nervous system and the reflexes in the human body free the mind for its higher functions, so this new kind of mechanical order should bring about a similar freedom, a similar release of energy for the creative processes. Because of our achievement of mechanical order throughout the planet, the dream of Isaiah might in fact come true: the dream of a universal society in which men shall be weaned from habits of hostility and war. Originally these aggressions were perhaps the natural outcome of anxiety for the future, in periods when there was never enough food or goods to go round: periods when only the powerful could arrogate to themselves all the resources men needed to be fully human.

But the good fairy who presided over the development of technics did not succeed in forestalling the curse that accompanied this genuine gift: a curse that came from this very overcommitment to the external, the quantitative, the measurable. . . . the external. For our inner life has become impoverished: as in our factories, so throughout our society, the automatic machine tends to replace the person and to make all his decisions—while, for its smoother working, it anesthetizes every part of the personality that will not easily conform to its mechanical needs.

All these are the veriest commonplaces of our "interesting age"; I remind you only of what you already know. On one side, the highest degree of scientific and technical refinement, as in the atomic bomb; on the other side, moral depravity, as in the use of that bomb not to conquer armies, but to exterminate defenseless people at random. . . . External order: internal chaos. External progress: internal regression. External rationalism: internal irrationality. In this impersonal and overdisciplined machine civilization, so proud of its objectivity, spontaneity too often takes the form of criminal acts, and creativeness finds its main open outlet in destruction. If this seems like an exaggeration, that is due only to the illusion of security. Open your eyes and look around you!

Now I put these paradoxes and contradictions before you . . . , dismaying though they may be, because I believe that the relations between art and technics give us a significant clue to every other type of activity, and may even provide an understanding of the way to integration. The great problem of our time is to restore modern man's balance and wholeness: to give him the capacity to command the machines he has created instead of becoming their helpless accomplice and passive victim; to bring back, into the very heart of our culture, that respect for the essential attributes of personality, its creativity and autonomy, which Western man lost at the moment he displaced his own life in order to concentrate on the improvement of the machine. In short, the problem of our time is how to prevent ourselves from committing suicide, precisely at the height and climax of our one-sided mechanical triumphs. . . .

Art, Technics, and Cultural Integration

. . . Why has our inner life become so impoverished and empty, and why has our outer life become so exorbitant, and in its subjective satisfactions even more empty? Why have we become technological gods and moral devils, scientific supermen and aesthetic idiots—idiots, that is, primarily in the Greek sense of being wholly private persons, incapable of communicating with each other or understanding each other? . . .

Art . . . is only one of the ways in which man re-orders, reflects upon, and re-presents his experiences to himself, attempting to arrest life in its perpetual flux and movement, so that human experience can detach itself, in the aesthetic object, in its final perfection and fulfillment. And what does art say, in all its manifestations, from a child's song to a symphony, from a scratch on a cave wall to a great complex mural like the Orozco mural at Dartmouth College? In the work of art the artist, first of all, says: "I am here and in me life has taken a certain form. My life must not pass till I master its meaning and value. What I have seen and felt and thought and imagined seems to me important: so important that I will try to convey it to you through a common language of symbols and forms, with something of the concentration, some of the intensity, some of the passionate delight that I carry to the highest pitch in myself through the very act of expression. With the aid of art I give you, in the present, the experience of a lifetime: the potentialities of many life-times. These aesthetic moments endow life with a new meaning; and these new meanings, heighten life with other aesthetic moments."

So says the artist. And though the symbols that are used in any culture must, to be understood and experienced, have some common ground, each fresh work of art is unique, because it is the representation, not of other artists' symbols—only mediocre and imitative art is that—but of the unique experience of a creative moment in life. With the expression of a true work of art the goodness of life is affirmed, and life itself renewed. The work of art springs out of the artist's original experience, becomes a new experience, both for him and the participator, and then further by its independent existence enriches the consciousness of the whole community. In the arts, man builds a shell that outlasts the creature that originally inhabited it, encouraging other men to similar responses and similar acts of creativity; so that, in time, every part of the world bears some imprint of the human personality. Art, so defined, has no quarrels with either science or technics, for they, too, as Shelley long ago recognized, may become a source of human feelings, human values. The opposite of art is insensibility, depersonalization, failure of creativity, empty repetition, vacuous routine, a life that is mute, unexpressed, formless, disorderly, unrealized, meaningless.

All that art is and does rests upon the fact that when man is in a healthy state, he takes life seriously, as something sacred and potentially significant; and he necessarily takes himself seriously, too, as a transmitter of life and as a creator, through his own special efforts, of new forms of life not given in the natural world. With his capacity for symbolization, man re-thinks, re-presents, re-patterns, re-shapes every part of the world, transforming his physical environment, his biological functions, his social capacities into a cultural ritual and drama full of unexpected meanings and climactic fulfillments. What exists outside man, as raw nature, the artist takes into himself and transmutes: what exists in himself, as sensation, feeling, emotion, intuition, insight, rationality, he projects outside himself in forms and sequences not given in nature. . . .

Man truly lives only to the extent that he transforms and creates out of the raw materials of life a world whose meanings and values outlast his original experience and transcend its limitations. That is, essentially, one of the great tasks of art; though art is not alone in performing that function, since it feeds and grows on man's other modes of self-explication and cosmic insight. For art to perform this function, however, at least one condition is necessary: man must respect his own creativity. As soon as man loses faith in his own potential significance and value, he reduces himself to the status of an animal who has lost the sureness of his elemental instinctual responses and must therefore take refuge in some even simpler mechanical pattern of order.

Does this not explain why the failure of art in our own time and the overvaluation of the machine have gone hand in hand; and why both of these facts have been symptoms of a more general social and personal disruption?

Now, the disintegration of modern Western culture, so well exemplified in the present breach between our superrefined technics and our primitive or infantile aesthetic symbols, between our overactive technical organization and our empty, discredited selves, can be interpreted in more than one way. At the end of the First World War, a German philosopher of history, Oswald Spengler, attempted a universal explanation of the facts that we are now confronting, in a book that prophesied, not without a certain sadistic elation, the downfall of the Western world. Spengler divided the development of every culture into two phases: first, a humane organic phase, the springtime of culture, when man's powers ripen and the arts flourish as a natural expression of his inner life and creativity; and, second, an arid mechanical phase, with life on the downward curve, a phase in which men become extraverted and externalized, given to organization and to the creation of hardened forms of life, creating a shell of empty custom and habit that prevents any further growth, so that, if the civilization that so takes form continues for any length of time, it is given over merely to vain repetitions, with no fresh content or meaning. In our own particular culture, Spengler believed, this tendency to subjective emptiness and external fixity was abetted by Western man's mastery of mechanical inventions; and in the final phase, now upon us according to his formula, those who understood their fate would give up lyric poetry in favor of business enterprise, painting and music in favor of engineering. This suicide of the inner man was but the prelude of a more general devaluation of life and a more widespread movement toward nihilism and self-extinction. . . .

... However accurate his intuitions were in some respects as to the immediate forces that have been at work in our own day, the fact is that his division between culture and civilization, between the organic and the mechanical, between (in our immediate terms of reference) art and technics, transfers to the beginning and the end of the cultural cycle processes that are in fact constantly in operation at every stage. Only a very misty, sentimental eye would fail to see in the lush overgrowth of medieval and Renaissance fortifications, for example, or the over-development of medieval armor, the same overweighting of technical facilities at the expense of life that the overdevelopment of subways and multiple express highways and atom bombs does in our civilization today. Only a very obstinate dogmatist would fail to see in the behavior of the mass of Londoners under bombing—not what Spengler pre-dicted—the bloodless cowardice and pacifism of the life-renouncing denizen of Megalopolis—but the same heroic qualities of selfless cour-age we associate with the springtime of chivalry. And if this is true even in war and engineering, it is equally true in a hundred other depart-ments of life. The fact is that the organic and creative, the mechanical and automatic, are present in every manifestation of life, above all within the human organism itself. If we tend to exaggerate one phase and neglect the other, it is not because civilization inexorably develops in this fashion, but because, through a philosophic foundation of mainly false beliefs, we have allowed our balance to be upset, and have not actively regained that dynamic equilibrium in which state alone the higher functions—those that promote art, morality, freedom—can flourish. This failure of balance can take place at any stage of develop-ment; and sometimes ... it is the overdevelopment of the inner life, the overproliferation of symbols, and the excessive claims of subjectivity that are responsible for the mischief. In our time, however, we suffer chiefly because of the result of the unlimited license we have given to the machine.

Those who took Spengler's thesis seriously—and many who never heard of it accepted it in practice—were in effect preparing to com-mit suicide; for they were transferring meaning and value to only one part of the environment, to only one process and function, to only one aspect of the human personality. That part, no matter how vastly one magnifies it or energizes it, can never become an adequate substitute for the whole. If technical achievements were alone capable of ab-sorbing human interest and manifesting creativity, if the machine were in fact the only reputable source of value for modern man, that would mean that his biological and social and personal activities would all shrink and shrivel. They would be otiose and purposeless in such a world and even when they persisted, as of course they must persist in some form, they would themselves become subject to a similar kind of specialization and segregation, which would, in the end, be their death.

We see something of this sort happening during the last generation among the painters. To begin with, a disturbing absence of the symbols of life and an equally disturbing multiplication of images of disorganization and destruction—ruined buildings, blasted landscapes, deformed figures, like Max Ernst's women with beards or dust brushes instead of faces, corpselike figures dissected by aesthetic Bluebeards. One must not blame the painter for bringing forth these symbols. Just because of his acute sensitiveness to the emotional currents of his period, he would need spiritual powers of the greatest magnitude—or a capacity for retreating into himself and encapsulating himself—in order to produce anything different. Let me reinforce this point by an historic example. Certainly two of the healthiest painters who ever lived were Peter Brueghel the Elder and Francisco José de Goya: strong, healthy, well-balanced spirits. But they both lived in an age of disintegration; and because they were honest enough to face every part of their experience, they both produced surrealist pictures of the most macabre kind, recording the horrors of war, the starvation and misery and torture they had witnessed and, what is more, had agonized over. Fortunately for themselves, fortunately for their contemporaries, fortunately for us, they knew heaven as well as hell: the delights of erotic love, of parenthood, of honest labor in tune with nature, the joy of the hunter and the plowman and the harvest hand. So, though they sensitively recorded the degradations of the day, they were still capable in their art of testifying to a fuller and better life.

Our period, unhappily, has not yet produced many Brueghels or Goyas in painting. The healthy art of our time is either the mediocre production of people too fatuous or complacent to be aware of what has been happening to the world—or it is the work of spiritual recluses, almost as withdrawn as the traditional Hindu or Christian hermits, artists who bathe tranquilly in the quiet springs of traditional life, but who avoid the strong, turbid currents of contemporary existence, which might knock them down or carry them away. These artists no doubt gain in purity and intensity by that seclusion; but by the same token, they lose something in strength and general breadth of appeal. Marsden Hartley in the older generation or Morris Graves in our own day would be examples of this self-contained art: an art filled, indeed, with symbols of life, quivering with sensitiveness in the case of Graves, or knit together by an inner composure, with Hartley, symbols that point to deeply felt and deeply meditated experiences of tenderness, passion, and love—all precious qualities in a grim and calloused age. The fact that such artists live and quietly sustain themselves is in itself a good sign, though it reveals nothing about our further social development, since this kind of artist has always found a cranny to grow in under the most unfavorable personal or social conditions. . . .

Our failure so far to regain the initiative for the human spirit, our inability, in general, to produce symbols that would help restore our inner composure and confirm our hidden desires and give buoyancy to sunken hopes, . . . these failures are not peculiar to the arts: they afflict in similar ways almost every other activity. In a world whose need for peace and brotherhood and planetary cooperation is now close to absolute—since a false move here may bring about a swift downfall of civilization—most of our deliberate collective actions on both sides of the Iron Curtain are in the direction of isolation, noncommunication, and destruction. . . .

Certainly, the present state of our civilization is not a self-perpetuating one. If modern man does not recover his wholeness and balance, if he does not regain his creativity and his freedom, he will be unable to contain the destructive forces that are now conspiring, almost automatically, to destroy him; and even if they were held in check, he will, if he continues along the present route, in the end go completely out of his mind. It will require only a little further commitment to machines already in existence, a little further devaluation of the person, a little more contempt for life and the values of life, before modern man out of his boredom and purposelessness, if not out of destructive malice, will let loose his weapons of total extermination. He may do this, though everyone knows . . . that there can be no victory for either side in a third world war. No victory and no peace. If our present state of unbalance continues, with "art degraded and imagination denied," our present society, for all its powers of organization, will bring on its own downfall. Given a little more time, even a war would not be necessary to effect this negation of life. A congealed condition of enmity, a "deep-freeze war" prolonged for a generation, would be sufficient to produce the same result. And what, then, would become of our triumphs in technics?

Once life becomes entirely valueless, once good and bad have ceased in our minds to exist, along with art and its happy symbols of life —when this happens why should anyone exert himself to achieve technical proficiency, as if power however immense could be of value in a valueless world? Already the fatal words that would bring the businessman and the engineer and the soldier down in the same dust heap as the artist and the poet have been spoken. From the gutters rises a cynical question: *So what?* Unless you believe that life transcends all its instruments and mechanisms, there is no answer to that question. Irrationality, criminality, universal nihilism, suicide—along that road we shall march until our inner powers flourish again sufficiently to command the machine we have created. To avert a tragic end, the human person must come back onto the center of the stage: not as chorus or spectator, but as actor and hero, indeed as dramatist and demiurge, summoning the forces of life to take part in a new drama.

So we come to our final question. Is there then no humane and life-giving alternative to the present process of helpless mechanization and purposeless materialism? Yes; I believe that there is a viable alternative, which is embedded in the very nature of man, for his nature has many other capacities besides the gift for exploiting scientific curiosity, for performing regular work, and for fabricating machines. Furthermore, I believe that at a critical point we shall make a series of new choices, just as deliberate as those which made the machine itself a dominating factor in our lives; and that if we make these choices in time to ward off disaster we shall bring about a general renewal of life. Collective changes of this nature are not the sudden result of some dictatorial fiat: they are the cumulative outcome of many little day-to-day decisions, arising out of a new method of approach, a new set of values, a new philosophy. . . . Once more the human person is coming back into the center of the picture.

[This] change is nothing less than a change of interest in the direction of the whole organism and the whole personality. A shift of values; a new philosophic framework; a fresh habit of life. Such a change has often happened before in history—most notably in the case of Rome, when the classic world fell under the sway of the Christian way of life. As you will recall, when that change took place, people ceased to build the mighty works of engineering that had made old Rome famous, the viaducts and aqueducts and sewers and concrete-surfaced roads; they built churches and monasteries. They ceased to devote themselves to empirical knowledge; they turned to theology and mysticism. They ceased to be profiteers and extortioners, gambling with men's daily necessities; they bought and sold at a just price. On this new basis, they built a great civilization and enacted a great collective drama that came to its own climax in the thirteenth century.

Do you think perhaps that all this cannot happen again? That is a quaint belief for an age that believes that change alone is absolute, for why should people who hold this view believe that their own scheme of life, built so exclusively around the machine, is immune from the processes its philosophy holds to be outside human control? . . . We are not . . . prisoners of the machine; or if we are, we built the prison, we established the prison rules, *we* appointed ourselves the jailers: yes, we even condemned ourselves to a life term within this grim place of confinement. But those prison walls are not eternal. So far from being given by nature, as the more pious believers in the machine have almost fooled themselves into believing, they are the outcome of the human imagination, concentrating upon one particular aspect of experience; and they can be broken down as fast as the walls of Jericho, as soon as the human spirit blows its horn and gives primacy, not to things but to persons.

The renewal of life is the great theme of our age, not the further dominance, in ever more frozen and compulsive forms, of the machine. And the first step for each of us is to seize the initiative and to recover our own capacity for living; to detach ourselves sufficiently from the daily routine to make ourselves self-respecting, self-governing, persons. In short, we must take *things* into our own hands. Before art on any great scale can redress the distortions of our lopsided technics, we must put ourselves in the mood and frame of mind in which art becomes possible, as either creation or re-creation: above all, we must learn to pause, to be silent, to close our eyes and wait.

One of the truly original spirits of the nineteenth century, a great logician, the Abbé Gratry, advocated as an act of mental hygiene dedicating a half hour each day—a half hour, no more—to complete retirement from the world, not using it even to think quietly in, but clearing one's spirit of all burdens and pressures, so that, as he put it, God might speak to one, or, if you prefer to put such matters in naturalistic terms, so one's hidden potentialities, one's buried unconscious processes, would have a chance to come to light. Now, God does not speak very often; but this act of detachment itself, even when no visible results directly come from it, is one of the first useful moves in reasserting the primacy of the person. Mahatma Gandhi, who was a saint as well as an astute politician, used to spend a whole day every week in complete retirement and silence, and perhaps no man in his time ever exerted so much influence over his contemporaries with so little visible apparatus to support him.

Once we have formed the habit of looking within, listening to ourselves, and responding to our own impulses and feelings, we shall not let ourselves be so easily the victims of uncontrollable emotions and affects: the inner life, instead of being either a gaping void or a ghoulish nightmare, will be open to cultivation and in both personal conduct and in art will bring us into more fruitful and loving relations with other men, whose hidden depths will flow, through the symbols of art, into our own. At this point, we can nourish life again more intensely from the outside, too, opening our minds to every touch and sight and sound, instead of anesthetizing ourselves continually to much that goes on around us, because it has become so meaningless, so unrelated to our inner needs. With such self-discipline, we shall in time control the tempo and the rhythm of our days: control the quantity of stimuli that impinge on us: control our attention, so that the things we do shall reflect our purposes and values, as human beings, not the extraneous purposes and values of the machine. At first, we shall make headway slowly and be perpetually frustrated, because our ways will be a challenge—not merely a challenge but an affront—to those of our community. But even our smallest negations and inhibitions will help to give back the initiative to the human spirit; and in time we shall be able to make more positive choices, not merely rejecting the irrelevant, the trivial, the repetitious, but affirming with new vigor all the significant goods of our age, because even when those goods come to us only with the aid of the machine, they will be ours to command: ours to reflect upon and to enjoy.

What I am saying here, in effect, is that the problems we have inquired into within the special realms of art and technics are illustrative of much larger situations within modern society; and that, therefore, we cannot solve these problems until we have achieved a philosophy that will be capable of re-orienting this society, displacing the machine and restoring man to the very center of the universe, as the interpreter and transformer of nature, as the creator of a significant and valuable life, which transcends both raw nature and his own original biological self. Man is not merely a creature of the here and now: he is a mirror of infinity and eternity. Through his own experience of life, through his arts and sciences and philosophies and religions, the brute world of nature rose to self-consciousness and life found a theme for existence other than endless organic transformation and biological reproduction. When man ceases to create he ceases to live. Unless he constantly seeks to surpass his animal limitations, he sinks back into a creature lower than any other brute, for his suppressed creativity, at that moment, will possess with irrational violence all his animal functions. Since wholeness and balance are the very conditions for survival, no less than for creation and renewal, these concepts must take the place of a philosophy based on isolation, specialization, the displacement of the personal, the one-sided emphasis of the external and the mechanical. . . .

So let me now sum up. Going back to the earliest forms of art and technics that anthropological research has turned up, I pointed out that man is both a symbol-maker and a tool-maker from the very outset, because he has a need both to express his inner life and to control his outer life. But the tool, once so responsive to man's will, has turned into an automaton; and at the present moment, the development of automatic organizations threatens to turn man himself into a mere passive tool. Fortunately, that does not mean either the end of art or the end of man. For the creative impulses that stirred in the human soul hundreds of thousands of years ago, when man's inquisitiveness and manipulativeness and growing intelligence and sensitivity caused him to throw off his animal lethargy—these deep impulses will not vanish because, temporarily, one side of his nature, that disciplined by tool and machine, has gotten out of hand. That is a momentary distortion of growth; and it is in the nature of life itself, after a period of growth, to seek to resume equilibrium, in order to be ready for the next act of growth. While life persists, it holds the possibility of circumventing its errors, of surmounting its misfortunes, of renewing its creativity.

We are now at a critical moment of history, a moment of great danger, but also of splendid promise. The burden of renewal lies heavily upon us; for there is no going on with the rigidities and compliances that have so far disintegrated our culture, without finally undermining the basis of life itself. . . .

Yes: the burden of renewal lies upon us; so it behooves us to understand the forces making for renewal within our persons and within our culture, and to summon forth the plans and ideals that will impel us to purposeful action. If we awaken to our actual state, in full possession of our senses, instead of remaining drugged, sleepy, cravenly passive, as we now are, we shall reshape our life to a new pattern, aided by all the resources that art and technics now place in our hands. At that decisive point we shall perhaps lay the foundations for a united world, because we shall aim to join together, not merely the now hostile tribes and nationalities and peoples, but the equally warring and conflicting impulses in the human soul. If that happens, our dreams will again become benign and open to rational discipline; our arts will recover form, structure, and meaning; our machines, however highly organized, will be responsive to the demands of life. And in the end, proudly reversing Blake's dictum, we shall, I hope, be able to say: *Art elevated, imagination affirmed, peace governs the nations.*

VII

EPILOGUE

CALL ME JONAH!

Friends and Colleagues: I don't know how to face this bestowal of the National Book Award. With all my due preparation for this event I'm now left speechless. And yet this literary honor, the National Medal for Literature, is in many ways the climax of all my earlier honors: nothing less than the celebration of my Golden Jubilee. Some fifty-odd years ago, my wife and I got married. Those fifty years have left a mark on everything that I have written. When I spoke to a large audience in Dublin, the summer before last, the chairman in introducing me said: "I am happy to say that Mrs. Mumford, too, is here with us tonight, and you will be interested to know that they recently celebrated their Golden Wedding." And the whole audience broke into applause; they were so surprised that two Americans could live together that long!

Then I realized a little while ago while putting together some essays and reviews of mine, that this was the fiftieth anniversary, too, of my being a writer of books. My first book, *The Story of Utopias*, (which I wouldn't recommend to anybody!) is still in print. It came out in 1922. . . .

Facing my fifty years as a writer of books, I put together a book of my own, a quite new book, though composed entirely of published material. A . . . highly organized assemblage of "Interpretations and Forecasts" from 1922 to 1972. About those interpretations and particularly about those forecasts, I can only repeat what I have said more than once to my wife: "I would die happy if I knew that on my tombstone could be written these words, "This man was an absolute fool. None of the disastrous things that he reluctantly predicted ever came to pass!' Yes: then I could die happy."

You see what's happened to my well-prepared "impromptu" talk!

It is already turning into something quite different; and in order to stress that I am tempted to add some seasoning to Dr. [René] Dubos's eulogy, and perhaps also to Senator [Eugene] McCarthy's remarks. Grateful though I am to both speakers, I am going to give a brief but quite different account of the man in front of you. To begin with, his name is Jonah. This places him as one of the minor prophets, not to be mentioned in the same breath as Amos or Isaiah. Jonah has become one of my favorite books in the Bible, though he figures in my personal life, not as a character to imitate, but as an admonitory figure, exposing my failings, taking me down when I am too elated by some minor success, jeering at my most acute forecasts.

This private Jonah is of course quite different from the stock character still visible in folklore. You know what Jonah stands for in the mind of the ordinary man today. The popular conception of Jonah is principally that of a bringer of bad luck. If anything goes wrong, Jonah is to blame for it. Jonah is that terrible fellow who keeps on uttering the very words you don't want to hear, reporting the bad news and warning you that it will get even worse unless you yourself change your mind and alter your behavior. What can people do with such a nuisance? Well, what happened to Jonah when he took the ship from Joppa? And why to begin with did he want to escape from Nineveh? Because he was fleeing from the voice of the Lord. Jonah did not want to tell the people of Nineveh, that mighty metropolis, what the Lord commanded him to say. *"If you go on this way you will be destroyed."* So Jonah abandoned his mission and fled as fast as he could for a distant port. But once at sea a violent storm arose, and everyone on board cursed Jonah for bringing bad luck to the ship. Then the crew threw him overboard, and he was swallowed by a whale. There the straightforward account of events takes a fresh turn, and the whale now becomes an important part of the story; for it turns out that the whale was sent by God to succor Jonah. What must have seemed to Jonah to have been desperate bad luck turns out in fact to be his salvation.

At this point something very strange happens in my own imagination. First I begin to identify my own life with Jonah's, and then Jonah himself turns into the whale, not the biblical whale but the whale in Herman Melville's stormy sea drama, *Moby-Dick*. What kind of a whale is this transmogrified Jonah? Does he resemble Moby-Dick, that tortured monster of the deep? No: not closely; for he is plainly no Leviathan. Perhaps he is nearest to the Right Whale, another species of whale that Melville describes. The human term for the Right Whale would be the Righteous Whale. Strangely the very day this notion came to me I had been reading a passage in Samuel Butler where he said: "If a man doesn't want to destroy his reputation entirely for the future, he mustn't be right too often." My identification with the Right Whale, or to put it more honestly, the Righteous Whale, exposes an unpleasant temptation every prophet must guard against: the temptation to remember how often he has been right.

Closely related to the Right Whale in my imagination is still another species, the Narwhale. If any of you know German, you will appreciate this identification. In German "Narr" means fool; and the Jonah-Whale is a fool whale, an idiot whale. That is an understandable aspect of Jonah: he ventures to defy prudence and common sense, to point to evils that people have learned to close their eyes to, and blurt out truths they are trying to hide from themselves. Anyone who has something new and important to say must be brazen enough, self-confident enough, to outface those Ibsen called the "compact majority," who will regard his readiness to speak out as a proof that he is either crazy or an "Enemy of the People." Only a fool would be vain enough to suppose that what he alone says now will some day seem important, no matter how many people reject it, or how scornfully they continue to dismiss it. So much for my private transformation of the story of both Jonah and the Whale.

But there is a more telling version of this singular story in *Moby-Dick*: the classic interpretation of Jonah's moral dilemma that one finds in Father Mapple's sermon. In that parable the whale has not the slightest importance. The important fact is that Jonah, who was a dedicated prophet, had heard the voice of the Lord, and in a cowardly panic ran away from it. He didn't dare to deliver the awful message he got directly from the Lord's mouth. Jonah fled from Nineveh as far as he could, and almost welcomed being buried in the belly of the whale; that, at least, got him out of his unwelcome duty to admonish the people of Nineveh about changing their ways.

This betrayal of his mission as a prophet is what Father Mapple properly denounces and castigates in that most magnificent passage. I have read his words aloud again and again, and each time the sermon gets better and better. It teaches something we must all learn if and when Truth calls us. For what is the lesson of science? What is the lesson of religion? Whenever Truth commands us, we must obey it and utter it aloud whether our friends and neighbors and countrymen like it or not.

There is a special lesson in the Book of Jonah which Melville chose to pass over. It comes out only at the end in Jonah's petulant complaint to God. This querulous conversation contrasts unfavorably with that incredible earlier dialogue Abraham had with God over the terms on which Sodom and Gomorrah, those cities of violence, bestiality, and hardcore pornography, might be saved from God's wrathful destruction. In a wonderful scene, a perfect example of Oriental bargaining, Abraham gets God to admit that perhaps these cities would be worth saving if as few as fifty righteous people could be found there. Agreed! But if not fifty, what about forty? If not forty, then perhaps thirty? And so, finally, by wheedling and needling, Abraham gets God to promise that those cities might be saved if as few as ten decent people could be found there. To their honor, it is plain that neither God nor Abraham wanted these cities destroyed, whether the majority repented of their sins or not. If a saving remnant could be found—that no doubt is where we get the phrase "a saving remnant"—even Sodom and Gomorrah could survive.

Jonah comes off badly in comparison with the wise and wily old patriarch, who didn't set out to be a prophet. Jonah actually feels let down by God because God didn't carry out his threat any more than he had punished Jonah for having failed the first time to deliver his message, but gave him another chance. In effect, God made a fool of Jonah by acting more mercifully than Jonah had guessed he would; and the people of Nineveh had made a double fool of him by tearfully repenting of their sins, from the king down. No wonder Jonah feels so humiliated that he wants to die. Jonah's monstrous error was to imagine that he knew in advance how badly both the people of Nineveh and God would behave.

In the final passage of this account it is plain that God had no more confidence than had Jonah that the people of Nineveh would permanently change their ways; but he was touched by at least their public remorse over their violence and villainy. That was something: so perhaps in the future the garbage would be collected more regularly and officials would blush when they took a bribe or broke a law. That was all God seems to have expected from this proud city of six score thousand people—and here I quote—"who could not tell their right hand from their left." The moral need not be spelled out. Woe to the prophet who confuses his own voice with the voice of the Lord and who thinks he knows in advance what God has up his sleeve!

Now you know why I have told you this story. In a sense it is the story of my life, because I am much closer to the mythic Jonah in all his ways, not least his temptations, than I am to any utopian dreamer. If anything, I am an anti-utopian, who knows that a blessing repeated too often may become a curse, and that a curse faced bravely may become a blessing. I wrote a whole chapter in one of my earlier books, *Faith for Living*, entitled "Life Is Better than Utopia." Long ago John Ruskin taught me that "there is no wealth but life." So long as consciousness remains up to the point where it is obliterated by bodily injury or intolerable pain, life is, as Henry James once said, the most precious thing, one might say the only precious thing, we truly possess.

That is the sort of man who is talking to you tonight: neither a pessimist nor an optimist, still less a utopian or a futurologist. And now, at the end, I want to say an almost unsayable thing, to record the depth of my thanks for what you have done on this occasion—to express my gratitude, not alone to those who are here, not just to those who have sung my praises, or who have bestowed this award, but also to those nameless voices coming from the distance and the deep, when I was entombed in the belly of the whale. Their response to my words has given me the faith to struggle out of that darkness and rise up into the sunlit air again. In the name of Jonah, the biblical Jonah, Melville's Jonah, my private whale of a Jonah, and above all God's Jonah, I thank you.

List of Sources

I. A Child of the City

East Side, West Side: *Sketches from Life: The Autobiography of Lewis Mumford: The Early Years* (New York: Dial Press, 1982), 3–10.

All Around the Town: Ibid., 13–24.

Our Metropolitan Pageants: Ibid., 120–30.

II. Architecture as a Home for Man

The Brooklyn Bridge: Selected from "The Renewal of the Landscape," in *The Brown Decades: A Study of the Arts in America, 1865–1895* (New York: Harcourt, Brace, 1931); this is reprinted from the revised edition (New York: Dover Publications, 1951), 43–48.

Towards Modern Architecture: *The Brown Decades,* 49–82.

The Case against "Modern Architecture": "The Case against 'Modern Architecture,'" *Architectural Record* 131, no. 4 (April 1962): 155–62.

Symbol and Function in Architecture: *Art and Technics,* Bampton Lectures in America, no. 4 (New York: Columbia University Press, 1952; paperback, 1960), 111–35.

III. The City in Civilization

What Is a City?: Selected from the Introduction to *The Culture of Cities* (New York: Harcourt, Brace, 1938), 3–10.

The Disappearing City: "The Future of the City: Part 1—The Disappearing City," *Architectural Record* 132, no. 4 (October 1962): 121–28; reprinted in *The Urban Prospect: Essays* (New York: Harcourt, Brace and World, 1968), 108–15.

The Medieval City: Selected from "Medieval Urban Housekeeping," in *The City in History: Its Origins, Its Transformations, and Its Prospects* (New York: Harcourt, Brace, 1961), 299–314.

The Baroque City: Combines selections from "The Structure of Baroque Power" and "Court, Parade, and Capital," in ibid., 345–51, 363–71, 391–95, 399–403.

The Lessons of Washington, D.C.: Originally "The Lessons of Washington," from "Court, Parade, and Capital," in ibid., 403–9.

IV. The Urban Prospect

The Ideal Form of the Modern City: Originally "The Modern City," in Talbot Hamlin, ed., *Forms and Functions of Twentieth-Century Architecture,* vol. 4, *Building Types* (New York: Columbia University Press, 1952), 797–817.

Yesterday's City of Tomorrow: "The Future of the City: Part 2—Yesterday's City of Tomorrow," *Architectural Record* 132, no. 5 (November

1962): 139–44; reprinted in *The Urban Prospect: Essays* (New York: Harcourt, Brace and World, 1968), 116–27.

Home Remedies for Urban Cancer: Appeared as "The Sky Line: Mother Jacobs' Home Remedies" in the *New Yorker*, December 1, 1962, 148ff; reprinted with the title "Home Remedies for Urban Cancer," in *The Urban Prospect*, 182–207.

Restored Circulation, Renewed Life: Appeared as "The Sky Line: The Roaring Traffic's Boom—III" in the *New Yorker*, April 16, 1955, 78ff; reprinted, with the title "Restored Circulation, Renewed Life," in Mumford, *From the Ground Up: Observations on Contemporary Architecture, Housing, Highway Building, and Civic Design* (New York: Harvest Books, Harcourt, Brace, 1956), 219–29.

The Regional Framework of Civilization: Combines selections from "Regions—To Live In," *Survey Graphic* 54 (May 1, 1925): 151–52, and "Regional Planning" (July 8, 1931, Address to Round Table on Regionalism, Institute of Public Affairs, University of Virginia), manuscript in Avery Library, Columbia University. Both essays reprinted in Carl Sussman, ed., *Planning the Fourth Migration: The Neglected Vision of the Regional Planning Association of America* (Cambridge, Mass.: MIT Press, 1976), 89–93, 199–208.

The Foundations of Eutopia: Selected from chapter 12 of *The Story of Utopias*, with an introduction by Hendrik Willem Van Loon (New York: Boni and Liveright, 1922), 267–72, 276–91, 297–308; reprinted with a new preface by Mumford and without the introduction by Van Loon (New York: Peter Smith, 1941; Gloucester, Mass.: Peter Smith, 1959; New York: Compass Books, Viking Press, 1962).

The Choices Ahead: *The Urban Prospect*, 227–55.

V. Visions of America

The Origins of the American Mind: *The Golden Day: A Study in American Experience and Culture* (New York: Boni and Liveright, 1926); this selection is taken from Mumford's *Interpretations and Forecasts, 1922–1972: Studies in Literature, History, Biography, Technics, and Contemporary Society* (New York: Harcourt Brace Jovanovich, 1973), 3–16.

The Golden Day: Combines selections from "The Golden Day" and "Envoi," in *The Golden Day*, 40–68, 140–42.

The New World Promise: "The New World Promise," *American Institute of Architects Journal*, n.s., 44, no. 2 (August 1965): 43–47 (First Annual Purves Memorial Lecture, delivered at the joint convention of the American Institute of Architects and the Pan American Congress of Architects held in Washington, D.C., June 14–18, 1965; simultaneously translated into Spanish).

VI. Technology and Culture

Technics and Human Development: *The Myth of the Machine*, vol. 1, *Technics and Human Development* (New York: Harcourt, Brace and World, 1967), 3–13.

The First Megamachine: "The First Megamachine," *Diogenes*, no. 55 (Fall 1966): 1–5; reprinted in *The Myth of the Machine*, vol. 1, *Technics and Human Development* and in Mumford's *Interpretations and Forecasts, 1922–1972: Studies in Literature, History, Biography, Technics, and Contemporary Society* (New York: Harcourt Brace Jovanovich, 1973), 259–69.

The Monastery and the Clock: *Technics and Civilization* (New York: Harcourt, Brace, 1934); reprinted with a new introduction by Mumford (New York: Harbinger Books, Harcourt, Brace, 1963); this selection is taken from the reprint, titled "Mechanization of Modern Culture," in *Interpretations and Forecasts,* 270–78.

The Reinvention of the Megamachine: Selected from "Reflections: The Megamachine—I," *New Yorker,* October 10, 1970, 50ff, taken from *The Myth of the Machine,* vol. 2, *The Pentagon of Power* (New York: Harcourt, Brace and World, 1970), 243–62.

Art and Technics: Combines "Art and the Symbol" and "Art, Technics, and Cultural Integration," from *Art and Technics,* Bampton Lectures in America, no. 4 (New York: Columbia University Press, 1952; paperback, 1960), 3–11, 136–62.

VII. Epilogue

Call Me Jonah!: Address delivered December 13, 1972, and published in Mumford's *My Works and Days: A Personal Chronicle* (New York: Harcourt Brace Jovanovich, 1979), 527–31.

Permissions Acknowledgments

Grateful acknowledgment is made to the following for permission to reprint previously published material:

Architectural Record: "The Case Against 'Modern Architecture,' " *Architectural Record*, 131, April 1962, pp. 155–162. "The Disappearing City" ("The Future of the City," Part I), *Architectural Record*, 132, October 1962, pp. 121–28. "Yesterday's City of Tomorrow," ("The Future of the City," Part II) *Architectural Record*, 132, November 1962, pp.139–44.) Copyright © 1962 by McGraw-Hill, Inc. All rights reserved. Reprinted from *Architectural Record* by permission.

Columbia University Press: "Art and the Symbol," "Art, Technics, and Cultural Integration," and "Symbol and Function in Architecture," from *Art and Technics* by Lewis Mumford (Bampton Lectures in America, No. 4), Columbia University Press, 1952. "The Ideal Form of the Modern City" (originally "The Modern City") from *Form and Functions of Twentieth Century Architecture*, vol. 4: *Building Types*, edited by Talbot Hamlin. Columbia University Press, 1952.

Doubleday & Company, Inc.: "A Child of the City," from *Sketches from Life* by Lewis Mumford. Copyright © 1982 by Lewis Mumford. Reprinted by permission of Doubleday & Company, Inc.

Dover Publications: "The Origins of the American Mind" and "The Golden Day," from *The Golden Day* by Lewis Mumford. Reprinted by permission of Dover Publications.

Harcourt Brace Jovanovich, Inc.: "The Roaring Traffic's Boom," from *From the Ground Up* by Lewis Mumford. Copyright © 1956, 1984 by Lewis Mumford. "The Choices Ahead" and "Home Remedies for Urban Cancer," from *The Urban Prospect* by Lewis Mumford. Copyright © 1968 by Lewis Mumford. "The Reinvention of the Megamachine" and "The Modern Megamachine," from *The Myth of the Machine*, vol. 2, *The Pentagon of Power* by Lewis Mumford. Copyright © 1970 by Lewis Mumford. "What Is a City?" from *The Culture of Cities* by Lewis Mumford. Copyright 1938, © 1966 by Lewis Mumford. "The Medieval City," "The Baroque City," and "The Lessons of Washington, D.C." from *The City in History* by Lewis Mumford. Copyright © 1961 by Lewis Mumford. "Technics and Human Development" and "The First Megamachine" from *The Myth of the Machine*, vol. 1, *Tech-*

Index

Abercrombie, Patrick, 174, 233
abolition movement, 271, 282–3
Abrams, Charles, 189
abstraction, 132–3, 135–7, 254–7, 260, 265, 319, 327, 328, 331
acceleration, concept of, 332
acoustics, 92
Adams, Henry, 90, 199, 245, 301, 351
Adler, Dankmar, 61, 62, 68
Agassiz, Louis, 272, 275
agriculture, 104, 106–7, 166, 167, 209, 212, 214, 266, 286, 313
Ahearn, Nellie, 27
airplane, invention of, 332
Albany (N.Y.) Cathedral, 52
Alberti, Leone Battista, 116, 121, 129, 130, 134, 138, 139, 150
Albertus Magnus, 127
Albright, W. F., 321
Alcott, Bronson, 265
Alessi, Galeazzo, 131
Alton estate (Roehampton, Eng.), 180
American Architecture (Schuyler), 35, 47, 56, 57
American Indians, 277, 289, 290, 274–5
American Museum of Natural History, 32
American Revolution, 36, 148, 261, 262
Amsterdam (Neth.), 146, 174, 175, 203
Amsterdam Avenue (N.Y.C.), 22, 27
animal behavior, 306–7, 308, 346
Appalachian Trail, 278
Arabs, Arab culture, 326, 332
arcades, in medieval cities, 122
archaeology, 135, 251–2, 309
architectural orders, 129, 136
architectural schools, 83, 233
architecture: and aesthetic experience, 89; baroque forms, 130–2; and civilization, 41, 75–6; modernism in, 42–3, 50–1, 67, 73–83; 19th-century

eclecticism in, 49–53 *passim*, 58–9, 65, 87; Renaissance forms, 130; as social expression, 65, 66, 75–6, 84–5, 92; social responsibilities of, 8, 42, 43, 66, 67, 69, 72
Aristotle, 214, 218–19, 252
Arsenal (Venice), 121
art, 6, 10, 272, 287, 348–61; applied to architecture, 54, 89; baroque, 133, 135, 136; and contemporary world, 350, 351, 356–7; exact arts, 251, 262; functions and message of, 160, 223–4, 245, 283, 310, 352–4; medieval, 329, 330; picturesque in, 223; Protestant rejection of, 252, 255, 259, 263; Renaissance concepts of, 134–5, 330–1; specialization in, 222–3
Ashbee, Charles Robert, 73
Assyria, 313, 335
Astor family, 25
astronomy, 312, 313, 318, 319, 327
Athens, 209
atomic bomb, 7, 300, 337, 338–40, 352, 355
Atomic Energy Commission, 341
Auditorium Building (Chicago), 57, 61, 64, 67
Austin Hall (Cambridge, Mass.), 53
Australopithecines, 306–7
authoritarian regimes, 148, 149, 312–14, 319–20; in ancient Egypt, 315–19, 321, 322; in 17th-century Europe, 127, 128, 133, 136, 137, 140–4. *See also* fascism; totalitarian states
Autobiography of an Idea (Sullivan), 59, 67
automation, 29
automobile traffic, 153, 201–6, 293, 294. *See also* wheeled vehicles

377

ABOUT THE AUTHOR AND EDITOR

Born in New York City in 1895, Lewis Mumford has produced over thirty books in the course of his sixty-year career as a writer. He was awarded the National Medal for Literature in 1972, and in 1962 won the National Book Award for *The City in History*. Among his other books are *Technics and Civilization, Sticks and Stones, The Brown Decades, Herman Melville,* and *The Culture of Cities*. He lives with his wife of over fifty years in Amenia, New York.

Donald L. Miller is Lewis Mumford's literary executor and chairman of the American Civilization Program of Lafayette College in Easton, Pennsylvania. He is the author of *The New American Radicalism* and, with Richard Sharpless, *The Kingdom of Coal*. He spent the last year at Oxford University completing a biography of Lewis Mumford.